CHRISTIANITY
AND THE
SOCIAL CRISIS
IN THE
21ST CENTURY

CHRISTIANITY

AND THE

SOCIAL CRISIS

IN THE

21ˢᵀ CENTURY

The Classic That Woke Up the Church

WALTER RAUSCHENBUSCH

HarperOne
An Imprint of HarperCollinsPublishers

HarperOne

All scriptural quotations, unless otherwise noted, are from NRSV.

HarperCollins Web site: http://www.harpercollins.com
HarperCollins®, ♣®, and HarperOne™ are
trademarks of HarperCollins Publishers.

FIRST HARPERCOLLINS PAPERBACK EDITION PUBLISHED IN 2007

Designed by Joseph Rutt

Library of Congress Cataloging-in-Publication Data is available upon request.

ISBN 978-0-06-149726-1

HB 01.26.2021

To

The Women Who Have Loved Me

My Mother

My Sisters Frida and Emma

My Dear Wife Pauline

And

My Little Daughters Winifred and Elizabeth

This Book Is Lovingly Inscribed

Thy Kingdom Come!

Thy Will Be Done On Earth!

Contents

Contents

Foreword

Pastors dedicate their lives to caring for the spiritual, ethical, and physical well being of people who are in their congregation. Walter Rauschenbusch, the product of seven generations of pastors, started his career serving a small church of immigrants in New York City in what was then aptly called Hell's Kitchen. Through his congregation, he was introduced to overcrowded tenements with high rent, horrendous working conditions rewarded by intolerably low wages, lack of heat in the winter, and lack of recreational facilities in the summer, all accompanied by consistent hunger and substandard health facilities. As a pastor, Rauschenbusch realized that in order to serve the spiritual needs of his congregation he had to address the whole of their lives.

As a Christian, Walter Rauschenbusch naturally turned to the Bible to see what it had to say about the harsh reality with which he had been confronted. *Christianity and the Social Crisis* is the result of his findings. With his new vision granted by the poor of his church, he saw the kingdom of God as the centerpiece of Jesus's teaching and the hope of his earthly ministry. Pastor Rauschenbusch was struck by how Jesus's kingdom of God contrasted with the lives of his congregation: "Instead of a society resting on coercion, exploitation, and inequality," he wrote, "Jesus desired to found a society resting on love, service, and equality." Rauschenbusch was convinced that the kingdom of God was not an apocalyptic vision that could be passively postponed, but a prophetic call for society's transformation in the here and now.

The radical message of *Christianity and the Social Crisis* is hard to appreciate today because his critique has become so intrinsic to Christianity's voice for the last century. But we can gauge its impact by the extraordinary response to the book's release in 1907. For the next three years, it was the best-selling religious book after the Bible, selling fifty thousand copies in its first few printings. Arriving home after a sabbatical in Germany, Rauschenbusch was surprised to find himself a national figure. He spoke at forums and churches around the country in places as diverse as the Northern Baptist National Convention in Chicago, Stephen Wise's Free Synagogue in New York, and historically black Fisk College in Tennessee. His book inspired the largest denominations to begin to incorporate social justice commitments into their statements of faith, including the Federal Council of Churches, the precursor to the National Council of Churches, which was founded the year after the release of *Christianity and the Social Crisis*. The Church's new enthusiasm for the kingdom of God powered many of the reform movements that swept the nation over the next century, including the fight for child labor laws, a manageable workweek with a minimum wage, FDR's New Deal, the Great Society, and the civil rights movement. Six decades after the book's original release, Martin Luther King Jr. would write, "In the early 50's I read Walter Rauschenbusch's *Christianity and the Social Crisis*, a book which left an indelible imprint on my thinking."

I am Walter Rauschenbusch's great-grandson, and the first in my family to return to the ministry after his extraordinary contribution. Yet, as familiar and revered a figure as he is to me, when I sit down with this book I am struck not only by the beauty and accessibility of the writing but also by the unapologetically radical Christian assertions for justice and equality. I am invigorated to read someone arguing so forthrightly, and with such deep religious passion, about something as elemental as dignity and respect for the poor. And I am both surprised and encouraged to read a book written one hundred years ago that acknowledges that in order to understand the full meaning of Jesus's teachings, we must look at the social context in which he lived.

Rauschenbusch identified the economic exploitation of the poor as nothing less than a national sin. As a pastor to the nation, Rauschenbusch preached both personal and societal repentance. He called upon Christians and the Church to lead the fight to redeem the nation through both personal and national regeneration in accordance with the social principles of Jesus. But kingdom building was not something that individuals or society were going to do alone, as Rauschenbusch readily admitted: "It is true that any regeneration of society can come only through the act of God and the presence of Christ; but God is now acting, and Christ is now here. To assert that means not less faith, but more." *Christianity and the Social Crisis* is a testimony of faith and hope in the power of God to work within society if citizens would open their hearts to the Lord's redeeming message.

The twenty-first century is a time of unprecedented capability and possibility, yet we, too, live in a time of social crisis and are in need of the power of God and the vision of Jesus. As a pastor, and as a minister of the gospel, what is my responsibility in this time? What is the responsibility of every Christian? Just as Rauschenbusch awoke to the social message of the gospel through his direct experience of poverty, Christians today must not be afraid to face the most pressing issues of our day—war, terrorism, poverty, globalization, religious fanaticism, AIDS, the rights of women—and to confront these challenges firsthand. Guided by the vision of the kingdom of God, we must recognize that it is not enough to help the afflicted; we must influence the systems that cause the affliction. It is not enough to help the assaulted man on the road to Jericho; we must stop the assaults. We are called to dedicate ourselves to the task of doing the work that Jesus set us here to do: to love God with all our heart, soul, mind, and strength, and to love our neighbor as ourselves in concrete and practical ways.

"The kingdom of God is always but coming," wrote Rauschenbusch in the last chapter of *Christianity and the Social Crisis.* Rauschenbusch understood that we would never perfect this world, but he also knew that was not an excuse not to try: "It is true that any effort at social regeneration is dogged by perpetual relapse and doomed forever to fall short of its aim. But the same is true of our personal efforts to live a Christian life; it is true also of every local church, and of the history of the Church at large. Whatever argument would demand the postponement of social regeneration to a future era will equally demand the postponement of personal holiness to a future life."

This profound equation between faith and the world is today's challenge, as it was one hundred years ago. As associate dean of religious life at Princeton University, I work with students from various religious traditions. The Christian students, whom Walter Rauschenbusch would have called "from the evangelical school," have a wonderfully vibrant spiritual connection with Jesus but do not, to my mind, take

Jesus's social teachings as literally as they do the apostle Paul's dictums on personal religion. Their approach to changing society is sometimes limited to individual religious conversion, or fixed on abortion and homosexuality. However, this seems to be shifting. Recently, more evangelical students have been inspired to take on issues such as preserving the environment, securing religious freedom, and stopping the trafficking of women.

On the flip side, students who point to Jesus's teachings on social justice as the primary motive for their work on hunger, poverty, or discrimination sometimes downplay their spiritual connection to the living Christ who is working and acting now in the world. They are hesitant to proclaim Jesus as Lord publicly. The same is true beyond our campus, and my own family is a good example. The past two generations of Walter Rauschenbusch's descendants have made remarkable contributions in art, law, education, philosophy, and economics. However, I was the first to restart the long legacy of pastors in the Rauschenbusch family and publicly proclaim the gospel. Likewise, in many social justice churches that over the past decades have done admirable advocacy work on behalf of the poor, peace, racial equity, and women's and gay rights, only recently can one sense the rekindling of the religious fervor that was the genesis of the Social Gospel movement. It is time to reclaim both the evangelical and the social element in Rauschenbusch's original work and put the power of the gospel back into the social gospel.

The individuals who have contributed to this book represent the best of the Social Gospel tradition—they combine a deep religious commitment to the Lord while working tirelessly for the kingdom. For their generous contributions to this one-hundred-year edition of *Christianity and the Social Crisis,* I humbly thank: Dr. Phyllis Trible, Rev. Dr. Tony Campolo, Sister Joan Chittister, Dr. Stanley Hauerwas, Dr. Cornel West, Rev. Dr. James A. Forbes Jr., and Rev. Jim Wallis. A special thanks to my cousin Dr. Richard Rorty, whose extraordinary contribution to philosophy and social commitment has been unparalleled in our lifetime. His afterword gives us a wistful perspective from the secular humanist world and challenges us to consider how well we Christians are practicing what we preach.

I have avoided responding to the various critiques of this book put forward throughout the last century or offering apologetics for any of Rauschenbusch's miscalculations or omissions. The responses to each chapter have done an excellent job of highlighting both strengths and weaknesses throughout the book. The criticism that I personally reject is that Rauschenbusch lost the spiritual center of the Christian faith because he challenged theological and social orthodoxies. Even one hundred years later, Rauschenbusch is still being targeted by conservative evangelicals such as Rick Warren, the Christian pastor and author of *The Purpose-Driven Life*, who wrote in his blog: "Rauschenbusch was a liberal theologian and he basically said we don't need this stuff about Jesus anymore." My great-grandfather dedicated his entire life to Jesus, and he lost his hearing and his health in the service of his congregation. His writings on the Social Gospel were marked by love for both his admirers and his detractors, a generosity not always returned. To understand his work one must read his prayers and meditations, which convey the mystical quality to his belief. As a benediction, I offer my favorite Rauschenbusch poem, written at the end of his life.

The Little Gate to God
In the castle of my soul
Is a little postern gate,
Whereat, when I enter,
I am in the presence of God.
In a moment, in the turning of a thought,
I am where God is.
This is a fact.
This world of ours has length and breadth,
A superficial and horizontal world.
When I am with God
I look deep down and high up.
And all is changed.
The world of men is made of jangling noises.
With God it is a great silence.
But that silence is a melody
Sweet as the contentment of love,

Thrilling as a touch of flame.
In this world my days are few
And full of trouble.
I strive and have not;
I seek and find not;
I ask and learn not.
Its joys are so fleeting,
Its pains are so enduring,
I am in doubt if life be worth living.
When I enter into God,
All life has a meaning.
Without asking, I know;
My desires are even now fulfilled,
My fever is gone
In the great quiet of God.
My troubles are but pebbles on the road,
My joys are like the everlasting hills,
So it is when I step through the gate of prayer
From time into eternity.
When I am in the consciousness of God
Those whom I love
Have a mystic value.
They shine, as if a light were glowing within them.
Even those who frown on me
And love me not
Seem part of a great scheme of good.
(Or else they seem like stray bumble bees
Buzzing at a window,
Headed the wrong way, yet seeking the light.)
So it is when my soul steps through the postern gate
Into the presence of God.
Big things become small, and small things become great.
The near becomes far, and the future is near.
The lowly and despised is shot through with glory,
And most of human power and greatness
Seems as full of infernal iniquities
As a carcass is full of maggots.

God is the substance of all revolutions;
When I am in him, I am in the Kingdom of God
And the Fatherland of my Soul.
Is it strange that I love God?
And when I come back through the gate,
Do you wonder that I carry memories with me,
And my eyes are hot with unshed tears for what I see.
And I feel like a stranger and a homeless man
Where the poor are wasted for gain,
Where rivers run red,
And where God's sunlight is darkened by lies?

May God's sunlight shine again. Thy kingdom come, God!

Paul Brandeis Raushenbush
Princeton University
2006

Introduction

Western civilization is passing through a social revolution unparalleled in history for scope and power. Its coming was inevitable. The religious, political, and intellectual revolutions of the past five centuries, which together created the modern world, necessarily had to culminate in an economic and social revolution such as is now upon us.

By universal consent, this social crisis is the overshadowing problem of our generation. The industrial and commercial life of the advanced nations is in the throes of it. In politics all issues and methods are undergoing upheaval and realignment as the social movement advances. In the world of thought all the young and serious minds are absorbed in the solution of the social problems. Even literature and art point like compass-needles to this magnetic pole of all our thought.

The social revolution has been slow in reaching our country. We have been exempt, not because we had solved the problems, but because we had not yet confronted them. We have now arrived, and all the characteristic conditions of American life will henceforth combine to make the social struggle here more intense than anywhere else. The vastness and the free sweep of our concentrated wealth on the one side, the independence, intelligence, moral vigor, and political power of the common people on the other side, promise a long-drawn grapple of contesting forces which may well make the heart of every American patriot sink within him.

It is realized by friend and foe that religion can play, and must play, a momentous part in this irrepressible conflict.

The Church, the organized expression of the religious life of the past, is one of the most potent institutions and forces in Western civilization. Its favor and moral influence are wooed by all parties. It cannot help throwing its immense weight on one side or the other. If it tries not to act, it thereby acts; and in any case its choice will be decisive for its own future.

Apart from the organized Church, the religious spirit is a factor of incalculable power in the making of history. In the idealistic spirits that lead and in the masses that follow, the religious spirit always intensifies thought, enlarges hope, unfetters daring, evokes the willingness to sacrifice, and gives coherence in the fight. Under the warm breath of religious faith, all social institutions become plastic. The religious spirit removes mountains and tramples on impossibilities. Unless the economic and intellectual factors are strongly reinforced by religious enthusiasm, the whole social movement may prove abortive, and the New Era may die before it comes to birth.

It follows that the relation between Christianity and the social crisis is one of the most pressing questions for all intelligent men who realize the power of religion, and most of all for the religious leaders of the people who give direction to the forces of religion.

The question has, in fact, been discussed frequently and earnestly, but it is plain to any thoughtful observer that the common mind of the Christian Church in America has not begun to arrive at any solid convictions or any permanent basis of action. The conscience of Christendom is halting and groping, perplexed by contradicting voices, still poorly informed on essential questions, justly reluctant to part with the treasured maxims of the past, and yet conscious of the imperious call of the future.

This book is to serve as a contribution to this discussion. Its first chapters are historical, for nothing is more needed than a true comprehension of past history if we are to forecast the future correctly and act wisely in the present. I have tried to set forth the religious development of the prophets of Israel, the life and teachings of Jesus, and the dominant tendencies of primitive Christianity, in order to ascertain what was the original and fundamental purpose of the great Christian movement in history. Every discussion of the question which appeals to history has to cover this ground, but usually only detached fragments of the material are handled at all, and often without insight adequate to give their true meaning even to these fragments. I am in hopes that these chapters will contribute some facts and points of view that have not yet become common property.

The outcome of these first historical chapters is that the essential purpose of Christianity was to transform human society into the kingdom of God by regenerating all human relations and reconstituting them in accordance with the will of God. The fourth chapter raises the question why the Christian Church has never undertaken to carry out this fundamental purpose of its existence. I have never met with any previous attempt to give a satisfactory historical explanation of this failure, and I regard this chapter as one of the most important in the book.

The fifth chapter sets forth the conditions which constitute the present social crisis and which imperatively demand of Christianity that contribution of moral and religious power which it was destined to furnish.

The sixth chapter points out that the Church, as such, has a stake in the social movement. The Church owns property, needs income, employs men, works on human material, and banks on its moral prestige. Its present efficiency and future standing are bound up for weal or woe with the social welfare of the people and with the outcome of the present struggle.

The last chapter suggests what contributions Christianity can make and in what main directions the religious spirit should exert its force.

In covering so vast a field of history and in touching on such a multitude of questions, error and incompleteness are certain, and the writer can claim only that he has tried to do honest work. Moreover, it is impossible to handle questions so vital to the economic, the social, and the moral standing of great and antagonistic classes of men, without jarring precious interests and convictions, and without giving men the choice between the bitterness of social repentance and the bitterness of moral resentment. I can frankly affirm that I have written with malice toward none and with charity for all. Even where I judge men to have done wrong, I find it easy to sympathize with them in the temptations which made the wrong almost inevitable, and in the points of view in which they entrench themselves to save their self-respect. I have tried—so far as erring human judgment permits—to lift the issues out of the plane of personal selfishness and hate, and to put them where the white light of the just and pitying spirit of Jesus can play upon them. If I have failed in that effort, it is my sin. If others in reading fail to respond in the same spirit, it is their sin. In a few years all our restless and angry hearts will be quiet in death, but those who come after us will live in the world which our sins have blighted or which our love of right has redeemed. Let us do our thinking on these great questions, not with our eyes fixed on our bank account, but with a wise outlook on the fields of the future and with the consciousness that the spirit of the Eternal is seeking to distill from our lives some essence of righteousness before they pass away.

I have written this book to discharge a debt. For eleven years I was pastor among the working people on the West Side of New York City. I shared their life as well as I then knew, and used up the early strength of my life in their service. In recent years my work has been turned into other channels, but I have never ceased to feel that I owe help to the plain people who were my friends. If this book in some far-off way helps to ease the pressure that bears them down and increases the forces that bear them up, I shall meet the Master of my life with better confidence.

The Historical Roots of Christianity

The Hebrew Prophets

It seems a long start to approach the most modern problems by talking of men who lived before Lycurgus and Solon gave laws to Sparta and Athens. What light can we get on the troubles of the great capitalistic republic of the West from men who tended sheep in Judea or meddled in the petty politics of the Semitic tribes?

History is never antiquated, because humanity is always fundamentally the same. It is always hungry for bread, sweaty with labor, struggling to wrest from nature and hostile men enough to feed its children. The welfare of the mass is always at odds with the selfish force of the strong. The exodus of the Roman plebeians and the Pennsylvania coal strike, the agrarian agitation of the Gracchi and the rising of the Russian peasants—it is all the same tragic human life. And in all history it would be hard to find any chapter so profoundly instructive, and dignified by such sublime passion and ability, as that in which the prophets took the leading part.

Moreover, the life and thought of the Old Testament prophets are more to us than classical illustrations and sidelights. They are an integral part of the thought-life of Christianity. From the beginning the Christian Church appropriated the Bible of Israel as its own book and thereby made the history of Israel part of the history of Christendom. That history lives in the heart of the Christian nations with a very real spiritual force. The average American knows more about David than about King Arthur, and more about the exodus from Egypt than about the emigration of the Puritans. Throughout the Christian centuries the historical material embodied in the Old Testament has been regarded as not merely instructive, but as authoritative. The social ideas drawn from it have been powerful factors in all attempts of Christianity to influence social and political life. Insofar as men have attempted to use the Old Testament as a code of model laws and institutions and have applied these to modern conditions, regardless of the historical connections, these attempts have left a trail of blunder and disaster. Insofar as they have caught the spirit that burned in the hearts of the prophets and breathed in gentle humanity through the Mosaic Law, the influence of the Old Testament has been one of the great permanent forces making for democracy and social justice. However our views of the Bible may change, every religious man will continue to recognize that to the elect minds of the Jewish people God gave so vivid a consciousness of the divine will that, in its main tendencies at least, their life and thought carries a permanent authority for all who wish to know the higher right of God. Their writings are like channel-buoys anchored by God, and we shall do well to heed them now that the roar of an angry surf is in our ears.

We shall confine this brief study of the Old Testament to the prophets, because they are the beating heart of the Old Testament. Modern study has shown that they were the real makers of the unique religious life of Israel. If all that proceeded from them, directly or indirectly, were eliminated from the Old Testament, there would be little left to appeal to the moral and religious judgment of the modern world. Moreover, a comprehension of the essential purpose and spirit of the prophets is necessary for a comprehension of the purpose and spirit of Jesus and of genuine Christianity. In Jesus and the primitive Church the prophetic spirit rose from the dead. To the ceremonial aspects of Jewish religion Jesus was either indifferent or hostile; the thought of the prophets was the spiritual food that he assimilated in his own process of growth. With them he linked his points of view, the convictions which he regarded as axiomatic. Their spirit was to him what the soil and climate of a country are to its flora. The real meaning of his life and the real direction of his purposes can be understood only in that historical connection.

Thus a study of the prophets is not only an interesting part in the history of social movements but it is indispensable for any full comprehension of the social influence exerted by historical Christianity, and for any true comprehension of the mind of Jesus Christ.

For the purposes of this book it is not necessary to follow the work of the prophets in their historical sequence. We shall simply try to lay bare those large and permanent characteristics which are common to that remarkable series of men and which bear on the question in hand.

RELIGION ETHICAL AND THEREFORE SOCIAL

The fundamental conviction of the prophets, which distinguished them from the ordinary religious life of their day, was the conviction that God demands righteousness and demands nothing but righteousness.

Primitive religions consisted mainly in the worship of the powers of nature. Each tribe worshiped its local tribal god, who dwelt in some gloomy ravine or on some mountaintop and sent rain and fertility to his people when he was pleased, or drought and pestilence on crops and herds when he was offended. Like every other despot, the god had to be kept in good humor by valuable gifts and prayers, offered in the right places, in the right manner, and by the duly qualified persons. If the sacrifices were neglected, the god was sure to be angry and then had to be propitiated by redoubled offerings, incantations, and dances. There was always some connection between religion and morality. It was always understood that the tribal god had instituted the tribal customs and was displeased with any violation of them. But the essential thing in religion was not morality, but the ceremonial method of placating the god, securing his gifts, and ascertaining his wishes. He might even be pleased best by immoral actions, by the immolation of human victims, by the sacrifice of woman's chastity, or by the burning of the firstborn.

In the primitive life of the Israelite tribes the religion of the common folk was probably much of this kind. Jehovah was the tribal god of Israel. Fortunately he was stronger and more terrible than the gods of the neighboring tribes, so that he was able to drive them out and give their land to his own people, but he was not fundamentally different from them and they were believed to be quite as real as Jehovah. There were certain forms of moral evil which he hated and certain social duties which he loved and blessed, but the surest way of remaining in his favor was to sacrifice duly and plentifully. If a man had offended against his fellow or his tribe, Jehovah would forgive when the rich smell of burnt meat filled his nostrils.

Against this current conception of religion the prophets insisted on a right life as the true worship of God. Morality to them was not merely a prerequisite of effective ceremonial worship. They brushed sacrificial ritual aside altogether as trifling compared with righteousness, nay, as a harmful substitute and a hindrance for ethical religion. "I desire goodness and not sacrifice," said Hosea (6:6), and Jesus was fond of quoting the words. The Book of Isaiah begins with a description of the disasters which had overtaken the nation, and then in impassioned words the prophet spurns the means taken to appease Jehovah's anger. He said the herds of beasts trampling his temple-court, the burning fat, the reek of blood, the clouds of incense, were a weariness and an abomination to the God whom they were meant to please. Their festivals and solemn meetings, their prayers and prostrations, were iniquity from which he averted his face. What he wanted was a right life and the righting of social wrongs: "Your hands are full of blood. Wash you, make you clean; put away the evil of your doings from before mine eyes; cease to do evil; learn to do well; seek judgment, relieve the oppressed; judge the fatherless; plead for the widow" (Isaiah 1:15–17, KJV).

Perhaps the simplest and most beautiful expression of that reformatory conception of true religion is contained in the words of Micah: "Wherewith shall I come before Jehovah, and bow myself before the high God? shall I come before him with burnt offerings, with calves of a year old? Will Jehovah be pleased with thousands of rams, or with ten thousands of rivers of oil? shall I give my firstborn for my transgression, the fruit of my body for the sin of my soul? He hath shewed thee, O man, what is good; and what doth Jehovah require of thee, but to do justly, and to love mercy, and to walk humbly with thy God?" (Micah 6:6–8, KJV).[1]

Amos (5:25) and Jeremiah (7:22–23) even tried to cut away the foundation of antiquity on which the sacrificial system rested, by denying that God had commanded sacrifices at all when he constituted the nation after the exodus from Egypt. Obedience was all that he had required.

This insistence on religious morality as the only thing God cares about is of fundamental importance for the question before us. The social problems are moral problems on a large scale. Religion is a tremendous generator of self-sacrificing action. Under its impulse men have burned up the animals they had laboriously raised; they have sacrificed their firstborn whom they loved and prized; they have tapped their own veins and died with a shout of triumph. But this unparalleled force has been largely diverted to ceremonial actions which wasted property and labor, and were either useless to social health or injurious to it. Insofar as men believed that the traditional ceremonial was what God wanted of them, they would be indifferent to the reformation of social ethics. If the hydraulic force of religion could be turned toward conduct, there is nothing which it could not accomplish.

This is still a living question. Under the influence of non-Christian customs and conceptions Christianity early developed its own ceremonial system. It is, of course, far more refined. Our places of worship have no stench of blood and entrails; our priests are not expert butchers. But the immense majority of people in Christendom have holy places, where they recite a sacred ritual and go through sacred motions. They receive holy food and submit to washings that cleanse from sin. They have a priesthood with magic powers which offers a bloodless sacrifice. This Christian ritual grew up, not as the appropriate and aesthetic expression of spiritual emotions, but as the indispensable means of pleasing and appeasing God, and of securing his favors, temporal and eternal, for those who put their heart into these processes. This Christian ceremonial system does not differ essentially from that against which the prophets protested; with a few verbal changes their invectives would still apply. But the point that here concerns us is that a very large part of the fervor of willing devotion which religion always generates in human hearts has spent itself on these religious acts. The force that would have been competent to "seek justice and relieve the oppressed" has been consumed in weaving the tinsel fringes for the garment of religion.

The prophets were the heralds of the fundamental truth that religion and ethics are inseparable, and that ethical conduct is the supreme and sufficient religious act. If that principle had been fully adopted in our religious life, it would have turned the full force of the religious impulse into the creation of right moral conduct and would have made the unchecked growth and accumulation of injustice impossible. This assertion can be verified by history. The Calvinistic Reformation stripped off a large part of the traditional ceremonial of the Church and it turned religious energy into political and intellectual channels. As a consequence the Calvinistic peoples at once leaped forward in the direction of democracy and education, and received such an increment of social efficiency that in spite of terrible handicaps they outstripped the stronger nations which failed to make this fuller connection between religion and social morality.

PUBLIC AND NOT PRIVATE MORALITY

It is important to note, further, that the morality which the prophets had in mind in their strenuous insistence on righteousness was not merely the private morality of the home, but the public morality on which national life is founded. They said less about the pure heart for the individual than of just institutions for the nation. We are accustomed to connect piety with the thought of private virtues; the pious man is the quiet, temperate, sober, kindly man. The evils against which we contend in the churches are intemperance, unchastity, the sins of the tongue. The twin-evil against which the prophets launched the condemnation of Jehovah was injustice and oppression.

The religious ideal of Israel was the theocracy. But the theocracy meant the complete penetration of the national life by religious morality. It meant politics in the name of God. That line by which we have tacitly separated the domain of public affairs and the domain of Christian life was unknown to them.

The prophets were not religious individualists. During the classical times of prophetism they always dealt with Israel and Judah as organic totalities. They conceived of their people as a gigantic personality which sinned as one and ought to repent as one. When they speak of their nation as a virgin, as a city, as a vine, they are attempting by these figures of speech to express this organic and corporate social life. In this respect they anticipated a modern conception which now underlies our scientific comprehension of social development and on which modern historical studies are based. We shall see that it was only when the national life of Israel was crushed by foreign invaders that the prophets began to address themselves to the individual life and lost the large horizon of public life.

The prophets were public men and their interest was in public affairs. Some of them were statesmen of the highest type. All of them interpreted past history, shaped present history, and foretold future history on the basis of the conviction that God rules with righteousness in the affairs of nations, and that only what is just, and not what is expedient and profitable, shall endure. Samuel was the creator of two dynasties. Nathan and Gad were the political advisers of David. Nathan determined the succession of Solomon. The seed of revolutionary aspirations against the dynasty of David was dropped into the heart of Jeroboam by the prophet Ahijah of Shiloh. Some of the prophets would get short shrift in a European State as religious demagogues. The overthrow of the dynasty of Omri in the Northern Kingdom was the result of a conspiracy between the prophetic party under Elisha and General Jehu, and resulted in a massacre so fearful that it staggered even the Oriental political conscience. On the other hand the insight of Isaiah into the international situation of his day saved his people for a long time from being embroiled in the destructive upheavals that buried other peoples, and gave it thirty years of peace amid almost universal war. The sufferings of Jeremiah came upon him chiefly because he took the unpopular side in national politics. If he and others had confined themselves to "religion," they could have said what they liked.

Our modern religious horizon and our conception of the character of a religious leader and teacher are so different that it is not easy to understand men who saw the province of religion chiefly in the broad reaches of civic affairs and international relations. Our philosophical and economic individualism has affected our religious thought so deeply that we hardly comprehend the prophetic views of an organic national life and of national sin and salvation. We usually conceive of the community as a loose sand-heap of individuals and this difference in the fundamental point of view distorts the utterances of the prophets as soon as we handle them. For instance, one of our most beautiful revival texts is the invitation: "Though your sins be as scarlet, they shall be as white as snow; though they be red like crimson, they shall be as wool." The words are part of the first chapter of Isaiah, to which reference has been made. The prophet throughout the chapter deals with the national condition of the kingdom of Judah and its capital. He describes its devastation; he ridicules the attempts to appease the national God by redoubled sacrifices; he urges instead the abolition of social oppression and injustice as the only way of regaining God's favor for the nation. If they would vindicate the cause of the helpless and oppressed, then he would freely pardon; then their scarlet and crimson guilt would be washed away. The familiar text is followed by the very material promise of economic prosperity, and the threat of continued war: "If ye be willing and obedient, ye shall eat the good of the land; but if ye refuse and rebel, ye shall be devoured with the sword." Of course the text is nobly true when it is made to express God's willingness to pardon the repentant individual, but that was not the thought in the mind of the writer. He offered a new start to his nation on condition that it righted social wrongs. We offer free pardon to individuals and rarely mention social wrongs.

We have seen that the prophets demanded right moral conduct as the sole test and fruit of religion, and that the morality which they had in mind was not the private morality of detached pious souls but the social morality of the nation. This they preached, and they backed their preaching by active participation in public action and discussion.

THE CHAMPIONS OF THE POOR

We advance another step in our study when we emphasize that the sympathy of the prophets, even of the most aristocratic among them, was entirely on the side of the poorer classes. Professor Kautzsch says: "Since Amos it was the alpha and omega of prophetic preaching to insist on right and justice, to warn against the oppression of the poor and helpless."[2] The edge of their invectives was turned against the land-hunger of the landed aristocracy who "joined house to house and laid field to field" (Isaiah 5:8, KJV),[3] till a country of sturdy peasants was turned into a series of great estates; against the capitalistic ruthlessness that "sold the righteous for silver, and the poor for a pair of shoes" (Amos 2:6, KJV), thrusting the poor freeman into slavery to collect a trifling debt; against the venality of the judges who took bribes and had a double standard of law for the rich and the poor.[4] This dominant trait of their moral feeling reacted on their theology, so that it became one of the fundamental attributes of their God that he was the husband of the widow, the father of the orphan, and the protector of the stranger. The widows and the fatherless were those who had no concrete power to back their claims, no "influence," no "financial interest," no "pull" with the police judges and aldermen of that time. The "stranger" was the immigrant who had no part in the blood-kinship of the clan, and hence no share in the land and no voice in the common affairs of the village. His modern brother is the proletarian immigrant of our cities, who also has no share in the modern means of production and no political power to protect his interests. When the prophets conceived Jehovah as the special vindicator of these voiceless classes, it was another way of saying that it is the chief duty in religious morality to stand for the rights of the helpless.

A man's sympathy is a more decisive fact in his activity than his judgment. One man today may disapprove of a given action of a railway or of a coal-combine, but his instinctive sympathy is always with "property" and "the vested interests." Another man may lament and condemn a foolish strike or headlong violence, but he will dwell on the extenuating circumstances and hold to the fundamental justice of "the cause of labor." This division of sympathy is now coming to be the real line of cleavage in our public affairs. There is no question on which side the sympathy of the prophets was enlisted. Their protest against injustice and oppression, to the neglect of all other social evils, is almost monotonous. To the more judicial and scientific temper of our day their invective would seem overdrawn and their sympathy would seem partisanship. In Jeremiah and in the prophetic psalms the poor as a class are made identical with the meek and godly, and "rich" and "wicked" are almost synonymous terms.

How did the championship of the oppressed come to be so essential a part of prophetic morality? It would be hard to find a parallel to it anywhere. What other nation has a library of classics in which the spokesmen of the common people have the dominant voice? If anyone cares to assert that divine inspiration alone will account for the fact, I should have no quarrel with the assertion. If the people ever come to their own in days to come, it may be that this trait of the Old Testament will come to be a stronger proof of its inspiration than the arguments that have hitherto done duty in theology.

But there were good historical causes for the attitude of the prophets in contemporary social movements.

When the nomad tribes of Israel settled in Canaan and gradually became an agricultural people, they set out on their development toward civilization with ancient customs and rooted ideas that long protected primitive democracy and equality. Some tribes and clans claimed an aristocratic superiority of descent over others. Within the tribe there were elders and men of power to whom deference was due as a matter of course, but there was no hereditary social boundary line, no graded aristocracy or caste, no distinction between blue blood and red. The idea of a *mèsalliance*, which plays so great a part in the social life of European nations and in the plots of their romantic literature, is wholly wanting in the Old Testament.[5] When the Bible became the property of the common man in the age of the Reformation, the total absence of a feudal nobility in the divinely instituted social life of Israel struck the people as an astonishing fact. It contributed greatly to emancipate them from their feudal reverence and added force to the democratic movements of that revolutionary age. The impression of primitive democracy made by the Bible is expressed in the old saying on which John Ball preached to the English peasants in Wat Tyler's rebellion:

When Adam dalf and Eve span,
Where was thanne a gentilman?

The great Alexandrian Jew Philo expressed the same impression about the Law: "If there is anyone in the world who is a praiser of equality, that man is Moses."[6] It was the decay of the primitive democracy, and the growth of luxury, tyranny, extortion, of court life and a feudal nobility, which Samuel wisely feared when the people demanded a king (1 Samuel 8:10–18).

The ownership of the land is the fundamental economic fact in all communities. Unequal distribution of the land and a hereditary aristocracy have always been inseparable facts. Approximately equal distribution of the land is the necessary basis for political and social democracy. Like all primitive peoples, Israel set out with a large measure of communism in land. It was used in severalty, but owned by the clan. At the conquest it was distributed to the tribes and there were ancient customs to prevent its alienation from the tribe. The principle was recognized that every family should have a freehold in land.

In this absence of social caste and this fair distribution of the means of production, the early times of Israel were much like the early times in our own country. America, too, set out with an absence of hereditary aristocracy and with a fair distribution of the land among the farming population. Both the Jewish and the American people were thereby equipped with a kind of ingrained, constitutional taste for democracy which dies hard. In time Israel drifted away from this primitive fairness and simplicity, just as we are drifting away from it. A new civilization arose, based on commerce and mobile wealth. Capital controlled the food supply. Great landed estates displaced the peasantry. The poor man, without the natural footing on the land, was often pushed over the precipice of want by any special emergency of war, famine, or sickness, and was sold into slavery for debt. The cities grew in size and importance. Rich men built stone houses and summer villas, and feasted daily on meat and wine, which the poor man tasted perchance thrice a year at the great feasts. Wealthy women robed their persons with the wealth wrung from the poor. As everywhere, this condition, when once created, tended to perpetuate itself and to guard against any reversal. The rich controlled the administration of the law. Priests and magistrates shared in the thirst for the most attractive of all narcotics—wealth. The rich in their well-fed optimism were lifted out of the natural human sympathy with the poor.

This rapid increase in wealth, with the usual unequal distribution of it, set in during the forty years preceding Amos. The old democratic instinct of the people angrily resented this upstart tyranny. It is a popular fallacy that long-continued oppression and misery cause revolutionary impatience. On the contrary, it is while the bit is new in the mustang's mouth that it rears and plunges. When a well-fed and independent people, with fresh memories of better days, are forced under the yoke, they are sure to protest. To the fellahin of Egypt poverty and exploitation seem as inevitable as the fall of night and the coming of death. In the United States the reaction against injustice is setting in swiftly and unanimously, though our working people are still in a condition that would seem paradise to the poor of other nations. So it was in Israel, and in that deeply religious age the protest was made in the name of God and by his spokesmen, the prophets. Amos, the first of the great social prophets, was a herdsman of Tekoa. He uttered the message of God, but he also expressed the feelings of the agrarian class to which he belonged. Abraham Lincoln in the contest against the slaveholding power, Henry George and Father McGlynn[7] in their protest against the alienation of the land, revived the earlier democracy of the Declaration of Independence and taught once more that all men are created free and equal, and are endowed with the inalienable right to life, liberty, and the pursuit of happiness. Similarly the championship of the poor by the prophets was not due to the inflow of novel social ideals, but to the survival of nobler conceptions to which they clung in the face of the distorted social conditions created by the new commercialism. They were the voice of an untainted popular conscience, made bold by religious faith.

We have an excellent illustration of this in the story of Ahab and Naboth's vineyard. Ahab knew the tenacity with which the Israelite clung to his freehold, and the sanctity which attached to the ancestral inheritance, and hence, when Naboth refused to sell, the king could only fume helplessly at the failure of his pretty plans for a private park. His wife was from Tyre, where royal power was older and accustomed to move roughshod over the fancied rights of the common herd. She sneered at his feeble grip and gave him a lesson in handling the judiciary. But the judicial murder of Naboth brought Elijah out to face the king, a grim incarnation of justice and of the divine rights of the people. Ahab had collided with the primitive land-system of Israel and the prophetic sense of justice, and it cost his dynasty the throne and Jezebel her life (1 Kings 21).

Another cause for the keen interest of the prophets in social justice deserves mention. The belief in a future life and future reward and punishment was almost absent in Hebrew religion. To live to an honored old age, to see his children and children's children, to enjoy the fruit of his labor in peace under his own vine and fig tree—that was all the heaven to which the pious Israelite looked forward. If social oppression robbed him of that, it robbed him of all. It even cheated him of his faith in the justice of God. On the supposition of a future life we can adjourn the manifest inequities of this life to the hereafter and trust that good and evil will yet be balanced justly when time and eternity are put together. In early Hebrew theology there were no such adjourned assizes for the individual. God must prove his justice here or never. If the wicked waxed fat and the pious were robbed with impunity, the moral order of the universe was under indictment. In Christianity, faith in the future life has to some extent subdued the demand for social justice, as we shall see later. The absence of this belief in Hebrew religion served to make the desire for earthly prosperity more direct and impatient, and belief in the divine justice lent religious sanction to the demand for economic justice.

The full strength of the humane social conceptions prevailing in Israel can be gauged only if we draw the Law into our discussion. We do not turn away from the prophets when we turn to the Law. According to the old interpretation, the entire Law contained in the Pentateuch was given by Jehovah to Moses and thus from the birth of the nation formed the foundation on which its whole life rested. In that case the prophets drew their ideals from the Law and their preaching was but a summons to the people to obey it. According to the modern critical interpretation only a small part of the Law was of very ancient origin. The Book of Deuteronomy was the outgrowth of prophetic ideas and agitation in the seventh century before Christ. The other portions of the Law did not originate till the Exile or after it, when the life of Judah had been long and deeply saturated with the teaching of the prophets. Thus on the one hypothesis the Law created the prophets; on the other hypothesis the prophets created the Law. In either case the relation is very close and causal. For any thorough discussion of the social ideals embodied in the Law it would be necessary to decide between these two hypotheses. For our purpose it is sufficient to point out that the Law and the prophets are a deposit of the same strong current of historical life, related to each other as cause and effect.

The Law, of course, recognized such fundamental customs and institutions of primitive Oriental civilization as slavery, polygamy, and blood-revenge. Insofar as it gives formal sanction to these institutions, it drops below the conceptions of human rights to which we have now attained. But its general drift and purpose, its regard for the rights of the poor, and its tenderness even for their finer feelings of self-respect are so noble and humane that one cannot study the social features of the Hebrew Law without a thrill of sympathy and admiration. By swift moral intuition, by the instinct of human fellow-feeling under the impulse of religious faith, regulations were conceived there which anticipated and outran the rudimentary protective legislation of our day. We shall glance at a few points only.

The land belonged to Jehovah, the national god. That is only another way of saying that it belonged to the community. It was not individual property, but clan and family property. There were various provisions to protect the right of the family to its ancestral holding and to prevent any permanent alienation. If land was sold under stress of need, it could be purchased back under favorable terms. In an agricultural community and before the introduction of machinery in farming, the land is by far the most important means of production. It is one of the highest problems of statesmanship how to plant and root the people evenly and wisely in the land. If the land is owned by the men who till it, there is social health and strength. If it is owned by wealthy proprietors and tilled by landless agricultural laborers, a curse is on the people. All the provisions of the Hebrew Law were meant to counteract the separation of the people from the land. It sought to prevent the growth of great estates and a landed aristocracy on the one side, and the growth of a landless proletariat on the other side (Leviticus 25).

Every seven years the fields were to lie fallow (probably in rotation) and their untilled harvests were to belong to all alike, like the berries that grow along our country roadsides or in our forests (Leviticus 25:1–7).[8] Of course the poor were benefited most by such liberty to picnic. When the grain, the grapes, and the olives were harvested, the poor had the right to glean, and the owner was forbidden to be too careful in harvesting the corners or to go over the vines and trees a second time (Deuteronomy 24:19–22).[9] A hungry man passing through the fields was always free to eat of grain or fruit (Deuteronomy

23:24–25). These provisions doubtless were based on ancient customs, which in turn were remnants of primitive communism in land, a lingering recognition that the entire community has rights in the land which limit those of the individual owner. This right of the hungry man to help himself was not like the coin flung to a beggar in pity. It was the claim to joint-ownership. It was his right. There is a fundamental moral distinction between the two things.

The laborer was to be paid at sundown (Deuteronomy 24:14–15).[10] That recognizes the importance of prompt payment of wages, for which modern labor legislation has had to contend. The principle for which the Eight-hour Movement and the Early-closing Movement now agitate was embodied in the Sabbath law. The Decalogue emphatically throws the protection of that law over those whose laborforce was most in danger of being exploited, the slaves, the immigrant stranger, and the beasts of burden. It was quite within the bounds of human nature for the frugal farmer to send them to work, while he sent himself to rest; hence they are especially enumerated. The earliest form of the Sabbath law is the most purely humane in its wording: "that thine ox and thine ass may rest, and the son of thy handmaid, and the stranger may be refreshed" (Exodus 23:12, KJV).[11] In a noncapitalistic community loans would usually be asked only to relieve need and therefore no advantage was to be taken of a neighbor's necessities by making his distress profitable. Interest was forbidden, so that debt could not breed more hopeless debt. This also counteracted the tendency to inequality in mobile capital. If an Israelite through debt or misfortune became slave to another, he was not a pariah, but was still to be treated as a member of the family, with a right to share in the family feasts. His servitude was not to become perpetual and when its term was over, he was to be loaded with gifts that he might have a start in shifting for himself. A fugitive slave was to be protected. Israel had no "Fugitive Slave Law." There is no record of any slave riots or of any burning slave question in its history (Deuteronomy 15, 23:15–16).[12]

Thus the Law, like the preaching of the prophets, manifests a striking sympathy for the poorer classes and an unflagging respect for their equal humanity. The manhood of the poor was more sacred to it than the property of the rich. In this fundamental attitude the Hebrew law differs widely from the Roman law, which was formulated in a despotic

State and amid a flagrant monopoly of wealth, and is responsible for much of the excessive reverence for private property rights in our Western civilization.

Some of the laws were purely ideal conceptions. The Year of Jubilee provided for a universal shakeup and a new start all around every fifty years; it was to restore the slave to liberty and the peasant to his land, and lift to the saddle again those families that had been thrown by a stumble in some gopher-hole of misfortune (Leviticus 25:8–17, 47–55). We know that this beautiful scheme remained a Utopia which even post-exilic zeal for the Law managed to disregard. Other laws were set aside by the ruthlessness of the strong. Only those were likely to be really effective which were firmly based on ancient custom. But in any case these were the ideals of social life that lived in the nobler hearts of Israel, and these ideals either created the prophetic convictions, or they were the product of the prophetic preaching.

THE EFFECT OF THE SOCIAL INTEREST ON THE RELIGIOUS LIFE

We rightly hold that social ideals of such moral value could grow only out of a religious life of high value. But the reverse is also historically true: that the high religious life of Israel could develop only within a nation that cherished and maintained such social ideals.

We have seen that the religion of the prophets was not the quiet devoutness of private religion. They lived in the open air of national life. Every heartbeat of their nation was registered in the pulse-throb of the prophets. They made the history of their nation, but in turn the history of their nation made them. They looked open-eyed at the events about them and then turned to the inner voice of God to interpret what they saw. They went to school with a living God who was then at work in his world, and not with a God who had acted long ago and put it down in a book. They learned religion by the laboratory method of studying contemporary life. Consequently their conception of God and of God's purposes was enlarged and clarified as their political horizon grew wider and clearer.

The first rise of widespread prophetism of which we have any record in Israel was historically connected with the raids and invasions of the

Philistines (about 1020 BC). Against their united and disciplined forces the scattered tribes were helpless. The national calamity created a religious revival. We catch glimpses of bands of prophets moving about in rhythmical processions, with music and song, spreading a contagious religious ecstasy. In Samuel the popular emotion found a practical, statesmanlike expression. The result was the election of the first king, the most important step toward organized national unity. As in the case of the American colonies and of the German States, the pressure of a great war was the only force sufficient to crystallize the loose ingredients of Israel into a nation. But the same national crisis which created the kingship also inaugurated the higher career of the prophetic order. There had been prophets in Israel before; they were a religious phenomenon common to all the Semitic peoples. But they had been mainly soothsayers, using their clairvoyant powers for anyone who needed them and paid them for their service. Their ecstatic raptures and their predictions had not been based on any fundamental moral convictions. The patriotic enthusiasm of the uprising against Philistine domination began to lift the prophets clear of the function and the magical implements of soothsaying, and cut them loose from ceremonial ritual in general. These functions now fell to the priests. This was "probably the very greatest relief which prophecy experienced in the course of its evolution."[13] Henceforth they were free to take that independent or hostile attitude to ritual religion to which we have referred, and their predictions henceforth were national in scope and based on fundamental moral laws and convictions. Thus patriotism was the emancipating power which set the feet of the prophetic order on that new and higher path which was destined to lift them far above the soothsayers of other nations with whom they started on a common level. That religious passion which had turned against a foreign invader was equally ready to turn against the domestic oppressors of the people.

The new series of prophets which began with Amos about 755 BC was summoned to action by a vaster danger than that of the Philistine invaders. The empire of Assyria was rising on the eastern horizon like a cyclone-cloud. It moved down on the cluster of little kingdoms in Syria and Palestine with irresistible force. Assyria was the first of those great powers which were destined to grind up the tribal nationalities of the ancient Orient and out of the detritus to form new conglomerate formations on a grander scale. What Assyria began, Chaldea and the Greeks continued and the Romans completed. We can see now that the process was inevitable and necessary for the development of a wider and higher civilization, but for those who got between the millstones, it was terror and agony. Napoleon playing at nine-pins with the kingdoms of Europe, or the white race dividing the earth during the nineteenth century, are mild modern parallels.

Now, to all the nations their gods were fundamentally the national gods. Every tribe had its god and every god had his tribe. Each people relied on the national god to preserve the nation. If the nation suffered some temporary defeat and disaster, the people were either angry with their god because he was inefficient and idle, or they cringed before him because he was angry. But when a nation was annihilated, it meant the collapse of the national faith and religion. Such a nation would hear the scoff of its neighbors: "Where is now thy god?"

This catastrophe of despair and disillusionment which brought other national religions to the ground amid the wreck of the nations that held them, threatened Israel too. The prophets saved the faith of the people. They even taught the people to rise on the ruins of their national past to a higher faith. The religion of the prophets was not based on local shrines or sacrifices, but on moral law. They asserted that Jehovah is fundamentally a god of righteousness, and a god of Israel only insofar as Israel was a nation of righteousness. The popular feeling was that if the people stood by Jehovah, he was in duty bound to stand by them against all comers. They expected their god to act on the maxim: "My country, right or wrong." The prophets denied it. They repudiated the idea of favoritism in the divine government. God moves on the plane of universal and impartial ethical law. Assyria belongs to him as well as Israel. He would live and be just even if Israel was broken. Israel was not a pet child that would escape the rod. Its prerogative was the revelation of God's will and not any immunity from the penalties of the moral law. The relation of the nation to Jehovah was not a natural right and privilege, but rested on moral conditions.

Thus the same historical catastrophe which wrecked the faith of others lifted the prophets to a higher faith. Their religion became international in its horizon and more profoundly ethical. Had their piety previously been narrow in its outlook and ritual in its character, it would now have suffered shipwreck. The Assyrian riddle would have been insoluble. Because they were men of large interest, new occasions under the inspiration of God were able to teach them new duties and new truths. They added new terms to the synthesis of truth. Their new faith at first seemed to the people a blasphemous denial of religion. When the events which they had foretold were actually fulfilled, the prophetic books became the support and stay on which popular religion slowly climbed to new life.

We are often told that ministers who concern themselves in political and social questions are likely to lose their spiritual power and faith. Professor George Adam Smith, in discussing the development of prophetic religion, says on the contrary: "Confine religion to the personal, it grows rancid, morbid. Wed it to patriotism, it lives in the open air, and its blood is pure."[14] I do not think so sweeping a generalization about purely private religion is just. But those who hold that the flower of religion can be raised only in flowerpots will have to make their reckoning with the prophets of Israel. The very book on which they feed their private devotion and that entire religion out of which Christianity grew, took shape through a divine inspiration which found its fittest and highest organs in a series of political and social preachers. It is safe to say that the "ethical monotheism" which has been Israel's invaluable contribution to the religious life of humanity would never have developed and survived if the prophets had from the outset limited their religion in the way in which we are nowadays advised to limit it.

THE LATER RELIGIOUS INDIVIDUALISM

That virility and humaneness of the prophets and that capacity for growth which stir our enthusiasm were largely due to the breadth and inclusiveness of their religious sympathy and faith. All the world was God's field; all the affairs of the nation were the affairs of religion. Every great event in history taught them a lesson in theology.

This type of religion was destroyed when the national life itself was destroyed by the foreign conquerors. The nation had been the subject of prophecy, and now the nation as such was blotted out. How could the prophets any longer appeal for national righteousness, when it was not at the option of the people to be righteous? Political agitation among a people under jealous foreign despotism would mean revolutionary agitation and would never be tolerated. Thus all the religious passion and reflection which had formerly flowed into social and political channels was dammed up and turned back. Prayer and private devoutness in pious individuals and in groups of pious men was the only field left to the religious impulse. The religious history and the ceremonial worship of Israel were the only bond of national unity that survived.

Jeremiah began the turn toward individual piety. The nation was breaking up about him. His prophetic activity had failed; the people refused to believe that his words were the word of Jehovah. But he heard the insistent inner voice of God, and the consciousness of this personal communion with Jehovah was his stay and comfort. Through his very failure and sufferings a tender personal relation developed between the soul of the prophet and his God. Other choice spirits were in the same situation. The influence of Jeremiah's writings reproduced in others that personal piety which was the outcome of his peculiar experience. For religious experience has a remarkable capacity for perpetuating and reproducing its type; witness the Confessions of Saint Augustine and the mysticism of Saint Bernard. Jehovah had been the God of the nation, and the God of the individual insofar as he was part of the nation. Now the nation was gone, and the righteous and lowly in their suffering and isolation stretched the lonely hand of faith to him and found him near with a personal touch of love and comfort. Thus the death-pangs of the national life were the birth-pangs of the personal religious life.

This was a wonderful triumph of religion, an evidence of the indestructibility of the religious impulse. It was fraught with far-reaching importance for the future of religion and of humanity in general. The subtlest springs of human personality were liberated when the individual realized that he personally was dear to God and could work out his salvation not as a member of his nation, but as a man by virtue of his humanity.

The value of this religious achievement has so impressed the students of Hebrew religious history that they have frequently assumed that this change in religion was pure gain. The real edifice of religion in the individual soul was now ready to stand for itself, they say, and the scaffolding of political and social religion could be torn down and its planking abandoned. It is assumed that Jeremiah and those who followed him recognized that the external means of realizing the ideal theocracy had failed, and they now set themselves deliberately to build a new religious community of regenerate souls. They turned their back on the Jewish nation and created the Jewish church.

That seems to me a misleading construction of the historical situation. It is true that the progress of religion toward spirituality was sure to make religion more personal. But every new religious synthesis should contain all that was good and true in the old. If the religious value of the individual was being discovered, why should the religious value of the community be forgotten? As a matter of fact, this concentration of religious life in the individual was not a deliberate step of progress, freely taken, but was forced upon these men by dire necessity. Religion found the broad plains of national life destroyed and in possession of the enemy, and it retreated into the mountain fastnesses of individual soul-life. It is a triumph of religious faith if a man who is crippled for life, and confined to a hopeless bed of pain and uselessness, still keeps his faith in God intact, or even develops so strong a trust in him who has slain him that others come to his bedside to draw faith from his mere look and existence. But that is not normal religion. Religion is the hallowing of all life, and its health-giving powers are always impaired if it is denied free access to some of the organs through which it fulfills its functions. Moreover, even with the prophets of the Exile, the restoration of the nation was the controlling desire. They insisted on personal holiness, not because that was the end of all religion, but because it was the condition and guarantee of national restoration. Personal religion was chiefly a means to an end; the end was social.

We can appreciate to the full the significance and value of the personal religion developed under the abnormal conditions of foreign domination and national prostration, and yet recognize frankly that this gain had involved a tremendous loss and that a religion developed under abnormal conditions is likely itself to be abnormal. This view is confirmed by the subsequent development of religious thought and life. Ezekiel, who lived during the Exile, shows the effect of the separation between the political and religious interests. He too still cherishes the national hope. At the end of his book he describes his vision of Jerusalem as he hoped it would be when restored and rebuilt. The old social convictions still persist; for instance, he takes care to provide for the just distribution of the land. And yet the political commonwealth and the king have become shadowy; the memory of them was growing dim and therefore the hope of them was vague and colorless. On the other hand the community of worshipers and the priests as their leaders were now vividly in the foreground. As a consequence the moral and religious emphasis had changed. His ideal city was no longer a city of justice so much as a city of the true worship. The older prophets had condemned the sins of man against man, especially injustice and oppression. Ezekiel dwelt on the sins of man against God, especially idolatry. Not justice but holiness had become the fundamental requirement, and holiness meant chiefly ceremonial correctness. The righteous nation was turned into a holy church. Ezekiel was a prophet by calling, but he was a priest by birth and training, and in comparing his literary style, his outlook on life, and his spiritual power with that of the older prophets, it is impossible to avoid a sense of religious decadence. The classical age was past. Religion had grown narrower and feebler when it was forced back from the great national and human interests into an ecclesiastical attitude of mind.

This impression deepens as we follow the little colony of Jewish Puritans who returned to their home and rebuilt the temple and the city amid poverty and fear. We shall have occasion hereafter to point out how intimately the religious life is connected with the secular life in which it develops. It is unjust to expect that the religious life which took form in the contracted circle that gathered about the rebuilt shrine of Jehovah would have the same bold originality and genius that swept through a hopeful and autonomous nation. But it is also unwise to hold that type of religion up to us as a higher development of religion.

It was an earnest, solid community of sifted and picked religious men, with a great preponderance of priests. There was marvelous courage and tenacity, heroic loyalty to conviction, a tenderness of personal piety, and a devotion to religion surpassing that of better times. But on its serious brow this religion wore a pallid complexion. It became legal, fixed, monotonous, a thing by itself, shut off from the spontaneity and naturalness of the general life. The prophetic voice was hushed and the prophetic fire died out. The scribe now sat where the prophet had stood, and the sacred book took the place of the living Voice. There was greater insistence on holiness than ever, but the conception of holiness had insensibly been lowered. The prophets had lifted the expression of religion to the ethical plane. The strong ethical ingredient was never again lost from Jewish religion, but the ceremonial ingredient began to mix with it in larger proportions and to become almost the chief constituent of holiness. Religion became once more priestly and ritual, with a timid and legal reverence for externals. It was coming to be dominated by those influences which Jesus and Paul opposed. This was a development similar to that of Christianity when the primitive spirituality of Paul passed into the ecclesiasticism and ceremonialism of the Catholic Church. This is not the classical period of Israel to which we turn for inspiration. Yet this is the period when personal religion was cultivated and when the teachers of religion did not preach politics, but devoted themselves to questions of worship and to church affairs.

THE PROPHETIC HOPE OF NATIONAL PERFECTION

In our personal Christian life every call to duty is immensely strengthened by the large hope of ultimately attaining a Christ-like character and the eternal life. That creates the atmosphere for the details of the religious life. In the social movement of our time the single reformatory demands are drawing a new and remarkable power from the larger conception of a reconstitution of social life on a cooperative basis. It takes a great and comprehensive hope to kindle the full power of enthusiasm in human lives.

The prophets too cherished a large ideal of the ultimate perfection of their people. Their specific demands for justice were reinforced by the conviction that these were at the same time an approximation to that wider national regeneration and a condition of its final completion.

In the earliest age of prophetism there was no distant outlook. Religious patriots were content if the nation was victorious over its enemies and could live in peace and prosperity under just kings. The development of a larger national hope was due to a double cause. On the one hand the ethical development of the nation and of its prophetic spokesmen furnished a higher ideal standard by which to measure the present. As long as a man has a low conception of what a perfect human character would imply, his idea of salvation will consist in slight reforms of conduct. The higher the conception of personal or social possibilities, the larger is the task set for us. On the other hand the doom of the nation, first impending and then actual, developed and enlarged the hope of the prophets. The less they lived by sight, the more they had to live by faith in the future. The more acute the present misery, the intenser the longing for the better day of God. We can find a ready illustration of this process in modern life. Those classes which are in practical control of wealth and power have practically no reformatory program; they are anxious to maintain the present situation intact. The middle classes, which share only partially in the advantages of the present social adjustments, have a list of grievances under which they chafe, but their social ideals do not differ very radically from the actual condition. They want reforms on the basis of the present social order, and they can reasonably hope to secure them by peaceful and gradual methods. But when we descend to the disinherited classes, or to those nations which are forcibly held back from political liberty and social betterment, the chasm between their actual condition and their desires grows so wide that only a revolutionary lift can carry them across. Thus under the double influence of a rising ethical life and a declining national life, the hope of the prophets became wider and more inclusive, and also more remote, separated from the present by a sharper line.

With the older prophets their social ideal was not a Utopian dream detached from present conditions, not a fair mirage floating in the air. It was within realizable distance. Its feet were planted on the actual social and political situation. The poetic imagery used by these Oriental patriots is apt to put a rainbow around their ideas, and our prosaic minds fail to see that they dealt with stern realities in a sober way. They had a clear-eyed outlook on contemporary events. They were religious men and as such expected no great crisis to come except through God's action. In any national regeneration God would have to be the real cause and force. They pictured his interference under the sublime image of a royal advent, God coming to his people on the wings of thunder and revealing his majesty to all the nations. This "day of Jehovah" would be the decisive turning-point, the inauguration of a new epoch of history. It meant vengeance on the foreign oppressor, punishment for the wicked, the sifting of Israel, the rescue of the weak. Beyond that day lay the golden age, in which all men would know God and his will, and the suffering of the just would be over forever. This day of Jehovah was to the prophets what the social revolution is to modern radical reformers, but expressed in terms of fervent religious faith; therefore its real goal was moral justice rather than economic prosperity, and it was to come by divine help and not by mere social evolution.

When the life of the nation withered away under the mailed fist of an alien power and the attainment of future improvements was torn from its control, the character of the national hope underwent a gradual change. It was never surrendered. However individualistic religion became, it never abandoned the collective hope as the real consummation of religion. The restoration of the temple after the Exile was hailed as a pledge of the national restoration that was to follow. The tense personal obedience to the minutiae of the Law in post-exilic Judaism was only the condition for the full blessing of God on the nation. Jehovah was always the God of an organized society and not of a disconnected mass of individuals. The Book of Daniel is an interpretation of international relations and events, a program for history to follow. But when the weight of foreign empire was so overwhelming and crushing that even the boldest hope could see no adequate resources in the people, the catastrophe that would break this power was conceived as a supernatural cataclysm out of all relation to human activity. By contact with foreign religious life during the Exile the belief in a great organized kingdom of evil had become a vital part of Jewish thought, and the Jews saw behind the oppressive human forces the shadowy and sinister forms of demon powers that could be overcome only by archangels and heavenly armies. When religion was driven from national interests into the refuge of private life, it lost its grasp of larger affairs, and the old clear outlook into contemporary history gave way to an artificial scheme. Instead of reading present facts to discern

God's purposes, men began to pore over the sacred books, and to piece the unfulfilled prophecies of the dead prophets into a mosaic picture of the future. The sunlight of the prophetic hope gave way to the lime-light of the apocalyptic visions of later Judaism.

It is profoundly pathetic to see how a people paralyzed, broken on the rack, and almost destroyed, still clung to its national existence and believed in its political future. Even the crudest dreams of apocalypti-cism have a tragic dignity and a lingering touch of vital force. In those dreams the Jewish people kept alive both their memories and their hopes, much as an impoverished aristocratic family will preserve the tarnished swords and the faded uniforms worn by illustrious ancestors and nurse the hope in its sons that they may someday regain the old position. But it is a mistake to look for political wisdom in a people that had no politics. Bands of foreign political refugees gathered in England have often dreamed intensely of the liberation of their father-land, but they have rarely planned wisely, and usually fail to take ac-count of changes since they left their home. Yet the unhistorical and artificial schemes of apocalypticism have been and are now more in-fluential in shaping the imagination of Christian men about the future course of history than the inspired thoughts of the great prophets. Men still rival the rabbis in learned calculations that somehow never turn out correct, and follow wandering lights which have thus far disap-pointed and led astray all that have ever followed them.

THE "PESSIMISM" OF THE PROPHETS

Social preachers nowadays are very commonly charged with being "too pessimistic." The same charge was made against the Hebrew prophets. Their people, like ours, was filled full of cheerful and egotis-tic optimism, with this distinction in favor of the Hebrews, that their optimism was based on religious faith, while ours is based mainly on material wealth. Israel had the strongest of all the gods for its cham-pion, and he would surely see his people through all trouble. Was not Israel his dwelling-place and did not his people supply him with the sacrifices which he loved?

It is significant that Amos first appeared at a festival at Bethel and interrupted its revels with a jarring note, crying that the fall of the

Northern Kingdom and the exile of its people were impending. These prophets continued to be disturbers of religious pleasure. To the people this seemed not only unpatriotic and disagreeable pessimism, but treason and blasphemy combined, for the nation and Jehovah were one, and the downfall of the one implied the downfall of the other. Amos came close to denying that Israel had any special religious prerogative at all.

As Amos and Hosea proclaimed the doom of the Northern Kingdom in the eighth century, Jeremiah proclaimed the fall of the Southern Kingdom a century and a half later. After the great reformation under Josiah (623 BC), the people were full of confidence. They had the temple; they had the Law. Jeremiah called their faith a delusion. Their temple would suffer the same fate as the ancient sanctuary of Shiloh. He denied that Judah was any better than the sister-kingdom had been. He ridiculed the optimistic prophets who prophesied the "smooth things" which the people loved to hear. He set it up as a general principle that the true prophets had always been prophets of disaster.

Ezekiel continued the same strain. He had been among the first prominent exiles deported in 597 BC. These men were full of hope for their own speedy return. Those who were left in Jerusalem were also full of confidence because they were now the sifted remnant. As long as Jerusalem was standing, Ezekiel made it his task to batter down and discourage this complacent confidence and to foretell the complete destruction of the national life.

How would we feel if a preacher should use a public gathering on Decoration Day or Thanksgiving Day to predict that our country for its mammonism and oppression was cast off by God and was to be parceled out to the Mexicans, the Chinese, and the negroes? In the sense of our security and strength we should probably simply laugh at him. But suppose that our country was bleeding through disastrous foreign wars and invasions, shaken by internal anarchy, terrified and angry at blows too powerful for us to avert, and in that condition a preacher should "weaken public confidence" still further by such a message? The vivid Oriental imagery of the prophets must not give us the impression that the injustice and corruption of that day were unique. It is impossible to make accurate comparisons of human misery, but it may well be that the conditions against which the moral sensibility of the prophets revolted could be equaled in any modern industrial center. And the same sins ought to seem blacker nineteen centuries after Christ than eight centuries before Christ.

Our prophetic books contain constant reference to the "false prophets." These were not the preachers of an idolatrous religion, but men who claimed to deliver the word of Jehovah. Neither were they always conscious liars. They were the mouthpiece of the average popular opinion, and they drew their inspiration from the self-satisfied patriotism which seemed so very identical with trust in Jehovah and his sanctuary. They were apparently the great majority of the prophetic order; the prophets of our Bible were the exceptional men.[15] The "false prophets" corresponded to those modern preachers who act as eulogists of existing conditions, not because they desire to deceive the people, but because they are really so charmed with things as they are and have never had a vision from God to shake their illusion. The logic of events proved to be on the side of those great Hebrews who asserted that black is really black, even if you call it white, and that a wall built with untempered mortar and built out of plumb is likely to topple. Because history backed their predictions, they are now in the Bible and revered as inspired.

It is well to note, however, that the prophets took no vindictive pleasure in prophesying evil, as some modern prophets enjoy beating the broom of God's vengeance about the ears of the people. While Jeremiah was foretelling the destruction of Jerusalem, his heart was breaking. It is significant that as soon as the disaster had come, the tone of prophecy changed. As long as the people were falsely optimistic, the prophets persisted in destroying their illusions. When the people were despairing, the prophets opposed their false hopelessness. On the ruins of the temple Jeremiah foretold its restoration, the return of the people, and a new era for his desolated country. As soon as the news of the destruction of the temple reached Ezekiel in exile, his threats changed to comfort and promises. This was not instability; it was loyalty to facts and hostility to illusions. Because they believed in the immutability of the moral law, they had to tremble at any departure from it, but they could also feel its unshaken strength under their feet when all things went to pieces about them. These pessimists were really pro-

foundly and magnificently optimistic. They never doubted the ultimate victory of Jehovah, of his righteousness, and of his people. The
time may come in our own country, when the smiling optimists will
be the most frightened and helpless of all, and when the present "pessimists" will be the only ones who have any hopes to cheer and any
clear convictions to guide.

The great prophets whom we revere were not those whom their
own age regarded most. They were the men of the opposition and of
the radical minority. They probably had more influence over posterity
than over their own generation. Their attacks on existing conditions
brought dangerous attacks upon them in return. A later day can always
study with complacency the attacks made on the vested interests in a
previous epoch, and the championship of eternal principles always
seems divine to a generation that is not hurt by them. Jesus summed
up the impression left on him by Old Testament history by saying that
prophets have no honor in their own country and in their own generation. It is always posterity which builds their sepulchres and garnishes
their tombs.

The Hebrew prophets shared the fate of all leaders who are far
ahead of their times. They did not themselves achieve the triumph of
their ideas. It was achieved for them by men who did not share their
spirit, and who insensibly debased their ideals in realizing them. The
ethical monotheism of the prophets did not become common property
in Judah till the priests and scribes enforced it. That is part of the
Divine Comedy of history. The Tories carry out the Liberal programs.
The ideas preached by Socialists and Single Taxers are adopted by
Populists, radical Democrats, and conservative Republicans succes-
sively, and in coming years the great parties will take credit for championing ideas which they did their best to stifle and then to betray. It is
a beneficent scheme by which the joy of life is evened up. The "practical men" and conservatives have the pleasure of feeling that they are
the only ones who can really make reforms work. The prophetic minds
have the satisfaction of knowing that the world must come their way
whether it will or not, because they are on the way to justice, and justice is on the way to God.

SUMMARY

Here then we have a succession of men perhaps unique in religious history for their moral heroism and spiritual insight. They were the moving spirits in the religious progress of their nation; the creators, directly or indirectly, of its law, its historical and poetical literature, and its piety; the men to whose personality and teaching Jesus felt most kinship; the men who still kindle modern religious enthusiasm. Most of us believe that their insight was divinely given and that the course they steered was set for them by the Captain of history.

We have seen that these men were almost indifferent, if not contemptuous, about the ceremonial side of customary religion, but turned with passionate enthusiasm to moral righteousness as the true domain of religion. Where would their interest lie if they lived today?

We have seen that their religious concern was not restricted to private religion and morality, but dealt preeminently with the social and political life of their nation. Would they limit its range today?

We have seen that their sympathy was wholly and passionately with the poor and oppressed. If they lived today, would they place the chief blame for poverty on the poor and give their admiration to the strong?

We have seen that they gradually rose above the kindred prophets of other nations through their moral interest in national affairs, and that their spiritual progress and education were intimately connected with their open-eyed comprehension of the larger questions of contemporary history. Is it likely that the same attitude of mind which enlarged and purified the religion of the Hebrew leaders would deteriorate and endanger the religion of Christian leaders?

We have seen that the religious concern in politics ceased only when politics ceased; that religious individualism was a triumph of faith under abnormal conditions and not a normal type of religious life; and that the enforced withdrawal of religion from the wider life was one cause for the later narrowness of Judaism. Does this warrant the assumption that religion is most normal when it is most the affair of the individual?

We have seen that the sane political program and the wise historical insight of the great prophets turned into apocalyptic dreams and bookish calculations when the nation lost its political self-government and training. How wise is it for the Christian leaders of a democratic nation to take their interpretation of God's purposes in history and their theories about the coming of the kingdom of God from the feeblest and most decadent age of Hebrew thought?

We have seen that the true prophets opposed the complacent optimism of the people and of their popular spokesmen, and gave warning of disaster as long as it was coming. If they lived among the present symptoms of social and moral decay, would they sing a lullaby or sound the reveille?

No true prophet will copy a prophet. Their garb, their mannerisms of language, the vehemence of their style, belong to their age and not to ours. But if we believe in their divine mission and in the divine origin of the religion in which they were the chief factors, we cannot repudiate what was fundamental in their lives. If anyone holds that religion is essentially ritual and sacramental; or that it is purely personal; or that God is on the side of the rich; or that social interest is likely to lead preachers astray; he must prove his case with his eye on the Hebrew prophets, and the burden of proof is with him.[16]

A Rhetorician for Righteousness

Phyllis Trible

How fitting that Walter Rauschenbusch began his study of social ethics with the Hebrew prophets. He appealed to the predecessors whose views stimulated his own. In particular, he focused on Amos, Hosea, Isaiah, and Jeremiah, major figures in ancient Israel from the eighth to the sixth centuries BCE. These historical roots provided resources to prod the Christian community in the United States at the beginning of the twentieth century CE.

RHETORICAL RESONANCES

Reading this chapter of Rauschenbusch's book a century later, one delights in the eloquence of its language disclosing the depth of its content. Images, metaphors, and aphorisms abound. Whether by intuition or intention, he joins style and substance to produce a powerful rhetoric for righteousness. In the process, he appropriates the past to charge the present and challenge the future.

The prophets and their writings, he says, "are like channel-buoys anchored by God, and we shall do well to heed them now that the roar of an angry surf is in our ears." Moving such a description to land, we associate it with Jeremiah, whom God made "a fortified city, an iron pillar, and a bronze wall" as a warning against his people (Jeremiah 1:18), and with Amos, whom God set as a plumb line to measure the unrighteousness of the people (Amos 7:8). At another juncture, where Rauschenbusch limns prophets as "disturbers of religious pleasure," we recall King Ahab tagging Elijah as a "troubler of Israel" and "my enemy" (1 Kings 18:17; 21:20). Such images and epithets witness to the formidable presence of prophets in times out of joint.

Among the pithy sentiments of Rauschenbusch is a critique of Christian devotees who spend their time "weaving the tinsel fringes for the garment of religion" rather than denouncing social evil. This description echoes Amos's railing against worshipers who offered the hollow noise of solemn assemblies (Amos 5:21–23), Micah's condemning preachers who uttered "empty falsehoods" rather than address rampant societal abuses (Micah 2:1–11), and Jeremiah's assailing leaders who made inauthentic vows and sacrifices to avert doom (Jeremiah 11:14–17). Again, Rauschenbusch's trenchant critique of "those who hold that the flower of religion can be raised only in flowerpots" evokes Jeremiah's graphic censure of those who had forsaken "the fountain of living waters" to dig out for themselves "broken cisterns that can hold no water" (Jeremiah 2:13) and also Amos's punning use of a basket of summer fruit (Hebrew *qayits*) to forecast the end (Hebrew *qets*) of the people Israel (Amos 8:1–3). In these instances, quotidian objects become vehicles for exposing the inadequacies of religion.

The use of animal imagery similarly linked Rauschenbusch to the prophets. Commenting on the timing of revolutionary fervor—that is, on the speed of angry responses to oppression and misery—he observes that "it is while the bit is new in the mustang's mouth that it rears and plunges." Behind the language lie a wealth of references, ranging from the pouncing of lion and leopard (Hosea 13:7; Amos 3:4, 12) through the trampling by horses (Jeremiah 8:16; Ezekiel 26:10–11; Micah 5:10), to the growling and ravaging by bears (Isaiah 59:11; Hosea 13:8; Amos 5:19). Keen observers of animals, the prophets found in them revelatory significance. Rauschenbusch follows suit.

STERN REALITIES AND UNCOMPROMISING RIGHTEOUSNESS

Although immersed in the poetic speech of the prophets, Rauschenbusch cautions (in his own poetic speech) that such imagery "is apt to put a rainbow around their ideas" so that "our prosaic minds fail to see that they dealt with stern realities in a sober way." Stern realities (persisting to this day) included class struggles, rich over poor, the landed aristocracy against peasants, the mistreatment of immigrant strangers, the sexual exploitation of women, the neglect of widows and orphans, the promotion of slavery, and the venality of courts. Over against these realities, says Rauschenbusch, the prophets set God's demand for "nothing but righteousness." As the norm and goal of social ethics, God's demand entails, above all, justice for the poor in this life.

To delineate righteousness Rauschenbusch draws sharp boundaries. Never does he waver in setting forth opposites, even at the expense of nuance. Hearing the cadences of his language inspires a litany of uncompromising contrast, couched in alliterative form. Prophetic faith means

Not ceremony but conduct
Not sacrifice (burnt offering) but service
Not malice but morality
Not oppression but obedience
Not jactitation but justice
Not expediency but ethics
Not personal but political
Not solitary but societal
Not ritual but righteousness
Not priest but prophet

DIFFICULTIES

These definitive boundaries serve Rauschenbusch's belief that the prophets constitute "the beating heart of the Old Testament." According to him, if the prophets were eliminated from this scripture, "there would be little left to appeal to the moral and religious judgment of the modern world." But therein lie difficulties. Not unlike his contemporaries, Rauschenbusch fails to recognize ethical problems within the prophetic literature itself, problems such as violence and misogyny (see, for example, Hosea 1–3; Ezekiel 16, 23). More broadly, he fails to embrace the fullness of the scripture. To elevate the prophets, he downplays the pursuit of righteousness in the creation literature of affirmation and promise, in the narrative literature of familial and national journeys of faith, and in the wisdom literature of suffering,

despair, and struggle. In short, he minimizes the grand sweep of the
Bible that Jews and Christians share, as well as certain attendant problems.

Adopting a scheme proposed by some scholars, Rauschenbusch
holds that early Israel knew a primitive religion of nature worship focused on sacrifices to its tribal god; that the coming of the prophets,
with their message of morality and social righteousness aimed "entirely
on the side of the poorer classes," marked the high point of Old Testament faith; and that with the destruction of the nation in the late sixth
century BCE the prophetic voices were muted. Individual piety replaced social ethics, cultic activities replaced political vitality, priestly
power replaced prophetic authority, and sacred writing replaced living
voices. Thus, he disparages Judaism by claiming that true prophecy
survived in Christianity (though not in all Christians and not at all
times). "In Jesus and the primitive Church the prophetic spirit rose
from the dead," he writes. Whether by this analogy he makes Judaism
corpse or executioner he fails to explore.

LAW AND APOCALYPSE

Rauschenbusch's denigration of Judaism does not, however, include
the Law. To the contrary, he intertwines it with prophecy. Although
aware of the debate about the order and hence relationship of prophecy and law, he does not take sides but rather sees each phenomenon
drawing strength from the other. Like prophecy, the Law supported
the poorer classes. Yet covenant, particularly the Sinai covenant, is the
puzzling omission in his discussion. Nowhere does he acknowledge its
foundational place in the promulgation of law and the development of
prophecy.

Another notable feature of Rauschenbusch's exposition is its focus
on the relationship between prophecy and apocalypticism. Whereas
many scholars, past and present, Jewish and Christian, have accented
the continuities between the two (without denying differences), he
aligns himself with those who set them in opposition. (In varying ways,
Martin Buber and Gerhard von Rad later took a similar position.) He
views apocalyptic literature as the writing of the defeated who, having
lost their vision of national events, turned away from social justice.

They retreated into private religion with its rewards in a future outside of history. They rejected vital faith for artificial schemes, with deleterious effects on both Christianity and Judaism. Given the revival of apocalyptic thinking in this present century, especially in politics, Rauschenbusch's insights merit careful reflection.

RHETORICAL RESONANCES

On the whole, reading this chapter revives the stirring message of the Hebrew prophets. For Rauschenbusch, no ambiguity, no polyvalency, no verbal instability impedes the call, in the words of Micah, "to do justice, love mercy, and walk humbly with God" (Micah 6:8). For him, no distance between past and present, no social location, inhibits the imperative, in the words of Amos, to "let justice roll down like waters, and righteousness like an ever-flowing stream" (Amos 5:24). For him, no cultural differences obviate the need, in the words of Isaiah, to "cease to do evil, learn to do good, seek justice, rescue the oppressed, defend the orphan, plead for the widow" (Isaiah 1:16–17).

"No true prophet," Rauschenbusch declares, "will copy a prophet." Nonetheless, we must appropriate what is fundamental in their writings. So comes the provocative question, as relevant for this new century as for Rauschenbusch's new century: "If they [the prophets] lived among the present symptoms of social and moral decay, would they sing a lullaby or sound the reveille?" Most surely, the answer calls, now as then, for justice (especially for the poor) in the social and political life of the nation.

One hundred years after the publication of his monumental study, Walter Rauschenbusch the prophet remains a rhetorician for righteousness. In his eloquent appeal to his predecessors, he continues to challenge his successors.

The Social Aims of Jesus

THE NEW SOCIAL INSIGHT INTO THE GOSPEL

A man was walking through the woods in springtime.[1] The air was thrilling and throbbing with the passion of little hearts, with the love-wooing, the parent pride, and the deadly fear of the birds. But the man never noticed that there was a bird in the woods. He was a botanist and was looking for plants.

A man was walking through the streets of a city, pondering the problems of wealth and national well-being. He saw a child sitting on the curbstone and crying. He met children at play. He saw a young mother with her child and an old man with his grandchild. But it never occurred to him that little children are the foundation of society, a chief motive power in economic effort, the most influential teachers, the source of the purest pleasures, the embodiment of form and color and grace. The man had never had a child and his eyes were not opened.

A man read through the New Testament. He felt no vibration of social hope in the preaching of John the Baptist and in the shouts of the crowd when Jesus entered Jerusalem. He caught no revolutionary note in the Book of Revelation. The social movement had not yet reached him. Jesus knew human nature when he reiterated: "He that hath ears to hear, let him hear."

We see in the Bible what we have been taught to see there. We drop out great sets of facts from our field of vision. We read other things into the Bible which are not there. During the Middle Ages men thought they saw their abstruse scholastic philosophy and theology amid the simplicity of the gospels. They found in the epistles the priests and bishops whom they knew, with robe and tonsure, living a celibate life and obeying the pope. When the Revival of Learning taught men to read all books with literary appreciation and historic insight, many things disappeared from the Bible for their eyes, and new things appeared. A new language was abroad and the Bible began to speak that language. If the Bible was not a living power before the Reformation, it was not because the Bible was chained up and forbidden, as we are told, but because their minds were chained by preconceived ideas, and when they read, they failed to read.

We are today in the midst of a revolutionary epoch fully as thorough as that of the Renaissance and Reformation. It is accompanied by a reinterpretation of nature and of history. The social movement has helped to create the modern study of history. Where we used to see a panorama of wars and strutting kings and court harlots, we now see the struggle of the people to wrest a living from nature and to shake off their oppressors. The new present has created a new past. The French Revolution was the birth of modern democracy, and also of the modern school of history.

The Bible shares in that new social reinterpretation. The stories of the patriarchs have a new lifelikeness when they are read in the setting of primitive social life. There are texts and allusions in the New Testament which had been passed by as of slight significance; now they are like windows through which we see miles of landscape. But it is a slow process. The men who write commentaries are usually of ripe age and their lines of interest were fixed before the social movement awoke men. They follow the traditions of their craft and deal with the same questions that engaged their predecessors. Eminent theologians, like other eminent thinkers, live in the social environment of wealth and to that extent are slow to see. The individualistic conception of religion is so strongly fortified in theological literature and ecclesiastical institutions that its monopoly cannot be broken in a hurry. It will take a generation or two for the new social comprehension of religion to become common property.

The first scientific life of Christ was written in 1829 by Karl Hase. Christians had always bowed in worship before their Master, but they had never undertaken to understand his life in its own historical environment and his teachings in the sense in which Jesus meant them to be understood by his hearers. He had stood like one of his pictures in

Byzantine art, splendid against its background of gold, but unreal and unhuman. Slowly, and still with many uncertainties in detail, his figure is coming out of the past to meet us. He has begun to talk to us as he did to his Galilean friends, and the better we know Jesus, the more social do his thoughts and aims become.

JESUS NOT A SOCIAL REFORMER

Under the influence of this new historical study of Christ, and under the pressure of the intense new social interest in contemporary life, the pendulum is now swinging the other way. Men are seizing on Jesus as the exponent of their own social convictions. They all claim him. "He was the first socialist." "Nay, he was a Tolstoian anarchist." "Not at all; he was an upholder of law and order, a fundamental opponent of the closed shop." It is a great tribute to his power over men and to the many-sidedness of his thought that all seek shelter in his great shadow.

But in truth Jesus was not a social reformer of the modern type. Sociology and political economy were just as far outside of his range of thought as organic chemistry or the geography of America. He saw the evil in the life of men and their sufferings, but he approached these facts purely from the moral, and not from the economic or historical point of view. He wanted men to live a right life in common, and only insofar as the social questions are moral questions did he deal with them as they confronted him.

And he was more than a teacher of morality. Jesus had learned the greatest and deepest and rarest secret of all—how to live a religious life. When the question of economic wants is solved for the individual and all his outward adjustments are as comfortable as possible, he may still be haunted by the horrible emptiness of his life and feel that existence is a meaningless riddle and delusion. If the question of the distribution of wealth were solved for all society and all lived in average comfort and without urgent anxiety, the question would still be how many would be at peace with their own souls and have that enduring joy and contentment which alone can make the outward things fair and sweet and rise victorious over change. Universal prosperity would not be incompatible with universal *ennui* and *Weltschmerz*. Beyond the question of economic distribution lies the question of moral relations; and beyond the moral relations to men lies the question of the religious communion with that spiritual reality in which we live and move and have our deepest being—with God, the Father of our spirits. Jesus had realized the life of God in the soul of man and the life of man in the love of God. That was the real secret of his life, the well-spring of his purity, his compassion, his unwearied courage, his unquenchable idealism: he knew the Father. But if he had that greatest of all possessions, the real key to the secret of life, it was his highest social duty to share it and help others to gain what he had. He had to teach men to live as children in the presence of their Father, and no longer as slaves cringing before a despot. He had to show them that the ordinary life of selfishness and hate and anxiety and chafing ambition and covetousness is no life at all, and that they must enter into a new world of love and solidarity and inward contentment. There was no service that he could render to men which would equal that. All other help lay in concentric circles about that redemption of the spirit and flowed out from it.

No comprehension of Jesus is even approximately true which fails to understand that the heart of his heart was religion. No man is a follower of Jesus in the full sense who has not through him entered into the same life with God. But on the other hand no man shares his life with God whose religion does not flow out, naturally and without effort, into all relations of his life and reconstructs everything that it touches. Whoever uncouples the religious and the social life has not understood Jesus. Whoever sets any bounds for the reconstructive power of the religious life over the social relations and institutions of men, to that extent denies the faith of the Master.

HIS RELATION TO CONTEMPORARY MOVEMENTS

If we want to understand the real aims of Jesus, we must watch him in his relation to his own times. He was not a timeless religious teacher, philosophizing vaguely on human generalities. He spoke for his own age, about concrete conditions, responding to the stirrings of the life that surged about him. We must follow him in his adjustment to the tendencies of the time, in his affinity for some men and his repulsion of others. That is the method by which we classify and locate a modern thinker or statesman.

The Christian movement began with John the Baptist. All the evangelists so understood it.[2] John himself accepted Jesus as the one who was to continue and consummate his own work. Jesus linked John closely to himself. He paid tribute to the rugged bravery and power of the man, and asserted that the new religious era had begun with John as an era of strenuous movement and stir. "The law and the prophets were until John; since that time the kingdom of God is preached, and every man presseth into it" (Luke 16:16).[3]

Both Jesus and the people generally felt that in John they had an incarnation of the spirit of the ancient prophets. He wore their austere garb; he shared their utter fearlessness, their ringing directness of speech, their consciousness of speaking an inward message of God. The substance of his message was also the same. It was the old prophetic demand for ethical obedience. He and his disciples fasted (Matthew 11:18, 9:14) and he taught them certain forms of prayer (Luke 11:1), but in his recorded teaching to the people there is not a word about the customary ritual of religion, about increased Sabbath observance, about stricter washings and sacrifices, or the ordinary exercises of piety. He spoke only of repentance, of ceasing from wrongdoing. He hailed the professional exponents of religion who came to hear him, as a brood of snakes wriggling away from the flames of the judgment. He demolished the self-confidence of the Jew and his pride of descent and religious monopoly, just as Amos or Jeremiah did. If God wanted children of Abraham, they were cheap and easy to get; God could turn the pebbles of the Jordan valley into children of Abraham by the million. But what God wanted, and found hard to get, was men who would quit evil. Yet God was bound to get such and would destroy all others. Now was the time to repent and by the badge of baptism to enroll with the purified remnant (Matthew 3:5–12).

The people asked for details. What would repentance involve? "What then must we do?" He replied: "He that hath two coats, let him share with him that hath none; and he that hath food, let him do likewise." The way to prepare for the Messianic era and to escape the wrath of the Messiah was to institute a brotherly life and to equalize social inequalities. If John thus conceived of the proper preparation for the Messianic salvation, how did he conceive of the Messianic era itself? Luke records his advice to two special classes of men, the tax-gatherers

and the soldiers. The tax-gatherers had used their legal powers for grafting and lining their pockets with the excess extorted from the people.
The soldiers had used their physical force for the same ends, like a New
York policeman taking a banana from the pushcart while the Italian
tries to look pleasant. John told them to stop being parasites and to live
on their honest earnings (Luke 3:10–14).

Would any preacher have defined repentance in these terms if his
eyes had not been open to the social inequality about him and to the
exploitation of the people by the representatives of organized society?
Luke characterized John's purpose by quoting the call of Isaiah to
make ready the way of the Lord by leveling down the hills and leveling
up the valleys and making the crooked things straight. John would not
have been so silent about the ordinary requirements of piety, and so
terribly emphatic in demanding the abolition of social wrongs, if he
had not felt that here were the real obstacles to the coming of the kingdom of God. From this preaching, coupled with our general knowledge of the times, we can infer what his points of view and his hopes
and expectations were, and also what the real spring of the remarkable
popular movement was which he initiated. It was the national hope of
Israel that carried the multitudes into the desert to hear John. The
judgment which he proclaimed was not the individual judgment of
later Christian theology, but the sifting of the Jewish people prepara-
tory to establishing the renewed Jewish theocracy. The kingdom of
God which he announced as close at hand was the old hope of the
people, and that embraced the restoration of the Davidic kingdom, the
reign of social justice, and the triumph of the true religion. John was a
true descendant of the prophets in denying that Jewish descent constituted a claim to share in the good time coming. He put the kingdom
on an ethical basis. But it was still a social hope and it required social
morality. According to our evangelists the work of John came to an
end because he had attacked Herod Antipas for his marriage with
Herodias (Matthew 14:3–5). According to Josephus[4] it was because
Herod feared the great influence of John over the people and wanted
to forestall a revolutionary rising under his impulse. The two explanations are not incompatible. Josephus had very direct lines of information about John[5] and his intimation deserves the more weight because
his book was written for a Roman audience and his general tendency

was to pass with discreet silence the revolutionary tendencies in his people.

Now Jesus accepted John as the forerunner of his own work. It was the popular movement created by John which brought Jesus out of the seclusion of Nazareth. He received John's baptism as the badge of the new Messianic hope and repentance. His contact with John and the events at the Jordan were evidently of decisive importance in the progress of his own inner life and his Messianic consciousness. When he left the Jordan the power of his own mission was upon him. He took up the formula of John: "The kingdom of God has come nigh; repent!" He continued the same baptism. He drew his earliest and choicest disciples from the followers of John. When John was dead, some thought Jesus was John risen from the dead. He realized clearly the difference between the stern ascetic spirit of the Baptist and his own sunny trust and simple human love (Matthew 11:16–19; Mark 2:18–22), but to the end of his life he championed John and dared the Pharisees to deny his divine mission (Mark 11:27–33). It seems impossible to assume that his own fundamental purpose, at least in the beginning of his ministry, was wholly divergent from that of John. In the main he shared John's national and social hope. His aim too was the realization of the theocracy.

Moreover, in joining hands with John, Jesus clasped hands with the entire succession of the prophets with whom he classed John. Their words were his favorite quotations. Like them he disregarded or opposed the ceremonial elements of religion and insisted on the ethical. Like them he sided with the poor and oppressed. As Amos and Jeremiah foresaw the conflict of their people with the Assyrians and the Chaldeans, so Jesus foresaw his nation drifting toward the conflict with Rome, and like them he foretold disaster, the fall of the temple and of the holy city. That prophetic type of religion which we have tried to set forth in the previous chapter, and which constituted the chief religious heritage of his nation, had laid hold on Jesus and he had laid hold of it and had appropriated its essential spirit. In the poise and calm of his mind and manner, and in the love of his heart, he was infinitely above them all.[6] But the greatest of all prophets was still one of the prophets, and that large interest in the national and social life which had been inseparable from the religion of the prophets was part of his life, too.

The presumption is that Jesus shared the fundamental religious purpose of the prophets. If anyone asserts that he abandoned the collective hope and gave his faith solely to religious individualism, he will have to furnish express statements in which Jesus disavows the religious past of his people.

THE PURPOSE OF JESUS: THE KINGDOM OF GOD

The historical background which we have just sketched must ever be kept in mind in understanding the life and purpose of Jesus. He was not merely an initiator, but a consummator. Like all great minds that do not merely imagine Utopias, but actually advance humanity to a new epoch, he took the situation and material furnished to him by the past and molded that into a fuller approximation to the divine conception within him. He embodied the prophetic stream of faith and hope. He linked his work to that of John the Baptist as the one contemporary fact to which he felt most inward affinity.

Jesus began his preaching with the call: "The time is fulfilled, and the kingdom of God is at hand; repent ye and believe the gospel" (Mark 1:15). The kingdom of God continued to be the center of all his teaching as recorded by the Synoptic gospels. His parables, his moral instructions, and his prophetic predictions all bear on that.

We have no definition of what he meant by the phrase. His audience needed no definition. It was then a familiar conception and phrase. The new thing was simply that this kingdom was at last on the point of coming.

We are not at all in that situation today. Anyone who has tried to grasp the idea will have realized how vague and elusive it seems. It stands today for quite a catalogue of ideas.[7] To the ordinary reader of the Bible, "inheriting the kingdom of heaven" simply means being saved and going to heaven. For others it means the millennium. For some the organized Church; for others "the invisible Church." For the mystic it means the hidden life with God. The truth is that the idea in the sense in which Jesus and his audiences understood it almost completely passed out of Christian thought as soon as Christianity passed from the Jewish people and found its spiritual home within the great Greco-Roman world. The historical basis for the idea was wanting there. The phrase was taken along, just as an emigrant will carry a water-jar with him; but the water from the well of Bethlehem evaporated and it was now used to dip water from the wells of Ephesus or from the Nile and Tiber. The Greek world cherished no such national religious hope as the prophets had ingrained in Jewish thought; on the other hand it was intensely interested in the future life for the individual, and in the ascetic triumph over flesh and matter. Thus the idea which had been the center of Christ's thought was not at all the center of the Church's thought, and even the comprehension of his meaning was lost and overlaid. Only some remnants of it persisted in the millennial hope and in the organic conception of the Church.

The historical study of our own day has made the first thorough attempt to understand this fundamental thought of Jesus in the sense in which he used it, but the results of this investigation are not at all completed. There are a hundred critical difficulties in the way of a sure and consistent interpretation that would be acceptable to all investigators. The limits of space and the purpose of this book will not permit me to do justice to the conflicting views. I shall have to set down my own results with only an occasional reference to the difficulties that beset them.

We saw in the previous chapter that the hope of the Jewish people underwent changes in the course of its history.[8] It took a wider and more universal outlook as the political horizon of the people widened. It became more individual in its blessings. It grew more transcendent, more purely future, more apocalyptic and detached from present events, as the people were deprived of their political autonomy and health. Moreover it was variously understood by the different classes and persons that held it. Because this hope was so comprehensive and all-embracing, every man could select and emphasize that aspect which appealed to him. Some thought chiefly of the expulsion of the Roman power with its despotic officials, its tax-extorters, and its hated symbols. Others dwelt on the complete obedience to the Law which would prevail when all the apostates were cast out and all true Israelites gathered to their own. And some quiet religious souls hoped for a great outflow of grace from God and a revival of true piety; as the hymn of Zacharias expresses it: "that we being delivered out of the hand of our enemies might serve him without fear, in holiness and righteousness before him, all the days of our life" (Luke 1:74–75). But even in this spiritual ideal the deliverance from the national enemies was a condition of a holy life for the nation. Whatever aspect any man emphasized, it was still a national and collective idea. It involved the restoration of Israel as a nation to outward independence, security, and power, such as it had under the Davidic kings. It involved that social justice, prosperity, and happiness for which the Law and the prophets called, and for which the common people always long. It involved that religious purity and holiness of which the nation had always fallen short. And all this was to come in an ideal degree, such as God alone by direct intervention could bestow.

When Jesus used the phrase "the kingdom of God," it inevitably evoked that whole sphere of thought in the minds of his hearers. If he did not mean by it the substance of what they meant by it, it was a mistake to use the term. If he did not mean the consummation of the theocratic hope, but merely an internal blessedness for individuals with the hope of getting to heaven, why did he use the words around which all the collective hopes clustered? In that case it was not only a misleading but a dangerous phrase. It unfettered the political hopes of the crowd; it drew down on him the suspicion of the government; it actually led to his death.

Unless we have clear proof to the contrary, we must assume that in the main the words meant the same thing to him and to his audiences. But it is very possible that he seriously modified and corrected the popular conception. That is in fact the process with every great, creative religious mind: the connection with the past is maintained and the old terms are used, but they are set in new connections and filled with new qualities. In the teaching of Jesus we find that he consciously opposed some features of the popular hope and sought to make it truer.

For one thing he would have nothing to do with bloodshed and violence. When the crowds that were on their way to the Passover gathered around him in the solitude on the eastern shore of the lake and wanted to make him king and march on the capital, he eluded them by sending his inflammable disciples away in the boat, and himself going up among the rocks to pray till the darkness dispersed the crowd (Matthew 14:22–23; John 6:14–15). Alliance with the Messianic force-revolution was one of the temptations which he confronted at the outset and repudiated (Matthew 4:8–10); he would not set up God's kingdom by using the devil's means of hatred and blood. With the glorious idealism of faith and love Jesus threw away the sword and advanced on the entrenchments of wrong with hand outstretched and heart exposed.

He repudiated not only human violence, he even put aside the force which the common hope expected from heaven. He refused to summon the twelve legions of angels either to save his life or to set up the kingdom by slaying the wicked. John the Baptist had expected the activity of the Messiah to begin with the judgment. The fruitless tree would be hewn down; the chaff would be winnowed out and burned; and there was barely time to escape this (Matthew 3:10–12). Jesus felt no call to that sort of Messiah-ship. He reversed the program; the judgment would come at the end and not at the beginning. First the blade, then the ear, and then the full corn in the ear, and at the very last the harvest. Only at the end would the tares be collected; only when the net got to shore would the good fish be separated from the useless creatures of the sea. Thus the divine *finale* of the judgment was relegated to the distance; the only task calling for present action was to sow the seed.[9]

The popular hope was all for a divine catastrophe. The kingdom of God was to come by a beneficent earthquake. Someday it would come like the blaze of a meteor, "with outward observation," and they could say: "Lo, there it is!" (Luke 17:20–21). We have seen that the prophetic hope had become catastrophic and apocalyptic when the capacity for political self-help was paralyzed. When the nation was pinned down helplessly by the crushing weight of the oppressors, it had to believe in a divine catastrophe that bore no causal relation to human action. The higher spiritual insight of Jesus reverted to the earlier and nobler prophetic view that the future was to grow out of the present by divine help. While they were waiting for the Messianic cataclysm that would bring the kingdom of God ready-made from heaven, he saw it growing up among them. He took his illustrations of its coming from organic life. It was like the seed scattered by the peasant, growing slowly and silently, night and day, by its own germinating force and the food furnished by the earth. The people had the impatience of the uneducated mind which does not see processes, but clamors for results, big, thunderous, miraculous results. Jesus had the scientific insight which comes to most men only by training, but to the elect few by divine gift. He grasped the substance of that law of organic development in nature and history which our own day at last has begun to elaborate systematically. His parables of the sower, the tares, the net, the mustard-seed, and the leaven are all polemical in character. He was seeking to displace the crude and misleading catastrophic conceptions by a saner theory about the coming of the kingdom. This conception of growth demanded not only a finer insight, but a higher faith. It takes more faith to see God in the little beginnings than in the completed results; more faith to say that God is now working than to say that he will someday work.

Because Jesus believed in the organic growth of the new society, he patiently fostered its growth, cell by cell. Every human life brought under control of the new spirit which he himself embodied and revealed was an advance of the kingdom of God. Every time the new thought of the Father and of the right life among men gained firmer hold of a human mind and brought it to the point of action, it meant progress. It is just as when human tissues have been broken down by disease or external force, and new tissue is silently forming under the old and weaving a new web of life. Jesus incarnated a new type of human life and he was conscious of that. By living with men and thinking and feeling in their presence, he reproduced his own life in others and they gained faith to risk this new way of living. This process of assimilation went on by the natural capacities inherent in the social organism, just as fresh blood will flow along the established arteries and capillaries. When a nucleus of like-minded men was gathered about him, the assimilating power was greatly reinforced. Jesus joyously felt that the most insignificant man in his company who shared in this new social spirit was superior to the grandest exemplification of the old era, John the Baptist (Matthew 11:11). Thus Jesus worked on individuals and through individuals, but his real end was not individualistic, but social, and in his method he employed strong social forces. He knew that a new view of life would have to be implanted before the new life could be lived and that the new society would have to nucleate around personal centers of renewal. But his end was not the new soul, but the new society; not man, but Man.

The popular hope was a Jewish national hope. Under the hands of
Jesus it became human and therefore universal. John the Baptist had
contradicted the idea that a Jew was entitled to participation in the
good time coming by virtue of his national descent. Every time Jesus
met a Gentile, we can see the Jewish prejudices melt away and he
gladly discovered the human brotherhood and spiritual capacity in the
alien. "Verily I say unto you, I have not found so great faith, no, not in
Israel," and he immediately makes room at the Messianic table-round
for those who shall come from the East and the West to sit down with
the patriarchs, while the sons of the kingdom, the Jews who were properly entitled to it, would be cast out (Matthew 8:10–12). He reminded
the indignant audience at Nazareth that the great Elijah had found his
refuge with a heathen Phoenician and Elisha had healed only a Syrian
leper. When one leper out of ten thanked him, he took pains to point
out that this one was a Samaritan foreigner (Luke 17:11–19), and
when he wanted to hold up a model of human neighborliness, he
went out of his way to make him a Samaritan, an alien, and a heretic
(Luke 10:25–37). Thus the old division of humanity into Jews and
Gentiles began to fade out in his mind, and a new dividing line ran
between the good and the evil, between those who opened their heart
to the new life and those who closed it. He approached the bold cos-
mopolitanism of Paul, that "in Christ Jesus there is neither Jew nor
Greek" (Galatians 3:28). But as soon as religion was thus based, not on
national prerogatives, but on human needs and capacities, the kingdom of God became universal in scope, an affair of all humanity. This
was a modification of immense importance.

Another subtle and significant change in the conception of the
kingdom came through the combination of all these changes. If the
kingdom was not dependent on human force, nor on divine catastrophes, but could quietly grow by organic processes; if it was not dependent on national reconstruction, but could work along from man to
man, from group to group, creating a new life as it went along; then
the kingdom in one sense was already here. Its consummation, of
course, was in the future, but its fundamental realities were already
present.

This is the point on which scholars are most at odds. Was the kingdom in Christ's conception something eschatological, all in the future,

to be inaugurated only by a heavenly catastrophe? Or was it a present reality? There is material for both views in his sayings. It is important here to remember that the sayings of Jesus were handed down by oral repetition among Christians for thirty or forty years before they were recorded in our gospels. But anyone can test for himself the fact that with the best intentions of veracity, a message or story changes a little when it passes from one mind to another, or even when it is repeated often by the same man. Something of his tastes and presuppositions flows into it. Unless we assume an absolute divine prevention of any such change, we must allow that it is wholly probable that the Church which told and retold the sayings of Jesus insensibly molded them by its own ideas and hopes. And if that is true, then no part of the sayings of Christ would be so sure to be affected as his sayings about his return and the final consummation of the kingdom. That was the hottest part of the faith of the primitive Church and anything coming in contact with it would run fluid. But any modifications on this question would all be likely to be in the direction of the catastrophic hope. That was the form of the Jewish hope before Christ touched it; he certainly did not succeed in weaning his disciples from it; it was the form most congenial to cruder minds; it chimed best with the fervid impatience of the earliest days; its prevalence is attested by the wide circulation of the Jewish apocalyptic literature among Christians. It is thus exceedingly probable that the Church spilled a little of the lurid colors of its own apocalypticism over the loftier conceptions of its Master, and when we read his sayings today, we must allow for that and be on the watch against it.

Like the old prophets, Jesus believed that God was the real creator of the kingdom; it was not to be set up by man-made evolution. It is one of the axioms of religious faith to believe that. He certainly believed in a divine consummation at the close. But the more he believed in the supreme value of its spiritual and moral blessings, and in the power of spiritual forces to mold human life, the more would the final act of consummation recede in importance and the present facts and processes grow more concrete and important to his mind. It was an act of religious faith for John the Baptist to assert that the long-desired kingdom was almost here. It was a vastly higher act of faith for Jesus to say that it was actually here. Others were scanning the horizon with the telescope to see it come; he said, "It is already here, right in the midst of you" (Luke 17:21). Anyone who reversed the direction of his life and became as a child could enter into it (Matthew 18:1–4). Anyone who saw that love to God and man was more than the whole sacrificial ritual was not far from the kingdom. The healing power going out to the demonized was proof that a stronger one had come upon the lord of this world and was stripping him of his property, and that the kingdom was already come upon them (Matthew 12:28). Thus the future tense was changing to the present tense under the power of faith and insight into spiritual realities. In the gospel and epistle of John we have a confirmation of this translation of the future tense into the present. The expected antichrist is already here; the judgment is now quietly going on; the most important part of the resurrection is taking place now. The discourse about the future coming of the Lord in the Synoptists is replaced in John by the discourse about the immediate coming of the Comforter (1 John 2:18; John 3:16–21, 5:19–29).

This, then, is our interpretation of the situation. Jesus, like all the prophets and like all his spiritually minded countrymen, lived in the hope of a great transformation of the national, social, and religious life about him. He shared the substance of that hope with his people, but by his profounder insight and his loftier faith he elevated and transformed the common hope. He rejected all violent means and thereby transferred the inevitable conflict from the field of battle to the antagonism of mind against mind, and of heart against lack of heart. He postponed the divine catastrophe of judgment to the dim distance and put the emphasis on the growth of the new life that was now going on. He thought less of changes made *en masse*, and more of the immediate transformation of single centers of influence and of social nuclei. The Jewish hope became a human hope with universal scope. The old intent gaze into the future was turned to faith in present realities and beginnings, and found its task here and now.

Luke says that the boy Jesus "advanced in wisdom and stature, and in favor with God and men"; that is, he grew in his intellectual, physical, religious, and social capacities. It is contrary to faith in the real humanity of our Lord to believe that he ever stopped growing. The story of his temptation is an account of a forward leap in his spiritual insight when he faced the problems of his Messianic task. When a growing and daring mind puts his hand to a great work, his experiences in that work are bound to enlarge and correct his conception of the purpose and methods of the work. It is wholly in harmony with any true conception of the life of Jesus to believe that his conception of the kingdom became vaster and truer as he worked for the kingdom, and that he moved away from the inherited conceptions along the lines which our study has suggested.

But after all this has been said, it still remained a social hope. The kingdom of God is still a collective conception, involving the whole social life of man. It is not a matter of saving human atoms, but of saving the social organism. It is not a matter of getting individuals to heaven, but of transforming the life on earth into the harmony of heaven. If he put his trust in spiritual forces for the founding of a righteous society, it only proved his sagacity as a society-builder. If he began his work with the smallest social nuclei, it proved his patience and skill. But Jesus never fell into the fundamental heresy of later theology; he never viewed the human individual apart from human society; he never forgot the gregarious nature of man. His first appeal was to his nation. When they flocked about him and followed him in the early Galilean days, it looked as if by the sheer power of his spirit he would swing the national soul around to obey him, and he was happy. There must have been at least a possibility of that in his mind, for he counted it as guilt that the people failed to yield to him. He did not merely go through the motions of summoning the nation to fealty, knowing all the while that such a thing lay outside of his real plan. No one will understand the life of Jesus truly unless he has asked himself the question, What would have happened if the people as a whole had accepted the spiritual leadership of Jesus? The rejection of his reign involved the political doom of the Galilean cities and of Jerusalem (Matthew 11:20–24; Luke 19:41–44); would the acceptance of his reign have involved no political consequences? The tone of sadness in his later ministry was not due simply to the approach of his personal death, but to the consciousness that his purpose for his nation had failed. He began then to draw his disciples more closely about him and to create the nucleus of a new nation within the old; it was the best thing that remained for him to do, but he had hoped to do better. He also rose then to the conviction that he would return and accomplish in the future what he had hoped to accomplish during his earthly life. The hope of the Coming and the organization of the Church together enshrine the social element of Christianity; the one postpones it, the other partly realizes it. Both are the results of a faith that rose triumphant over death, and laid the foundations of a new commonwealth of God even before the old had been shaken to ruins.

THE KINGDOM OF GOD AND THE ETHICS OF JESUS

All the teaching of Jesus and all his thinking centered about the hope of the kingdom of God. His moral teachings get their real meaning only when viewed from that center. He was not a Greek philosopher or Hindu pundit teaching the individual the way of emancipation from the world and its passions, but a Hebrew prophet preparing men for the righteous social order. The goodness which he sought to create in men was always the goodness that would enable them to live rightly with their fellow-men and to constitute a true social life.

All human goodness must be social goodness. Man is fundamentally gregarious and his morality consists in being a good member of his community. A man is moral when he is social; he is immoral when he is antisocial. The highest type of goodness is that which puts freely at the service of the community all that a man is and can be. The highest type of badness is that which uses up the wealth and happiness and virtue of the community to please self. All this ought to go without saying, but in fact religious ethics in the past has largely spent its force in detaching men from their community, from marriage and property, from interest in political and social tasks.

The fundamental virtue in the ethics of Jesus was love, because love is the society-making quality. Human life originates in love. It is love that holds together the basal human organization, the family. The physical expression of all love and friendship is the desire to get together and be together. Love creates fellowship. In the measure in which love increases in any social organism, it will hold together without coercion. If physical coercion is constantly necessary, it is proof that the social organization has not evoked the power of human affection and fraternity.

Hence when Jesus prepared men for the nobler social order of the kingdom of God, he tried to energize the faculty and habits of love and to stimulate the dormant faculty of devotion to the common good. Love with Jesus was not a flickering and wayward emotion, but the highest and most steadfast energy of a will bent on creating fellowship.

The force of that unitive will is best seen where fellowship is in danger of disruption. If a man has offended us, that fact is not to break up our fraternity, but we must forgive and forgive and forgive, and always stand ready to repair the torn tissues of fellowship (Matthew 18:21–22). If we remember that we have offended and our brother is now alienated from us, we are to drop everything, though it be the sacrifice we are just offering in the temple, and go and re-create fellowship (Matthew 5:23–24). If a man hates us or persecutes and reviles us, we must refuse to let fraternity be ruined, and must woo him back with love and blessings (Matthew 5:43–48). If he smites us in the face, we must turn the other cheek instead of doubling the barrier by returning the blow (Matthew 5:38–42). These are not hard and fast laws or detached rules of conduct. If they are used as such, they become unworkable and ridiculous. They are simply the most emphatic expressions of the determination that the fraternal relation which binds men together must not be ruptured. If a child can be saved from its unsocial self-will only by spanking it, parental love will have to apply that medicine. If a rough young fellow will be a happier member of society for being knocked down, we must knock him down and then sit down beside him and make a social man of him. The law of love transcends all other laws. It does not stop where they stop, and occasionally it may cut right across their beaten tracks. When Mary of Bethany broke the alabaster jar of ointment, the disciples voiced the ordinary law of conduct: it was wasteful luxury; the money might have fed the poor. Jesus took her side. While the disciples were thinking of the positions they were to get when their master became king, her feminine intuition had seen the storm-cloud lowering over his head and had heard the mute cry for sympathy in his soul, and had given him the best she had in the abandonment of love. "This is a beautiful deed that she has done." The instinct of love had been a truer guide of conduct than all machine-made rules of charity (Mark 14:3–9).

Jesus was very sociable. He was always falling into conversation with people, sometimes in calm disregard of the laws of propriety. When his disciples returned to him at the well of Samaria, they were surprised to find him talking with a woman! (John 4:27). Society had agreed to ostracize certain classes, for instance the tax-collectors. Jesus refused to recognize such a partial negation of human society. He accepted their invitations to dinner and invited himself to their houses, thereby incurring the sneer of the respectable as a friend of publicans and a glutton and wine-drinker (John 4:27). He wanted men to live as neighbors and brothers and he set the example. Social meals are often referred to in the gospels and furnished him the illustrations for much of his teaching (Luke 14). His meals with his disciples had been so important a matter in their life that they continued them after his death. His manner in breaking the bread for them all had been so characteristic that they recognized him by it after his resurrection (Luke 24:30–31). One of the two great ritual acts in the Church grew out of his last social meal with his friends. If we have ever felt how it brings men together to put their feet under the same table, we shall realize that in these elements of Christ's life a new communal sociability was working its way and creating a happy human society, and Jesus refused to surrender so great an attainment to the ordinary laws of fasting (Mark 2:18–19).

Pride disrupts society. Love equalizes. Humility freely takes its place as a simple member of the community. When Jesus found the disciples disputing about their rank in the kingdom, he rebuked their divisive spirit of pride by setting a little child among them as their model (Mark 9:33–37); for an unspoiled child is the most social creature, swift to make friends, happy in play with others, lonely without human love. When Jesus overheard the disciples quarreling about the chief places at the last meal, he gave them a striking object lesson in the subordination of self to the service of the community, by washing their dusty sandaled feet (Luke 22:24–30; John 13:1–20).

All these acts and sayings receive their real meaning when we think of them in connection with the kingdom of God, the ideal human society to be established. Instead of a society resting on coercion, exploitation, and inequality, Jesus desired to found a society resting on love, service, and equality. These new principles were so much the essence

of his character and of his view of life, that he lived them out spontaneously and taught them in everything that he touched in his conversations or public addresses. God is a father; men are neighbors and
brothers; let them act accordingly. Let them love, and then life will be
true and good. Let them seek the kingdom, and all things will follow.
Under no circumstance let them suffer fellowship to be permanently
disrupted. If an individual or a class was outside of fraternal relations,
he set himself to heal the breach. The kingdom of God is the true
human society; the ethics of Jesus taught the true social conduct
which would create the true society. This would be Christ's test for any
custom, law, or institution: does it draw men together or divide them?

INSISTENCE ON CONDUCT AND
INDIFFERENCE TO RITUAL

In our study of the Old Testament prophets, we saw that indifference
or hostility to ritual religion was a characteristic of prophetic religion,
and that this turned the full power of the religious impulse into the
sluice of ethical conduct. Jesus was a successor of the prophets in this
regard.

He used the temple as a place to meet men. He valued the temple as
a house of prayer and fiercely resented the intrusion of the money-
making spirit within it (Mark 11:15–19). But otherwise it was of no religious importance to him. According to the Gospel of John he foretold
a stage of religion in which the old burning issue of the true place of
worship would be antiquated and dead (John 4:19–24). Stephen, who
understood Jesus better than most of the apostles, had scant reverence
for the temple (Acts 6:14, 7:44–50). The temple sacrifices are mentioned by Jesus only to say that the duty of fraternal reconciliation
takes precedence of the duty of proceeding with sacrificial ritual
(Matthew 5:23–24).

Since the Exile and the dispersion of the people, the minor and
personal acts of ritual had really become of greater practical importance in the life of the Jews than the temple sacrifices. About some of
these minor ritual acts Jesus was in perpetual collision with the guard-
ians of customary piety. They did violence to human needs to keep the
Sabbath intact. They wanted men to look solemn and fast in contri-

tion even when they were happy in God. They concentrated attention on the things that a man must not touch and eat for fear of ceremonial defilement, and thereby made men indifferent to moral defilement. Jesus on the other hand held that the Sabbath was made to serve man, not to break him; that a man should fast only when fasting was the fit outward expression of his inward state of mind; and that no outward contact with tabooed things would make any difference in the moral status of a man, for that is determined only by the good or evil thoughts and impulses which proceed from his own soul. In his indifference to the law of clean and unclean food he not only brushed aside the traditions of the elders, but contradicted the sacred Law itself.[10]

These religious duties were supposed to serve God. Jesus was indifferent to them when they did not serve men, and hostile to them when they harmed men. He ridiculed the models of piety who were so punctilious about ritual observances and so indifferent to wrong moral relations. They faithfully gave a tithe of everything to religion, down to the mint, anise, and cumin in their garden-beds, but such little things as justice and mercy and good faith, the qualities on which human society rests and which constitute the real burden of the Law, they quite overlooked (Matthew 23:23). When he saw a Pharisee straining the milk lest haply he should swallow a drowned gnat and so transgress the Law in eating a strangled beast, he saw there a type of what these religious men were doing all the time: straining out gnats and swallowing camels (Matthew 23:24). They wiped the outside of the platter, but within it was "filled with extortion and excess"; their food was acquired by injustice and consumed in luxury (Matthew 23:25–26). Thus religion, which ought to be the source of morality, drugged and blinded the moral judgment, so that the very teachers of religion locked the door of the kingdom of God in men's faces (Matthew 23:13). They even nullified the fundamental obligation of the child to the parent by teaching that if a man gave money to the temple, and thus supported the ritual worship of God, he was free from the duty of supporting his parents (Mark 7:1–13). Thus religion had become a parasite on the body of morality and was draining it instead of feeding it.

This revolutionary attitude to inherited religion, which so jarred the earnest and painstaking representatives of traditional piety, is explained by Christ's conception of the kingdom of God. They thought it was a

Jewish affair and would rest on careful religious observances. He
thought it was a human affair and would rest on right human relations.
He would tolerate nothing that hallowed wrong, not even religion. He
had no patience with religious thought which hampered the attainment of a right social life. To them the written Law inherited from the
past was the supreme thing; to Jesus the better human life to be established in the future was the supreme thing.

HIS TEACHING ON WEALTH

Like all the greatest spiritual teachers of mankind, Jesus realized a profound danger to the better self in the pursuit of wealth. Whoever will
watch the development of a soul that has bent its energies to the task
of becoming rich, can see how perilous the process is to the finer sense
of justice, to the instinct of mercy and kindness and equality, and to
the singleness of devotion to higher ends; in short, to all the higher
humanity in us. It is a simple fact: "Ye cannot serve God and
mammon"; each requires the best of a man. "The cares of this life and
the deceitfulness of riches"—note that quality of deceitfulness—will
choke the good seed like rank weeds which appropriate soil and sunshine for their own growth (Matthew 13:22). When a man lays up
treasure, his heart almost inevitably is with his treasure. Then gradually the inner light in him is darkened; the eye of his conscience is
filmed and blurred (Matthew 6:19–34). Wealth is apt to grow stronger
than the man who owns it. It owns him and he loses his moral and
spiritual freedom. The spirit of the world is always deluding men into
thinking that "a man's life consisteth in the abundance of the things
which he possesseth" (Luke 12:15), but when he builds his life on that
theory, he is lost to the kingdom of God. And the worst of it is that he
does not know it. The harlot and the drunkard have their hours of re-
morse and self-abasement; the covetous man does not even know that
he is on the downward way. Saint Francis Xavier, the noble Jesuit missionary, said that in the confessional men had confessed to him all sins
that he knew and some that he had never imagined, but none had ever
of his own accord confessed that he was covetous.

But Jesus did not fear riches merely as a narcotic soul-poison. In his
desire to create a true human society he encountered riches as a prime

divisive force in actual life. It wedges society apart in horizontal strata between which real fellow-feeling is paralyzed. It lifts individuals out of the wholesome dependence on their fellows and equally out of the full sense of responsibility to them. That is the charm of riches and their curse.

This is the key to the conversation of Jesus with the rich young man, who was so honestly and lovably anxious to have a share in the Messianic salvation (Mark 10:17–31). He could truthfully say that he had lived a good life. Jesus accepted his statement, but if he would be perfect, he bade him get rid of his wealth and join the company of the disciples. This demand has been understood either as a test or as a cure. Some think that it was merely a test; if he had consented to give up his wealth, it would not have been necessary to give it up. Some think it was a cure for the love of money which was really needed in this exceptional case. On either supposition the advice concerned merely this young man's soul; it was medicine to be swallowed by him for his own good alone. But Jesus immediately rises from this concrete case to the general assertion that it is hard for any rich man to enter the kingdom of God, harder than for a camel to wedge through the eye of a needle. The young man who was departing with clouded face was simply a demonstration of a general fact. Clearly here was a case where the heart was anchored to its treasure.

The solution for this "hard saying" has been sought in the remark quoted only in Mark (10:23): "How hard it is for them that *trust* in riches to enter the kingdom." A man may have riches safely, if only he will not trust in them for salvation. It is easy to satisfy that requirement. But unfortunately the best manuscripts do not contain the phrase about trusting. The critical editions of the Greek text drop it or place it in the margin. Some early copyist probably felt as anxious to dull the sharpness of the saying as some modern preachers.

The solution lies in another direction. We think of the salvation of the individual in the life to come, and find it hard that so fine a young fellow should be barred out of heaven because he was rich. Jesus was thinking of the righteous society on earth which he was initiating and of the young man's fitness for that. Suppose the young man had kept his property and had thus joined the discipleship. How would that have affected the spirit of the group? Would not the others have felt jealously that he was in a class by himself? If Jesus had shown him favor, would not even the Master's motives have been suspected? If he had replenished the common purse from his private wealth, it would have given them all a more opulent living; it would have attracted self-ish men and would have paralyzed the influence of Jesus on the poor. Then the crowds would have been at his heels, not merely for healing, but for the loaves and fishes—with dessert added. Judas would have been deeply pleased with such a reinforcement of the apostolate, but Jesus would have gone through the same sorrow which came upon Francis of Assisi when property was forced upon his Order and its early spirit was corrupted. It is all very well to say that rich and poor are alike in Christ, but in fact only exceptional characters, like Jesus himself, can sit at a rich man's table and be indifferent to the fact that he is rich. Others can forget it for a while under the pressure of a great common danger or sorrow or joy, but in general the sense of equality will prevail only where substantial equality exists. The presence of the rich young man would have been ruinous to the spirit of the disciple-ship and would have put a debased interpretation on the hope of the kingdom. Jesus did not ask him to hand over his property for the common purse, as the Church in later times did constantly, but simply to turn it back to social usefulness and come down to the common level.

The meeting of Jesus and the rich young man has often been painted, but always as a private affair between the man and Jesus. At the St. Louis Exposition there was a painting representing Jesus sitting in a barnlike building with a group of plain people about him, women, old men, and the disciples. Before him stands the young man richly dressed, a bird of very different feather. Jesus by his gesture is evidently drawing in the listening group. It was not a matter between the man and God, but between the man and God and the people. The theo-logical interpretations of the passage, like the artistic, have failed to take account of this third factor in the moral situation. If the kingdom of God is the true human society, it is a fellowship of justice, equality, and love. But it is hard to get riches with justice, to keep them with equality, and to spend them with love. The kingdom of God means normal and wholesome human relations, and it is exceedingly hard for a rich man to be in normal human relations to others, as many a man has discovered who has honestly tried. It can be done only by an act of renunciation in some form.

It gives a touch of cheerful enjoyment to exegetical studies to watch the athletic exercises of interpreters when they confront these sayings of Jesus about wealth. They find it almost as hard to get around the needle's eye as the camel would find it to get through. The resources of philology have been ransacked to turn the "camel" into an anchor-rope, and Oriental antiquarian lore has been summoned to prove that the "needle's eye" was a little rear-gate of the Oriental house through which the camel, by judiciously going down on its knees, could work its way. There is a manifest solicitude to help the rich man through. There has not been a like fraternal anxiety for the Pharisee; he is allowed to swallow his camel whole (Matthew 23:25). In the case of the parable of the unjust steward (Luke 16:1–9) there are something like thirty-six different interpretations on record. They differ so widely in their allegorical explanations that we are left in doubt if the lord of the steward is God or the devil. Yet the parable seems simple if one is not afraid of breaking crockery by handling it as Jesus did.

A rich man had farmed out his lands to various tenants on shares. A steward managed the whole and collected the rents. His master became suspicious of him and gave him notice of dismissal. It would take effect as soon as his accounts were made up. The steward confronted a painful situation. He looked at his white hands and concluded that manual labor was not in his line. His social pride would not permit him to beg. So he concluded, as others have done, to "graft." He used the brief term of authority still left him to get on the right side of the tenant farmers by reducing on paper the amount of their harvests and consequently of the shares due to the proprietor. He could hope to enjoy their comfortable hospitality for some time in return for the substantial present he made them out of his master's pocket. In fact they would have to "stand in" with their confederate to keep him silent. When his master learned of it, he could not help admiring the cleverness of the rascal, even though it was at his expense.

Jesus, too, admired the shrewdness and foresight which the men of the present social order exhibit within their plane of life. If only the children of light would be as wise in theirs! His application is that the men who hold the dishonest money of the present era will do well to use the brief term of power left to them before the Messianic era begins. Let them do kindness to the children of the kingdom, and they may hope by their gratitude to get some sort of borrowed shelter when the situation is reversed and the pious poor are on top.[11]

The story shows a very keen insight into the contemporary methods of grafting and into the state of mind of the grafter. No one could have told the story who had not thought incisively about social conditions. Interpreters have found it necessary to defend Jesus because he holds up an immoral transaction for admiration and imitation. Probably Jesus never imagined that a teacher of his well-known bent of mind would be supposed to approve of financial trickery. It is precisely because he was so completely outside of and above this whole realm of dealing that he could play with the material as he did, just as a confirmed socialist might use the watering of stock or the "promotion" of a mining company as an illustration of the beauties of socialism. It is hard to imagine Jesus without a smile of sovereign humor in advising these great men to get a plank ready for the coming deluge.

The parable of the steward has often been so allegorized and spiritualized that the application to the rich has almost evaporated. His contemporary hearers saw the point. "The Pharisees, who were lovers of money, heard all this and they ridiculed him." The Greek verb means literally: "they turned up their nose at him" (Luke 16:14). Jesus replied to their scoff by telling the story of Dives and Lazarus (Luke 16:19–31). It was not intended to give information about the future life. Its sting is in the reference to the five brothers of Dives, who were living as he had lived and were in imminent peril of faring as he fared. They were the men who refused to do what the parable of the steward advised them to do.

There is a notable difference between our gospels in regard to the amount of teaching on wealth which they report, and in regard to the sharpness of edge which it bears. The Gospel of John is at one extreme; we should hardly know that Jesus had any interest in questions of property if we had only the fourth gospel. There the center of his teaching is not the kingdom of God, but the eternal life; his interests are religious and theological. The divine figure of the Son of God moves through the doubts and discussions of men like the silver moon sailing serene through the clouds. Luke is at the other extreme. He alone reports the parables of the rich fool, the unjust steward, and Dives and Lazarus. He also gives a sharper social turn to sayings reported by the other gospels. For instance, in the beatitudes of Matthew, Jesus blesses the poor in spirit, those who hunger and thirst after righteousness, the meek, and the pure in heart. In Luke he cheers the socially poor, the physically hungry, and puts his meaning beyond question by following up his blessings on the poor with corresponding woes to the rich, the satiated, and the frivolous.[12]

Many critics doubt that Jesus taught as Luke reports him. They think that Luke drew this class of material from a Jewish Christian source which was tainted with Ebionitic tendencies. I fail to be convinced by their arguments. The other evangelists report so much of a similar nature that the sections reported by Luke alone seem quite in keeping with the mind of Jesus. The material in question seems to bear the literary and artistic coinage of Christ's intellect as much as any other material in the gospels. The "Ebionitic sections" run all through the narrative of Luke, so that they were not drawn from some brief document covering a small portion of Christ's life. The critical suspicions seem to rest on a moral dislike for the radical attitude toward wealth taken by Jesus according to Luke, rather than on sound critical principles. But if it is a question of moral insight, we may fairly doubt who saw more truly, Jesus or the modern middle-class critics.

An ascetic distrust of property and the property instinct very early affected the Christian Church after its transition to the Greek world, and it is important to be on the watch against any influence of this alien tendency on those who reported the sayings of Christ. But the radical teachings of Jesus are not ascetic, but revolutionary, and that distinction is fundamental. What is called Ebionitic[13] is simply the strong democratic and social feeling which pervaded later Judaism. The probability is rather that the later reporters softened this social radicalism and spiritualized his thought, than that some Ebionitic followers of Jesus imported their social unrest into his spiritual teaching.

In any case, Luke put his endorsement on this conception of Christ's thought. He was the only writer in the New Testament, so far as we know, who was of Greek descent and character. He had a singular affinity for all that was humane, generous, heroic, and humanly stirring and touching, and he tells his stories with a distinct artistic note. Men like Stephen, Barnabas, and Paul were his heroes. To him alone we owe the parable of the good Samaritan, of the prodigal son, of the Pharisee and publican, and the story of the great sinner and the penitent thief. The socialist among the evangelists was also the one who has given us the richest expressions of the free grace of God to sinful men, without which our evangel would be immeasurably poorer. If he was tainted with Ebionitic and Jewish spirit in reporting the teachings on wealth, how did he escape being tainted with the legal and narrow spirit of Jewish Christianity which must have saturated his supposed Ebionitic sources?

THE SOCIAL AFFINITIES OF JESUS

As with the Old Testament prophets, the fundamental sympathies of Jesus were with the poor and oppressed. In the glad opening days of his preaching in Galilee, when he wanted to unfold his program, he turned to the passage of Isaiah where the prophet proclaimed good tidings to the poor, release to the captives, liberty to the bruised, and the acceptable year of the Lord for all. Now, said Jesus, that is to be fulfilled (Luke 4:16–22). To John in prison he offered as proof that the Messiah had really come, that the helpless were receiving help, and the poor were listening to glad news (Matthew 11:2–5). The Church has used the miracles of Jesus for theological purposes as evidences of his divine mission. According to the Synoptic gospels, Jesus himself flatly refused to furnish them for such a purpose to the contemporary theologians (Matthew 12:38–39, 16:1–4). His healing power was for social help, for the alleviation of human suffering. It was at the service of any wretched leper, but not of the doubting scribes. To get the setting of his life we must remember the vast poverty and misery of Oriental countries. It threatened to engulf him entirely and to turn him into a traveling medical dispensary.

It is often possible nowadays to detect the social studies and sympathies of a public speaker by an unpurposed phrase or allusion which shows where his mind has been dwelling. This is constantly true of Jesus. If he had not known how much a strayed sheep or a lost coin meant to the poor, he would not have told the anecdotes about their joy in recovering them (Luke 15:1–10). If he had not appreciated the heroic generosity of the poor, he would not have breathed more quickly when he saw the widow dropping her two mites in the temple treasury (Mark 12:41–44). He knew how large a share the lawyers get in settling an estate and how little is left for the widow (Mark 12:40). He knew how bitterly hard it is for the poor to set the judicial machinery of organized society in motion in their favor; hence he used the illustration of the widow and the judge (Luke 18:1–8). He knew the golden rule of "society": dine those by whom you want to be dined. Those who most need a dinner are never asked to have a dinner. He suggested to his hosts a reversal of this policy (Luke 14:12–14), and he loved to think of the Messianic salvation as an actual reversal on a grand scale, in which the regular guests would be left out in the cold, while the halt and blind were gathered from the highways and hedges to enjoy the fat things (Luke 14:15–24; Matthew 22:1–14). No man would have laid on the colors in the opening description of Dives at his feasting and Lazarus among the dogs as Jesus did (Luke 16:19–21), who had not felt vividly the gulf that separates the social classes. If that parable came from the lips of Jesus, that is enough to mark his social spirit. *Ex ungue leonem.*[14]

Jesus proceeded from the common people. He had worked as a carpenter for years, and there was nothing in his thinking to neutralize the sense of class solidarity which grows up under such circumstances. The common people heard him gladly (Mark 12:37) because he said what was in their hearts. His triumphal entry into Jerusalem was a poor man's procession; the coats from their backs were his tapestry, their throats his brass band, and a donkey was his steed. During the last days in Jerusalem he was constantly walking into the lion's cage and brushing the sleeve of death. It was the fear of the people which protected him while he bearded the powers that be. His midnight arrest, his hasty trial, the anxious efforts to work on the feelings of the crowd against him, were all a tribute to his standing with the common people.

Dr. W. M. Thomson, in his *Land and the Book*, beautifully says: "With uncontrolled power to possess all, he owned nothing. He had no place to be born in but another man's stable, no closet to pray in but the wilderness, no place to die but on the cross of an enemy, and no grave but one lent by a friend." That, perhaps, overstates his poverty. But it is fair to say that by birth and training, by moral insight and

conviction, by his sympathy for those who were down, and by his success in winning them to his side, Jesus was a man of the common
people, and he never deserted their cause as so many others have
done. Whenever the people have caught a glimpse of him as he really
was, their hearts have hailed Jesus of Nazareth as one of them.

THE REVOLUTIONARY CONSCIOUSNESS OF JESUS

There was a revolutionary consciousness in Jesus; not, of course, in the
common use of the word "revolutionary," which connects it with violence and bloodshed. But Jesus knew that he had come to kindle a fire
on earth. Much as he loved peace, he knew that the actual result of his
work would be not peace but the sword. His mother in her song had
recognized in her own experience the settled custom of God to "put
down the mighty and exalt them of low degree," to "fill the hungry
with good things and to send the rich empty away" (Luke 1:52–53).
King Robert of Sicily[15] recognized the revolutionary ring in those
phrases, and thought it well that the Magnificat was sung only in
Latin. The son of Mary expected a great reversal of values. The first
would be last and the last would be first (Mark 10:31). He saw that
what was exalted among man was an abomination before God (Luke
16:15), and therefore these exalted things had no glamour for his eye.
This revolutionary note runs even through the beatitudes where we
should least expect it. The point of them is that henceforth those were
to be blessed whom the world had not blessed, for the kingdom of God
would reverse their relative standing. Now the poor and the hungry
and sad were to be satisfied and comforted; the meek who had been
shouldered aside by the ruthless would get their chance to inherit the
earth, and conflict and persecution would be inevitable in the process
(Matthew 5:1–12).

We are apt to forget that his attack on the religious leaders and authorities of his day was of revolutionary boldness and thoroughness.
He called the ecclesiastical leaders hypocrites, blind leaders who fum-
bled in their casuistry, and everywhere missed the decisive facts in
teaching right and wrong. Their piety was no piety; their law was inadequate; they harmed the men whom they wanted to convert.[16] Even
the publicans and harlots had a truer piety than theirs (Matthew

21:23–32). If we remember that religion was still the foundation of the Jewish State, and that the religious authorities were the pillars of existing society, much as in medieval Catholic Europe, we shall realize how revolutionary were his invectives. It was like Luther anathematizing the Catholic hierarchy.

His mind was similarly liberated from spiritual subjection to the existing civil powers. He called Herod, his own liege sovereign, "that fox" (Luke 13:32). When the mother of James and John tried to steal a march on the others and secure for her sons a pledge of the highest places in the Messianic kingdom (Matthew 20:20–28), Jesus felt that this was a backsliding into the scrambling methods of the present social order, in which each tries to make the others serve him, and he is greatest who can compel service from most. In the new social order, which was expressed in his own life, each must seek to give the maximum of service, and he would be greatest who would serve utterly. In that connection he sketched with a few strokes the pseudo-greatness of the present aristocracy: "Ye know that they which are supposed to rule over the nations lord it over them, and their great ones tyrannize over them. Thus shall it not be among you."[17] The monarchies and aristocracies have always lived on the fiction that they exist for the good of the people, and yet it is an appalling fact how few kings have loved their people and have lived to serve. Usually the great ones have regarded the people as their oyster. In a similar saying reported by Luke, Jesus wittily adds that these selfish exploiters of the people graciously allow themselves to be called "benefactors" (Luke 22:25). His eyes were open to the unintentional irony of the titles in which the "majesties," "excellencies," and "holinesses" of the world have always decked themselves. Every time the inbred instinct to seek precedence cropped up among his disciples he sternly suppressed it. They must not allow themselves to be called Rabbi or Father or Master, "for all ye are brethren" (Matthew 23:1–12). Christ's ideal of society involved the abolition of rank and the extinction of those badges of rank in which former inequality was incrusted. The only title to greatness was to be distinguished service at cost to self (Matthew 20:26–28). All this shows the keenest insight into the masked selfishness of those who hold power, and involves a revolutionary consciousness, emancipated from reverence for things as they are.

The text, "Give to Caesar what is Caesar's" (Matthew 22:21), seems to mark off a definite sphere of power for the emperor, coordinate with God's sphere. It implies passive obedience to constituted authority and above all guarantees Caesar's right to levy taxes. Consequently it has been very dear to all who were anxious to secure the sanctions of religion for the existing political order. During the Middle Ages that text was one of the spiritual pillars that supported the Holy Roman Empire.[18] But in fact we misread it if we take it as a solemn decision, fixing two coordinate spheres of life, the religious and the political. His opponents were trying to corner Jesus. If he said "pay the Roman tax," he disgusted the people. If he said "do not pay," Rome would seize him, for its patience was short when its taxes were touched. Jesus wittily cut the Gordian knot by calling for one of the coins. It bore the hated Roman face and stamp on it—clear evidence whence it issued and to whom it belonged. If they filled their pockets with Caesar's money, let them pay Caesar's tax. The significant fact to us is that Jesus spoke from an inward plane which rose superior to the entire question. It was a vital question for Jewish religion; it did not even touch the religion of Jesus. Moreover, it was not purely a religious question with them; matters that concern money somehow never are purely religious. In paying tribute to Caesar, they seemed to deny the sovereignty of Jehovah, Israel's only king; that was, indeed, one point for grief. But another point was that they had to pay, pay, pay; and money is such a dear thing! Jesus felt none of their fond reverence for cash. Hence he could say, Give to Caesar the stuff that belongs to him, and give to God what he claims.

We have another incident in which his inward attitude to taxation comes out (Matthew 17:24–27). The Jews annually paid a poll-tax of half a shekel for the support of the temple worship, which sufficed to maintain it in splendor. The collector met Peter and asked if his master did not intend to pay. Peter, probably knowing his custom hitherto, said, "Certainly." When he came into the house, Jesus, who seems to have overheard the conversation, asked him from whom the kings of the earth usually exacted taxes, from their subjects or their sons. Peter rightly judged that the subjects usually did the paying, and the members of the royal family were exempt. "Then," said Jesus, "as we are sons of God and princes of the bloodroyal, we are exempt from

God's temple-tax. But lest we give offense, go catch a fish and pay the tax." We all know by experience that the expression of the face and eye are often quite essential for understanding the spirit of a conversation. We must think of Jesus with a smile on his lips during this conversation with his friend Peter. Yet something of his most fundamental attitude to existing institutions found expression in this gentle raillery. He was inwardly free. He paid because he wanted to, and not because he had to.

Camille Desmoulins, one of the spiritual leaders of the French Revolution, called Jesus *"le bon sansculotte."* Emile de Laveleye, the eminent Belgian economist, who had the deepest reverence for Christianity as a social force, said, "If Christianity were taught and understood conformably to the spirit of its Founder, the existing social organism could not last a day" (*Primitive Property*). In his essay on "The Progress of the World," James Russell Lowell said, "There is dynamite enough in the New Testament, if illegitimately applied, to blow all our existing institutions to atoms."

These men have not seen amiss. Jesus was not a child of this world. He did not revere the men it called great; he did not accept its customs and social usages as final; his moral conceptions did not run along the grooves marked out by it. He nourished within his soul the ideal of a common life so radically different from the present that it involved a reversal of values, a revolutionary displacement of existing relations. This ideal was not merely a beautiful dream to solace his soul. He lived it out in his own daily life. He urged others to live that way. He held that it was the only true life, and that the ordinary way was misery and folly. He dared to believe that it would triumph. When he saw that the people were turning from him, and that his nation had chosen the evil way and was drifting toward the rocks that would destroy it, unutterable sadness filled his soul, but he never abandoned his faith in the final triumph of that kingdom of God for which he had lived. For the present, the cross; but beyond the cross, the kingdom of God. If he was not to achieve it now, he would return and do it then.

That was the faith of Jesus. Have his followers shared it? We shall see later what changes and limitations the original purpose and spirit of Christianity suffered in the course of history. But the Church has never been able to get entirely away from the revolutionary spirit of

Jesus. It is an essential doctrine of Christianity that the world is fundamentally good and practically bad, for it was made by God, but is now
controlled by sin. If a man wants to be a Christian, he must stand over
against things as they are and condemn them in the name of that
higher conception of life which Jesus revealed. If a man is satisfied
with things as they are, he belongs to the other side. For many centuries the Church felt so deeply that the Christian conception of life and
the actual social life are incompatible, that anyone who wanted to live
the genuine Christian life, had to leave the world and live in a monastic community. Protestantism has abandoned the monastic life and
settled down to live in the world. If that implies that it accepts the present condition as good and final, it means a silencing of its Christian
protest and its surrender to "the world." There is another alternative.
Ascetic Christianity called the world evil and left it. Humanity is waiting for a revolutionary Christianity which will call the world evil and
change it. We do not want "to blow all our existing institutions to
atoms," but we do want to remold every one of them. A tank of gaso-
line can blow a car sky-high in a single explosion, or push it to the top
of a hill in a perpetual succession of little explosions. We need a combination between the faith of Jesus in the need and the possibility of
the kingdom of God, and the modern comprehension of the organic
development of human society.

We saw at the outset of our discussion that Jesus was not a mere
social reformer. Religion was the heart of his life, and all that he said
on social relations was said from the religious point of view. He has
been called the first socialist. He was more; he was the first real
man, the inaugurator of a new humanity. But as such he bore within
him the germs of a new social and political order. He was too great to
be the Savior of a fractional part of human life. His redemption ex-
tends to all human needs and powers and relations. Theologians have
felt no hesitation in founding a system of speculative thought on the
teachings of Jesus, and yet Jesus was never an inhabitant of the realm
of speculative thought. He has been made the founder and organizer
of a great ecclesiastical machine, which derives authority for its offices
and institutions from him, and yet "hardly any problem of exegesis is
more difficult than to discover in the gospels an administrative or organizing or ecclesiastical Christ."[19] There is at least as much justification

in invoking his name today as the champion of a great movement for a more righteous social life. He was neither a theologian, nor an ecclesiastic, nor a socialist. But if we were forced to classify him either with the great theologians who elaborated the fine distinctions of scholasticism; or with the mighty popes and princes of the Church who built up their power in his name; or with the men who are giving their heart and life to the propaganda of a new social system—where should we place him?

A Response by an Evangelical

Tony Campolo

As I reread this Christian classic, I was both thrilled and troubled by what Walter Rauschenbusch had to tell us. Of overwhelming importance to all Christians is his clear declaration that the central message of Jesus concerned the kingdom of God as a socio-historical reality. For Rauschenbusch, the gospel Jesus proclaimed was all about the realization in this world of the kingdom of God—a kingdom marked by economic justice; an end to the racist, sexist, and ethnic prejudices and discriminatory practices of our present age; and glimpses of an emerging new humanity.

Rauschenbusch offers us a clear and pronounced alternative to any attempt to place the kingdom of God solely in another world after this life is over. Understanding Jesus as a prophet in the tradition of Amos and Isaiah, Rauschenbusch makes a clear case that Jesus was committed to the transformation of this present world into a new societal system in which God's will would be done on earth even as it is done in heaven.

It has taken Evangelicals like me far too long to come around to embracing Rauschenbusch's kind of holistic gospel that not only promises eternal life to individuals but also offers hope for dramatic positive changes in our present social order.

The way in which Rauschenbusch views the coming of God's kingdom on earth is of vital importance. He teaches that the kingdom will emerge in evolutionary fashion as Christians, imbued with the spirit of Christ, work together to make it happen. He rejects the belief that the evils of our present age will come to a sudden and climactic end through an apocalyptic intervention of God, as so many present-day

Evangelicals would contend. Fans of the famous Left Behind books by Tim LaHaye and Jerry Jenkins would be very disturbed to learn that Rauschenbusch clearly does not believe that God's kingdom comes through a sudden eschatological event. Instead, he believes the kingdom of God comes on earth through a gradual process facilitated by people of God infused with the ethics and social vision of Christ. When godly people are mobilized into a movement that permeates all the institutions of society with the values of Christ, then, he contends, the gates of hell cannot prevail against it.

Rauschenbusch viewed Jesus in much the same way as did the Catholic theologian Pierre Teilhard de Chardin. Teilhard declared Jesus to be what he called "the Omega man." By that, he meant Jesus was an incarnation of the fully actualized human being that God wills for all of us to become. Jesus was the person who embodied the highest expressions of God's love and justice and, as such, was a full manifestation of a new kind of humanity that could create the kingdom of God. This man Jesus, whose personhood had eschatological dimensions, lived among us—and as we spiritually relate to him and surrender to his influence in our lives, we will be transformed into people through whom God's kingdom becomes a historical reality. Though Teilhard had a much stronger mystical dimension to his teachings, his thinking about the role of Jesus in bringing in the kingdom was similar to Rauschenbusch's teaching.

It is important to recognize that Rauschenbusch, though he embraced a Hebraic view of God's kingdom being in this world, rejected the belief that it would come about through a violent overthrow of the present socioeconomic order. While expressing great sympathies for a socialist vision in which all economic inequalities would be abolished, he totally rejected the kind of violence evident in the Bolshevik Revolution. He can better be understood as a precursor of Mahatma Gandhi and Martin Luther King Jr. He was a pacifist who rejected violence as an instrument for God's revolution.

Rauschenbusch considered John the Baptist to be the beginning of the Christian movement. He saw that Jesus, while connecting with John's vision for a new humanity in which there would be a redistribution of wealth, transcended the belief that the kingdom would come through God breaking into history with an abrupt cataclysmic judgment on the present age. God would not bring in the kingdom, according to Rauschenbusch, through the violent overthrow of the present kingdoms of this world, but through organic, evolutionary development. As individuals "assimilated" the spirit of Christ and lived out his ethics, the kingdom of God would break loose in the world. As persons relinquished their individualism and embraced a community spirit that made them one, they would, according to Rauschenbusch, become a force for social change.

To say that Rauschenbusch had a big impact on Christian thinking would be an understatement. His call for Christians to become instruments of God working to change our world into one that embodies the ethical values of the kingdom of God is an essential part of our thinking today. It is hard to imagine that Christians ever thought otherwise. Yet, in the not too distant past, a good part of American Christendom posited God's kingdom as belonging only to another world. Some of us Evangelicals still hold to this belief, but most share Rauschenbusch's view that we are called to take up the challenge of bringing about social transformation. Furthermore, over the past few decades an increasing number of Evangelicals have come to believe, as Rauschenbusch did, that in our efforts to be kingdom builders, we must give priority to addressing the needs of the poor and oppressed. It is hard for most current Evangelicals to understand how our predecessors could have missed the more than two thousand biblical admonitions to seek justice and well-being for those whom Jesus called "the least of these."

While we may embrace much of Rauschenbusch's thinking, it is easy to understand why so many Evangelicals are troubled by the writings of this twentieth-century prophet. First and foremost, Evangelicals are concerned about his understanding of the personhood and work of Jesus. He does not clearly affirm the traditional church belief that Jesus was fully God incarnate. There is no doubt that Rauschenbusch affirms divine qualities in Jesus, but it is not at all clear that he views Christ as the second member of the Trinity.

Second, there is a sense in which Rauschenbusch fails to grasp the radical sinfulness of the human race. It would remain for Reinhold Niebuhr and others of later decades to raise the awareness that there is something desperately wrong with all of us, and that assimilating the spirit of Christ as some kind of transforming moral influence is not enough to create the new humanity Rauschenbusch envisioned. I wish Rauschenbusch had asserted the need for personal conversion in which an individual enters into a dialogical and transforming relationship with a living Christ. We Evangelicals believe that what is needed is infinitely more than a noble ethic that is assimilated as we yield to the influence of Christ's teachings. Rather, we affirm the need for a miraculous transformation of who we are into what we should be, a transformation that comes as Christ himself invades our hearts and minds and souls—as mystical as that might sound. It may be that Rauschenbusch is deserving of the criticism of Reinhold Niebuhr's brother, Richard Niebuhr, who spoke out against those who would preach a gospel in which "a God without wrath brought men without sin into a kingdom without judgment through the ministrations of a Christ without a cross."

We Evangelicals also have trouble with Rauschenbusch's view of Scripture. As he developed his understanding of the ethics of Jesus, Rauschenbusch used Scripture very much in accord with the teachings of biblical scholars of his day, who understood the Bible as being powerfully conditioned by the political circumstances of the writers. Since we Evangelicals view the Bible as inspired by the Holy Spirit, we are less willing to accept the overriding influence of such external forces. We accept the established canon of the Bible and believe the Holy Spirit was at work in the authors of Scripture, guiding them as they wrote so as to give us an infallible guide for faith and practice. Therefore, we cannot accept Rauschenbusch's belief that parts of the Bible need not be taken seriously since they are more reflections of the political pressures under which they were written than revelations from God.

Finally, I do not believe there is necessarily a contradiction between Rauschenbusch's idea that the kingdom of God emerges as individuals come together to form a movement through which God effects change and the traditional evangelical belief that God intervenes at the eschaton, bringing history to a dramatic and apocalyptic end. Personally, I believe both are true. I contend that to be Christian is to surrender to the leading of Christ to work for social justice, but that we do so in the hope that one day Christ will physically return and bring to a triumphant conclusion the good work he initiated in us and is carrying out through us (Philippians 1:6).

It is easy to understand why Rauschenbusch thought the way he did concerning the organic, progressive evolution of society, ameliorated by godly people who sacrifice individual egoism for the collective good. Sociologists of the time, such as Lester Ward, had made this kind of thinking prevalent. The naive optimism that marked the early part of the twentieth century supported this way of looking at the future. Since those heady visionary days, we have been shaken back to the reality that demonic "principalities and powers" are at work in the world, increasing the kingdom of evil.

While Rauschenbusch saw the Church's potential to provide the volunteers and financial resources for a positive social movement, he nevertheless failed to recognize its mystic nature as the living organism in which Christ is personally alive. You cannot help but sense that Rauschenbusch believed the Church had become a social institution bogged down by self-interests and that he questioned whether or not, with its rituals and legalisms, it really could become the moral force in history that God intended for it to be. That the kingdom will emerge in history was never doubted by Rauschenbusch, but I sense that he suspected God might build the kingdom via people outside the Church who espouse the moral influence of Jesus because the Church fails in its calling. We Evangelicals do not have such doubts and agree with the Scripture that it will be in and through the Church, in spite of its shortcomings, that all social institutions will become subject to God's will (Ephesians 1:21–23). The bride of Christ will strive to create the kingdom of God here on earth, doing so in anticipation of the coming of our Bridegroom, who will complete the task. Maranatha!

THREE

The Social Impetus of Primitive Christianity

To what extent were the social aims of Jesus seized and carried out by the Church which called itself by his name? Did his early followers have the same all-embracing and lofty conceptions of the kingdom of God, the same passionate love for justice, and the same humane tenderness and brotherly freedom which make the soul of Jesus the luminous center of our moral and spiritual world?

It would be miraculous if they had. "What hand and brain went ever paired?" There is a gap even between the ideal cherished by any lofty mind and the realization which he can give to it in his own action. There are few men who maintain their first love unchilled to their colder age and their early purposes untarnished by policy and concession to things as they are. But as soon as the thoughts of a great spiritual leader pass to others and form the animating principle of a party or school or sect, there is an inevitable drop. The disciples cannot keep pace with the sweep of the master. They flutter where he soared. They coarsen and materialize his dreams. They put their trust in forms and organization where he dared to trust in the spirit. They repeat his words, but they make mere formulas of his prophetic figures of speech. They may join the Order of St. Francis, but they will not call the birds their sisters and the Sun their brother. Belike Brother Elias[1] becomes the head of the "little brothers" whom the poet-saint of Assisi called out to serve the Lady Poverty.[2] That is the tragedy of all who lead. The farther they are in advance of their times, the more will they be misunderstood and misrepresented by the very men who swear by their name and strive to enforce their ideas and aims. If the followers of Jesus had preserved his thought and spirit without leakage, evaporation, or adulteration, it would be a fact unique in history.

But they did not. Few held fast his spiritual liberty; the Jewish Christians remained in some measure of servility to the old Law; the Gentile Christians early fashioned a new Law and obeyed it in the old spirit of legalism. Few rose to his conception of worshiping God simply by a reverent and loving life; the Church early developed Christian sacraments and superstitious rites with which to placate and appease the Father of Jesus. Few made his conceptions of the right human life their inward possession. Imagine Jesus, with the dust of Galilee on his sandals, coming into the church of St. Sophia in Constantinople in the fifth century, listening to *dizzy* doctrinal definitions about the relation of the divine and human in his nature, watching the priests performing the gorgeous acts of worship, reciting long and set prayers, and offering his own mystical body as a renewed sacrifice to their God! Has anyone ever been misunderstood as Jesus has?

If the religious and moral thoughts and aims of Jesus were thus paralyzed and distorted from the outset, we may take it for granted as a matter of course that his social aims and ideas suffered a similar diminution in scope, force, and purity. If, on the other hand, we should find that primitive Christianity was still inspired by high social aims and still instinct with social energy, it would furnish an added argument of the highest significance for the strength of the social impetus originally imparted by Jesus and inherent in the historical movement inaugurated by him.

THE LIMITATIONS OF OUR INFORMATION

It is necessary to remind ourselves that our information for the purposes of such an inquiry is meager and incomplete. The early Christians did not belong to the literary class with whom the impulse to record its doings on paper is more or less instinctive. They had no motive for making elaborate historical records of their life. They expected the speedy end of the world and never dreamed of a posterity that would cherish every scrap of information about them. Even the sayings of the Master were not recorded till years had gone by. Whatever was written, was to serve some immediate and passing occasion, and in writings of that sort the most important facts, which really make up the bulk of the common life, are often not even mentioned, because they are so well understood by all parties concerned that they go without saying. We have no document whatever which sets out to furnish a coherent account of the moral or social life of the early Christian communities.

Moreover, if there were any radical political or social ideas current in early Christianity, there was good cause for not writing them down or publishing them freely. The Roman government was tolerant and almost indifferent on questions of religious belief and worship, but suspicious and alert against anything that smelled like smoldering revolutionary fire.[3] Even social clubs and benevolent associations were under sharp surveillance lest they mask political designs. There is one relic of primitive Christianity which embodies revolutionary hopes and passions, and it is significant that it purposely veils its meaning. The contemporary political powers are described under the image of beasts; the capital city is called by the mystic name of Babylon; the keyword of its allegories is hidden in the number 666, in which the letters of the word are translated into their numerical equivalents (Revelation 13). Political thought and utterance are so absolutely free in England and America that we can scarcely conceive along what subterranean channels political and social ideas have to move under more despotic conditions; how unsigned letters and poems pass from hand to hand; how a whisper, an innocent name, or a sprig of flowers will convey a world of meaning. But what is meant to evade contemporary scrutiny, is likely also to escape the knowledge of later times and to perish without trace. We make much of those passages of the New Testament which prove the political loyalty of the early Christians to the Roman Empire. But possibly one purpose in Luke's mind when he wrote the Book of Acts for the use of Theophilus was to present an apologetic of Christianity to the upper classes; and when Paul exhorted the Romans to obey the government, he may have had in mind the possibility that in the capital of the world his letter might drop into influential hands. If there was even a shade of such a side-motive in these writings, we must allow for it in constructing our conception of the political attitude of primitive Christianity.

The suggestion just made is somewhat conjectural. The following is quite certain. No books of the first century have reached us unless later times had interest enough in them to copy them. The survival of a book depended, not on the interest it awakened in the first century, nor on the interest it would awaken today, but on the interest which the third or fourth century took in it. If it was written by some man whom that subsequent age revered as a Christian authority, or if it lent welcome support to doctrines or institutions then struggling for the mastery, it was copied and quoted and had a chance of coming to our hands. If not, the material on which the earliest copies were written was sure to perish in some one of a hundred ways, and the book itself disappeared from human sight forever. There were books which were widely read and loved in the Church of the second century, but which fell into disrepute and oblivion because they did not suit the tastes and standards of the age schooled by the great doctrinal controversies. It is wholly likely that the same fate would befall any popular literature in which the social feelings and hopes of the earliest generations were embodied. They, too, became antiquated and uncongenial to the churchmen of the later age, especially after the Church had emerged from its oppressed condition and was fostered and fed by the Empire.

There were various important drifts and movements in early Christianity, but only those which were finally victorious in Catholic Christianity secured a fair and permanent historical record. For instance, the great Gnostic movement, which was as important in the world of thought in the second century as the evolutionary idea is in our own age, was finally thrust out by the Church, and of all its rich literature we have only one book left; otherwise we are dependent for our information on the partisan statements and garbled quotations of its enemies.

The Jewish Christian Church was at first the whole of the Christian Church. Gradually it was outstripped by the rapid growth of the Gentile churches, and through its doctrinal conservatism and prejudices, and through the force of outward events, it was left in the lurch of the larger movement and gradually separated from it in sympathy. Jewish Christian bodies survived to the fifth century, but they were then regarded as heretical and their literature had little chance of survival. The Epistle of James and the Revelation of John are more or less directly the product of this Jewish Christianity. They were saved from the deluge of oblivion because they were admitted into the ark of the Canon; and they were thus admitted only because they bore the names of apostles, and then only reluctantly.

Now, the Jewish Christian churches represented the radical social wing of the primitive Church. They were leavened by the ancient democracy of the Hebrew prophets and of post-exilic Judaism. In popular Jewish thought the poor and the godly were simply identified, and there was a frequent and strident note of hostility to the upper classes. The Epistle of James shares this Jewish spirit. It is one of the most democratic books of the New Testament. "Let a brother in humble circumstances boast of his exalted rank, and a rich brother of his humble rank, for like the flower of the grass will he pass away. In the midst of his business will he wilt away" (James 1:9–11). He describes indignantly how the rich man is ushered obsequiously into a front pew, while the poor man is sent into the gallery. That seems to him a reversal of God's judgment, for the poor as a class have been chosen by God to be rich in the Christian faith and heirs of the coming kingdom, while the rich as a class are the oppressors of the Christians and the enemies of the name of Christ (James 2:1–9). He pronounces an invective against the rich which would seem intolerably denunciatory in the mouth of a modern socialist preacher: "Here now, you rich men, weep and wail for the calamities coming upon you! Your wealth is rotted and your garments are moth-eaten! Your gold and silver have rusted, and their rust shall accuse you and eat into your flesh like fire. You have foolishly piled up wealth just before the world ends. Look now, the wages of the workingmen who have reaped your fields, which you have fraudulently retained, cry out against you and the outcries of the reapers have come to the ears of the Lord of Hosts. You have lived in luxury and wantonness on earth. You have fattened your hearts like cattle for a day of slaughter. You have condemned in the courts and done to death the just man who offers no resistance to you" (James 5:1–6). The significance of such a passage lies not in itself, but in the body of sentiment of which it is a manifestation.

The Apocalypse of John is part of the popular apocalyptic literature which flourished both among the Jews and the Jewish Christians, and the hope of a revolutionary overturning is the essence of the apocalyptic hope, as we shall see later.

The radical social spirit of the Jewish Christian churches can also be gauged in a measure by the sayings of Jesus. These sayings were kept alive and transmitted by word of mouth for years before any larger attempt was made to record them in writing, and the Jewish churches furnished the collective memory which treasured and preserved them. It is safe to say that in the main only those portions of the teachings of Jesus which in some way were dear and congenial to these churches were thus preserved. If, therefore, the Synoptic teachings of Jesus as we now have them are saturated with social thought, it is because such thought echoed the sentiment of the Jewish Christian community.[4] In the preceding chapter I have declined to follow those scholars who ascribe much of the radical social teaching in Luke to Ebionitic, that is, to Jewish Christian influence. If it should be true that any part of that material is not due to Jesus, but to those who, in transmitting his thoughts, consciously or unconsciously infused something of their own social passion into them, Jesus would be relieved in part of the charge of radicalism, but the Jewish Christian Church would be dyed with a deeper scarlet. We have an interesting example of such an editorial intensification of the social animus. The "Gospel according to the Hebrews" was a very ancient gospel, which originated and circulated in Jewish Christian circles. Only a few fragments of it are preserved. One of them tells the story of the rich young ruler in this form:

Said to him the other rich man, "Master, what good thing must I do to live?" He said to him, "Man, do the law and the prophets." He replied, "I have." He said to him, "Go, sell all thou possessest and distribute it to the poor and come follow me." But the rich man began to scratch his head and it pleased him not. And the Lord said to him: "How sayest thou, I have done the law and the prophets? For it is written in the law: thou shalt love thy neighbor as thyself; and see, many of thy brothers, sons of Abraham, are covered with filth, dying of hunger, and thy house is full of much goods, and nothing at all comes out of it to them." And turning he said to his disciple Simon, who sat by him, "Simon, son of John, it is easier for a camel to enter through the eye of a needle than for a rich man to enter into the kingdom of heaven."[5]

The point of our argument is this. The Jewish Christian communities were numerically and spiritually an important part of earliest Christianity. In many respects they most faithfully preserved the direct impress of Jesus, for they were the product of the same moral environment which had nurtured his mind. But the main current of Christian life, which finally resulted in Catholic Christianity, followed other channels and left Jewish Christianity like a landlocked bay, and of its literary products only a few remnants were preserved. Consequently the social spirit which glowed in that part of the Christian Church is not adequately represented in early Christian literature as we now know it, and our general impression of the social impetus in primitive Christianity is to that extent weakened and imperfect. It is not at all unlikely that a similar fate befell other writings which shared the same qualities.

Again, of those writings which did survive, only a limited number were embodied in the Canon of the New Testament, and only those that were embodied are known to the mass of Christian readers today. They have to form their judgment of the nature of original Christianity solely from their impressions of the New Testament. But an impression based only on that material is bound to be one-sided. If the gospels and the writings of one man were eliminated from our New Testament, the compass of what remains would be very slight. Paul immensely preponderates in the bulk of our material, and so we get the impression that his ideas and points of view were those generally prevailing in the apostolic age. That is probably far from true. In many respects Paul was a free lance, the propagandist of a new theology, a great dissenter and nonconformist, who was viewed with distrust or hostility by the representatives of an older theology and a more authoritative organization. He was a mind of immense stature and virility, but it was impossible that so intense a spirit should embody all sides of Christianity with equal vigor and in rounded harmony. Paul was a radical in theology, but a social conservative, a combination frequently met today. If we assume that in this respect he is an exponent of the whole of primitive Christianity, we may be misled. Yet even Paul was not as apathetic toward social questions as is usually assumed.

And finally the same caution with which we began our study of the social aims of Jesus applies to any study of the social contents of early

Christianity. We have not been accustomed to read the records from this point of view. We have read them for spiritual devotion. We have studied them from the theological and ecclesiastical point of view. The records as they lie before us are incomplete and one-sided, and even what does bear on our purposes is overlaid for us by other interests, by preconceptions and long-standing habits of mind. We must stretch a sympathetic hand back to our brothers of the first and second century and see if they do not respond with the warm and mystic clasp that belongs to the order of social Christians of all times. Of course this discussion will be one-sided too. There is no intention of presenting a rounded picture of the moral and religious life of primitive Christianity. We shall simply try to do justice to the force of the social impetus quivering in it.

THE HOPE OF THE COMING OF THE LORD

The hope of the immediate return of Christ dominated the life of primitive Christianity. Its missionary zeal, its moral energy, its theological conceptions and its outlook on the world, the interests it cherished and the interests it repudiated, can all be understood only under the high atmospheric pressure of that expectation. This great culminating event was believed to be very near. Paul, too, believed that. It is often asserted that he modified his expectations as time went on. It would be strange if he did not, but there is no change traceable in his thought on this point sufficient to modify his conception of the historic mission of Christianity. The possibility that he personally might depart before the Lord returned, deepened into probability and then into certainty; but it was always a question of years and decades with Paul, and never of centuries.

The return of the Lord meant the inauguration of the kingdom of God. What the prophets had foretold, what the people had longed for, and what John the Baptist had proclaimed as close at hand, would come to pass when Jesus returned from heaven to reign. He had not achieved his real mission during his earthly life; the opposition of the rulers had frustrated that; it had been God's will so. But he was still the Messiah of Israel; the national salvation was bound to come; the kingdom would yet be restored to Israel. In a very short time he would descend from heaven and then all their hopes would be fulfilled in one glorious and divine act of consummation. Their preaching was with a view to that event. They sought to do for his second coming what John the Baptist had sought to do for his first coming: to proclaim repentance to the people and to gather a holy remnant. The Christian hope of the Parousia was the Jewish hope of the Messianic kingdom, except that the person of the Messiah had gained wonderfully in concreteness and attractiveness, and the hope had become far more vivid and intense. The coming Messiah was the Master whom they knew and loved. He had ascended on high to receive the kingdom from his Father, and soon they would see him again, perhaps tomorrow or the day after.

Ideas could well differ as to what the kingdom implied and the return of Christ would usher in. Some would place the emphasis on the spiritual blessings, others on the social justice and emancipation that would be involved in the perfect reign of God. It was an ideal, and a very capacious and elastic ideal. The early Christians were no more unanimous about their eschatology than the Jews had been, and than we are today.

Paul expected an immediate spiritualization of the entire Cosmos.[6] The dead would be raised in a spiritual body; the living would be transformed into the same kind of body; for flesh and blood in the nature of things could not share in that spiritual kingdom. Death would cease. Nature would be glorified, and the long travail of all creation would end when the children of God would be manifested in their glory. In Paul's program of the future there is no room for a millennium of happiness on this present earth. Only the dogmatic theory that all scripture writers must hold the same views can wedge the millennium into Paul's scheme of the coming events. His outlook is almost devoid of social elements. To him the spirit was all. This material world could be saved only by ceasing to exist.

But there were others to whom the life in the spirit was not so intense and experimental a reality as to Paul. They clung more lovingly to this old earth and to the human intercourse which made their happiness. The material world would, of course, end some day, but first there would be a really good life on earth. When Satan and his hosts were chained and imprisoned, and Christ and his saints reigned instead, then injustice and oppression would cease at last. Nature would be free from the stunting power of sin and the splendid fertility of paradise before the fall would return.[7] Death would come late and gently. If anyone had suffered death for the testimony of Jesus, that would not deprive him of his share in that happy time; he would come to life and be invulnerable to death till the thousand years were over. At the end of that time there would be a last rallying of the powers of evil, a final spasm of judgment, and then this earth would pass away.

This is the type of the Christian hope expressed in the Apocalypse of John. The twentieth chapter describes this intermediate stage of salvation before the new heavens and the new earth appear in the twenty-first chapter. And even that new earth is only a glorified old earth, with a shining city and ever-bearing fruit trees and a crystal river and nations that pass in and out through its gates.

The eschatology of the Apocalypse was the orthodox eschatology of primitive Christianity. Most of the writers of the post-apostolic age express or endorse it. It was opposed on principle by the Gnostic teachers and by some of the Greek Church fathers; for them salvation consisted in the emancipation of the spirit from the deadly prison-house of matter, and they could not admit a glorification of the material world in millennial splendor. Gradually as the years rolled on and the Lord failed to come, this hope grew fainter. Montanism in the second half of the second century sought to revive it by strenuous insistence on it, but only brought it into discredit. When the Empire accepted Christianity as the State religion, and the peace and power which, under the pressure of persecution, had seemed possible only through the direct intervention of God, had come in other ways, the millennial hope was practically abandoned by the leaders of the Church. They had their millennium. Eusebius pleased the courtiers of Constantine by suggesting that perhaps the marble and gold of the Church ordered by Constantine over the Savior's tomb was the new Jerusalem.[8] The common people long clung to the millennial hope; they were still disinherited and longed for their inheritance.

Now, the millennial hope is the social hope of Christianity. There are two personalities to which religion holds out a hope of salvation: the little personality of man, and the great collective personality of mankind. To the individual, Christianity offers victory over sin and death, and the consummation of all good in the life to come. To mankind it offers a perfect social life, victory over all the evil that wounds and mars human intercourse and satisfaction for the hunger and thirst after justice, equality, and love. One or the other of these two may be emphasized in the religious life of an individual or a nation. Ancient Israel believed intensely in the divine consummation for the community; the hope of a future life for the individual had very little influence in Jewish religious life before the Exile. On the other hand, in the Greek world of the first Christian centuries the longing for eternal life was exceedingly strong, and the hope for any collective salvation almost nonexistent. In the Synoptic teaching of Jesus all turns on the kingdom of God, and the life hereafter is rarely referred to; in the Gospel of John "eternal life" is the central word and the "kingdom of God" scarcely occurs. Many men today longed for heaven when they were young, and the idea of a salvation for society never occurred to them; now they are almost indifferent whether they personally will survive death or not; but they would gladly give their life if it could help forward the salvation of society. A perfect religious hope must include both: eternal life for the individual, the kingdom of God for humanity.

In early Christianity we see a gradual change of emphasis from the one hope to the other. From its Hebrew origin it brought the social hope; from its Greek environment it accepted the intensification of the individual hope. The former waned as primitive Christianity disappeared; the latter waxed as Catholic Christianity developed. Each hope was deeply and organically connected with all the other features of worship and church life characteristic of primitive Christianity on the one hand and Catholic Christianity on the other. But insofar as Christianity retained the first impact coming from Jesus and the Baptist and the prophets of Israel, its hope was predominantly the social hope.

THE REVOLUTIONARY CHARACTER OF
THE MILLENNIAL HOPE

The millennium was the early Christian Utopia. It occupied the same place in the imagination and hope of the first generations of Christians which the cooperative commonwealth occupies in the fancies of modern socialists. The "woes" which always preceded the inauguration of the golden age corresponded to that forcible clash of the contending interests which is expected as inevitable in the coming transition of power from the possessing classes to the proletariat. It is true, all hope was put in the intervention of God and none at all in economic development or the forcible or political action of Christians. But their hope was a revolutionary hope, even though the revolutionists were as passive as sheep led to the slaughter and as meek as their Master. They hoped for a change complete and thorough; for an overturning swift and catastrophic; for an absolute transition of power from those who now rule to those who now suffer and are oppressed. What else is a revolution?

The entire complexion of this hope had been inherited from Judaism. The general framework of the successive eras, the woes, the angelic hosts, the mystic arithmetic of sevens and tens, were common to Jewish and Christian apocalypticism. With slight changes Christians could adapt and Christianize Jewish apocalyptic writings, and they did so.[9]

One most important point in which the Jewish attitude was copied by some Christians was the hostility to Rome. The oppressed and tortured spirit of post-exilic Judaism had turned in fierce hatred against the nations that oppressed Israel. Rome was the last and most terrible of them all. They were all but agents of great demon powers who hated Israel and thwarted its God. When the hurricane of God's judgment should come at last, it would mean deliverance to Israel, but necessarily it would mean also vengeance and overthrow for Rome.

This attitude toward the dominant political power was readily imported into Christian thought with the apocalyptic literature which embodied it. Jews who became Christians could hardly help retaining that philosophy of contemporary history. Was not Rome built up by the aid of its gods? And what were its gods but the demons whom Christ was to overthrow and strip of their power? As surely as the true God was in irreconcilable conflict with the demon powers of idolatry, so surely would there have to be a death-struggle with the Empire before the kingdom of Christ could be set up. In the Apocalypse of John, before the shout of the multitude could proclaim the final "Hallelujah! For the Lord our God the Almighty reigns!" the other shout had to go up, "Fallen, fallen is Babylon the great!" (Revelation 19:6, 18:2).

In the Middle Ages the whisper began to go abroad that the scarlet woman that rides on the beast, the great city seated on the seven hills, was papal Rome. That interpretation has been so useful in the long battle of Protestantism with Romanism that it has acquired a kind of canonical authority, so that to many readers of the Bible it seems a self-evident matter that the Apocalypse prophesies the anti-Christian power of papal Rome. But neither the writer nor the early readers of the book had the faintest conception of the papacy or its far-off corruption. Not even the tiniest germ of that institution was in existence when the book was written. To any contemporary reader the great city enthroned on the seven hills, ruling over all nations, the luxurious market for all the merchants of silver and pearls and purple and silk and scarlet, could mean only one thing: the capital of the Empire. Her fall and ruin meant the overthrow of the Empire (Revelation 17–19). But surely the shout of triumph hailing that event was not expressive either of political indifference nor political loyalty.

Not all Christians shared this attitude of hostility to the State. Paul certainly did not regard the Empire as Satanic in character, but as a divine instrument of order and justice (Romans 13:1–7), a power holding the anti-Christian malignity in check (2 Thessalonians 2:1–12). But Paul wrote his commendation of Roman justice during the early and happy years of Nero's reign, when that gifted and impressionable mind was still under the influence of Seneca. Up to that time the persecution of the Christians had all proceeded from the hatred of the Jews, and the strong arm of the Roman government had often served to protect the Christians from the influential malice of the Jews. On the other hand, the Apocalypse was written when the iron hand of Rome had turned against the Christians as such under Nero and perhaps under Domitian.[10] All the world had listened aghast to the news of the burning of great Rome. But to the Christian communities the most significant fact was the death-moan of their brethren that followed. The glare of burning Rome and the blood of the Christian martyrs combine in the lurid colors of the seventeenth and eighteenth chapters of the Apocalypse. The prayer for vengeance against Rome was the answer in some Christian minds to the beginnings of persecution by Rome. It was not Christian, but it was very human.[11]

The hope of Christ's return dominated the thoughts of primitive Christianity. Christ's return was the inauguration of the kingdom of God. The kingdom of God was the hope of social perfection. The reign of Christ involved the overthrow of the present world-powers. Thus the millennial hope was necessarily a political hope and in antagonism to the existing political situation. As soon as the Roman Empire took an attitude of active hostility toward the followers of Christ, some at least of them took an attitude of passive hostility toward the Empire. This was neither wise nor Christian, but in estimating the social impetus of primitive Christianity we cannot overlook these revolutionary tendencies. If the broadening current of the Christian movement had such sucking whirlpools on one of its edges, it helps us to estimate the swiftness and force of the entire stream.

THE POLITICAL CONSCIOUSNESS OF CHRISTIANS

The apocalyptic hope expressed a tremendous sense of political destiny. All the world was to be made over and the Christians placed in the center of things. The reins of power were to be torn from the hands of the mighty and given to the followers of Jesus. The history of the world converged upon them. They had this proud consciousness of an exalted future, not because of their own worth, but because they believed in the worth of Jesus Christ and hoped to be lifted to power with him as his faithful adherents.

At the core this hope was sound, but we cannot help feeling that the form of the hope was largely visionary. It certainly did not come true. As we pointed out in an earlier chapter,[12] the apocalyptic hope was a debased form of the prophetic hope, developed at a time when the Jewish people were without political power or experience. The whole scheme of the future in the apocalyptic literature is artificial, unreal, unhistorical, and mechanical. Jesus turned away from it and emphasized the law of organic development,[13] but his followers did not generally rise to that higher view.

Yet we do find in early Christianity a different type of thought which had the same high sense of a historical mission, but which combined it with a saner and more philosophical outlook on the world.[14] It was evolutionary, while apocalypticism was catastrophic.

For those who believed in Christ his coming marked the fundamental epoch in human history. All that had gone before was but preparation. In Paul's philosophy it was a basal thought that Christ was the second Adam, the source and starting-point of a new and spiritual humanity, the originator of a new type of man (1 Corinthians 15:44–49; Romans 5:12–21). The Christian Gnostics, who were the Christian evolutionary philosophers of that age, went even farther and made the revelation of Christ the central cosmic event.[15]

And it was not simply a new kind of individual that was being produced within the sphere of Christ's influence, but a new people, a novel social unity. "You are a chosen race, a kingly priesthood, a consecrated nation, God's own people"—four terms in which organic solidarity is expressed with reiterated emphasis.[16] In their churches Christians had a visible demonstration of the fact that the old social unities were being broken up to build a new unity. The old dividing lines of Jew and Gentile, of civilized Greek and raw barbarian, of slave and freeman, of man and woman, were fading out; the only line that was left to their vision was the line that separated Christians from the rest of the world, and all who were in Christ were one new being (Galatians 3:26–28; Colossians 3:5–11).

This new race had a great past and a greater future. Reaching backward it claimed all the venerable history of Israel for its own. The patriarchs and prophets, the types, the promises, the whole scriptures, were not Jewish, but Christian. The Christians were the real Israel. By one daring act of expropriation the Jewish people were thrust out of their historic heritage and the Christian Church sat within the tents of Shem. Christianity was the original religion restored and completed. It was as old as mankind. By this appropriation of Hebrew history the Christians, looking backward, gained a profound sense of historic dignity and importance. They also gained a sense of being a corporate social body, a political entity. Looking forward, this new people realized that it was the people of destiny. As surely as Christ was destined to reign, so surely were the Christians the coming people. They were not only to be superior to the others, but to absorb all others.

When Christianity came on the stage of history, there were two distinct types in possession, the Gentiles and the Jews, with a deep and permanent cleavage between the two. Christianity added a third genus, and Christians were profoundly convinced that they were to assimilate and transform all others into a higher unity. The Epistle to the Ephesians is a tract reflecting on this aspect of the mission of Christ. Romans 9–11 is a philosophy of history, forecasting the method by which this process of absorption and solidification was to come about. There is a prophetic grandeur of vision in this large international outlook of the early Christians. The evolution of religion has always been intimately connected with the evolution of social organization. When tribes were amalgamated into a nation, tribal religions passed into a national religion.[17] In the Roman Empire nations were now being fused into a still larger social unity. The old national religions were incapable of serving as the spiritual support for this vaster social body. There was a crying need for an international and purely human religion. Christianity, as we now know, was destined to fulfill this function, and these early Christian thinkers had a prophetic premonition of this destiny. They often dwelt on the fact that Christianity had been born simultaneously with the Empire under Augustus.[18] The universal State and the universal religion were twins by birth. They ought, therefore, to be in helpful relations to each other in accordance with the manifest purpose of God. The Empire should cease to persecute the Church. The Church could be the best ally of the State in creating civil peace, because Christians had the highest morality, and because they alone had power over the demons who menaced the security of the Empire.[19] As the soul holds the body together, so Christians hold the world together.[20] They exert a conservative and unifying influence. This conception of Christianity as a penetrating, renewing, and unifying power, destined to control the future of the world, was just as full of triumphant hopefulness as the apocalyptic hope, but allowed of a quiet process of historic growth. It did not regard the existing State as Satanic and evil, yet had full room for moral criticism of existing conditions and the determination to contribute to a thorough moral change.

The apocalyptic hope was probably the dominant Christian conception of history in the very first generations. This other view gained power as time passed, as the number and influence of Christians increased, and as men of larger mental reach and higher education grew up in the Church. The fact that religious convictions are the living force in these theories must not blind us to the fact that they contain a consciousness of social solidarity, of social power, and of a social mission. This satisfaction for the dawning sense of a vaster human unity probably lent greater force than we now imagine to the missionary appeal of Christians among the lower and middle classes.

Today we have a similar process of international amalgamation very similar to that of the early Christian centuries. At that time a new and common civilization was growing up around the Mediterranean Sea; today it is growing up around all the oceans. It is significant that the prophets of the modern social movement are also the prophets of a new internationalism, which aims to supplant the narrow patriotisms and interests of a bygone stage of human development by the wider enthusiasms and outlooks of a vaster human brotherhood. There is a profound similarity between the consciousness and the aims of early Christianity and of modern social thought, wherever it has ethical and religious impetus in it.

THE SOCIETY-MAKING FORCE OF PRIMITIVE CHRISTIANITY

All that has been said so far bears intimately on the social contents of early Christianity, but it deals with its ideas and theories rather than its actual social achievements. But primitive Christianity was not in the least academic. Its distinctive quality was the passionate moral energy with which it pressed for action. Jesus had put a new spirit into his followers. That spirit spread with a noble contagion and sought expression and realization in a new society. The old social life was stubbornly hostile to it at some points and unresponsive at others. Therefore a new social life had to be created to be the fit environment for the new spirit. Hence, wherever Christianity came, we see a new society nucleating.

To create a new type of social organization is always a feat of strength. The higher the ideas and aspirations are which the organization embodies, the greater is the force needed to create and maintain the organization. Water seeks its level; so does man. It is not hard for a swimmer to keep his face above water; it is very hard to lift his shoulders above the water. The Christians at Corinth were Corinthians

before they were Christians. Their memories and habits, their imaginations and appetites, were in league with the common life about
them. They lived in the same houses and workshops and baths with
their fellows. Yet Christianity called on them to cut loose from their
social environment and to rise to an ethical standard which they had
neither recognized in theory nor practiced in life. It bade them cease
from that sexual indulgence which the Greeks regarded as a simple,
pleasurable satisfaction of a natural appetite. It called for unselfishness
and honesty in money affairs, and Greeks were not famous for that
either. It demanded peaceableness and gentleness of intercourse,
whereas the Greek took to factious debating as a duck to the water.

The results achieved were by no means ideal. But the religious
power of the new faith did succeed in gathering these people into organizations where such moral teachings were urged with immense
determination, and where the irresistible force of public opinion exerted its disciplinary power on all who manifestly contradicted in their
living the ideals accepted in their faith. The first generation of Christian teachers had to make a strenuous fight against the grosser forms of
sexual evil within the churches. In the following generations we hear
less about them in exhortations addressed to Christians and more in
writings addressed to the general public. Probably the moral standard
had been effectively raised within the Christian community, and these
outstanding vices had been practically left behind, much as intoxication and profanity in the American churches. A body of seasoned
Christians had grown up under lifelong Christian influences, and
their combined influence was more steady and powerful than the occasional warnings of the early apostles.[21] To curb the strongest and
therefore the most destructive physical desire; to put an edge on conscience in regard to honesty and generosity in the use of property; to
soften the hateful and factious spirit by a lovable gentleness—even a
slight success in these directions would be an invaluable contribution
to social life. But to draw men out of their social environment into an
organization expressly dedicated to the achievement of this high moral
standard, is a wonderful testimony to the society-making power of the
new religion.

Most social organizations follow natural lines of cleavage. Blood
kinship, tribal sympathies, neighborhood, financial profit, social pro-

tection or advancement—these are some of the forces that bind men together. Christianity cut across these natural and conventional lines. It tore down the existing barriers with irresistible force and brought men together by a new principle of stratification. Jews were wrenched loose from the firm hold of their race and religion; Greeks from their culture and pleasures; and both joined on a footing of equality. Spiritual affinity triumphed over the strongest bonds that hold men together. The call of Jesus to give up home and property, reputation and life, for his sake, was treasured in the collection of his sayings because it corresponded to the actual experience of so many of his followers. The society-making force can be measured by the obstacles it had to overcome.

It was the Christian policy to minimize the contact with the unhallowed life outside. It was this withdrawal which evoked so much hatred and resentment and brought on the Christians, as on the Jews, the charge of an *odium generis humani*, a general hatred for humankind. But within the charmed circle of the Christian name the love was all the more intense. Its strength was novel, inexplicable, and awakened sinister suspicions in outsiders. But it was not common crime, as the heathen suspected, but the common experience of the highest spiritual and ideal good which unfettered such new powers of human fellowship. Faith in a common Father made men brothers. When men had vowed allegiance to the same Master, had felt the inward compulsion of the same divine Spirit, and looked forward intently to the same great consummation in the return of Christ, all the old distinctions were puerile and outworn, and they locked hands as Christian brothers. The natural desire for social intelligence and intercourse, the inborn craving of man for man, was spiritualized, ennobled, and intensified by being put on such a basis. The fact that such a society was possible at all is splendid testimony to the good in man. The strength of its cohesion is prophetic of what human society may come to be when its higher dormant faculties are called into action.

The churches of the first generation were not churches in our sense of the word. They were not communities for the performance of a common worship, so much as communities with a common life. They were social communities with a religious basis. A common religious experience and hope brought them together, but the community of life extended to far more than that. They prayed together, but they also ate together. They had no church buildings, but met in the homes of their members. That in itself was an influence against ecclesiasticism and for social intimacy. They had a rudimentary organization, as every human society is sure to have, but they had no official clergy distinct from the laity. They were democratic organizations of plain people. Because they were separated from all other society, they had to find nearly all their social relations, pleasures, and interests within the Christian community. How far did this sharing of all life extend?

THE SO-CALLED COMMUNISM AT JERUSALEM

The church at Jerusalem will occur to everyone as the classical illustration of a larger sharing of life. "All who became Christians were together and held all they had for the common use. They sold their property and goods, and shared the proceeds according to their individual needs." They met for worship in the temple, and met for their meals in their homes. The outflow of this close fellowship was a simple-hearted gladness, so that they could praise God and win the goodwill of men (Acts 2:43–47, 4:32–5:11).

It is amusing to note how our popular expositors treat this Christian communism today. They approach it with a sort of deprecatory admiration. It is so useful for proving how noble and loving Christianity was, but it is so awkward if anybody should draw the conclusion that we today ought to share our property. They make much of the fact that we have no other instance of communism among the other churches of the New Testament, and that even at Jerusalem the mother of Mark still had a house of her own to live in. They seem more anxious to emphasize that it did not occur twice than to show that it did occur once. But many an ecclesiastical body would be happy if it had as much scripture to quote for its favorite church practices, and would treat with scorn any suggestion that after all it had "occurred only once." As a result of this anxiety, it is commonly asserted that the later poverty of the church at Jerusalem was due to its communism. The assertion has been made so often that it is accepted almost as self-evident. Yet there is not the slightest statement in the Bible connecting the two things; it is pure inference. Luke, who is our sole source of information, has not a breath of disapproval. To him it is evidently a beautiful fact, a wonderful demonstration of the power of the Holy Spirit in the Church. It is hard to escape the feeling that the bias of Luke and of modern Christians is somewhat divergent.

At the outset the disciples at Jerusalem simply continued the life they had lived with the Master. They went on doing as they had done with him. They had had a common purse. He had cared for the wants of his family like a father, and they acknowledged that they had never been in want while under him (Luke 22:35). They were now away from their old homes and occupations in Galilee. So they continued a family life among themselves and shared what they had.

As their number increased, the problem of providing for the common meals and for the poor and sick became difficult. Those who were better off, in the glow of brotherly love and religious self-sacrifice, and probably in the expectation of the speedy return of Christ, replenished the common purse by larger offerings. In a few memorable cases they even parted with real estate for this purpose. It is worthy of note that Luke was able to mention only a single instance of such generosity by name, and that was by a man of remarkable largeness of heart, Barnabas (Acts 4:36–37). All evidence indicates that Luke was not an eyewitness of this early life at Jerusalem. The purpose of his book was not to furnish an impartial and critical account of the beginnings of Christianity, but to give an edifying sketch of the wonderful progress of the gospel from Jerusalem to Rome. His tone is that of a modern pastor giving a centenary history of his church, or of a missionary describing the progress of Christianity in a Karen tribe. Writing at such a distance and for such a purpose it is very natural and right that he should dip his brush in the liquid gold of enthusiasm and say, "Not one of them claimed anything of his possessions as his own, but all things were common to them." Yet the fraternal fervor must have been strong, for even Ananias and Sapphira felt that they had to make at least a show of complete renunciation to measure up to the standard set by the Christian community.

But whatever the extent of this generosity may have been, it was always generosity, and not communism in any proper sense of the word. No one was required to turn his property into the common fund on admission, as in all communistic colonies. And above all there was no common economic production. In fact, there seems to be no trace of communistic production in ancient Christian literature. The rudimentary communism of primitive tribal life was gone and forgotten. The possibility of a higher communistic ownership of the instruments of production had not yet risen above the horizon of common thought. Individual and family production was the only kind commonly known. Thus these first Christians produced separately and consumed in common. It was religious and instinctive fraternity, but not communism in any strict sense. Wherever people meet closely on a footing of equality, sharing is inevitable. In the family we always hold most of our possessions for common use. Students in dormitory, soldiers on the march, sportsmen in camp, share freely. It is impossible to have a man sit by you as your brother and let him go hungry while you feed. Therefore as a usual thing we do not let him sit by us or we deny that he is our brother. But whenever calamity or joy sweeps away the artificial barriers, men at once begin to share. Religion had the same effect in Jerusalem, and often since.

The later poverty at Jerusalem may have been due in part to this generosity. If a man turned in his farm to be eaten up, he raised the standard of living of all for a while, but his private capital was gone without creating any capital for common production. On the other hand, the continued poverty may well have been due to other causes: to the general poverty of the lower classes in Palestine; to persecution and economic unsettlement; to the emigration of well-to-do and conspicuous members; to the separation of the Galilean Christians from their accustomed sources of earning; or to the amount of time devoted to religion and withdrawn from labor. It is at least hasty to charge a permanent situation to a single cause.

Thus the church at Jerusalem was not quite as communistic as is usually supposed. On the other hand, the other churches were not as completely devoid of communistic features as is commonly assumed.

THE PRIMITIVE CHURCHES AS
FRATERNAL COMMUNITIES

The disciples at Jerusalem had met in their homes and had eaten in common. The one act which might be called an act of distinctively

Christian ritual at the beginning, the reminder of the Lord's last meal with the disciples, was performed in connection with these common meals, and this ensured the homeliness and simplicity of the rite. These common meals were so essential a part of the earliest church life that this custom was established wherever Christianity came. This in itself is a strong proof that the churches were more than organizations for worship. We know from Paul's letter to the Corinthians (1 Corinthians 11:17–34) that the Christians met in the evening, the time for the chief meal of the day, and dined together. Such common meals were frequent in the Greek fraternal associations, and Greeks could easily fall in with the custom. These love-feasts did not consist of eating a wafer as a religious symbol, as is done in some modern churches; it was a downright meal to which people came hungry, so that Paul advised them to get a bite at home to take the edge off their appetites, if they were too hungry to wait for one another.

Now the assurance of one square meal means a great deal to a poor man physically. It means still more to his consciousness of human worth and his enjoyment of human intercourse to sit at a social function as the equal of all. To break bread in common brings men close to one another. At Corinth the social differences had obtruded themselves at the common meals. The well-to-do had drifted together in a coterie, had clubbed their well-filled baskets, and were in danger of getting hilarious together, while the poor brother sat on one side hungry and outside the pale of social enjoyment. Paul took this very seriously. It seemed to him a denial of the fundamental spirit of the churches.

These common meals persisted for centuries, though changed in character. The ritual act of the "Lord's Supper" became more ceremonial, mysterious, and awe-inspiring, and a meal where people were heartily satisfying their physical hunger did not seem the fit environment for the mystery of the eucharist. Hence that part was transferred to the morning service. But the evening meal continued. As wealthy men entered the churches, they often defrayed the expenses of a meal and made it an act of charity to the poor. The rich paid and the poor ate. That was a complete departure from the democracy of the common meal at the beginning. But the persistence of the custom, even when all the conditions had so completely changed, proves how deeply it was embedded in the traditions coming down from the origin of Christianity.

The provisions for the common meal were brought by each family, as in our basket picnics. When the Lord's Supper was transferred to the Sunday morning service, it still remained customary for the people to bring provisions along, and the material for the eucharist was taken from these offerings. What was left was distributed to all who were in need. As time went on, regular monthly offerings of money were introduced and under the ascetic enthusiasm of almsgiving, large properties were often turned over to the churches. It is significant that for a long time the churches did not accumulate property. If real estate was given, it was sold and the proceeds used up. If there was any special need, a collection had to be taken to meet it. In the Greek fraternal associations the accumulation of income-bearing property was essential. The later Church, too, derived its chief income from landed wealth. The primitive Church on principle was without property.[22]

Moreover, the income of the Church was wholly for those in need. In modern church life the bulk of the income goes for the support of the clergy and the expenses of worship, and even of the expenses for benevolence only a small fraction is for charitable help of the needy. In the primitive Church the officers were not paid, unless they temporarily went without earnings to serve the Church. In that case they were supported because they were needy, and not because they were officers. As the Church was ecclesiasticized and clericalized, an increasing clergy was needed to do what the people at first had done for themselves. The clergy became a separate and priestly class, for whom secular employment was not fitting, and who had to be maintained. An ever increasing proportion of the income of the Church was devoted to the clergy and the expenses of the ritual. In the fifth century it was regarded as a fitting division that one-fourth go to the bishop, one-fourth to the clergy, one-fourth for the maintenance of worship, and only one-fourth to the poor. Yet in theory the property of the Church long remained "the patrimony of the poor." This, too, was a survival of earlier traditions.

It is possible to get a very fair estimate of a man's character from the allotment of his expenditures. The same is true of a Church. If its income is largely devoted to appliances of aesthetic beauty, we may be sure that its heart is in its ritual. If the primitive churches could do with little income spontaneously offered, we may be sure that they were democratic bodies in which the people themselves did the work. If the income was wholly devoted to the help of the needy, we may be sure that fraternal helpfulness was essential to their church life.

This line of argument is confirmed by the history of the organization of the primitive churches.[23] We are apt to transfer our own conditions back to the first century and to assume that the elders and bishops, like the modern pastor, existed primarily for teaching and preaching. But religious utterance was the common right of all Christians. Whoever had the spiritual gift for it, could exercise it. It was not a duty attached to a church office. The officers of the primitive churches were executive and administrative officers, and not preachers. If they could also teach, it was simply an added advantage in their personal influence. The terms "bishop," "elder," "deacon," have to us a solemn and ecclesiastical significance. In the first century they were secular terms, taken from common life. *Episcopos* was equivalent to our superintendent or manager. The churches adopted the forms of organization to which their members were accustomed in their voluntary clubs and societies and in their village or city government, just as Americans in organizing any new society would instinctively organize with a president, secretary, treasurer, and executive committee, because that is the form of organization which we have always known. To get the atmosphere of the first century, we must strip these terms of their ecclesiastical and clerical significance and make them business terms.

These officers presided at the common meetings, and to that extent they were religious officers. They watched over the moral condition of the members and guided the discipline of the church, which was a very important part of its life, and to that extent they were moral officers. And they administered the finances and organized the fraternal care of the churches. The latter was probably the original function of the bishops insofar as they differed from the other elders. The bishop rose to power in the church not by virtue of his teaching, but because he managed the funds and controlled the extensive executive apparatus of the church. The man who held the purse-strings finally ruled the church. It was only toward the close of the second century that the bishops added the control of the teaching functions to their other growing powers.

It is the outcome of the close investigation which has been given to this subject in recent years that the framework of organization in the primitive churches was devised, not for the conduct of worship, nor for teaching and preaching, but for the administration of the common life. The first step in organization was the appointment of the Seven at Jerusalem, and they were appointed to administer the fraternal help of the church with greater fairness (Acts 6:1–6). It has usually been assumed that these Seven were the first "deacons." It now seems more probable that the deacons were a later contrivance for the purpose of rendering subsidiary assistance to the bishops, and that the Seven were the first elders.[24] In that case the original purpose of the presbyterate was not teaching, but organized helpfulness. The bishops of the early centuries were first of all great executive officers. They became teachers and theologians when doctrine and theology became so essential a part of church life.

If these results of modern historical investigation are to any extent correct, they furnish a powerful proof of the fact that in the early Christian communities the administration of mutual helpfulness was a very important part of their existence, and that their common life must have extended far beyond their common religious worship.

If we inquire in what directions this fraternal helpfulness manifested itself, our information is far richer about the third century than about the first and second.[25] By that time the organization of the churches had been centralized and perfected, and the charitable help was administered through this machinery. In the first century the methods were crude and more spontaneous, but the spirit of it was probably purer than later, more democratic and less debased by the desire to win merit by ascetic almsgiving.

From the outset widows and orphans were extensively cared for. The social conditions of the ancient world and the impulses inherited from Judaism laid this duty upon the churches. About AD 250, the church at Rome had fifteen hundred dependents of that kind under its care. When Christians were in prison for their faith or exiled to the mines, the churches cared for their needs and comfort, often in lavish degree. It was not uncommon to ransom Christians imprisoned for debt. The proper burial of the dead was even more important to the sentiments of the ancient world than to ours. Just as today, the poorer classes organized in societies which guaranteed their members an honorable burial. The churches performed this service for their members. In public calamities, like pestilence or the invasion of nomadic brigands, they stood by their members and sent aid to a distance.[26] The duty of working was strictly urged in the primitive Church; holy idleness was the outgrowth of later asceticism. But if a man was out of work, the churches assumed the responsibility either of finding him a job or of caring for him.[27] Thus the means of life were guaranteed him in either case. The church at Rome, living in the midst of vast pauperism, could boast that it had no beggar in its membership. The troubles coming upon them for their faith made Christians even more migratory than the rest of the city population of that day. But wherever they went, they were sure of Christian hospitality and the first aid needed to get a foothold in a strange place. Hospitality was one of the fundamental Christian virtues in primitive Christian life.[28] It was so open-handed that it invited exploitation by professional beggars. The heathen writer Lucian made the gullibility of the Christians part of the plot of his novelette, *On the Death of Peregrinus Proteus.*

By the end of the third century charity began to be institutionalized. There were Christian lodging-houses for strangers, homes for the aged, the sick, the poor. In the first and second century it was more a matter of direct neighborly help from man to man. Probably the chief help was not given in the form of money, but of human service and influence. In Paul's epistles we get glimpses of influential families in whose homes the church-groups met and upon whom the task of hospitality and watch-care chiefly devolved. They put their property, their influence and social standing, at the service of the Christian community. Paul speaks of such with deep respect. Stephanas, who came from Corinth to visit Paul at Ephesus, was a man of that kind (1 Corinthians 16:15–18). He probably made this journey on behalf of the Church at his own expense, just as men of wealth would undertake to defray some public function at Athens, or paid for common expenses in the voluntary associations of Greek social life. The poor and the alien were without political rights or social importance, and found protection by close relation to some citizen of wealth and standing. The relation of client and patron was widespread and of great social importance. It is interesting that where our conditions are similar to those of the ancient world, a similar relation of clientage has grown up in the protection given to the poor by the political boss and the service exacted by him in return. It is probable that the wealthier members of the Christian communities served as the *patroni* of their poorer brethren. Phoebe, of the Corinthian harbor-town Cenchreae, was probably not a poor deaconess, but a woman of social standing who had served Paul and many others as *patrona*.[29]

Christianity spread at first chiefly in the cities and among the lower middle class, the working class, and the slaves. The poorer classes of the Empire were a proletariat much like that of our great cities. They were largely composed of slaves and of freemen who were economically submerged through the competition of organized slave labor, through the drift of the peasantry toward the cities, and through the increasing economic breakdown of the Empire. The Christian Church was of immense social value to these people. It took the place in their life which life insurance, sick benefits, accident insurance, friendly societies, and some features of trade unions take today. The individual found in the community a hold when any wave of misfortune threatened to sweep him off his feet and drag him out to sea in the undertow of misery. It is now generally recognized that this element of mutual help was quite as strong a factor in the growth of the Christian movement as the attractiveness of the truth it presented. Harnack justly makes "The Gospel of Love and Charity" one of the chief chapters in his account of the missionary expansion during the first three centuries.[30] The historian Schiller in his history of the imperial age of Rome says: "As the gospel of the poor and oppressed, of the despairing and guilty, Christianity naturally sought its adherents first in the lower strata of population, and if we remember what moral degradation prevailed in the Greek seaports, we realize the more the power of the new faith, which was able to awaken a higher and somewhat more ideal conception of life even amid such surroundings. The fundamental idea of Christianity ... could unfold but slowly, and only a few of the nobler spirits could rise to such lofty conceptions. With the majority of believers the determining motives were the socialist elements on the one hand and the Messianic hope and the expectation of a better life beyond on the other hand."[31] Karl Kautsky, in his history of socialism, thinks the practical aid was a stronger element than the hope of the golden age. "Like the Social Democracy today, primitive Christianity grew to a power irresistible by the ruling classes of that day because it became indispensable to the masses of the population." Speaking of the decay of communistic enthusiasm in the Church after Constantine, he says: "But even in this weakened form Christianity for centuries accomplished great things in counteracting pauperism. Though it did not abolish poverty, it was the most effective organization for alleviating the misery growing out of the general poverty within its reach. And that was perhaps the strongest lever which lifted it to success."[32]

THE LEAVEN OF CHRISTIAN DEMOCRACY

The history of Christian charity has been a favorite part of popular church history. It is delightful to think of heathen men coming under the influence of Jesus and the Christian Church and developing such tenderness of affection and such ardor of self-sacrifice amid "a world without love." But Christianity was not simply the culture of the faculty of love. It brought with it a strong leaven of democracy and protest which unsettled men. It created social unrest and carried disturbance in its train.

Shortly after Paul left the little church at Thessalonica he got word that some of the Christians there had quit working. They seem to have been unusually poor. Consequently the hope of the Lord's coming had taken powerful hold on them and they expected it immediately (2 Thessalonians 2:1–12). But if relief was coming so soon, why go on breaking their backs? It is all very well for men in comfortable armchairs to write about the dignity of labor, but those who have had nothing but labor in their life have an instinctive hankering for the dignity of leisure. Grinding social pressure and tense millennial expectations have again and again in the history of Christianity caused crowds to drop their work and wait for the Lord, who would be their emancipator from drudgery. Paul very wisely explained to them that the Lord's coming was not quite as near as they supposed, and that in any case "he that will not work, shall not eat" (2 Thessalonians 3:6–15).

At Corinth the social unrest seized the women. They felt the hot promptings of the Spirit in their souls just like the men, and rose to prophesy. They, too, felt their intellectual life enriched with new thoughts and a wider outlook; why should they not have the right to teach in the Church? They felt the emancipating sense of equality and the glad sweep of the new brotherhood in the meeting and put off the veil, which the lustfulness of men and long-standing social inferiority had compelled women to wear when in the presence of strangers. Paul in one of his bold, prophetic strains asserted that in Christ all the old distinctions of race and social standing would disappear, including the difference between man and woman. The spirit of Christianity has accomplished that result in the slow progress of centuries, and our women are now free and our equals. If these Corinthian women tried to take at once that heritage of liberty which was to be theirs eventually, we cannot help sympathizing with them. But we can also understand the unusual vexation and distress in Paul's mind when he heard of this disorder, and agree with his prudence in bidding them keep within the bounds of customary modesty and restraint (1 Corinthians 11:2–16, 14:33–36).

The social unsettlement even reached family relations and created a religious tendency to divorce. There were Christians who felt that it was impossible for them to live a Christian life while married to a heathen. The question whether it was not the right or even the duty of a Christian to sever so incompatible a relation had become so pressing at Corinth that it was one of the chief subjects on which the Church consulted Paul by letter and committee. There were others with whom the new passion for sexual purity had awakened scruples even about the relations within wedlock, and who were ready to assert the right of the individual to himself on high religious grounds. Here, too, we have the anticipation of later results of Christian influences: a keener feeling that marriage should rest on spiritual affinity and sympathy and not on physical or conventional grounds, and a finer sense of the right of the soul to its own body. Of course it is exceedingly likely, as human nature goes, that in some cases old dislikes and aversions were simply seeking cover under these new religious pleas. But in any case it must have been a leaven of unrest in various families (1 Corinthians 7).

We catch a glimpse, too, of a new stirring among the Christian slaves. In discussing the question whether Christians ought to sever marriages with heathen, Paul sets up the general principle that a Christian can be a Christian in any outward set of circumstances, and that he ought to remain in that condition in which the call of God found him. In that connection he turns to address the slaves: "Were you a slave when you were called? Do not let that trouble you. Nay, even if you have the chance to gain your freedom, prefer to remain as you are. For he that was called to be a Christian while a slave, is henceforth a freed-man of the Lord; likewise he that was called in freedom, is henceforth the slave of Christ" (1 Corinthians 7:21–24). Evidently there were Christian slaves who were troubled by their servile status. They were dependent on the permission of their masters for the right to be Christians at all. They were liable to be commanded to perform immoral or idolatrous acts, and they had no legal right to refuse. But Paul's argument indicates that the cause of unrest lay even deeper, in a newly awakened sense of dignity and human worth. How could a soul belonging to Christ still bend to the yoke of man? Paul says it can be done; the Christian slave is spiritually free in Christ and that ought to content him. Let him wear the badge of slavery with that inward sense of emancipation. There are other passages in the New Testament touching on the relations of Christian slaves to their masters. In heathen literature the commonest vice of slaves was stealing. The most serious danger of Christian slaves apparently was the independence and aggressiveness begotten of a new sense of equality and worth. Especially if their masters were also their brethren in Christ, the moral problem thereby created was not always satisfactorily solved.[33]

We have already touched on the views taken by Christians about the Roman Empire. These theoretical views were sure to manifest themselves at least occasionally in practical conduct. Christians were citizens of a higher kingdom. The Empire was not their highest good. It was soon to come to naught by God's hand. Its laws were not to them the supreme laws, nor in any sense identical with the moral law. They were often placed in a position where it was their religious duty to disobey the commands of the public officers. Even Paul, who takes so respectful an attitude toward the moral value of government, had no real use for the State so far as Christians were concerned. He did not think of trying to bring Christian influences to bear on the State; but neither did he want any influence of the State in the affairs of Christians. If brethren had trouble between them, they were not to begin litigation before the courts of the Empire, but to settle by the arbitration of other brethren (1 Corinthians 6:1–11). Christians withdrew from the surrounding heathen life and minimized all contact with it. This involved that they had to reproduce and parallel the necessary institutions of society within their own community. The churches legislated for their members and exercised judicial functions, enforcing them with various grades of disciplinary punishments. In heathen life the religious and civil organizations were one; the officers of the State as such performed the public religious acts. Through the hostile relation of the Christian Church and the heathen State, which continued for nearly three centuries, the Church developed a permanent organization of its own, which controlled and directed the life of its members with a pressure often more insistent and searching than that of the State. The Church was, in fact, a State within the State. The ecclesiastical courts and the canon law of later times were an outgrowth of this situation. It was the realization of this which finally roused the Empire to active hostility against the Church. There were only two persecutions in which the Empire took the initiative and exerted its vast strength to destroy the Church, the one beginning AD 250 and the other AD 303, each lasting about ten years. Each of these was directed, not against the belief of Christians, but against this all-pervading, tenacious organization which paralleled and rivaled the organization of the Empire and seemed to threaten its sovereignty.

With such an inward emancipation from the ordinary patriotism and enthusiasm for the Empire; with such a parallel organization to absorb the obedience and devotion of Christians; and under the painful pressure of unjust persecutions and frequent chicanery, it would be strange if practical revolutionary sentiments had never sprouted within the fenced acreage of the Church. It is true, in all documents intended for the general public, especially in the writings of the apologists, there are emphatic assurances of the harmlessness and patient obedience of Christians. These writings had the very practical purpose of lightning rods to draw off the electricity that might gather in high places and be discharged in sudden strokes of persecuting anger. Doubtless all that the apologists said was true. Doubtless Christians did pray for the emperor. So do the persecuted sectarians in Russia or the Christian Armenians in Turkey; but perchance the cloth of their sentiments shows a different pattern and color on the lower side. The repeated injunctions in the New Testament to give honor to the emperor and to pay taxes wherever they were due, may indicate that these duties were not self-evident to all. Paul clearly goes out of his way in his letter to the church at Rome to urge respect for the government and willing payment of taxes (Romans 13:1–7). The psychological motive for that passage must have been either to conciliate the goodwill of influential men at the capital into whose hands the letter might fall, or the knowledge and fear that contrary sentiments existed either at Rome or in other places with which Paul was acquainted. Christians who were brought before Roman officials did not always manifest the ideal meekness with which we are apt to invest their memory; they displayed their human nature by taunts and prophecies of disaster. During the Decian persecution, when the vacant seat of the Roman bishop was once more filled, an eminent Christian leader boasted that the emperor would rather have heard of a rival emperor being proclaimed than of a bishop being seated at Rome. The tone of pugnacity and antagonism is unmistakable.[34]

Thus the spirit of primitive Christianity did not spread only sweet peace and tender charity, but the leaven of social unrest. It caused some to throw down their tools and quit work. It stirred women to break down the restraints of custom and modesty. It invaded the intimacies of domestic relations and threatened families with disruption. It awakened the slaves to a sense of worth and a longing for freedom which made slavery doubly irksome and strained their relations to their masters. It disturbed the patriotism and loyalty of citizens for their country, and intervened between the sovereign State and its subjects.

All this is neither strange nor reprehensible. No great historic revolution has ever worked its way without breaking and splintering the old to make way for the new. New wine is sure to ferment and burst the old wineskins. Moreover, it is likely to taste sour and yeasty, and some will say, "The old is better." Jesus foresaw that the Christian movement would work incidental harm and pain. He had come to cast a fire upon the earth. He had not come to bring peace but the sword. Families would be riven in twain and set in antagonism, two against three. But he was willing to pay the cost of the kingdom of God in tears and blood if need be. Our argument here is simply this, that Christianity must have had a strong social impetus to evoke such stirrings of social unrest and discontent. It was not purely religious, but also a democratic and social movement. Or, to state it far more truly: it was so strongly and truly religious that it was of necessity democratic and social also.

THE OUTCOME

In spite of the defectiveness and one-sidedness of the historical sources furnishing the material for our study, we have found an abundant and throbbing social life in primitive Christianity.

All of its theories involved a bold condemnation of existing society. Whether that society was to be overthrown by a divine catastrophe of judgment or displaced and absorbed in the higher life of the Christian community, in any case it was to go. The future of society belonged to that new life originated by Christ. Christianity was conscious of a far-reaching and thorough political and social mission. This is the more remarkable because it was weak in numbers, apparently withdrawn from the larger life of society, and without any present or any apparent future influence on the organized life of the civilized world. Such convictions, cherished in the face of such odds, argue that it was launched with a powerful and invincible social impetus, and that the consciousness of a regenerating mission for social life is inseparable from the highest form of religion.

The strength of its social tendencies was not exhausted by its hopes for the future. It immediately began to build a society within which the new ideals of moral and social life were to be realized at once, so far as the limitations of an evil environment permitted. The primitive Christian churches were not ecclesiastical organizations so much as fraternal communities. They withdrew their members from the social life outside and organized a complete social life within their circle. Their common meals expressed and created social solidarity. Their organization at first was executive and was devised to meet social and moral, rather than religious and doctrinal, needs. Their income was completely devoted to fraternal help. As organizations for mutual help and fraternal cooperation the Christian churches became indispensable to the city population and invincible by the government.

This fraternal helpfulness was more than mere religious kindliness. It was animated by the consciousness of a creative social mission and accompanied by a spirit of social unrest which proves the existence of powerful currents of democratic feeling. Under the first impact of its ideas and spirit, men and women tried to realize at once those social changes which have actually been accomplished in centuries of development. This impulse proves that a reconstructive social dynamic inheres in Christianity and must find an outlet in some form, slow or swift.

We were prepared to find a long drop downward when we passed from Jesus to the thoughts and doings of his followers. We did find it so. In their religious life not even the greatest maintained his level, and the lowest groped in a density of superstition and puerile legalism which makes it seem queer to put the great name of Jesus upon them. And yet the higher impulse was implanted. Give it time! Humanity is an organism that passes through a long series of metamorphoses, and it measures its seasons by centuries. The purification of the religious life, the comprehension of the real meaning and spirit of Christ, have made marvelous progress in recent times.

In the social direction of the religious spirit we found a like decline. There is not the same unerring penetration of judgment on social morality, not the same eagle-eyed boldness of hope and faith for the future, not the same sweet reasonableness about the slow methods of realizing the ultimate goal, not the same lovable love nor the same power to heal and save the broken and diseased members of the social body. There is a good deal of crude thinking, of sectarian narrowness and pride, of ecclesiastical ambition, of complete forgetfulness of the high mission to the world. And yet there is the germ of a new social life for humanity, the conception of a social morality based on love and worldwide in its obligation. Give it time! This, too, under ever changing forms, may work its way, and triumph yet. The modern emancipation of the intellectual life began in the Renaissance of the fifteenth century and is not finished yet. The modern emancipation of the religious life began in the Reformation

of the sixteenth century and is not finished yet. The modern emancipation of the political life began in the Puritan Revolution of the
seventeenth century and is not finished yet. The modern emancipation of the industrial life began in the nineteenth century and is not
finished yet. Let us have patience. Let us have hope. And above all
let us have faith.

Unless the Call Be Heard Again

Joan Chittister

"God is not nice," the proverb teaches. "God is not an 'uncle.' God is an earthquake." Maybe that's why so many of us try to avoid the voice of God in the world—or at the very least, to tame it.

But not all. There are those with an ear for both the personal and the public dimensions of faith, for both contemplation and action, for both the cultivation of the presence of God within us and fidelity to the will of God for the world.

Walter Rauschenbusch, in the style of the prophets before him, set out in the nineteenth century neither to domesticate the gospel nor to promote the civil religion. Most of all, he was speaking to the Church at a time when both forms of faith were not only popular but taken for granted.

Religion in a pluralistic society, the purists proclaimed, was for the practice of the faith, not the practice of the gospel. It was for the spiritual welfare of the Christian, not the critique of the government. Religion was to be seen but not heard. Separation of church and state, they called it, while the church got more and more quiescent and the democratic state became more and more of an oligarchy, run by the rich on the backs of the laboring poor.

Prophetic presence and personal piety, however, were of a piece in Christian life for Walter Rauschenbusch. One was not distinct from the other. The function of religion was not simply to believe what we were told we must. The function of religion, he taught, was to prod us to do what had to be done in this world because of what we believed. It was to save lives as well as souls.

Most telling of all, he drew his model of Christianity from the Church of Acts. In the early Church he saw both the love of Jesus and—as a result of it—justice in action. It was the servant church—not the clerical church, the credal church, or the canonical church—to which Rauschenbusch pointed in his attempt to bring personal commitment to Jesus to the point of white-hot zeal for the kingdom of God.

Personal piety alone, the inner conviction of having come to know Jesus, was simply not enough for him. Salvation, he taught, was about more than individual redemption. Like the early Church, he waited for the return of Jesus, for the coming of the kingdom—but until then, he reasoned, the Christian was obliged to do something to bring it.

Walter Rauschenbusch believed that the function of the Christian life was to bring the kingdom of God to a world far too satisfied, it seemed, to live in a godless kingdom here on earth and to wait quietly, sanctimoniously, for the kingdom of God to come later, and somewhere else. He was a religious man, not simply a pious one. There is a chasm of difference, a depressing disparity, between the two.

Rauschenbusch did not live his spiritual life in the fear of an angry God. He lived it in thrall to a just one. In an era darkened by poverty and rugged individualism, unconscionable gain for some and pathetic poverty for others, his commitment to the social gospel was, in a dark time of desperate transition from an agricultural society to an industrialized one, light on a mountaintop, a cloud of fire in darkness.

In the face of a society where money trumped position and greed trampled on ideals, Rauschenbusch taught an ethic of Christian care rather than an ethic of legal rights. He ripped away the veil from the eyes of a people, a Church, for whom being spiritually compliant and routinely spiritual, had become a superficial, if not simplistic, sign of sanctity.

The inner life, Rauschenbusch reasoned, was not for its own sake. He looked head-on at the social system in the early Church and its relationship to the Jesus who had walked from Galilee to Jerusalem doing good—curing lepers, giving sight to the blind, feeding thousands, and raising the dead to life—and saw in the early Church a template for the entire Christian life.

This was a people, he instructed his own generation and reminds us yet, who were themselves acutely aware of social oppression, who structured themselves precisely to care for one another, who were marginal to the society around them, and who were devoted to living an alternative community lifestyle in the midst of a ruthless and unwelcoming world. The early Church, he argued, was neither a theocratic church nor a quiescent church. Not yet.

In fact, it may have been exactly when the Roman world welcomed them that Constantinian Christians began to be more Constantinian—more part of the system—than Christian. Then the Church became part of the State, and the State began to be seen as the secular arm of the Church.

Over and over again, Rauschenbusch called the Church beyond the politics of the Church to the purpose of the Church: the bringing of the kingdom—here, in our own time, and to the poorest of the poor. Why? Because the early Church, he reminded modern society, had a reputation for upsetting social mores, for irritating social systems, for breaking down social, sexist, and political boundaries to such a degree that it became legendary, even in its own time, for both its generosity and its justice.

No doubt about it: Walter Rauschenbusch challenged a Church that had for far too long been simply one more state institution in both Europe and the Americas to remember of what it was really made, to what it had really been called. The struggle of the early Church to bring moral righteousness, the kingdom of God, to the public arena, it seemed, had not been accomplished.

Rauschenbusch concentrated on the conversion of the Church at least as much as he concentrated on the conversion of churchgoers. As a result, the role of the Church in society is still a burning question, perhaps more now than ever before in U.S. history. With pluralism have come mosques and temples and shrines of every sort where once only crosses had been. Now the identity of Church with State is more and more at issue. Now the Church must stand on its own—without state identity, without legal preeminence, without assumed privilege—for all the world to see.

As a result, the question for the Christian Church now goes far beyond whether or not the Community of Acts gives us any kind of model of what the Church must be if it is to embody the life of Christ in our own time. The question for us now is whether or not in our own time, this model is still real, whether or not this model is still needed— whether or not we are still it.

Rauschenbusch makes two major points that remain eerily true. The first is the fact that every century brings in its wake both greater progress and greater poverty than the century before it. The second is that the Church itself is called to be a model of the life to come, a model of justice and peace, an intimation of the kingdom of God on earth.

The Church, we come to understand, must itself make choices. And from century to century, the Church has. History is certain: deciding whether the Church as we know it is political, pastoral, or prophetic becomes the choice and the challenge of every generation.

But the Church has stepped and stuttered throughout time from one model to the next.

First, political and aligned with the State, the Church failed century after century to challenge the State. The Church itself either played political games with the great powers or was a political power in its own right.

Later, the pastoral church became an agent of the State to comfort the oppressed but too often failed to challenge the oppressors.

Finally, prophetically speaking as the voice of conscience in the midst of the State, the Church came late to many issues—slavery, sexism, segregation—but it also came early to others–the labor movement, peace, nuclearism, and global communism.

Now, in our century, ecological sustainability, life issues, pluralism, sexism, and globalism command the concerns of the entire shrinking globe. The Church must decide again how to function as a voice of conscience and a voice of caution in a century in which science is outrunning morality, wealth is overrunning the poorest people on earth, and force is running rampant from one continent to another.

The tension of these things threatens the very existence of the globe, the very dignity of human life. Now the Church must remember again the Church of Acts and the voice of Walter Rauschenbusch calling it to bring the kingdom—as did the voice of Jesus on the Mount of Beatitudes.

We are not here as a church to manipulate the State or to live in it with privilege and pomp. We are not called simply to bind up the wounds of those the system oppresses. We are surely called as the Church of Acts to be prophetic presence in its midst, the voice of the prophets in our time.

Why? Because we pray daily, "Thy kingdom come, thy will be done," and so must do something to bring it.

Why? Because time changes nothing; people do.

FOUR

Why Has Christianity Never Undertaken the Work of Social Reconstruction?

In the preceding chapters we have studied the origins of Christianity. It rested historically on the religion of the Hebrew prophets, and the great aim of the prophets was to constitute the social and political life of their nation in accordance with the will of God. The fundamental purpose of Jesus was the establishment of the kingdom of God, which involved a thorough regeneration and reconstitution of social life. Primitive Christianity cherished an ardent hope of a radically new era, and within its limits sought to realize a social life on a new moral basis.

Thus Christianity as a historical movement was launched with all the purpose and hope, all the impetus and power, of a great revolutionary movement, pledged to change the world-as-it-is into the world-as-it-ought-to-be.

The organization in which this movement was embodied, after three centuries of obscurity and oppression, rose triumphant to be the dominant power of the civilized world. Christian churches were scattered broadcast over the Roman Empire. Their numbers were so great and their organization so flexible and tenacious that the final attempts of the Empire to uproot the Church proved futile and the Empire capitulated and made terms. Christianity supplanted heathenism as the State religion of the Empire. Its churches were endowed with the ancient properties and rights of the temples. Its clergy were given immunity from the taxes and exactions which crushed all other classes. Its members filled the civil service. Its great bishops had the ear of the men in power. The population of the ancient world entered the Church *en masse*, and though the great majority may have had little experience of the inner power of the new faith, yet the people lay open to the instruction and guidance of the Church. The bishops came to be the leaders of the local nobility which controlled the municipal life of the Roman cities. In the East the great Justinian formally placed the administration of public charity and the supervision of the public officials under the bishops.

When the machinery of imperial administration broke down in the provinces under the invasion of the barbarians in the fifth century, the machinery of the Church remained unbroken. The provincial cities rose like islands of the old Roman civilization amid the flood of barbarian life that covered the provinces, and in the cities the bishops were the leaders, the protectors of the poor, and the organizers of the forces of law and order. Amid the general disorder and insecurity the Church offered the stable points and thereby gathered power to itself. Ancient families became extinct and the Church became the heir of their lands and slaves and serfs. Small proprietors sought security by committing their lands to the Church and becoming its tenants. The landed wealth of the Church alone sufficed to make it a power of the highest rank in the feudal system of the Middle Ages, in which all power finally rested on the possession of the land. Bishops and abbots became feudal dignitaries, sometimes almost sovereign princes in their own domains, and always with a potent voice in the government of their nations. The pope became a sovereign over a large part of Italy, and his material power and spiritual influence were so vast that he could wrestle on even terms for supremacy with the emperors. The Church was the preserver of the remnants of intellectual culture, the sole schoolmistress of the raw peoples. Her clergy long had almost a monopoly of education, and were the secretaries of the nobles, the chancellors and prime ministers of kings. The Church had its own law code and its own courts of law which were supreme over the clergy, and had large rights of jurisdiction even over the laity, so that it could develop and give effect to its own ideas of law and right. Throughout the Middle Ages the sway of the Church over the moral and spiritual life of the people, her power to inspire and direct their enthusiasms and energies, her chance for molding their conceptions of life, were amazing and un-paralleled by any other force.

In modern life the relation between Church and State has grown looser, the reverence for the Church has sensibly waned, and other intellectual and spiritual forces have risen by her side and successfully claimed part of the field which she formerly held alone. But the potential efficiency of the Church in affecting public opinion and custom is still almost incalculable, even in the least religious countries of Europe. In our own country, if the Church directed its full available force against any social wrong, there is probably nothing that could stand up against it.

Here, then, is a vast force which by all the tradition of its origin and by its very essence is committed to the moral reconstruction of human society. It has had time and opportunity. Why, then, has it not reconstituted the social life of Christendom?

Two answers may be given to this question, each the opposite of the other.

It may be replied that in spite of the spread and power of the Church any actual reconstruction was impossible. Christianity was rising when the ancient world was breaking down. By the time the Church had gained sufficient power to exercise a controlling influence, the process of social decay, like the breakdown of a physical organism in a wasting disease, was beyond remedy. The unsolved social questions of pagan centuries had created a despotic government, a venal and rapacious bureaucracy, a vicious and parasitic aristocracy of wealth, and a vast mass of nerveless and hopeless hereditary paupers. The impact of the Teutonic barbarians merely crumpled up an organization that was hollow within. What power could save a State that was rotten to the core? A similar huge task confronted it in working on the raw clay of that new human material which covered the ancient civilization like a landslide in the great migration of nations. Amid the general anarchy, against the coarse vice and brutality of the barbarians, herself harried by the rapacity of the nobles and weakened by the ignorance and barbarism of her own clergy, the Church did what she could, but a thorough social reconstruction was impossible. In modern life her power is broken by the prevalent doubt and apostasy, and the current of materialism and mammonism is now too great to be stemmed.

Such a statement of the case deserves a more sympathetic consideration than it is likely to get from either friend or foe of the Church. Impetuous Christians are apt to see only the duty that has been left undone, and not the difficulties which beset the stout hearts of the past. Those who are no friends of the Church often have no realizing experience themselves what a task it is to counteract even a single, deep-rooted moral evil or to quicken a single group of human beings to a nobler life. Whoever thinks that Christianity ought to have accomplished more than it did, confesses great faith in its potency. I have that faith. I feel so deeply the inexhaustible powers of renewal pulsating in it, that its very achievements only make me ask: Why has it never done what it was sent to do?

Others again will return the opposite reply. If we ask why Christianity has not reconstituted society, they will say it has done so. Has it not lifted woman to equality and companionship with man, secured the sanctity and stability of marriage, changed parental despotism to parental service, and eliminated unnatural vice, the abandonment of children, blood revenge, and the robbery of the shipwrecked from the customs of Christian nations? Has it not abolished slavery, mitigated war, covered all lands with a network of charities to uplift the poor and the fallen, fostered the institutions of education, aided the progress of civil liberty and social justice, and diffused a softening tenderness throughout human life?[1]

It has done all that, and vastly more. The influence of Christianity in taming selfishness and stimulating the sympathetic affections, in creating a resolute sense of duty, a stanch love of liberty and independence, an irrepressible hunger for justice and a belief in the rights of the poor, has been so subtle and penetrating that no one can possibly trace its effects. We might as well try to count up the effect in our organism of all the oxygen we have inhaled since our first gasp for breath. Insofar as humanity has yet been redeemed, Christianity has been its redemption. Many of us have made test of that regenerating power in our personal lives. Many, too, have marked the palpable difference in the taste of life between some social circle really affected by Christian kindliness and a similar circle untouched by Christian motives and affections. What is true within such small spheres of social life has been true in the large area of Western civilization. And yet human society has not been reconstituted in accordance with the principles of Jesus Christ.

In the first place, it is necessary to remind ourselves that Christian writers who describe the influence of Christianity on human life are always tempted to emphasize the contrast between heathenism and Christian society by selecting the darkest aspects of the former and the brightest sides of the latter.[2] The witticisms of heathen satirists and the somber invectives of Christian moralists are quoted to characterize heathen life. But if some socialist historian of the twenty-fifth century should ransack the files of our comic papers and of our "muckraking" magazines, what an appalling, unrelieved, and unfair picture he would get of society under our individualistic regime! On the other hand, in describing Christian society we are apt to assume that Christian theory was identical with Christian practice; that the declamations of some ancient Christian rhetorician were sober scientific estimates; and that the highly moral edicts of Christian emperors were enforced better than the highly moral laws of Kansas or New York. We are apt, also, to forget that the moral force of Christianity was usually only one factor in producing such a change as the abolition of slavery or piracy, and that over against the benign influences of the Church must be set the malign and divisive influences which she created by persecuting zeal, intellectual intolerance, or religious wars. In short, we must soberly face the fact that a good many deductions have to be made from the popular panegyrics, and that the Church has not accomplished all that is often claimed for her.

In the next place, the social effects which are usually enumerated do not constitute a reconstruction of society on a Christian basis, but were mainly a suppression of some of the most glaring evils in the social system of the time. For instance, amid the incessant feuds of the Middle Ages the Church for a short time and within a limited area succeeded in imposing the Truce of God and so giving the harassed people a chance to breathe. In our own time it has aided in mitigating the suffering entailed by war through the Red Cross conventions and otherwise. But it has never yet turned more than a fragment of its moral force against war as such. The Church is rendering some service today in opposing child labor and the sweatshop system, which are among the culminating atrocities of the wages system, but its conscience has not at all awakened to the wrongfulness of the wages system as a whole, on which our industry rests. Thus, in general, the Church has often rendered valuable aid by joining the advanced public conscience of any period in its protest against some single intolerable evil, but it has accepted as inevitable the general social system under which the world was living at the time, and has not undertaken any thoroughgoing social reconstruction in accordance with Christian principles.

In the third place, the most important effects of Christianity went out from it without the intention of the Church, or even against its will. For instance, the position of woman has doubtless been elevated through the influence of Christianity, but by its indirect and diffused influences rather than by any direct championship of the organized Church. It is probably fair to say that most of the great churches through their teaching and organization have exerted a conservative and retarding influence on the rise of woman to equality with man. Similarly Christianity has been one of the most powerful causes of democracy, but the conscious influence of the Church has more widely been exerted against democracy than for it. A volatile spirit has always gone out from organized Christianity and aroused men to love freedom and justice and their fellow men. It is this diffused spirit of Christianity rather than the conscious purpose of organized Christianity which has been the chief moral force in social changes. It has often taken its finest form in heretics and freethinkers, and in non-Christian movements. The Church has often been indifferent or hostile to the effects which it had itself produced. The mother has refused to acknowledge her own children. It is only when social movements have receded into past history so that they can be viewed in the larger perspective and without the irritation created by all contemporary disturbance of established conditions, that the Church with pride turns around to claim that it was she who abolished slavery, aroused the people to liberty, and emancipated woman.

The facts of history are so clear on this point that the indirectness of the social influence of Christianity has been set up as a kind of doctrine. We are told that Christianity is sure to affect society, but that Christianity must not seek to affect it. The mission of the Church is to implant the divine life in the souls of men, and from these regenerated individuals forces of righteousness will silently radiate, and evil customs and institutions will melt away without any propaganda.

That is certainly one of the most important means of social transformation. Put a new moral standard and a new moral motive into a human heart, and it will unconsciously affect all it touches. A Christian woman will make a home sweet and Christian, even if she has no theory about Christianizing the home-life. But would it not be more effective still if she added the conscious purpose to make her home a little kingdom of God, and intelligently set herself to counteract all customs and outside influences that expressed the selfishness and ostentation and gluttony of the life surrounding her home? If a result gives us joy and pride after it is attained, why should it not be our conscious object before it is attained? Why should the instinctive and unpurposed action of Christian men be more effective than a deeply rooted and intelligent purpose? Since when is a curved and circuitous line the shortest distance between two points? Will the liquor traffic disappear if we say nothing about it? Will the atrocities on the Congo cease if we merely radiate goodness from our regenerate souls?

We suspect that this theory was devised to put the best face on an uncomfortable fact. It is a fact that there has been a startling absence of any thorough and far-seeing determination or effort to transform and Christianize the social life of humanity. But that lack has not been due to the wise self-restraint of the Church, which knew a better way, but to a series of historical causes which have paralyzed its reconstructive purpose and power. These causes I shall try to set forth in this chapter and it can then be judged whether the past failure of the Church to undertake the reconstruction of social life justifies a present refusal to undertake it consciously.

This brief survey will have to run back and forth over nineteen centuries of Christian history. Its brevity will have to excuse the abruptness and the lack of due qualifications in many of the statements.

IMPOSSIBILITY OF ANY SOCIAL PROPAGANDA IN THE FIRST CENTURIES

It is correctly asserted that the apostles undertook no social propaganda. Paul held no antislavery meetings, and Peter made no public protest against the organized grafting in the Roman system of tax-farming. Of course they did not. Even the most ardent Christian socialist of our day would have stepped softly if he had been in their place. The right of public agitation was very limited in the Roman Empire. Any attempt to arouse the people against the oppression of the government or the special privileges of the possessing classes, would have been choked off with relentless promptness. If, for instance, anyone had been known to sow discontent among the vast and ever threatening slave population—which was not negro, but white—he would have had short shrift. Society was tensely alert against any possible slave rising. If a slave killed his master, the law provided that every slave of that household should be killed, even if there was no trace of complicity. Upper-class philosophers might permit themselves very noble and liberal sentiments only because there was no connection between them and the masses, and their sentiments ended in perfumed smoke.

Under such circumstances any prudent man will husband his chances of life and usefulness, and drop the seeds of truth warily. If the convictions of William Lloyd Garrison had burned in Paul, we should probably not know that Paul had ever existed. There is no parallel between such a situation and our own in a country where we are ourselves the citizen-kings, and where the right of moral agitation is almost unlimited. The parallel would have to be sought with American missionaries working among the Armenians in Turkey, or with evangelical sectarians in Russia before the present revolution. Our missionaries in China are in a privileged position, yet they have to let official corruption alone or their consuls are likely to hear from the mandarins.

POSTPONEMENT TO THE LORD'S COMING

Paul was not an antislavery man. He doubtless realized the oppressive conditions of many slaves, just as we recognize the hard lot of miners or oyster-dredgers. But to his lofty idealism outward conditions were almost indifferent. He himself bore poverty and homelessness almost with equanimity for Christ's sake. Let the slave realize that he is Christ's free-man, and he can hold his head as erect as any (1 Corinthians 7:17–24). This is sublime, but it is too rare an atmosphere for the mass of men, and even the few can maintain such victorious elevation of soul only under the tension of unusual feelings and only for a limited time.

Paul and the entire primitive Church were under such tension. They expected the very speedy coming of the Lord. Paul expected that this event would signalize the transformation and spiritualization of all the material world (1 Corinthians 15; Romans 8), and what did our transient earthly troubles matter in the face of so tremendous a change? Others, as we have seen,[3] expected the coming of the Lord to usher in an earthly millennium of justice and happiness, which would solve all social questions in one blessed catastrophe. They were then in the same position as those revolutionary socialists who refuse to dabble with social palliatives because the people are almost on the point of seizing control of all. We know now that the Christians of the first century were at the beginning of Christian history; they thought they were at the end.

This expectation, to anyone who took it seriously, affected all relations and outlooks on life. Paul even advised against marriage on account of the nearness of the end and the upheavals sure to precede it. He counseled an attitude of inner detachment. Let those who had wives be as if they had none, and those who purchased property as if they did not own it; let those who had dealings with the world make them as slight as possible; for the time was short, and the present makeup of the world was soon to pass away (1 Corinthians 7:25–35). Given that conviction of the coming end, this was the language of a heroic soul. Anyone with that faith would be morally absolved from entering on any moral crusade that would take time. But without that honest faith the same attitude would be a shirking of responsibility. If a man spends only a single night in a shack in the woods, he does not mind if the stars shine through the roof or the rain leaks in, for in the morning he will strike camp. But if he occupies a house for years in which roof and drainage are defective, and if his children are perpetually sick in consequence, it is criminal for him to let things run on because someday it may happen that he will move.

HOSTILITY TO THE EMPIRE AND ITS CIVILIZATION

In the preceding chapter we discussed the attitude of primitive Christianity to the Empire and the civilization organized in it.[4] We saw that the hope of the Lord's coming necessarily involved the hope that the Empire and its social life would come to an end. The feelings inherited from Judaism and its apocalyptic literature, and the feelings generated by the persecution of the Christians, united in creating a clouded atmosphere of fear and distrust through which imperial Rome loomed threatening and detestable.

This feeling received a strong moral reinforcement by the awakened Christian conscience which felt keenly the immorality of heathen society, the lasciviousness of its pleasures, the unnaturalness of its ornaments and luxuries, the greed of its traffic, the factiousness and hatred prevalent in private and public life. How could the ideals of life which they carried in their hearts be realized in a world so incompatible with them? How could a social life so fundamentally wrong be reconstructed? Men usually undertake a hopeful reformatory activity only if betterment is somewhere within sight. In some of our cities in which local politics seemed bad beyond remedy, citizens were long in a state of pessimistic lethargy. Socialists are so profoundly convinced of the hopeless and fundamental injustice of the capitalistic system that they will cooperate in no reform which is simply to ameliorate or prolong a system that ought to cease. Similarly the political and moral outlook of Christians on the world about them was so dark and hopeless that the idea of a moral campaign could hardly have occurred to them, even if it had been permitted, and even if their hope of God's intervention had not made their efforts seem useless.

This moral outlook received a sinister reinforcement by the religious belief prevailing in early Christianity that the heathen world was under the control of demon powers.[5]

This was the common belief of the heathen world itself. Only the word *demon* did not have the exclusively evil significance which it has with us. Their demons were good, bad, or indifferent. The common man believed himself surrounded by them just as the medieval Christian felt himself protected by ministering angels and saints, or tempted by devils. For their favor the Roman merchant offered gifts and prayers. Against their anger or spite the Greek sailor wore his amulets. From their defilements men sought cleansing in the ritual of the heathen "mysteries" and the prevalent Oriental cults. For the educated man, with whom the conception of one God had shouldered aside the belief in the ancient gods, it was convenient to think that the traditional gods were real spiritual powers, though of an inferior rank.

The Christians simply retained this common belief of the second century, but by a process which has often been repeated in the history of religion this many-hued world of spirits was suddenly all dyed in uniform black. They were parts of that Satanic kingdom which opposes God and his kingdom. They were not figments of the imagination, but real and terrible seducing spirits who had for ages enthralled the world and persuaded men to offer them gifts and sacrifices. Whatever was good in pre-Christian civilization, or whatever was similar in heathen ritual to Christian rites or institutions, was a counterfeit devised in advance by the demons in order to thwart Christianity which threatened to rob them of their power. It is necessary to read the early Church Fathers and apologists to realize how fundamental this belief was in their theology and in their interpretation of history and contemporary life. A theology like ours, with no demons in it, would have seemed to Justin Martyr or Cyprian to knock the bottom out of the Christian faith.

But if heathen religion was the service of demons, all heathen life was under their control, for all heathen life was woven through with religious acts and ceremonies. Every official act of State, every military ceremony, every public or private festivity, was connected with sacrifices, libations, or prayers. No Christian could take part in them without defiling himself with the deadly sin of idolatry. The only course open to Christians was to diminish their points of contact with heathen society and constitute a little social world within the world. Such a mingling in the common life as an effort at social reconstruction would involve, was quite out of the question. The best social service which the Church could render to the heathen world was to counteract and break the power of the demons.

THE LIMITATIONS OF PRIMITIVE CHRISTIANITY AND THEIR PERPETUATION

The causes already enumerated were on the whole confined to early Christianity. The State was hostile, and any moral campaign against social wrongs was impossible. The Lord was coming to usher in the new era, and any human effort for a slow amelioration was needless. The heathen world was so corrupt, so hostile, and so penetrated by demon powers, that any hope of changing its evil life was paralyzed by the very magnitude of the task involved. Thus in spite of the powerful social impetus residing in primitive Christianity such a process of conscious moral reconstruction of society as we conceive today was both theoretically and practically out of the question in the first three centuries.

Moreover, these early Christians were subject to the same limitations of human nature to which we all are prone. They, too, were creatures of custom. Before slavery was abolished in our country, there were millions of genuine Christians, honestly willing to see and do the right in other matters, to whom it seemed a preposterous proposition that slavery is incompatible with Christianity. To them it was a necessary and fundamental human institution, like the family or the school. Today there are very few Christians who realize that it is a crying wrong to hold land idle for speculation in cities where men's lungs are rotting away, overgrown with tuberculosis bacilli for lack of air; few who realize that it is a flat denial of Christianity to take advantage of the needs of your fellow man to buy his labor cheaply or sell him your goods dearly. These things seem to us a necessary and inevitable part of the structure of society. If, therefore, the early Christians accepted the universal institution of slavery as part of the social universe; if it was centuries before we hear any straight declaration against the principle of slavery in the Church; and if the Church itself became a great slaveowner in the later days of its wealth—need we be surprised who have had nineteen centuries of Christian influences upon us and who are still so blind to wrong?

Moreover, in the early generations the churches were mainly composed of slaves and poor people whose minds were stunted by toil and lack of culture. The physical fear of persecution, the sense of social ostracism, the superstitious fear of demon powers, the self-righteous pride and narrowness inseparable from sectarian religious life, combined to shut them up in their own organizations and to rob them of the wide and free outlook on human life. It is quite possible for a flowerpot or a religious body to be exceedingly narrow, and yet to harbor the germinating seed of something very great. It is one of the most convincing testimonies to the Christian religion that within such human environment it was able to generate such religious thought and energy.

It was thus entirely natural and excusable if the reconstructive purpose inherent in Christianity did not find its largest application in the primitive beginnings of Christianity. It would be miraculous if it had. But the harm was done when subsequent generations took this failure as an excuse or even as a command for similar inaction. Since the end of the second century "apostolic" became the decisive word in the Church. Whatever the apostles had done or not done was binding precedent. In later times the opinions of the great Fathers received a similar authority, which almost throttled free initiative. Human life is always imitative and therefore conservative. But religion, by the very reverence which makes it noble, intensifies the conservative instinct. It embalms even insignificant usages and ideas and gives them binding authority. Thus the attitude of the primitive Church toward society tended to perpetuate itself when all the causes which had created that attitude had long disappeared. Paul lived under a hostile government and in view of the speedy end of the world. We live under our own government, free to think and speak as we will; we look backward on nineteen centuries of Christian history, and we look forward to an indefinite continuance of the present world. Yet it still passes as a clinching argument for Christian indifference to social questions that Paul never started a good government campaign. "When two do the same thing, it is not the same." We cling to the letter of primitive Christianity and are false to its spirit. We have turned the eagle-minded Paul, one of the greatest champions of freedom and progress in all history, into a personified code of law and precedent that bids us ever to remain where he stood. We have thrust the steel driving-rod of an old locomotive between the spokes of a new locomotive. There is the grim humor of human life!

THE OTHERWORLDLINESS OF CHRISTIANITY

There is another line of causes which set in very early, but which did not come to their full force in primitive Christianity. They swayed that "catholic" Christianity which developed out of primitive Christianity about the end of the second century and which ruled with unbroken power till the Reformation.

We have seen that the ancient Hebrew religion had been for this present life. The hope of blessedness or the fear of punishment in a life after death plays no appreciable part in Old Testament religion. The prophetic insistence on present social righteousness and the hope of a Messianic reign on earth developed in a national religion devoted to the present life.

On the other hand, in the Greco-Roman world there was an intense desire for the future life. A great revival of religion had begun in the pagan world before the Christian era and continued for several centuries to gather strength. The deep interest in religious philosophy, the popularity of the "mysteries," the eagerness with which old Oriental religions were welcomed in the West, and the swiftness with which religions made headway, were all symptoms of this new religious awakening. The chief hope held out by all these religious movements was the atonement and purification of sin and the attainment of immortal life.

It was natural that when Christianity spread in the pagan world, men should seize that part of its rich and varied contents which most appealed to their desires, and emphasize it to the exclusion of others. They saw in Christ the redeemer from earthliness. By his incarnation, his death, and resurrection he had implanted potential immortality in the human race. By baptism the immortal life could be imparted to the believer; by the eucharist, that "medicine of immortality," and by the mortification of the body, it could be nourished and strengthened to the final triumph over all that clogged it. Nearly all the early Fathers wrote on the resurrection. The gift of immortality was the great theme of early Greek theology. The Nicene Council was not merely the triumph of a Christological formula, but of that conception of Christianity which made it primarily redemption from death and impartation of immortality. The prayers for the dead and to the dead, the festivals of the martyrs and saints, the poetic speculation on heaven and hell and purgatory, the desire for a blessed death with all "the consolations of religion," the apparatus presented in the sacraments of the Church to attain security from hell and early release from purgatory, the churchyards crowding up to the churches and into them—all these testify to the place which the future world held in the thoughts of ancient and medieval Christianity.

But as the eternal life came to the front in Christian hope, the kingdom of God receded to the background, and with it went much of the social potency of Christianity. The kingdom of God was a social and collective hope and it was for this earth. The eternal life was an individualistic hope, and it was not for this earth. The kingdom of God involved the social transformation of humanity. The hope of eternal life, as it was then held, was the desire to escape from this world and be done with it. The kingdom was a revolutionary idea; eternal life was an ascetic idea.

We modern men, too, believe in eternal life, but the asceticism is almost drained out of it. We hold that this life is good and the future life will be still better. We feel that we must live robustly now and do the work God has given us to do, and at death we shall pass to a higher world in which we shall serve him in still higher ways. But in former stages of Christianity the feeling was rather that this is an evil world from which only death can free us: at the best a discipline to prepare us for the heavenly life; at the worst a snare to cheat us of it. The body is a sepulchre; the world a prison; from both the soul hopes to escape. The heaven-born spirit longs for emancipation from the grossness of matter.

This dualism of spirit and matter was not derived from the teaching of Jesus. It was in the intellectual atmosphere of the day, part of the general spiritual equipment of the times. Platonic and Stoic philosophy taught it. It was the strongest religious ingredient in Gnosticism, in Neo-Platonism, and in all the religious movements of that age. It was inevitable that Christianity, both in its theology and its popular religious feelings, should be deeply affected by it. But such a conception of present life and future destiny offered no motive for an ennobling transformation of the present life. Why should Christians labor to make this present life just and beautiful when by its very nature it was sensual and debasing? To make this life sweet and attractive would only rivet the chains which the soul should long to strip off, and would quench that longing for heaven which was the mark of earnest religion. It is significant that those Church Fathers who brought the eternal life to the front in the thought of the Church, either unconsciously or consciously parted company with the millennial hope.[6]

The hymns of the Church are like an auriferous sand-bed in which the intenser religious feelings of past generations have been deposited. They perpetuate what would otherwise be most fugitive: the religious emotions. If anyone will look over either the standard church hymnals or the popular revival collections, he will find very few hymns express-ing the desire for a purer and diviner life of humanity on earth. So far as I have been able to see, those hymns which have something of the ring of the social hope are either re-expressions of Hebrew hymns, or hymns about the millennial coming of Christ, or patriotic hymns, or foreign missionary hymns. From these four significant sources some joy of the social hope has streamed into Christian hymnology. On the other hand, the hymns expressing the yearning of the soul for the blessed life in the world to come are beyond computation.

The otherworldliness of Christians indirectly did affect social life for good. The fear of eternal punishment, the hope of eternal reward, the prospect of facing the great Judge of all things, held many a coarse nature from evil and to justice and mercy, who might not have done the right for the right's sake or through any higher motive. It helped to sensitize the conscience of the Christian nations up to a certain point. But that only confirms our general proposition, that the social effects hitherto produced by Christianity have been produced indirectly as by-products, and that the main current of its power has been deflected from the task of Christianizing social life.

THE ASCETIC TENDENCY

The otherworldliness of early Christianity was only one aspect of its general ascetic view of life. When ascetic piety turned its face to the future, it longed for complete release from the world and the body, and for the bliss of pure spirituality in heaven. When it turned its face to present duties and relations, it sought to lessen the contact with the world and to wear thin the body, in order to weaken the hold of the sensuous and material over the soul, to enjoy some foretaste of the rapturous contemplation in heaven, and to prepare the spirit for its final victory and escape. This attitude of mind was common to all ear-nest religious movements of the ancient world. Christian asceticism was not Christian; it was only a Christian modification of a general spiritual drift in contemporary life. All these movements in some measure identified evil with matter. The flesh that envelops the soul is the seat of evil; hence it must be opposed and worn down. The world with its glamour and entanglements is a kind of larger physical integument, enchaining the soul in material and temporal interests; the less of it, the better for the soul. The spirit that desires emancipation must not only avoid excess and wrongful pleasure, but cut down all satisfaction of the natural desires to a minimum. The perfect life would be the contradiction of nature.

The sexual instinct is the most insistent, powerful, and intimate form in which the soul encounters the power of the material life and the attractiveness of the world. Therefore ascetic religion turned against sexual desire as its chief enemy. Its fight against sexual evils is one of the Church's chief titles to honor. It was a fight against tremendous odds of hereditary abnormal passions, vicious customs and opinions, and the deposit of centuries of sensuality in literature, art, and religion. The Church branded all sexual intercourse outside of marriage as mortal sin, in man as well as in woman, and so protected the happiness of the family and the most important right of woman. It stood against concubinage and the divorce evil of the ancient world. Its influence on legislation in the Roman Empire was stronger in this domain of life than in any other.[7]

But this insistence on personal purity lost much of its social value by its disparagement of the sexual life in general. Marriage, too, was regarded by many of the early Church teachers as a lower moral condition, a relation necessarily involving physical defilement, a compromise with the fallen life of humanity, a concession to the weakness of the flesh. It was not a relation good in itself, but simply a preventive of licentiousness needed by the weak. Blessed were those who did not need it. Since the second century the Church honored voluntary virginity in man and woman. For a long time it frowned on a second marriage as a blemish on Christian character. Men who were already in the bonds of marriage might become priests, but none who was already in holy orders should descend to marry. Of its higher churchmen it early began to demand a life of abstinence, even if they were married. Finally celibacy was demanded of all priests in the Western Church. But the moral demands imposed on the clergy as a law were imposed on all men as an ideal, especially after monasticism captured the heart of the Church from the fourth century onward. Not only the young remained unmarried, but many left their families to join the "angelic choirs" of the ascetic. Women handed their children over to churches or monasteries and dedicated themselves to holiness. That enthusiastic propagandist of monkery, St. Jerome, said, "Though your mother with hair unbound and garments torn point to the breasts that nourished you, and though your father lie on the threshold, tread over him with dry eyes and take the flag of Christ," that is, become a monk.[8] "To be converted to God" came to mean entering a monastery. Even Chrysostom, the sensible, pictures the model husband as the one who lives almost like a monk.

Now, marriage is the fundamental social relation. The family is the social cell. It is society in miniature. If this was the attitude of ascetic Christianity toward the most natural and most loving of all social institutions, what chance of proper treatment did the other social relations have? Of course for the majority of men the common sense of nature was fortunately stronger than any ideal motives which religion could marshal to thwart nature. They continued to marry and to beget children and be happy. But with such views of the perfect Christian life, it would be with a feeling either of actual sin or at least of falling short of the highest life. It is true the Church in many ways took the family life under its special care. It made marriage a religious ceremony and declared it a sacrament. And yet marriage continued to be a second-best condition, and in that atmosphere a true Christianizing of even that simplest social relation was hardly possible. It was one of the greatest social services of the Reformation that it broke with the ascetic ideal so far as marriage was concerned, and ranked the married life as higher than the unmarried. The Catholic Church still theoretically views voluntary celibacy as the flower of virtue, but practically Catholics have shared with Protestants in the emancipation from the ascetic ideal, which was originally due to non-Christian influences, but which has so long been able to pose as almost the essence of Christian morality.

The attractiveness of this present world reaches us mainly through two channels—the family and property. The family comprises the people who are dear to us, and property the things that are dear to us.

Asceticism turned its vigor against both. If we are to be emancipated from the world, the hold of the property instinct must be broken. Under the pressure of the monastic movement men left their property altogether, and dedicated themselves to a life of poverty. The more absolute the poverty, the holier the monk or the order. For those who remained in their family and calling, the ideal was fundamentally the same. Let them at least limit their needs and give away the surplus saved.

Under the stimulus of this ascetic distrust of property very large amounts were set free for charity. In fact, the charitable activity of the Church was amazing. For sheer willingness to give, modern Christianity cannot match its beneficence with ascetic Christianity. But this giving was not essentially a social conflict with the moral evils of pauperism, but a religious conflict with the moral evil of the love of property. The aim was not primarily to lift the poor recipient to social health, but to discipline the soul of the giver. The Church Fathers of the fourth and fifth centuries condemned private property with such vigor that they have often been classed as communists. But they took this ground, not because they saw how valuable for the moral life a fair diffusion of property would be, but because they feared the seductive charm of property. They never proposed a communistic production of more wealth, but only called on men to share what wealth they had. If all had obeyed them, the productive capital of society would have been turned in for consumption, and society would have eaten its own head off.

The zeal for giving evoked by ascetic self-discipline was greatly reinforced by the desire to gain merit. Asceticism and the idea of religious merit are very closely connected. If the Christian who enjoys his family and property can be saved and get to heaven, the man who, for the love of God, strips himself of family and property surely must have something more than mere salvation. He would have a surplus with God, with which he could either pay up the debts contracted through former sins or which he could turn over to the general treasure of merit on which the weak and sinful could bank. It was one of the most important contributions of Paul to spiritual religion that he denied utterly that man could earn merit with God, but threw him naked and humble on the mercy of God. When the capitalistic impulse tries to accumulate a cash balance in heaven and do business with the Lord on a debit and credit basis, commercialism poisons religion.

The desire to discipline the soul and the desire to win merit united in making men give large amounts in charity, but they also vitiated the social effectiveness of the giving. The social effect was subsidiary. The giving was the main thing, not the help. Almsgiving was the best means of penitence, the most effective bath of the soul next to baptism—a means of holiness even stronger than prayer or fasting. The poor, through whom this virtue was acquired, were "the treasure of the Church," part of its equipment, a kind of gymnastic apparatus on which the givers increased their moral muscle. Hence begging was ennobled. It became a profession with its own class spirit. The mendicant orders almost glorified it. Since the effect produced by the alms was a secondary matter, men preferred to turn their alms over to the Church to be used at its discretion; their part was done with the giving. There were many organizations to elicit gifts, but no systematic organization of charity for the purpose of abolishing pauperism.

Of course a great deal of good was done. Human kindliness and good sense were never wholly paralyzed. The touch of brotherly love was warm in spite of all calculations of merit to be earned. But it is clear that the religion which elicited the charity, at the same time thwarted it, and that under these religious conceptions a sane Christianization of social relations would never be undertaken. As long as asceticism ruled in Christianity, the force of religion was exerted to lift men out of their social relations, instead of bringing them into normal relations. It would seek to suppress the natural instincts instead of finding the right and happy channels for them.

MONASTICISM

It is a remarkable demonstration of the incurably social nature both of man and of Christianity that when religion sought most earnestly to escape from social life, it turned its hand once more to build up a true social life. Every monastery proposed to be an ideal community.

The idea that society and the State were ruled by demons and were anti-Christian in their character was abandoned as a matter of course when the Church was supported by the State and society became

Christian in name. But this primitive pessimism was not supplanted by any true conception of this world as the very place in which the kingdom of God was to be built up by making all natural relations normal and holy. The older view was replaced by another pessimistic amalgamation of Greek philosophy and biblical ideas.

Philosophy had speculated about the original condition of humanity as a state of freedom and equality. The Bible told of a happy state in paradise before man fell. Man then must have been by nature free from those evils from which ascetic piety now painfully strove to free him once more. Originally man was free from sexual desire and from covetousness; there was no family nor private property, no commercial machinery for money-getting, no difference of rich and poor, or of master and slave. The ideal life, then, would consist in the abandonment of all these social institutions. Their abolition was out of the question for the mass of fallen humanity, but the chosen few at least could leave the sinful social life and create a little world apart in which they would live out the holy life which God originally ordained for man. These social ideas blended with the ascetic desire for self-discipline to create the monastic community. Here the foundations of civil society, the family, property, and worldly profession, were annihilated, and here the life of Christian perfection was to be lived.

Throughout the Middle Ages an incalculable quantity of moral and spiritual energy was put into the organization and reformation of monastic communities. Whoever desired to live a consecrated Christian life became a monk as a matter of course. Every monastic order was a society for Christian endeavor. The noblest and greatest minds spent themselves in summoning men to a still higher type of ascetic community life, or in repairing these fragile human edifices which were built on a contradiction of nature and persisted in obeying the law of gravitation and sliding down to ruin. In turn, all the great moral movements of medieval Christianity were led by monks and fostered in the monasteries where all the idealists gathered. In ever widening circles the monastic ideal laid hold of men. The mendicant orders immensely increased the numbers, because they made the support of the monks so cheap. And beyond the regular orders were the lay brotherhoods, the members of which approximated the monastic life as nearly as their family and calling permitted.

Monasticism was rich in beneficent social effects. Many of the monks were sympathetic and wise counselors and friends of the people. Every monastery was a center for charitable aid of travelers and the poor. The monasteries founded in wild and desert districts became pioneers of civilization, models of better agricultural methods and simple horticultural experiment stations.

But they rendered this social aid without any intention to reconstitute the social community about them. That was impossible. If anyone desired to live in a really Christian community, let him come into the monastery. The monks aided the poor and sick, because that was part of ascetic Christianity; in doing so they gave away the property of the order, and giving was salutary. They preferred the barren and wild places for their monasteries, not in the spirit of the modern missionary or the social settlement, because they were most needed there, but because they were farthest away from human society and therefore nearest to God. The Irish monks, for instance, first settled the lonely islands in their rivers; then the islands of the sea; then the strange countries with alien tongue—all to be pilgrims for Christ. Then incidentally they came in contact with the inhabitants of these foreign countries and became missionaries by force of their humane Christianity and in spite of their ascetic Christianity. If the monks became pioneers of agriculture, it was not because they were anxious to enrich the peasants. They had to work to get a living for their monastic colony and the poor supported by it, and to be independent of the world. Moreover, work was a salutary means of subduing the sensual desires begotten by idleness, and of giving the vagrant thoughts a definite task. Usually they selected trades that were compatible with meditation and that did not minister to luxury. But since they were a community working under a single management and having a continuous economic life, they had division of labor, gradual accumulation of wealth and improvement of methods, and contact with the experience and resources of distant regions. Thus the latent socialism in their community life worked a blessing in spite of their ascetic religion. In fact, every monastic body was a communistic colony. That was an essential part of its attempt to revive the apostolic and ideal life.

Now these institutions, founded usually with noble devotion to God, with an honest desire to live the perfect life, carrying with them so many admirable effects for the religious and social life of men, were nevertheless one potent cause for the failure of Christianity to undertake its reconstructive social mission.

The finest and most elevated natures were picked out of society as by a spiritual magnet and placed in communities by themselves, isolated from common society. The energy which they ought to have devoted to making society normal, they employed in making themselves abnormal. The power that might have lifted mankind up was used in wearing themselves down. The good men among the monks served mankind even as monks; but would men of that stamp not have served it if they had remained in the natural bonds of family and neighborhood?

When the monastic movement first swept over the ancient Church, it is certain that many went out to the hermit colonies at least partly because they were weary of the burdens of taxation and service imposed by the tottering Empire, and of the lack of freedom that hemmed all men in. They shook off the burdens of civilization at a time when civilization was desperately in need of all its human resources, and especially of all moral energy. They necessarily unloaded on those who remained the burdens which they refused to carry longer. Thus a social organism, wasted by disease and attacked by external dangers, was further bled of some of its best blood corpuscles. Ascetic and monastic Christianity contributed not a little to the fall of the Roman Empire and the destruction of ancient civilization.

During the Middle Ages some of the best organizing ability, which might have sufficed to meet the social anarchy and disorganization of society, was devoted to the organization of local monasteries or new orders, or to the reformation of old orders. When occasionally some great monastic leader took hold of a real moral and social task, the effect was sometimes wonderful.

One of the worst consequences of monasticism was the sterilizing of the best individuals. The minds of ideal bent were not allowed to propagate. The monks and nuns were condemned to childlessness. The enthusiasm of the monastic movement dragged the common priesthood into celibacy also. Aside from the considerations of ecclesiastical politics, it was chiefly the reaction of monasticism which made celibacy compulsory for the priest. But the sterility of monks and nuns

and priests for so many centuries turned the laws of heredity against
the moral progress of the race. It was just as if an agricultural experiment station should nip off all the flowers that showed unusual color
and fragrance and should develop seed from the rest. It has been truly
asserted that the most draining effect which war has on the life of nations is that it kills off the capable and lets the incapable propagate.
Monasticism eliminated the morally capable, just as war eliminates
the physically capable. God alone knows where the race might be
today if the natural leaders had not so long been made childless by
their own goodness. The wonderful fecundity of the Protestant parsonage in men of the highest ability and ideality is proof of what has been
lost. If those who were vowed to celibacy still followed the desires of
nature, they begot children under a sense of sin and shame. What that
may signify for the psychical development of the child, we are not wise
enough to tell. The Catholic Church has always had an instrument of
immense mobility and resourcefulness in the priests and monks and
sisters who were not burdened with family cares and ties, and therefore
able to give their thought and service wholly to the interests of the
Church. When this instrument is turned to social purposes, it is exceedingly effective and noble. But a married ministry is more likely as
a body to share the point of view and social interests of the common
mass of men who also have women to love and children to provide for.
A celibate ministry is perhaps more efficient for the Church; an
equally good married ministry is of more service to the kingdom of
God.[9]

Thus the monastic movement deflected and paralyzed the forces
which might have contributed to a Christian reconstruction of society. It also made the very idea of such a reconstruction impossible.
Every monastery was a concrete assertion that the ordinary life of men
was not only evil and far removed from Christian conditions, but also
that it was inherently so and incapable of real Christianization. If a
man wanted to live a really Christian life, he must get out of civil
society and into monastic society. Thereby the common social life
was condemned like a rotten hulk, and the most potent spiritual
authority of that age declared any effort to reconstruct it to be useless
in the nature of things. Thus the reconstructive aim of Christianity
was declared impossible, and the indomitable reconstructive energy

of Christianity was turned to the building of ideal communities out-side of the common life.

SACRAMENTALISM

It was one of the fundamental characteristics of prophetic religion in Israel that the service of God was sought in ethical conduct and not in ceremonial performances.[10] Christianity in its original purity was even more a religion of absolute spirituality, almost wholly emancipated from ceremonial elements, insisting simply on right relations to men as the true expression of religion. If this attitude had been maintained, it would have turned the force of the religious impulse toward social righteousness, and would inevitably have resulted in a progressive in-sight into moral wrong, and a progressive reconstruction of social rela-tions in conformity with Christian ideas.

But even in the first generation few were able to rise to the spiritual-ity of Jesus and Paul. The Jewish Christians clung to their inherited ceremonial and tried to bind Christianity down to it. Christians who had come out of paganism were imbued with the customs, the in-stincts, the points of view created by the entire religious past of the race. It would have been an almost inconceivable leap forward in social and religious evolution if Christianity for the mass of men had remained purely ethical and spiritual. As a matter of fact, Christianity did not displace paganism, but penetrated its bulk with a kind of chemical force which was destined in the slow processes of human history ultimately to disintegrate and eliminate paganism from human thought and conduct. In a large sense the entire history of Christianity to our day may be understood as an effort of the spirit of Christianity to overcome the inheritance of ethnic ideas and superstitions. The Refor-mation was an important epoch in that process, but it is not yet com-pleted.

Christianity in the heathen world rapidly relapsed toward the pre-prophetic stage of religion. The material furnished by Christianity was worked over into a new ceremonialism, essentially like the magic ritual of the Greek mysteries and Oriental cults, only more wonderful and efficacious. Baptism was a bath of regeneration, cleansing the guilt of all pre-baptismal sins, and making the soul like that of a newborn child. In the sacrament of the eucharist in some mysterious way the very body and blood of the Lord were present, and the divine could be physically eaten and its powers received to transform the material into the spiritual and immortal. The formulas of baptism and the Lord's Supper were fraught with magic powers. Worship became a process of mystagogic initiation into the divine mysteries. All the old essentials of pagan religion were reproduced in Christian form, but with scarcely a break in their essence: the effort to placate God by sacrifice, the amulets, vows, oracles, festivals, incense, candles, pictures, and statues. It was like a tropical jungle sprouting again after it is cut down. In Neo-Platonism, the highest and most refined product of the old pagan religion, we observe precisely the same process. The whole system of popular superstition was adapted in that, too. In religion the superstitions and feelings of the lower strata usually soak upward and saturate the higher. The leaders of religious thought will hallow by theological thought and ecclesiastical institutions the coarse and superstitious desires appealing to them from the lower masses.

But when Christianity turned its deepest interest from ethical conduct to sacramental ritual, it thereby paralyzed its power of moral transformation. Ritualism numbed the ethical passion of primitive Christianity. There was a vast loss of force even in the effects exerted in private morality. Of course the loss was still greater in the less intimate and pressing duties of the wider social life. The parasitic growth of ritualism and sacramentalism on the body of Christianity is one great historical cause why Christianity has never addressed itself to the task of social reconstruction.

THE DOGMATIC INTEREST

A parallel fact is the deflecting influence of dogma. Primitive Christianity had strong convictions and was very productive in religious thought, but it was undogmatic. In the Epistle of Barnabas, written near the beginning of the second century, we find the noble words, "There are three dogmas of the Lord: the hope of life, ... and righteousness ... and love."[11] Contrast with that the opening words of the so-called Athanasian Creed: "Whosoever will be saved, before all things it is necessary that he hold the catholic faith; which faith except every one do keep whole and undefiled, without doubt he shall perish ever-lastingly." It then proceeds to set forth that catholic faith in a number of subtle definitions on the relation between the persons of the trinity.

Since the second century, and especially since the great doctrinal controversies of the fourth century, dogma came to be regarded as the essence of Christianity. A man must assent to the true doctrine, and if he held that, the fundamental requirement of religion was fulfilled. But when dogmatic and speculative questions absorbed the religious interest, less of it was left for moral and social questions. The polemic bitterness and intolerance engendered by the dogmatism of the Church have been antisocial forces of the first importance. But it was probably an even greater loss to the race that its ablest intellects, the natural leaders of humanity, concentrated their abilities on compara-tively fruitless speculation and on the formulation and defense of dogmas which too often were not even true.

The mass of men are not able to comprehend speculation; but if they see their intellectual leaders vociferating about the incomprehen-sible, they will echo the catchwords with an ardor equal to their igno-rance. In them the constant insistence on dogma induced an unthinking submission of intellect which dried up those powerful springs of free faith and will that had made primitive Christianity so productive. In that respect dogmatism cooperated with ritualism, which likewise requires no intelligence in the worshiper, and which always acts as a narcotic on the intellect of the people. But intellectual independence and determination are absolutely necessary if the moral forces are to make headway against deeply rooted wrongs.

A type of Christianity in which pagan superstition and Greek intel-lectualism had paralyzed the original social and ethical impetus was in no condition to undertake the immense task of reorganizing social re-lations on a Christian basis. Even the personality of Jesus, which is the unceasing source of revolutionary moral power in Christianity, was almost completely obscured by the dogmatic Christ of the Church.

THE CHURCHLINESS OF CHRISTIANITY

One of the profoundest changes in the history of Christianity took place when the simple groups of Christian believers, who were bound together in intimate social life by the same faith and hope, were transformed into a firmly organized, authoritative, and international ecclesiastical organization. Correct doctrine, as we have seen, came to be essential to salvation. But the Church alone was the teacher of true doctrine. She alone preserved the deposit of faith received by apostolic tradition and had the promise of Christ that she would be kept in the truth. The sacraments alone could mediate salvation, and the Church and her priesthood by apostolic succession and ordination alone had the power to administer the sacraments, to pronounce the magic words that would change the bread and wine into the mysterious vehicle of the body and blood of Christ, and to absolve from guilt and save from hell. Thus the Church was the great channel of salvation; apart from the Church there was no salvation. If a man wanted to be saved—and men wanted it intensely—he must remain in contact with the Church, obedient to her teaching and spiritual direction. Perhaps the most distinctive characteristic of Christianity down to our own time has been its churchliness.

Christian ethics became churchly ethics. An action was good or bad mainly because the Church said so. It was good always if it served the Church, for the cause of the Church was the cause of God.[12] There was no higher exercise of piety than to build churches or endow monasteries. Avarice was refusal to enrich the Church. Charity to the Church covered a multitude of sins. If a king served the cause of the Church, he was a blessed man, though he might betray the cause of his people in doing so. Gregory of Tours freely narrates the shameful life of the Frankish kings, but he naively calls them men of God on whom the divine blessing rested, because they were zealous for the catholic cause and confessed the blessed trinity. Clovis prospered because he was a supporter of the Orthodox Church. Alaric sought the same ambitious ends, but lost his kingdom, his people, and eternal life, because he was an Arian heretic.[13] The medieval clergy were often notoriously immoral; but the people were kept in awe of them because they were the representatives of the Church, and through them alone could the sacraments and the absolution of the Church be obtained. They might not have the spirit of Christ, but they had the ordination of the Church. Churchly correctness took precedence of Christ-like goodness. If sin profited the Church, even sin might be holy. The amount of distortion of facts, falsification of history, and forging of documents practiced in order to advance the cause of the Church is quite incredible. The sale of indulgences, which finally unfettered the popular protest of the Reformation movement, was merely a glaring instance of prostituting the spiritual welfare of the people to the financial enrichment of the Church organization.

Christian morality finds its highest dignity and its constant corrective in making the kingdom of God the supreme aim to which all minor aims must contribute and from which they gain their moral quality. The Church substituted itself for the kingdom of God, and thereby put the advancement of a tangible and very human organization in the place of the moral uplifting of humanity. By that substitution the ethical plane of all actions was subtly but terribly lowered. The kingdom of God can never be advanced by cruelty and trickery; the power of the organized Church can be and has been advanced by persecution and forgery.

By that substitution the Church could claim all service and absorb all social energies. It has often been said that the Church interposed between the soul of man and God. It also interposed between man and humanity. It magnified what he did for the Church and belittled what he did for humanity. It made its own organization the chief object of social service.

The more churchly Christianity is, the more will the Church be the only sphere of really Christian activity. Only those portions of daily life which are related to the Church will be illuminated by the consciousness of serving God. The rest is secular, natural, permissible; it is not religious and holy. The secular calling in the home, the workshop, or the town is left unhallowed by religion and void of that joy and enthusiasm which come through the consciousness that God loves our work. If a man takes his religion seriously, he will then want to devote his life to the Church.

The property of the primitive Church was entirely devoted to the needy. The officers of the Church lived by their own labor unless the service of Christ compelled them to forgo their earnings. As Christianity became ecclesiastical, the Church made itself the chief recipient and its clergy the chief beneficiaries of Christian giving. If a man helped a friend in need, he did a moral act. If he gave to the Church, he did a religious act. The Church was able to offer the most enticing eternal rewards to those who gave to her. Thus she discouraged the giving of aid from man to man and encouraged the concentration of giving on herself. To some extent this systematized charity, but it also eliminated the salutary human element from charity, and an ever larger percentage of the gifts never reached the poor. Charitable institutions are apt to use an increasing share of their income for salaries and incidentals. Trustees are apt to regard themselves as the practical owners of the funds they have long administered. The charity of the Church was perhaps the most distinctly social service which it rendered. That service was diverted the more Christianity became churchly in its essence.

Since the progress of Christianity was identical with the progress of the Church, the ablest men consumed their strength in building up the power and influence of the Church and in working their way to the places in the Church from which they could direct its policies. The organizing ability which might have reconstituted social life was expended on the organization of the hierarchy and the monastic orders.

The State is the organization through which men cooperate for the larger social ends. If men conceive of political duties as a high religious service to man and God, the State can be a powerful agent in the bettering of human life. As long as the Church was in opposition to the State, the Church denied that the functions of the State had any sacredness and deterred its members from entering political service. But even when the Church and the State had entered into a compact of friendship, the Church did not infuse the moral vigor and enthusiasm into the political life which it might have imparted. It turned aside many of the ablest and choicest spirits to the monastic life and to hierarchical careers. It has often been said that when the organization of the Empire was tottering to its fall, a new social edifice was rising in the organization of the Church. But the question may fairly be asked if the Church did not hasten the fall of the Empire by draining off so much of the best strength from civil life and using it for her own organization.

The influence of the Church on humane legislation was neutralized by her anxiety to secure benefits for herself. The historian Schiller, in speaking of the failure of the Church to act against slavery, says, "In general it is astonishing how little influence the Church always exerted on the development of law."[14] But the laws conferring financial gifts on the Church herself and exemptions on her clergy were very numerous and important. In the perpetual conflicts between the civil and ecclesiastical powers in the Middle Ages it is often difficult for us to see that the cause of Christianity was in any sense at stake. Doubtless the great fighting princes of the Church, men of the granite quarry like Hildebrand, were convinced that the supremacy of the Church was essential to the supremacy of spiritual interests and the reign of God over man. Doubtless they were partly right, and every good churchman of today, if he had lived then, would have gone with enthusiasm into the fight about lay investiture. But from our present perspective we see clearly enough that the cause of the Church was not at all identical with the cause of God, and that the power of Christ over humanity did not advance at even pace with the power of the pope over the princes. It was largely a class struggle, the conflict of an ecclesiastical aristocracy with a secular aristocracy, and the welfare of the people was not the real issue. When the Church fought for her own political interests, and not for the cause of the people, her influence on the State was often a disturbing and disastrous one. Where clericalism is a political power, it thrusts an alien influence into every political question. Civic questions are not decided on their own merit, but according to the profit the clerical machine may get out of them. This disturbing influence is greatly increased if the Church is not a national body, but is governed from a foreign center. In that case Roman schemes or the ambitions of Italian upstarts may determine the civil policies of Germany or France.

Thus when Christianity was embodied in an all-absorbing and all-dominating ecclesiastical organization, its social effectiveness was crippled. Its ethical influence was lowered and vitiated. Its fraternal helpfulness was largely absorbed by the clerical machine. Its organizing ability was spent on strengthening its own organization. Its influence on the State was used to secure benefits for itself rather than for the people. By connecting all religious life with its own organization, it left the common life unhallowed and unrenewed.

In making these historical criticisms on ecclesiasticism, I do not belittle the immense value and importance of Christian churches.

Religion demands social expression like all other great human impulses. Without an organization to proclaim it, to teach it, to stimulate it, the religious life would probably be greatly weakened in the best, and in many would be powerless and unknown. The mischief begins when the Church makes herself the end. She does not exist for her own sake; she is simply a working organization to create the Christian life in individuals and the kingdom of God in human society. She is an agent with large powers, and like all other agents she is constantly tempted to use her powers for herself. Our modern political parties were organized to advocate certain political principles and realize them in public life. Gradually they have come to regard their perpetuation as an end in itself, and public welfare is subordinated to party victory. Our public-service corporations exist for the public, but we know how these our servants have become our masters, so that the public exists for their dividends. This slow, historical embezzlement of public powers, this tendency of organizations and institutions to aggrandize themselves at the expense of the ends for which they were called into existence, is one of the most important phenomena in moral life. There is no permanent institution but has succumbed to this temptation. The organization of the Church is simply one sinner among many, and not the worst by any means. Her history is the story of how she fell by rising, and rose by falling. No one who loves her can serve her better than by bringing home to her that by seeking her life she loses it, and that when she loses her life to serve the kingdom of God, she will gain it.

SUBSERVIENCE TO THE STATE

Ideally the State is the organization of the people for their larger common interests. Actually all States have been organizations of some section of the people to protect their special interests against the rest. Ideally the chief function of the State should be the maintenance of justice. Actually the chief function of most States has been the maintenance of existing conditions, whatever they happened to be. The State is the representative of things as they are; the Church is the representative of things as they ought to be. Insofar as it is loyal to this duty, it must be in perpetual but friendly conflict with the State, pushing it on to ever higher lines of duty. Nothing better could happen to any State than to have within it a Church devoted, not to its own selfish corporate interests, but to the moral welfare of humanity, and nudging the reluctant State along like an enlightened pedagogue.

Before Constantine the Church was, of course, unable to fulfill any such friendly office as moral monitor. After Constantine the Church was in many respects less free than it had been before. The Christian emperors considered the apparatus of the Church as an important part of the machinery of the Empire, and kept a firm and coercing hand on the legislative councils and the episcopal executives of the Church. Their favors were even more deadly than their decrees of banishment. The leaders of the Church learned to be courtiers in order to further the interests of their sees and of orthodoxy in general, and the atmosphere of courts is not healthy for any who are to champion the cause of the people in the spirit of Christ. During the Middle Ages the landed wealth of the Church made her a part of the feudal system. She was on the whole a conservative and merciful landlord, but her interest was with the landed aristocracy and the governing powers. When she antagonized the State, it was in her own interest. The Reformation did not directly remedy the dependence of the Church on the State, but in some countries made the Church an even more servile tool of the princes. To our own day, wherever the Church leans on state protection and lives on state aid, she is expected to lend her moral support to the State to maintain existing conditions, and she does so. Both in England and Germany, for instance, the Established Church is a Tory influence. But when she is thus allied with the powers that be, she can make no effective protest against the wrongs that be. The Church supported by the State is in the position of the office-holders appointed by the party in power. They have to support the policy of the administration, praising it when it is good, and defending it when it is bad. The separation of Church and State has the double advantage of removing the clerical influence from political life, and the political influence from church life. It leaves the Church unmuzzled to speak out, if it has anything to say. It does its best work when it is the party in opposition, poor but vociferous.

The Church as a body has been dependent on the State and therefore subservient to it. The members of the Church individually have been politically disfranchised and subject to their rulers, and that has made them passive on questions of political morality.

While the Church lived in the hostile and heathen Empire, its members had to keep aloof from public life and to find all their interests in the narrow circle of the family and the churches. Hence, so far as asceticism permitted, the ethics of the family was developed and leavened with Christian ideas. The early narrowness of interest left its record in the writings of the apostles and the early Fathers, and set a precedent for later times.

But even when Christianity was tolerated and encouraged, the mass of men were shut out from active participation in government. Politics was the occupation of a privileged class. But where there are no political rights, there are no political duties, and the sense of political obligation is not developed. A man is not likely to take a keen and intelligent interest in a sphere of action over which he has no control and in which he is never called to act.

Moreover, if a preacher had an audience of subject peasants, he had no incentive to preach politics to them, unless he was a popular agitator. What political duties could he preach to them except to render obedience to the king and their feudal lord, and to be content in the station in which it had pleased God to place them? And of that kind of political preaching there has always been more than enough. There has never been any feeling of treading on ground alien to religion when the few but invaluable texts were reached in which law and order are enjoined. It was only when a preacher spoke before kings and gentry like Latimer, or before the citizens of free cities like Savonarola, or when some great national movement stirred all classes in a common interest against a foreign enemy, that social or political preaching could be attempted, and right valiantly did many a Christian man use such opportunities.

But the limits set by a despotic age have continued into our democratic age. They have become theological tradition. The sermons of one generation are read and imitated by the next. Theological textbooks and teachers move along the trodden paths. The wider interests thrown open by the advent of the people to political power have very slowly called forth corresponding religious thought. The old historical conditions have evolved a theory by which a circle of short radius is drawn about the individual. The relations lying within that circle are supposed to be within the province of religious thought and church teaching; those lying beyond it are outside of the realm of religion. The ethics of the private life, of the family, and of friendly social intercourse, together with the interests of education, literature, and to some extent of art, lie within this circle. Industry, commerce, and politics in the main lie outside of it. "Religion has nothing to do with politics and sociology." This circular division has no rational justification. It is a historical product of an age when the common people were shut out from participation in public affairs. It is now out of date and its perpetuation is wholly bad. The people now have political and social rights, yet the Church is not giving adequate teaching on the duties corresponding to those novel rights. Industrial and political affairs press upon the life of every man with a force unknown formerly, yet the organization which ought to discuss the new moral problems is silent or inefficient in its teaching. The great sociologist Schaeffle, speaking of the slowness with which the larger relations of commerce and politics have been affected by Christianity, truly says, "The great need of our time is a public morality."

The dependence of the Church on the State, and the political passivity of the subject people, combined to cripple the social efficiency of the Church in former times, and the precedents and theories set up in the pre-democratic age continue to operate even where the causes which justified them have passed away.

THE DISAPPEARANCE OF CHURCH DEMOCRACY

The subjection of the Church to the State would have been neutralized and overcome if only the churches had preserved the Christian democracy of their own organization. The primitive churches set out with an organization as democratic and simply patriarchal as a Teutonic town-meeting. By the beginning of the second century they were passing under the limited monarchy of a single bishop, and the limited monarchy tended to shake off all limitations and thrust down all competing forces. In ever widening areas monarchical organization grew up, and this tendency finally culminated in the absolutism of the papacy, in which all power flows from the head downward. The clergy became a hierarchy graded on monarchical principles. At the same time the laity were gradually ousted from all the rights of election, church discipline, and self-government, which they had originally possessed, and reduced to the helpless passivity of a subject population under a bureaucratic despotism. This slow revolution was due partly to the ambition and lust for power inherent in human nature, but mainly to the assimilating influence of secular institutions.[15] The churches step by step copied the forms of organization prevalent about them.[16] The centralization of Church power in the clergy and the bishop in the third century took place simultaneously with a centralization of power in the organization of the Empire.[17] The Church poured its organization into the molds furnished by imperial Rome, and when the mold was broken and crumbled away, the Church in its system of government stood erect as an ecclesiastical duplicate of the Empire.

For the purposes of ecclesiastical aggrandizement it was worth a great deal to the Church that it inherited the results of the organizing genius of Rome, but the inheritance was deadly to the revolutionary social influence of the Church. Jesus had emphatically repudiated the principles on which political government is usually run: "You know that the rulers of the Gentiles lord it over them. . . . It will not be so among you" (Matthew 20:25–26). But the Church duplicated in its own organization the aristocracy and monarchy of the world, and therewith prepared a home for the despotic spirit within the edifice dedicated to democracy. A given spirit will create an institution adapted to itself; but in turn an institution will constantly evoke the spirit that fits it. The Catholic Church by its organization tends to keep alive and active the despotic spirit of decadent Roman civilization in which it originated. Even today, when the current of democracy is flowing so powerfully through the modern world, the Roman Church has a persistent affinity for the monarchical principle and an instinctive distrust of democracy. The chronic difficulty encountered by the Latin nations of Southern Europe and Southern America in making free institutions work, is probably not due to any inefficiency of blood or race, but partly to clerical interference in government, and partly to the antidemocratic spirit constantly flowing out from the Roman Church into the national life of peoples under her control.[18] If we ask why the Church failed to reorganize society on a basis of liberty and equality, we have here one of the most important answers.

The causal influences running back and forth between the civil and the ecclesiastical organization of the people are far more powerful than is generally understood. The monarchical government of the Roman Church originated in the despotic society of ancient Rome and then perpetuated itself by the conservatism of hallowed religious institutions. The aristocratic republicanism of the Calvinistic churches originated in the Swiss republics, and then perpetuated itself wherever Calvinism went. The democracy of the Congregational church bodies originated in the democratic passions of the English Revolution and also perpetuated itself. Thus the Church borrows from the State.

But in the same manner the State borrows from the Church. "The action of religion on the minds of men is so profound that they are always led to give to the organization of the State forms which they have borrowed from that of religion."[19] If a people is accustomed to the spirit and practice of self-government in its local churches, it will find self-government in the civil community that much easier, and any government from above will be unpalatable. The Congregational churches of New England and the town-meetings of New England are causally related, just like the priest-ridden Church of Russia and her political autocracy. The maxim of King James I, "No bishop, no king," was quite right in the perception that one kind of monarchy strengthens the other. In the English Revolution the political attitude of each section was quite accurately graded according to its ecclesiastical radicalism. The Episcopalians were for the king; the Presbyterians were for a strong Parliament; the Independents were republicans, and vice versa.

Thus it seems likely that if the Christian churches had remained democratic and self-governing organizations, the spirit of Christian democracy would have been perpetuated, intensified, and practically trained among them, and would have turned with greater vigor and efficiency to all moral and social tasks lying about the Church. It is significant that with every turn toward a purer conception of worship and doctrine in the evangelical sects of the Middle Ages, there was also a turn toward democracy in church organization and toward radical social ideas. They all had communistic ideals.

THE LACK OF SCIENTIFIC COMPREHENSION OF
SOCIAL DEVELOPMENT

To undertake the gradual reconstruction of social life consciously and intelligently would have required a scientific comprehension of social life which was totally lacking in the past. Sociology is still an infant science. Modern political economy may be said to have begun with Adam Smith's *Wealth of Nations*, which was published in 1776. Modern historical science, which is interpreting the origins and the development of social institutions, is only about a century old.

For the ordinary man the social order as he finds it has all the sanctity and immutability of natural and divine law. Under feudalism both noble and peasant assumed that God himself had divided humanity into barons and serfs, and any contradiction of that seemed a sacrilege to the barons and a joyful surprise to the serfs. In monarchical countries the institution of kingship is regarded as the natural and divine order. In European thought it is treated as an axiom that there must be well-defined social classes. In our own country intelligent men assume that land has always been freely bought and sold by individuals as today; that a man has always had the power to dispose about his property even after he was dead; that businessmen have always bought in the cheapest market and sold in the dearest at whatever prices they could make; that workingmen have always competed with one another for wages; and that any attempt to change these social adjustments is an attempt to meddle with a natural law as universal as the law of gravitation. Yet our capitalistic organization is of comparatively recent origin, and would have been thought intolerable and immoral in times past. We are only now coming to realize that within certain limits human society is plastic, constantly changing its forms, and that the present system of social organization, as it superseded others, may itself be displaced by something better. Without such a conception of the evolution of social institutions any larger idea of social regeneration could hardly enter the minds of men. The modern socialist movement is really the first intelligent, concerted, and continuous effort to reshape society in accordance with the laws of social development.

The comprehension of the gradualness of social changes is also a late attainment. The childish mind wants swift results and loses interest if things move slowly. It wants the flower seeds which were planted last night to be above ground before breakfast. It finds the atmosphere of the fairy tales so congenial, because there great things happen at the waving of the fairy's wand. This is also the characteristic of the savage, and in lessening degree of every unscientific mind. It understands personal action, and so far as its personal powers will reach, it is willing to help in making things better. For anything beyond its immediate reach and power it trusts in divine intervention. For the slow molding of institutions by ideas and the slow creation of ideas to justify institutions, for the steady alternation of cause and effect in the development of society, there has been no trained observation.

The Church, as we have seen, had the conception of a thorough social regeneration. To that extent religion was prophetic and outran the political intellect by many centuries. But Jesus stood almost alone in the comprehension of the gradualness of moral conquest. The millennial hope was the modern social hope without the scientific conception of organic development. The Church Fathers were lacking in the historical sense for development. The educated men among them had been trained in the Roman rhetorical schools, and the educational system of that day was almost useless for producing historical insight.[20] The air of the miraculous which hung about Christian thought down to modern times was also directly hostile to any scientific comprehension of social facts. When all things happened by devils or angels, how could men understand the real causes of things?

In the Bible the Church always had a historical literature which might have opened its eyes to a multitude of social facts, and every time the Bible was in some way freshly comprehended, the social leaven hidden in it did begin to work. All the medieval evangelical movements which were based on renewed reading of the Bible involved some crude but noble attempt to live a life of social fraternity. When the Bible became the common property of the people through the invention of printing and the translations of the Reformation, it exerted a marked influence on the general social stir of that age. But in general the social enlightenment contained in the Bible was numbed by the dogmatic and ecclesiastical interests of the Church and by the allegorical method of interpretation. Theologians hunted for proof-texts of dogma. Churchmen were interested in the tithing system of the Old Testament because it helped them to exact ecclesiastical taxes, but not in the land system of the Mosaic Law. The allegorical method neutralized the social contents of the Bible by spiritualizing everything. For instance, the emancipation of the Israelite tribes from galling overwork and cruelty in Egypt, and their conquest of a good tract of land for settlement, is a striking story of social revolt, but it was turned into an allegory of the exodus of the soul from the world and its attainment of the Promised Land beyond the Jordan of death. The great social parable of the good Samaritan was "spiritualized" into an allegory of humanity, which leaves the divine city of Jerusalem and goes down to Jericho, the accursed. It falls into the hands of the devil and his angels, is stripped of the robes of its original righteousness, and left half dead in its sins. But Christ finds it, pours wine and oil, the blood of his passion and his Spirit, into its wounds, and commits it to the Church to be cared for till his second advent.[21] This method of interpreting sacred books is no Christian invention. The Jews used the Old Testament, and the Greek philosophers used Homer in the same way. It was an ingenious and swift way of getting ready-made spiritual and doctrinal results from the Bible. But like a sleight-of-hand performer taking ribbons and rabbits out of a silk hat, it never took anything out of the Bible that was not already in the mind of the interpreter, and thus it learned nothing new from the Bible. And by its tendency to seek for spiritual and mystical meanings it belittled and overlooked the homely social significance of the biblical stories and teachings.

The Church shared with all the rest of humanity the childlike view of the world, the lack of the historical sense, the inability to understand the facts and laws of social development. The moral intuition awakened by religion made it swifter and bolder to hope for a radical social change than those who traveled by common sense alone; but the prevalent belief in the miraculous and in constant divine interventions counteracted the enlightening effects of its moral vision.

These intellectual deficiencies would, perhaps, alone suffice to explain why the Church has never undertaken a clear-eyed and continuous reconstruction of society in any larger way.

THE OUTCOME OF THE DISCUSSION

We set out on this discussion with the proposition that the failure of Christianity to accomplish that task of social regeneration to which it seemed committed by its origins, was not due to the conscious and wise self-limitation of the Church, but to a series of historical causes. Some of the most important of these causes I have tried to set forth. I think that for anyone following this enumeration dispassionately and with previous comprehension of the historical facts alluded to, even so imperfect a résumé can hardly fail to make the main proposition at least probable. If any considerable portion of the argument has been correct it follows that the failure of the Church to undertake the work of a Christian reconstruction of social life has not been caused by its close adherence to the spirit of Christ and to the essence of its religious task, but to the deflecting influence of alien forces penetrating Christianity from without and clogging the revolutionary moral power inherent in it.

In primitive Christianity the failure is sufficiently accounted for by the impossibility of undertaking a social propaganda within the hostile Empire, and by the hostility to the existing civilization created through the protest against idolatry and through the persecutions suffered by Christians. The catastrophic element in the millennial hope was an inheritance from Judaism. The belief in the demon powers ruling in heathen society was partly Jewish, partly heathen.

The otherworldliness, the asceticism and monastic enthusiasm, the sacramental and ritual superstitions, were all derived from contemporary religious drifts in heathen society. The dogmatic bent was acquired mainly from Greek intellectualism. The union of Church and State was likewise a reversion to ethnic religion. The lack of political rights and interests among the mass of Christian people, and the disappearance of the original democracy of Church organization, were part of the curse of despotism which lay upon all humanity. The lack of a scientific comprehension of society was in the main inevitable in the past stages of intellectual progress.

At first sight such a conception of Christian history seems like a tremendous impeachment of the Church for apostasy and dereliction of duty. But not to anyone who understands the patience of God and the infinite slowness and imperfection of historical progress. It takes so long for new ideas to trickle down through the solid strata of human life; so long for new conceptions to get sufficient grip on the mass of men to sway them; so long for the moral nature of the social body to be sensitized. Anyone who has had experience in the training of children or young minds will realize how hard it is to build a lasting basis of independent intelligence and firm morality, and how opposing influences perpetually neutralize the best work of the parent or teacher. Anyone who has honestly tried to live a Christian life himself, will be ready to take a humble view of the success attending his efforts. Anyone who has tried to train a single church or club or trades-union to take high points of view and rise to nobler lines of action, will realize how hopeful and how disheartening the task is. When Jesus bent his soul to uplift humanity, he set his shoulders to a task which is not accomplished in a day. The modern intellect, which reckons with thousands of years in the evolution of the savage, with hundreds of thousands in the formation of geological deposits, and with eternities in astronomical evolution, ought to be ready to have patience if the full results of the Christian spirit have not yet come to fruitage.

If such a review of past failures leaves a feeling of condemnatory surprise, it is largely due to the false expectations raised in the past by religious rhetoric. Christian orators have scurried through history for edifying anecdotes. They have pictured the first three centuries as a golden age of Christian love and purity. They have assumed that the enthronement of Christianity as the state religion of the Empire and the apparent conquest of paganism meant the actual disappearance of pagan habits of mind and customs. As if anything set up by thousands of years of history could vanish into thin air! They have represented the progress of Christianity as a triumphal procession of the gospel, leaving regenerated nations and ages behind it. Then if we awake from that fictitious enthusiasm and face the sober facts of human imperfection, it is a sore and angry surprise.

To say that Christianity in the past has largely followed alien influences and has missed its greatest mission is not to condemn the men of the past. They followed the light they had and threw their lives into the pursuit of that light with an ardor that puts us to shame. If we have any zeal for the truth in us now, it is altogether likely that we would have shouted for the Homousios or the Homoiusios[22] had we walked the streets of Alexandria in the fourth century. If I had known St. Francis, I hope I should have had grace enough to become a Franciscan friar and to serve the Lady Poverty. If destiny had put me on the chair of St. Peter, I hope I should have made a good fight against the encroachments of the secular power on the sacred heritage of Christ and the vicar of Christ. But being a twentieth-century Christian, I hope I shall do nothing of the kind. If the men of the past flinched in following their ideals, they must answer to God for it. Also if they consciously taught what was un-Christian, or quenched the better light in others.

THE PASSING OF THESE CAUSES IN MODERN LIFE

The sadness of the failure hitherto is turned into brightest hopefulness if we note that all the causes which have hitherto neutralized the social efficiency of Christianity have strangely disappeared or weakened in modern life. Christianity has shed them as an insect sheds its old casing in passing through its metamorphosis, and with the disappearance of each of these causes, Christianity has become fitter to take up its regenerative work. Let us run over the causes of failure set forth in this chapter and note how they have weakened or vanished.

In the Roman Empire, as we have seen, social agitation would have been suppressed promptly. Today it still encounters the moral resentment of the classes whose interests are endangered by a moral campaign and, if necessary, these interests are able to use the political machinery to suppress agitation. But in the freer countries of Western civilization the dissemination of moral ideas is almost untrammeled. The prophet's message still brings the prophet's odium; but a man will have to go far if he wants to be stoned or put in the stocks.

Primitive Christianity did not work for social changes which required a long outlook, because it expected the immediate return of Christ. That the return of Christ will end the present world is still part of general Christian teaching; but the actual lapse of nineteen centuries has proved so plainly that we have to reckon with long reaches of time, that this expectation deters very few from taking a long look ahead in all practical affairs. There are, indeed, a number of Christian bodies and a great number of individuals who have systematized the apocalyptic ideas of later Judaism and early Christianity and have made them fundamental in their religious thought. They are placing themselves artificially in the attitude of mind which primitive Christianity took naturally. They are among the most devout and earnest people. By their devotional and missionary literature they exert a wide influence. They share with splendid vigor in evangelistic work, because evangelism saves individuals for the coming of the Lord, and in foreign missionary work, because it is an express condition that the Lord will not return "until the gospel has been preached to all nations." They take a lively interest in the destructive tendencies of modern life, because these are "signs of the times" which herald the end; but they do not feel called to counteract them. Such an effort would be predestined to failure, because the present world is doomed to rush through increasing corruption to moral bankruptcy, and Christ alone by his coming can save it. Historical pessimism is generally woven into the texture of this pattern of thought, and it is this pessimistic interpretation of history, more than the somewhat academic expectation of the immediate return of Christ, which neutralizes the interest of this school of thought in comprehensive moral reformation. So far as the influence of this drift goes, it is a deadweight against any effort to mobilize the moral forces of Christianity to share in the modern social movement. This is all the more pathetic because these men have a nobler ingredient of social hope for humanity than ordinary Christians. But outside of this sphere of thought the hope of the immediate millennium, which was once so influential, is no longer a factor to deter Christians from their wider mission to society.

The primitive attitude of fear and distrust toward the State has passed away. We do not regard the existing civilization and its governments as hostile to Christianity. The ancient feeling that demon powers inspire the State has vanished with the belief in demons. Some today regard the State as the organization of secular life, which, though in a sphere apart from religion, is good and useful in its way. Others take the more religious view of it, that it is one of the divinely constituted factors to train the race for the kingdom of God, of equal dignity with the family and the Church. Under either conception it is possible to cooperate with it and turn the regenerative moral power of religion into the channels of organized civil life.

The otherworldliness of Christian desire is strangely diminished. We all believe in immortality, but we are not weary of this world. The longing to die and go to heaven is not regarded as a test of spiritual life as it used to be, even within the memory of many of us. To us salvation means victory over sin rather than escape from hell. This change of attitude dignifies the present life. It is not, then, too paltry for earnest effort. The hope of personal salvation after death no longer monopolizes the Christian hope. There is now room beside it for the social hope.

The ascetic and monastic ideal, which dominated Christian life for a thousand years and more, has disappeared almost completely. If the saints that lie buried under the stone floor of some ancient European church could rise and listen to a modern sermon, they would find their gospel turned upside down. Instead of praise of virginity, they would hear eulogies of family life. Instead of the call to poverty, they would hear the praise of Christianity because it makes men and nations prosperous and wealthy. Instead of exhortations to wear their flesh thin with fasting and vigil, they would be invited to membership in the YMCA, with gymnasium and bath to keep their flesh in a glow of health. If the old gospel of individualism should hereafter change into the gospel of socialism, the change would not be half as great as that involved in the surrender of the ascetic ideal of the Christian life. Some ascetic practices still linger in the observance of Lent. The ascetic notion occasionally crops up that men are best turned to God by affliction, and that revivals follow on hard times. The distrust of the intellectual and artistic and political life in English evangelicalism and German pietism, the retirement of the Christian within the untroubled realm of family and business life, is a diluted Protestant form of the ascetic flight from the world. The Roman Church, by force of its strong medieval traditions, still exalts the monastic life as the crown of religious living; but its medieval saints would think their Church was dead if they saw the scarcity of monks in America. The current of modern religion does not run away from the world, but toward it. Religion no longer spends its immense force in tearing men out of social life and isolating them from family, property, and State. Therefore it is now free to direct that force toward the Christianizing of the common life. It no longer establishes monastic communities to live the truly

Christian and communistic life. Therefore it ought now to make the life of the entire community truly Christian. If the disappearance of ascetic enthusiasm means the evaporation of Christian self-sacrifice, it would mean a net loss and a surrender of Christianity to worldliness. If it means that the old enthusiasm is now directed toward the moral regeneration of society, it would mean a new era for humanity.

Ceremonialism, which early clogged the ethical vigor of Christianity, was broken in the Reformation and is slowly dying out. Greek and Roman Catholicism are faithful to it by virtue of their conservatism, but even there it is no longer a creative force. There are ritualistic drifts in a few Protestant bodies, but they are not part of modern life, but romantic reactions toward the past. The present tendency to a more ornate and liturgical worship in the radical Protestant denominations of America is aesthetic and not sacramental in motive. It is proof that sacramentalism is so dead that Protestant churches no longer need to fear the forms that might revive it. The priest is dying. The prophet can prepare to enter his heritage, provided the prophet himself is still alive with his ancient message of an ethical and social service of God.

It is a commonplace that Christianity has grown less dogmatic. There is probably just as much earnest conviction, but it is modified by greater respect for the conviction of others and by a deeper interest in right living. Men and churches fellowship freely with little regard to doctrinal uniformity. One of the chief antisocial forces has therewith disappeared from Christianity, and the subsidence of the speculative interest has to that extent left Christianity free to devote its thought to ethical and social problems.

Christianity in the past was almost wholly churchly. The organized Church absorbed the devotion, the ability, and the wealth of its members. To some degree that is still true. The churches need time and money and must strive to get their share. For very many men and women the best service they can render to the kingdom of God is really through the local church and its activities. In some measure, religion is still supposed to be bounded by the Church. What is connected with the churches is religious; what is apart from them is supposed to be secular. Even very worldly affairs, like bazaars and oyster suppers, are religious if they raise the support or increase the popularity of a church. On the other hand, efforts to fight tuberculosis or secure parks and playgrounds are viewed as secular, because they are not connected with a church. But there has been a great change. The wiser leaders of Christianity do not desire to monopolize the services of Christian men for the churches, but rejoice in seeing the power of religion flow out in the service of justice and mercy. Religion is less an institution and more a diffused force than ever before. The brazen vessel of the Church was fatally cracked and broken by the Reformation, and its contents have ever since been leaking away into secular life. The State, the schools, the charitable organizations, are now doing what the Church used to do. The Roman Church continues its traditions of churchly authority and exclusiveness. Some Protestant bodies try with more or less success to imitate her role, but Protestantism cannot compete with the Roman Catholic Church in churchliness. In spite of itself, Protestantism has lost its ecclesiastical character and authority. But at the same time Protestant Christianity has gained amazingly in its spiritual effectiveness on society. The Protestant nations have leaped forward in wealth, education, and political preponderance. The unfettering of intellectual and economic ability under the influence of this diffused force of Christianity is a historical miracle. Protestantism has even Protestantized the Roman Catholic Church. The Roman Church crumbles away before it in our country and can only save its adherents by quarantining its children in parochial schools and its men and women in separate social and benevolent societies. The churches are profoundly needed as generators of the religious spirit; but they are no longer the sole sphere of action for the religious spirit. They exist to create the force which builds the kingdom of God on earth, the better humanity. By becoming less churchly Christianity has, in fact, become fitter to regenerate the common life.

Modern Christianity everywhere tends toward the separation of Church and State. But when the Church is no longer dependent on the State for its appointments and its income and the execution of its will, it is by that much freer to champion the better order against the chief embodiment of the present order. We shall see later that even when Church and State are separated, the Church may still be in bondage to the powers of the world. It can still be used as a spiritual posse to read the Riot Act to the rebellious minds of men. But as the formal control of the Church by the State slackens, and the clerical interests are withdrawn from politics, the Church is freer to act as the tribune of the people, and the State is more open to the moral and humanizing influence of Christianity. At the same time the political emancipation and increasing democracy of the people is bound to draw the larger social and political problems within the interests of the masses, and there is sure to be a silent extension of the religious interest and motive to social and political duties.

In the past the Church was dominated by the clergy and it was monarchical in its organization. The Reformation brought a slow turn on both points. The power of the hierarchy was broken; the laity began to rise to increased participation in church life. That in itself ensured an increasing influence of Christianity on secular life. At the same time the Protestant bodies, in varying degrees, reverted toward democracy in organization. Those Protestant bodies which constitute the bulk of Protestantism in America and of the free churches in England all have the essence of Church democracy. Even the churches with episcopal government are affected by the spirit of democratic self-government. The Roman Church in America itself has not escaped this influence. All this lays the churches open to democratic sympathies, provided they are not merely organizations of the possessing classes.

The intellectual prerequisites for social reconstruction were lacking formerly. They are now at hand. Travel and history are breaking the spell of existing conditions and are telling even the common man that social relations are plastic and variable. We have the new sciences of political economy and sociology to guide us. It is true, political economy in the past has misled us often, but it, too, is leaving its sinful laissez-faire ways and preparing to serve the Lord and human brotherhood. All the biblical sciences are now using the historical method and striving to put us in the position of the original readers of each biblical book. But as the Bible becomes more lifelike, it becomes more social. We used to see the sacred landscape through allegorical interpretation as through a piece of yellow bottle-glass. It was very golden and wonderful, but very much apart from our everyday modern life. The Bible hereafter will be "the people's book" in a new sense. For the first time in religious history we have the possibility of so directing religious energy by scientific knowledge that a comprehensive and continuous reconstruction of social life in the name of God is within the bounds of human possibility.

CONCLUSION

To a religious man the contemplation of the larger movements of history brings a profound sense of God's presence and overruling power. "Behind the dim unknown standeth God within the shadow, keeping watch above his own."[23] Christ is immanent in humanity and is slowly disciplining the nations and lifting them to share in his spirit. By great processes of self-purification the alien infusions in Christianity have been eliminated, and Christianity itself is being converted to Christ.

But all these larger movements, by which the essential genius of Christianity is being set free, have also equipped it for a conscious regenerating influence on the common life of the race. It is now fitter for its social mission than ever before.

At the same time when Christianity has thus attained to its adolescence and moral maturity, there is a piercing call from the world about it, summoning all moral strength and religious heroism to save the Christian world from social strangulation and death. That call will be the subject of the next chapter. The converging of these two lines of development is providential. We are standing at the turning of the ways. We are actors in a great historical drama. It rests upon us to decide if a new era is to dawn in the transformation of the world into the kingdom of God, or if Western civilization is to descend to the graveyard of dead civilizations and God will have to try once more.

Repent. The Kingdom Is Here.

Stanley Hauerwas

Rauschenbusch told his first biographer, Dores Robinson Sharpe, "I have always regarded my public work as a form of evangelism, which called for a deeper repentance and a new experience of God's salvation." Rauschenbusch's description of his work as evangelism is extremely important for understanding *Christianity and the Social Crisis* and, in particular, his chapter explaining why Christianity has never undertaken the work of social reconstruction. Rauschenbusch was obviously a historian, and *Christianity and the Social Crisis* is certainly a book shaped by his work as a historian. But the book, I think, is best read as a sermon seeking to convict Christians of our sins as well as call us to the redeeming work of the kingdom of God.

Accordingly, Rauschenbusch, like a good evangelist, begins his book with the good news of God's kingdom exemplified by the prophet and the ministry of Jesus and embodied in the early Church. In the first chapter, he eloquently displays the prophetic hope that the kingdom of God is not some future ideal but a reality to be realized through the joining of religion and ethics. Jesus incarnated the spirit and the social teachings of the prophets, but he also "realized the life of God in the soul of man and the life of man in the love of God." Through his personality, Jesus made the reality of the kingdom of God an unavoidable force in human history.

Rauschenbusch was a Protestant liberal theologian, but it should not be forgotten that Protestant liberalism rightly assumed that Jesus matters. Therefore, Rauschenbusch begins *Christianity and the Social Crisis* with the good news of the gospel. Though often criticized for being "soft on sin," he rightly understood that to name sin rightly requires that we first hear the good news of the Kingdom. Accordingly, Rauschenbusch saw quite clearly that sin is not simply something we do but a power that possesses us. Therefore, in this chapter, "Why Has Christianity Never Undertaken the Work of Social Reconstruction?" Rauschenbusch not only seeks to explain historically why the kingdom incarnated in Jesus has not been realized but also to convict us of our sins. In short, this is the chapter in which Rauschenbusch seeks to mirror our sins and to call us to repentance.

I think it a very good thing that Rauschenbusch understood himself to be an evangelist. My problem with this chapter is not that he wanted to convict us of sin, but rather that the developments he quite understandably thought to be problematic can also be understood as crucial for the work of the reconstruction he thought so important. Monasticism, ritualism, sacramentalism, dogmatism, the churchliness of Christianity, and the subsequent subordination of the Church to the State did at times serve to still the passion for the kingdom. But as Rauschenbusch also recognized, each of these developments also provided the means for Christians to resist state power.

John Howard Yoder's criticisms of "Constantinianism" in many ways is quite similar to Rauschenbusch's account for why the Church failed to carry out the work of social reconstruction. Yoder, however, provides an account of the Church's relation to the kingdom of God that helps us see how some of the developments Rauschenbusch identifies as "failures" can be interpreted as resources for the Church to maintain a faithful witness to the kingdom. Yoder, no less than Rauschenbusch, insisted on the "politics of Jesus," but Yoder's eschatology helps us see, in a way Rauschenbusch does not, how the Church is constitutive of the kingdom. Rauschenbusch's inadequate ecclesiology was a correlative of his identification of the kingdom of God with progressive accounts of history that ironically meant his position could lead to the loss of the eschatological tension between Church and world that is a characteristic of Constantinianism.

The failure to maintain the tension between Church and world that is crucial for understanding how God has brought the world under judgment through the teaching and life of Jesus is, I think, one of the reasons some of Rauschenbusch's judgments in this chapter seem so dated. His suggestion, for example, that monasticism prevented the most talented from producing children for the good of the race has unwelcome eugenic implications. Moreover, his calling attention to the "wonderful fecundity" of the Protestant parsonage for the production of men of the highest ability and his celebration of the family as one of the most important contributions of Christianity to civilization suggest gender and class presumptions that we now rightly question.

That Rauschenbusch, like so many progressive thinkers of his day, was unduly impressed by the new science of eugenics was not accidental given his eschatology. He rightly insisted that Jesus had entered history, but he mistakenly thought history was also the history of race. Accordingly, he thought the progressive developments in that history were associated with Western civilization, and in particular with American democratic institutions. As a result, his understanding of the Church as a witness to the kingdom of God was not sufficiently robust.

Given the scholarship of the time, it is quite understandable that Rauschenbusch thought that the apocalyptic character of the early Church was one of the reasons the work of social reconstruction had been delayed. He criticized the Church for associating Christian hope with eternal life, which he thought resulted in an individualism that betrayed the social character of Jesus's proclamation of the kingdom. This kind of "otherworldliness" he thought was the result of Christians accepting the apocalyptic ideas of Judaism in which it was assumed that the end of the world was soon to come. Christians' acceptance of this pessimistic view of history therefore stills their desire to transform the world according to the kingdom. Rauschenbusch seems to have represented the oft-made claim that Jesus came proclaiming the kingdom but instead we got the church.

That said, however, it is important that those of us who have been influenced by Yoder's recovery of the significance of the Church not forget the lessons to be learned from Rauschenbusch. Rauschenbusch rightly insisted that the Church does not exist for herself, but rather for the transformation of the world. To proclaim the kingdom of God therefore demands that Christians never forget we have been called from the world to be of service to the world. No one better exemplified such service than Walter Rauschenbusch. This is why *Christianity and the Social Crisis* is as important for our day as it was one hundred years ago.

Walter Rauschenbusch was an evangelist of the kingdom of God. The sermon that is *Christianity and the Social Crisis* is as desperately needed in our day as it was in his. The passion for justice, his prayers for social awakening, the hymns of social solidarity, and the institutions for humane care he created cannot be taken for granted. The work he began we must continue. After Rauschenbusch, there is no gospel that is not "the social gospel." We are permanently in his debt.

FIVE

The Present Crisis

When the Nineteenth Century died, its Spirit descended to the vaulted chamber of the Past, where the Spirits of the dead Centuries sit on granite thrones together. When the newcomer entered, all turned toward him and the Spirit of the Eighteenth Century spoke: "Tell thy tale, brother. Give us word of the humankind we left to thee."

"I am the Spirit of the Wonderful Century. I gave man the mastery over nature. Discoveries and inventions, which lighted the black space of the past like lonely stars, have clustered in a Milky Way of radiance under my rule. One man does by the touch of his hand what the toil of a thousand slaves never did. Knowledge has unlocked the mines of wealth, and the hoarded wealth of today creates the vaster wealth of tomorrow. Man has escaped the slavery of Necessity and is free.

"I freed the thoughts of men. They face the facts and know. Their knowledge is common to all. The deeds of the East at eve are known in the West at morn. They send their whispers under the seas and across the clouds.

"I broke the chains of bigotry and despotism. I made men free and equal. Every man feels the worth of his manhood.

"I have touched the summit of history. I did for mankind what none of you did before. They are rich. They are wise. They are free."

The Spirits of the dead Centuries sat silent, with troubled eyes. At last the Spirit of the First Century spoke for all.

"We all spoke proudly when we came here in the flush of our deeds, and thou more proudly than we all. But as we sit and think of what was before us, and what has come after us, shame and guilt bear down our pride. Your words sound as if the redemption of man had come at last. Has it come?

"You have made men rich. Tell us, is none in pain with hunger today and none in fear of hunger for tomorrow? Do all children grow up fair of limb and trained for thought and action? Do none die before their time? Has the mastery of nature made men free to enjoy their lives and loves, and to live the higher life of the mind?

"You have made men wise. Are they wise or cunning? Have they learned to restrain their bodily passions? Have they learned to deal with their fellows in justice and love?

"You have set them free. Are there none, then, who toil for others against their will? Are all men free to do the work they love best?

"You have made men one. Are there no barriers of class to keep man and maid apart? Does none rejoice in the cause that makes the many moan? Do men no longer spill the blood of men for their ambition and the sweat of men for their greed?"

As the Spirit of the Nineteenth Century listened, his head sank to his breast.

"Your shame is already upon me. My great cities are as yours were. My millions live from hand to mouth. Those who toil longest have least. My thousands sink exhausted before their days are half spent. My human wreckage multiplies. Class faces class in sullen distrust. Their freedom and knowledge has only made men keener to suffer. Give me a seat among you, and let me think why it has been so."

The others turned to the Spirit of the First Century. "Your promised redemption is long in coming."

"But it will come," he replied.

THE INDUSTRIAL REVOLUTION

Man has always suffered want and the fear of want. His dangers have always come from two sources—nature and man.

Drought or flood, locusts or wild beasts, swept away his crops or herds. Earthquake and fire shook his home to ruin or ate up in the flare of an hour the toil of a lifetime. But there is a disciplining power in the adversities of nature. If man wrestles bravely with her, she will turn to bless him and make him more a man. By learning nature's laws and obeying them, he makes nature obey him.

The really grinding and destructive enemy of man is man. The roaming savage in famine and superstition hunted and ate his enemy as he hunted the beast. When men settled down to till the fields, they captured prisoners and made them drudge for them as slaves, just as they domesticated the horse and ox and made them work. Strong peoples conquered the weak and exacted forced labor or rent for the use of the land which the serf had once owned. Exploitation has changed its form from one stage of society to another, but it has always existed. "From the beginning until now man has divided his fellows into those who were to be fed and those who were, figuratively at least, to be eaten."[1]

There has always been social misery. The pyramids of Egypt were built on it; the Roman roads were cemented with it. But today we face a new form of it, which affronts all just conceptions of human life in new and peculiar ways. Modern poverty, strangely enough, began when man for the first time in history began to escape from poverty.

The American Declaration of Independence in 1776 and the French Revolution in 1789 were the birth of modern democracy. But about the same time another revolution set in beside which these great events were puny.[2] In 1769 James Watt harnessed the expansive power of steam for human use. Hitherto man had used only the localized power of falling water and the fitful power of blowing wind. The only ready force had been the vital energy of man and beast. Now at last the weary hum of the hand-spindle and the pounding of the hand-loom could cease. Nature bent her willing neck to the yoke, and the economic production of our race took a leap forward—as when a car has been pushed forward by hand on the level, and now grips the cable and rushes up a steep incline. If some angel with prophetic foresight had witnessed that epoch, would he not have winged his way back to heaven to tell God that human suffering was drawing to its end?

Instead of that a long-drawn wail of misery followed wherever the power-machine came. It swept the bread from men's tables and the pride from their hearts.

Hitherto each master of a handicraft, with his family and a few apprentices and journeymen about him, had plied his trade in his home, owner of his simple tools and master of his profits. His workmen ate at his table, married his daughters, and hoped to become masters themselves when their time of education was over. He worked for customers whom he knew, and honest work was good policy. He supplied a definite demand. The rules of his guild and the laws of his city barred out alien or reckless competition which would undermine his trade. So men lived simply and rudely. They had no hope of millions to lure them, nor the fear of poverty to haunt them. They lacked many of the luxuries accessible even to the poor today, but they had a large degree of security, independence, and hope. And man liveth not by cake alone.[3]

Then arrived the power-machine, and the old economic world tottered and fell like San Francisco in 1906. The machine was too expensive to be set up in the old home workshops and owned by every master. If the guilds had been wise enough to purchase and operate machinery in common, they might have effected a cooperative organization of industry in which all could have shared the increased profits of machine production. As it was, the wealthy and enterprising and ruthless seized the new opening, turned out a rapid flow of products, and of necessity underbid the others in marketing their goods. The old customs and regulations which had forbidden or limited free competition were brushed away. New economic theories were developed which sanctioned what was going on and secured the support of public opinion and legislation for those who were driving the machine through the framework of the social structure.

The distress of the displaced workers was terrible. In blind agony they mobbed the factories and destroyed the machines which were destroying them. But the men who owned the machines, owned the law. In England the death penalty was put on the destruction of machinery. Sullenly the old masters had to bow their necks to the yoke. They had to leave their own shops and their old independence and come to the machine for work and bread. They had been masters; henceforth they had a master. The former companionship of master and workmen, working together in the little shops, was gone. Two classes were created and a wide gulf separated them: on the one hand the employer, whose hands were white and whose power was great; on the other the wage-earner, who lived in a cottage and could only in rare and lessening instances hope to own a great shop with its costly machinery.[4]

This disintegration of the old economic life has slowly spread, reaching one trade after the other, one nation after the other. Today it is working its way in Russia and India. Longfellow, in his "Village Blacksmith," has described a master of the old kind. "The smith, a mighty man was he, with strong and sinewy hands." Today one son of the smith is nailing machine-made horseshoes on with machine-made nails, and repairing the iron-work of farmers which is wrought elsewhere. The other sons have gone into town and are factory hands. One worked in the fluff-filled air of a cotton mill and slept in a dark bedroom. He died of consumption.

Thus went the old independence and the approximate equality of the old life. The old security disappeared, too. A man could not even be sure of the bare wages which he received for his toil. The machine worked with such headlong speed that it glutted the market with its goods and stopped its own wheels with the mass of its own output. Periodical prostrations of industry began with speculative production, and a new kind of famine became familiar—the famine for work.

The machine required deftness rather than strength. The slender fingers of women and children sufficed for it, and they were cheaper than men. So men were forced out of work by the competition of their own wives and children, and saw their loved ones wilt and die under the relentless drag of the machine. The saying that "a man's foes shall be they of his own household" received a new application.

Under the old methods industry could be scattered over the country. The machine now compelled population to settle about it. It was the creator of the modern city. It piled the poor together in crowded tenements at night and in unsanitary factories during the day, and intensified all the diseases that come through crowding. Poverty leaped forward simultaneously with wealth. From 1760 to 1818 the population of England increased 70 percent; the poor relief increased 530 percent.

Here, then, we have the incredible paradox of modern life. The instrument by which all humanity could rise from want and the fear of want actually submerged a large part of the people in perpetual want and fear. When wealth was multiplying beyond all human precedent, an immense body of pauperism with all its allied misery was growing up and becoming chronic. England was foremost in the introduction of machine industry, and the first half of the nineteenth century was one of the darkest times in the economic history of England. While the nation was attaining unparalleled wealth and power, many of its people were horribly destitute and degraded. It is hardly likely that any social revolution, by which hereafter capitalism may be overthrown, will cause more injustice, more physical suffering, and more heartache than the industrial revolution by which capitalism rose to power.

That such an evil turn could be given to an event that held such a power for good is a crushing demonstration that the moral forces in humanity failed to keep pace with its intellectual and economic development. Men learned to make wealth much faster than they learned to distribute it justly. Their eye for profit was keener than their ear for the voice of God and humanity. That is the great sin of modern humanity, and unless we repent, we shall perish by that sin. But the first call to repentance comes to all those who have had this defective moral insight of humanity under their training, and whose duty it was to give a voice to the instincts of righteousness and brotherhood.

The first dire effects of the industrial revolution have been greatly mitigated in European countries: partly by the defensive organization of the workers; partly by the interposition of the State; partly by the awakened conscience of the people; and chiefly by the fear of the Social Democracy. In our own country the machine in the past wrought no such harm. Our industries were in their infancy when the machine arrived, and there was no old economic structure for it to destroy. Our people were an emigrant folk, less rooted in the ancestral soil than any other nation, and have been ready and able to seek employment elsewhere when economic readjustments broke up their old employment. What Kipling calls the "hideous versatility" of Americans, which is a result of life in a new country, has made it easy to turn from one trade to another, or to learn the work with a new machine. Above all, our free and cheap land has been a constant outlet for labor, and long kept labor scarce and wages high.

But there is nothing in the nature of our country that will permanently exempt us from the social misery created by the industrial revolution elsewhere. Popular orators have often asserted that the conditions of the effete monarchies could never come to a people with free institutions like ours. Developments in recent years have given them the lie. Capitalism is no respecter of governments; it will flourish in a republic as well as in a monarchy—perhaps better. The people cannot eat the ballot. It will serve them only if they are wise and strong enough to use it as a shield for their own defense and as a sword against the enemies of the republic. The influences which formerly protected us and gave us a certain immunity from social misery are losing their force. We are now running the rapids faster than any other nation. We do everything more strenuously and recklessly than others. Our machinery is speeded faster; our capital centralizes faster; we use up human life more carelessly; we are less hampered by custom and prejudice. If we are once headed toward a social catastrophe, we shall get there ahead of schedule time. No preventives against the formation of social classes written in a paper constitution can long save us from the iron wedge which capitalism drives through society. The existence of at least two distinct classes is inherent in the nature of capitalistic organization of industry, and essential to its very existence. Gustav Schmoller, the eminent professor of political economy at Berlin, says in his great work, "All experts agree that no country has such a plutocracy as the United States."[5]

The purpose of this chapter is to bring the present situation before us with a few rapid strokes in order to create a realizing sense of the present crisis. The main concern of the discussion will be with the moral element contained in the condition of society and in its drifts. In former chapters I have shown that the moral power generated by the Christian religion is available for the task of social regeneration. I wish here to show that it is needed, fully and immediately, if our Christian civilization is to stand and advance.

In the nature of the case the discussion will be a critique of present conditions. It will have to dwell on the adverse symptoms, like the diagnosis of a physician. If he is dealing with the breakdown of the digestive or nervous apparatus, he may fail to mention that the bones are all sound and that the patient has a splendid head of hair. Personally I am not a despiser of my age and its achievements. There is no other age in which I should prefer to have lived. The very fact that we can feel our social wrongs so keenly and discuss them calmly and without fear of social hatred is one of the highest tributes to be paid to our age. My appeal is made hopefully to the educated reason and the moral insight of modern Christian men.

THE LAND AND THE PEOPLE

Next to life itself the greatest gift of God to man is the land from which all life is nourished. The character of a nation cannot be understood apart from the country and climate in which it lives. The social prosperity, the morality, the rise or decline of a people, always fundamentally depend on the wisdom and justice with which the land is distributed and used.

In our country the land in its vastness and abundance, its variety and wealth, has been one of the most sanitary influences in our national life. The mass of independent farmers have been and still are the moral backbone of our nation. The "embattled farmers" won our independence and formed the incomparable armies of our Civil War on both sides, just as the marvelous army of Cromwell was composed of the sons of English yeomen. It was our land, fully as much as our institutions, which absorbed and assimilated the mass of our immigrants in the past, and formed an automatic safety-valve for the overheated machine of our commercial and political life.

Our system has been to distribute our farming land in severalty as the private property of the family which tilled it. This system has doubtless been of great use in the rapid settlement of our country. It has offered the individual every incentive to improve his land to the utmost, since it belonged absolutely to him and his descendants. It is often asserted that the secret of our prosperity lies in this private ownership of land in contrast to the land communism prevailing, for instance, in the Russian village community. It is overlooked that our method of assigning homestead claims from the public lands has in fact been a kind of gigantic communism in land.

Nearly all ancient communities with which we have historic connection recognized that the community is the real owner of the land.[6] In the old English village the woodland and pasture were common to all.[7] The meadowland was divided only till the hay-harvest was over and then was common once more. Only the plow-land was permanently divided, but subject to fresh division as new claimants were admitted to the commune. Only those entitled to a share in the common land were citizens with full political rights. This institution is one of the marks of the Aryan race and underlay the freedom and virility of the people. It was disturbed and destroyed by the same influences which sapped the primitive self-government of the people. Large remnants of it persisted down to our day in Europe. Previous to the industrial revolution vast tracts of common land still existed in England. The poor man could build on it free of rent and could till patches of it and pasture his sheep or geese. In our own law the principle that the land is the property of the community—a principle which has all good sense and political philosophy on its side—is still embodied in the "right of eminent domain." The State can condemn private property for public uses, because the community has a latent and superior right in the land which may at any time supersede the inferior right of the individual.

But in general our law treats land as private property. This institution is of comparatively recent origin.[8] It is due mainly to the influence of Roman law. Rome, too, in the early days of its strength had communal ownership. The herds were pastured on the *ager publicus*. If new land was conquered, the younger sons got their allotment there. But gradually the wealthy families crowded out the *plebs rustica*. They took the lion's share of land conquered. They turned their great herds into the common pasturage. They used their political power to suppress the popular demands for a redivision of land and for a maximum limit of landed wealth. Gradually they established ownership in severalty and fortified it by law. Then they sucked up the small estates and undermined the sturdy peasantry of Italy which had made Rome great. Six persons at one time owned the whole province of Africa. The great historian of Rome sums up the pernicious effects of this system in the terse sentence, *Latifundia perdidere Romam*, "the great estates have ruined Rome."

This system, which was the result of the ruthless displacement of public rights by the strong and one chief cause for the decay of Rome, was, of course, embodied in Roman law. That body of law was the product of a refined civilization, and in precision and subtlety was far superior to anything the medieval nations could produce. For this reason, and because it always magnified the powers of the ruling class, it was profoundly influential in the later development of law. Thus the conception of property rights which had helped to kill the Empire passed to other peoples and everywhere strengthened the hands of the strong and limited the communal rights over the land. It was as if a rug of exquisite weave had been taken from some village devastated by cholera and had been carried with its deadly infection to another city.

Our national homestead system was like the old village commune in allotting to everyone who asked for it in good faith a sufficient portion of land for the support of his family. The land set aside for the support of the public schools and the fund accruing from the sale of public lands were further communistic features. The salutary element in our system was not so much that the owner owned his land so absolutely, but that the land was so evenly distributed among the people and was so accessible to all who were able to use it.

But now that our free lands are almost exhausted, we have come to the point where the element of injustice in the system will begin to menace us. The first comers are well placed; but how about those who press up hungry through our ports and through the gates of birth? They will have the bitter cry of Esau when the blessing had been given to Jacob and nothing was left for him. Those who have the soil, have that and their bodies to work it. Those who have no soil, have only their bodies, and they must work for the others to get bread. They are the disinherited children of our nation. Of course in practice many who now own land will lose it, and many who now have none will secure it. But the land henceforth belongs to a limited number, not merely for use, but for complete possession, and the ever increasing remnant will have no right in it, nor income from it. What God gave for the support of all, will be the special privilege of some. Farmland will more and more come to have a monopoly value. As land grows dear, it will become harder for a young man without capital to secure his first foothold. He will have to mortgage himself heavily or become a tenant. There will be two layers of population drawing their living from the land—those who own the land and those who till it. Our farmers will become peasants. Their prosperity, their hopefulness and moral vigor, will decline, and therewith the moral strength of our nation will be indefinitely diminished. As the monopoly value of farmland increases, it will be a more profitable form of investment for the huge industrial capital anxiously seeking investment. Our rich men will become large owners of agricultural lands. In time we shall have three layers of population on the land, as in England and Eastern Germany—the great proprietor, the tenant farmer, and the agricultural laborer—and that means poverty and ignorance in the country.

This may seem a far-fetched fear to some, just as thirty years ago it seemed an idle fear that our great corporations might come to shackle our political democracy. But common sense and the experience of other nations teach a lesson plain enough to all except that not infrequent class which will learn only in the dear school of experience. Already thousands of our best young farmers are passing over our northwestern boundary to Canada to escape the conditions. If they have the choice between cheap land and loyalty to their country, they choose the cheap land. Already the current of immigration, which no longer finds a ready outlet to the land, is choking our great cities. Already the industrial laboring class is gasping under an increased pressure because the automatic outlet of the workers to the land is being stopped. Yet we are only at the beginning of things. The situation clamors for sufficient moral foresight to avoid the fate of Italy, Spain, or Ireland. The farmers ever cling with the grip of desperation to the land, like an unweaned child to its mother's breast. But when they have once been forced from it into the city, it is exceedingly hard to plant them on the soil once more. An agricultural population is hard to re-create. Yet without a sound agricultural population a nation declines in economic ability and in moral resourcefulness.

In the matter of ordinary agricultural land the monopolistic element inhering in private ownership has not yet made itself felt. But throughout our country those locations which give the access to special opportunities are rapidly being absorbed. The most beautiful locations along our seashore and on our lakes and rivers are bought up, and the people are fenced out from natural beauty and pleasure. The water rights on which great cities depend for life have to be jealously guarded against hands itching to get at them. The franchises by which the transportation of men, of freight, of gas, of electricity, is made possible, all rest on the grant of exceptional land rights. The anthracite mines are a striking demonstration of the effect of giving public rights into the absolute ownership of individuals or corporations. The coal stored in the cellar of our great American tenement was intended by its builder for the use of all. A few vigorous boys have secured the key to the cellar on the understanding that they would fetch the coal up for the rest. But they now claim that the entire supply is their own, and charge the tenants not only for the service of hoisting it up, but for the coal itself. They are using the key not only to get coal out, but to keep it in.

The most glaring evils of our land system are found in our cities. City land represents an opportunity to live and to make a living. Its value is created by the community that throngs over and around it. The more wealthy and moral the neighborhood, the more valuable the land. The value of an empty city lot is wholly a social product; the value of an improved lot is partly a social and partly a personal product. Moreover, additional value is created by the pressure of want. The more numerous the people, the greater the need of a place on which to live and breathe. Space is as much a necessity of life as air and water. People may perish for the lack of it. Hence they will pay heavily for the use of it. Thus the community, both by its labors and by its needs, creates an increasing value for city land. But our laws give this social product away to individuals. This encourages speculation in land. Men buy up land with the hope that its value will increase without their labor. If their forecast proves false, they suffer impoverishment or bankruptcy. If it proves correct, they have an unearned gain, like a shrewd card-player. In either case the process is demoralizing for the speculator.

It is far worse for the people. The naturally high price of city land is further enhanced by the artificial pressure of speculation. Around all our cities lies a ring of unused land held with the hope of a rise. The growing population either has to pay the price demanded, or crowd closer inside of the ring, or use its money and its precious time in traveling daily beyond the ring. If the city enjoys a rapid growth, rents and land prices rise, the landowners absorb a large part of the increase in wealth, and the boom is choked. The crowding of the cities increases the expenses for fire protection, police, and sanitation. It is responsible for many of the most deadly diseases, especially tuberculosis. It is also responsible for the moral deterioration accompanying the tenement house and the street life of the cities. The ramifications of these demoralizing effects are almost endless.

A boy dug a lot of angleworms and kept them in a small amount of earth in a tin can. After some days he returned to the neglected worms and found that most of them had died in their crowding, a few still lived limp and discolored, and maggots infested the rotting mass. Here were organisms taken out of their natural surroundings, in which they would have maintained their cleanliness and health, and crowded to their death. The parable is plain.

The values thus created by society and absorbed by individuals are enormous. An eminent and very conservative economist[9] estimates that the unearned increment in Berlin during the last fifty years certainly amounted to $500,000,000 or $750,000,000. Rental values in London increased in 1871–1891 from £24,000,000 to almost £40,000,000, and about £7,150,000 of this was unearned increase. The total of this for twenty years would be equal to the entire estimated wealth of Germany. Owing to the immense growth of our country, and the still more immense growth of our cities, this process has gone on faster in the United States than anywhere else. Successful land speculation has formed the nucleus of very many of our large fortunes. Our cities are poor, unclean, always pressing against the limits of indebtedness, and laying heavy burdens of taxation on the producing classes. At the same time these enormous values pass to individuals who have only contributed a fractional part to their creation.

There is a deep-rooted injustice here which must impress anyone who reflects upon it and whose judgment is not clouded by profit derived from the system. This does not, however, imply that those who profit by it are morally guilty. They may or may not be. Few as yet recognize any wrong in it. Law and custom sanction it. Even those who see the wrong are scarcely able to withdraw from it. They, too, need land to accomplish anything and must hold it in the established ways. But poison is poison, even if it is supposed to be a necessary food or drink. Slavery once had the sanction of human and divine law. It may be that the day will come when anyone claiming exclusive property right in land will be asked, like the slaveholder in Vermont, to "show a bill of sale signed by the Almighty."

The moral problem to be solved by us is how to safeguard the rights of the individual holder of the land who has increased its value by his labor and intelligence, and yet to extract for the community the value which the community creates. The latter right is now obscured and disregarded, and many of the most destructive and menacing evils of our civilization are directly or indirectly traceable to this legalized method of disinheriting the community.[10]

From an economic point of view all human history has turned on the possession of the land and its privileges. The conflicts of nation with nation have been like contests of herds for grazing ground. The conflicts of class with class have been struggles for equal rights on the grazing ground. While agriculture was the chief source of wealth, the burning social question was how to counteract the tendency toward the aggregation of land in a few hands. The intense social struggles of the Greek republics turned largely on the redistribution of the communal land. Where approximate equality was maintained, political liberty and efficiency continued. The contrary meant a decay of liberty and intelligence in the mass of the people, and finally death. Political power was always desired and used to secure special control over the natural resources. Land robbery on a large scale has been the sin of the mighty. In 1904 the Czar gave command to add certain state forests to his private possessions. They were valued at a hundred million rubles. He paid three hundred thousand.[11] The church and monastery lands which were "secularized" during the Reformation were the property of the people, held in trust by the Church. If they had been devoted to other public service, they might have endowed a wonderful system of education or freed Germany and England forever from the need of paying taxes. Instead they were seized by the possessing classes. In Germany they strengthened despotic power. In England they laid the foundation for the wealth of the great aristocratic families to this day. No nation can allow its natural sources of wealth to be owned by a limited and diminishing class without suffering political enslavement and poverty. Our system tends that way. "The abolition of private property in land in the interest of society is a necessity."[12]

WORK AND WAGES

In the agricultural stage of society the chief means of enrichment was to gain control of large landed wealth; the chief danger to the people lay in losing control of the great agricultural means of production, the land. Since the industrial revolution the man-made machinery of production has assumed an importance formerly unknown. The factories, the machines, the means of transportation, the money to finance great undertakings, are fully as important in the modern process of production as the land from which the raw material is drawn. Consequently the chief way to enrichment in an industrial community will be the control of these factors of production; the chief danger to the people will be to lose control of the instruments of industry.

That danger, as we saw in our brief sketch of the industrial revolution, was immediately realized in the most sweeping measure. The people lost control of the tools of industry more completely than they ever lost control of the land. Under the old system the workman owned the simple tools of his trade. Today the working people have no part nor lot in the machines with which they work. In capitalistic production there is a cooperation between two distinct groups: a small group which owns all the material factors of land and machinery; a large group which owns nothing but the personal factor of human labor power. In this process of cooperation the propertyless group is at a fearful disadvantage.

No attempt is made to allot to each workman his share in the profits of the joint work. Instead he is paid a fixed wage. The upward movement of this wage is limited by the productiveness of his work; the downward movement of it is limited only by the willingness of the workman to work at so low a return. His willingness will be determined by his needs. If he is poor or if he has a large family, he can be induced to take less. If he is devoted to his family, and if they are sick, he may take still less. The less he needs, the more he can get; the more he needs, the less he will get. This is the exact opposite of the principle that prevails in family life, where the child that needs most care gets most. In our family life we have solidarity and happiness; in our business life we have individualism and—well, not exactly happiness.

The statistics of wages come with a shock to anyone reading them with an active imagination. In my city of Rochester the average wage for males over sixteen reported by the United States Census of 1900 was $480.50 a year and for females $267.10. I do not know how accurate that was. It hardly matters. Fifty dollars one way or the other would mean a great deal to the families affected, but it would not change the total impression of pitiable inadequacy.

But the real wages are not measured by dollars and cents, but by the purchasing power of the money. That the necessaries of life have risen in price in recent years is familiar enough to every housekeeper. Wages, too, have risen in some trades. Very earnest efforts have been made by experts to prove that the rise in wages has kept pace with the rise in prices, but with dubious results. *Dun's Review* some time ago compared the prices of 350 staple commodities in July 1, 1897, and December 1, 1901, and found that $1,013 in 1901 would buy no more than $724 in 1897. Hence if wages had remained apparently stationary, they had actually declined.

The purchasing power of the wages determines the health and comfort of the workingman and his family. It does not decide on the justice of his wage. That is determined by comparing the total product of his work with the share paid to him. The effectiveness of labor has increased immensely since the advent of the machine. The wealth of the industrial nations consequently has grown in a degree unparalleled in history. The laborer has doubtless profited by this in common with all others. He enjoys luxuries that were beyond the reach of the richest in former times. But the justice of our system will be proved only if we can show that the wealth, comfort, and security of the average workingman in 1906 is as much greater than that of the average workingman in 1760 as the wealth of civilized humanity is now greater than it was in 1760. No one will be bold enough to assert it. The bulk of the increase in wealth has gone to a limited class who in various ways have been strong enough to take it. Wages have advanced on foot; profits have taken the Limited Express. For instance, the report of the Interstate Commerce Commission of June 1902 stated that from 1896 to 1902 the average wages and salaries of the railway employees of our country, 1,200,000 men, had increased from $550 to $580, or 5 percent. During the same period the net earnings of the owners had increased from $377,000,000 to $610,000,000, or 62 percent. Thorold Rogers, in his great work *Six Centuries of Work and Wages*, says: "It may well be the case, and there is every reason to fear it is the case, that there is collected a population in our great towns which equals in amount the whole of those who lived in England and Wales six centuries ago; but whose condition is more destitute, whose homes are more squalid, whose means are more uncertain, whose prospects are more hopeless, than those of the peasant serfs of the Middle Ages or the meanest drudges of the medieval cities." If the celebrated saying of

John Stuart Mill is true, that "it is questionable if all the mechanical inventions yet made have lightened the day's toil of any human being," it means that the achievements of the human mind have been thwarted by human injustice. Our blessings have failed to bless us because they were not based on justice and solidarity.

THE MORALE OF THE WORKERS

The existence of a large class of population without property rights in the material they work upon and the tools they work with, and without claim to the profits resulting from their work, must have subtle and far-reaching effects on the character of this class and on the moral tone of the people at large.[13]

A man's work is not only the price he pays for the right to fill his stomach. In his work he expresses himself. It is the output of his creative energy and his main contribution to the common life of mankind. The pride which an artist or professional man takes in his work, the pleasure which a housewife takes in adorning her home, afford a satisfaction that ranks next to human love in delightsomeness.

One of the gravest accusations against our industrial system is that it does not produce in the common man the pride and joy of good work. In many cases the surroundings are ugly, depressing, and coarsening. Much of the stuff manufactured is dishonest in quality, made to sell and not to serve, and the making of such cotton or wooden lies must react on the morals of every man that handles them. There is little opportunity for a man to put his personal stamp on his work. The medieval craftsman could rise to be an artist by working well at his craft. The modern factory hand is not likely to develop artistic gifts as he tends his machine.

It is a common and true complaint of employers that their men take no interest in their work. But why should they? What motive have they for putting love and care into their work? It is not theirs. Christ spoke of the difference between the hireling shepherd who flees and the owner who loves the sheep. Our system has made the immense majority of industrial workers mere hirelings. If they do conscientious work nevertheless, it is a splendid tribute to human rectitude. Slavery was cheap labor; it was also dear labor. In ancient Rome the slaves on the country estates were so wasteful that only the strongest and crudest tools could be given them. The more the wage worker approaches their condition, the more will the employer confront the same problem. The finest work is done only by free minds who put love into their work because it is their own. When a workman becomes a partner, he "hustles" in a new spirit. Even the small bonus distributed in profit-sharing experiments has been found to increase the carefulness and willingness of the men to such an extent that the bonus did not diminish the profits of the employers. The lowest motives for work are the desire for wages and the fear of losing them. Yet these are almost the only motives to which our system appeals. It does not even hold out the hope of promotion, unless a man unites managing ability to his workmanship. The economic loss to the community by this paralysis of the finer springs of human action is beyond computation. But the moral loss is vastly more threatening.

The fear of losing his job is the workman's chief incentive to work. Our entire industrial life, for employer and employee, is a reign of fear. The average workingman's family is only a few weeks removed from destitution. The dread of want is always over them, and that is worse than brief times of actual want. It is often said in defense of the wages system that while the workman does not share in the hope of profit, neither is he troubled by the danger of loss; he gets his wage even if the shop is running at a loss. Not for any length of time. His form of risk is the danger of being out of work when work grows slack, and when his job is gone, all his resources are gone. In times of depression the misery and anxiety among the workingpeople are appalling; yet periodical crises hitherto have been an unavoidable accompaniment of our speculative industry. The introduction of new machinery, the reorganization of an industry by a trust, the speeding of machinery which makes fewer men necessary, the competition of cheap immigrant labor, all combine to make the hold of the working classes on the means of life insecure. That workingmen ever dare to strike work is remarkable testimony to the economic pressure that impels them and to the capacity of sacrifice for common ends among them.

While a workman is in his prime, he is always in danger of losing his job. When he gets older, he is almost certain to lose it. The pace is so rapid that only supple limbs can keep up. Once out of a job, it is hard for an elderly man to get another. Men shave clean to conceal gray hairs. They are no longer a crown of honor, but an industrial handicap. A man may have put years of his life into a business, but he has no claim on it at the end, except the feeble claim of sympathetic pity. President Eliot[14] thinks that he has a just but unrecognized claim because he has helped to build up the goodwill of the business. There is a stronger claim in the fact that the result of his work has never been paid to him in full. If, for instance, a man has produced a net value of $800 a year and has received $500 a year, $300 annually stand to his credit in the sight of God. These dividends with compound interest would amount to a tidy sum at the end of a term of years and ought to suffice to employ him at his old wages even if his productive capacity declines.[15] But at present, unless his employer is able and willing to show him charity, or unless by unusual thrift he has managed to save something, he becomes dependent on the faithfulness of his children or the charity of the public. In England a very large proportion of the aged workingpeople finally "go on the parish." In Germany they have a socialist system of insurance for old age. The fact that so few Germans have emigrated in recent years is probably due in part to the hope held out by this slight capitalization of their life's labor. We are not even thinking of such an institution in America. Fear and insecurity weigh upon our people increasingly, and break down their nerves, their mental buoyancy, and their character.

This constant insecurity and fear pervading the entire condition of the workingpeople is like a corrosive chemical that disintegrates their self-respect. For an old man to be able to look about him on the farm or business he has built up by the toil of his life is a profound satisfaction, an antidote to the sense of declining strength and gradual failure. For an old man after a lifetime of honest work to have nothing, to amount to nothing, to be turned off as useless, and to eat the bread of dependence, is a pitiable humiliation. I can conceive of nothing so crushing to all proper pride as for a workingman to be out of work for weeks, offering his work and his body and soul at one place after the other, and to be told again and again that nobody has any use for such a man as he. It is no wonder that men take to drink when they are out of work; for drink, at least for a while, creates illusions of contentment and worth. The Recessional of Alcohol has the refrain, "Let us forget." Every great strike, every industrial crisis, pushes some men over the line of self-respect into petty thievery and vagrancy, and over the gate to the long road of hoboism is written, "Leave all hope behind, all ye that enter here." To accept charity is at first one of the most bitter experiences of the self-respecting workingman. Some abandon their families, go insane, or commit suicide rather than surrender the virginity of their independence. But when they have once learned to depend on gifts, the parasitic habit of mind grows on them, and it becomes hard to wake them back to self-support. They have eaten the food of the lotos-eaters and henceforth "surely, surely slumber is more sweet than toil." It would be a theme for the psychological analysis of a great novelist to describe the slow degradation of the soul when a poor man becomes a pauper. During the great industrial crisis in the 90's I saw good men go into disreputable lines of employment and respectable widows consent to live with men who would support them and their children. One could hear human virtue cracking and crumbling all around. Whenever work is scarce, petty crime is plentiful. But that is only the tangible expression of the decay in the morale of the working people on which statistics can seize. The corresponding decay in the morality of the possessing classes at such a time is another story. But industrial crises are not inevitable in nature; they are merely inevitable in capitalism.

A similar corrosive influence is the hatred generated by our system. The employees are often hot with smoldering resentment at their treatment by the employers, and the employers are at least warm with annoyance at the organizations of the men, and full of distrust for the honesty and willingness of their helpers. The economic loss to both sides in every strike is great enough, but the loss in human fellowship and kindliness is of far greater moment. It would be far better for a community to lose a million dollars by fire than to lose it by a strike or lockout. The acts of violence committed on both sides, by legalized means on the one, by spontaneous brutality on the other, are only the efflorescence of the inflamed feeling created. And the acute inflammation tends to become chronic. Every animal will fight other animals that trench on its feeding grounds. Every social class in history has used whatever weapons it had—sword, law, ostracism, or clerical anathema—to strike at any other class that endangered its income. Railways use lobbies; their employees use clubs; each uses the weapon that is handy and effective. But it is all brutalizing and destructive. Strikes are mild civil war, and "war is hell." If our industrial organization cannot evolve some saner method of reconciling conflicting interests than twenty-four thousand strikes and lockouts in twenty years, it will be a confession of social impotence and moral bankruptcy.[16]

THE PHYSICAL DECLINE OF THE PEOPLE

It used to be a fine thing to mark how the richer food and freer life in our country increased the stature and beauty of the immigrant families. America meant a rise in the standard of living, and hence an increase in physical efficiency. The rapid progress of our country has been due to the wealth of natural resources on the one side and the physical vigor and mental buoyancy of the human resources on the other side.

Today there are large portions of the wage-earning population of which that is no longer true. They are not advancing, but receding in stamina, and bequeathing an enfeebled equipment to the next generation.[17]

The human animal needs space, air, and light, just like any other highly developed organism. But the competitive necessities of industry crowd the people together in the cities. Land speculation and high car-fares hem them in even where the location of our cities permits easy expansion. High rents mean small rooms. Dear coal means lack of ventilation in winter. Coal-smoke means susceptibility to all throat and lung diseases. The tenement districts of our great cities are miasmatic swamps of bad air, and just as swamps teem with fungous growths, so the bacilli of tuberculosis multiply on the rotting lungs of the underfed and densely housed multitudes. The decline in the death-rate with the advance in sanitary science, the sudden drop of the rate after the destruction and rebuilding of slum districts in English cities,[18] prove clearly how preventable a great proportion of deaths are. The preventable decimation of the people is social murder.

The human animal needs good food to be healthy, just like a horse or cow. The artificial rise in food prices is at the expense of the vital force of the American people. The larger our cities, the wider are the areas from which their perishable food is drawn and the staler and less nourishing will be the food. Canned goods are a sorry substitute for fresh food. The ideal housewife can make a palatable and nourishing meal from almost anything. But the wives of the workingmen have been working girls, and they rarely have a chance to learn good house-keeping before they marry. Scorching a steak diminishes its nutritive value and the appetite of the eater, and both are essential for nutrition.

Poor food and cramped rooms lower the vitality of the people. At the same time the output of vitality demanded from them grows ever greater. Life in a city, with the sights and sounds, the hurry for trains, the contagious rush, is itself a flaring consumer of nervous energy. The work at the machine is worse. That tireless worker of steel, driven by the stored energy of the sun in forgotten ages, sets the pace for the exhausted human organism that feeds it. The speeding of machines is greater in America than anywhere in the world. Unless the food and housing remain proportionately better, the American workman is drained faster. Immigrants who try to continue the kind of food that kept them in vigor at home collapse under the strain.

Under such a combination of causes the health of the people inevitably breaks down. Improved medical science has counteracted the effects to a large extent, but in spite of all modern progress the physical breakdown is apparent in many directions. Diseases of the nerves, culminating in prostration and insanity; diseases of the heart through overstrain; diseases of the digestion through poor nutrition, haste in mastication, and anxiety; zymotic diseases due to crowding and dirt—all these things multiply and laugh at our curative efforts. Tuberculosis, which might be eradicated in ten years if we had sense, continues to cripple our children, to snuff out the lives of our young men and women in their prime, and to leave the fatherless and motherless to struggle along in their feebleness. Alcoholism is both a cause and an effect of poverty. The poor take to drink because they are tired, discouraged, and flabby of will, and without more wholesome recreation. When the narcotic has once gained control over them, it works more rapidly with them than with the well fed who work in the open. Tuberculosis and alcoholism are social diseases, degenerating the stock of the people, fostered by the commercial interests of landowners and liquor dealers, thriving on the weak and creating the weak.

This condition of exhaustion tends to perpetuate itself. Children are begotten in a state of physical exhaustion. Underfed and over-worked women in tenement and factory are nourishing the children in their prenatal life. During the years when a workingman's family is bringing up young children, before their earnings become avail-able, the family is submerged in poverty through these parental burdens, and neither the parents nor the growing children are likely to be well fed and well housed. Very early in life the children are hitched to the machine for life, and the vitality which ought to build their bodies during the crucial period of adolescence is used up to make goods a little cheaper, or, what is more likely, merely to make profits a little larger. Imagine that any breeder of livestock should breed horses or cows under such conditions, what would be the result in a few generations? Our apple orchards are planted in wide squares, so that every tree has the soil, the air, the sunshine, which it needs. If we planted a dense jungle of trees, we should have a dwarfed growth, scraggy and thorny, and only here and there a crabbed apple. What harvest of humankind will we have in the broad field of our republic if we plant men in that way?

The physical drain of which we have spoken is gradual and slow, and therefore escapes observation and sympathy. But it is the lot of the workingpeople in addition to this to suffer frequent mangling and mu-tilation. A workman who tends one of our great machines is pitted against a monster of blind and crushing strength and has to be ever alert, like one who enters a cage of tigers. Yet human nature is so con-stituted that it grows careless of danger which is always near, and cheerfully plucks the beard of death. Unless the machines are sur-rounded with proper safeguards, they take a large toll of life and limb. The state accident insurance system in Germany has revealed a terri-ble frequency of industrial accidents. We have never yet dared to get the facts for our country, except in mining and railroading; but it is safe to say that no country is so reckless of accidents as our own. It is asserted that one in eight of our people dies a violent death. The In-terstate Commerce Commission in October 1904 stated that 78,152 persons had been killed on the railroads in the previous ten years, and

78,247 had been injured in the single preceding year. Anyone who has ever been through a railway accident knows what a horrible total of bloody and groaning suffering these figures imply. Yet few railways voluntarily introduced automatic car-couplers to lessen one of the most frequent causes of accident. They resisted legislation as long as they could; introduced the automatic couplers as slowly as they could; and are now resisting the introduction of the block system in the same way. Yet automatic coupling reduced the number of men killed from 433 in 1893 to 167 in 1902, and the number injured from 11,277 to 2,864, in spite of the fact that the total number of employees had greatly increased during these ten years. The same resistance met the efforts to guard the lives of sailors by the Plimsoll mark and indeed almost every effort to compel owners to provide safety appliances, or to make them liable for accidents to their servants. It is dividends against human lives. All great corporations have agents whose sole business it is to look after accidents and see that the company suffers as little loss as possible through the claims of the injured. Yet many are injured in railway work and elsewhere because long hours in the service of those same corporations had so worn them down that their mind was numb and they were unable to look out for themselves.

I venture to give concreteness to these matters by telling a single case which I followed from beginning to end.

An elderly workingman, a good Christian man, was run down by a street car in New York City. His leg was badly bruised. He was taken to an excellent hospital nearby. His wife and daughter visited him immediately. After that they had to wait to the regular visiting day. On that day they came to me in great distress and said that he had been sent forward to Bellevue Hospital. I went with them and we found that he had been there only one night, and had again been sent on to the Charity Hospital on Blackwell's Island. At both hospitals they said the case was not serious and they had shifted him to make room for graver cases. The steamer connecting Bellevue and the Island had left on its last trip that day. If the two women had been alone, they would have been helpless in their anxiety till the next day. I got them across. After hours of fear, which almost prostrated them, we found the old man. He was fairly comfortable and reported that his night at Bellevue had been spent on the floor. A few days later gangrene set in; the leg was twice amputated, and he died. I am not competent to say if this result was due to neglect or not. I know of other cases in which that first hospital shipped charity patients elsewhere without giving any notice whatever to the relatives.

The agent of the street-car company promptly called on the family and offered $100 in settlement of all damages. I saw the manager on their behalf. He explained courteously that since the case resulted in death, $5,000 would be the maximum allowed by New York laws, and since the man's earnings had been small and he had but few years of earning capacity before him, the amount of damage allowed by the courts in his case would be slight. The suffering to the affections of the family did not enter into the legal aspect of the matter. The company paid its counsel by the year. If the family sued and was successful in the lower court, the manager frankly said they would carry it to the higher courts and could wear out the resources of the family at slight expense to the corporation. The president, a benevolent and venerable-looking gentleman, explained to me that the combined distance traveled by their cars daily would reach from New York to the Rocky Mountains. People were constantly being run over, and the company could not afford to be more generous. The widow concluded to submit to the terms offered. The $100 was brought to her in the usual form of single dollar bills to make it look like vast wealth to a poor person. The daughter suffered very serious organic injury through the shock received when her father had disappeared from the hospital, and this was probably one cause for her death in childbirth several years later.

The officers of the hospitals and the officers of the street-railway company were not bad men. Their point of view and their habits of mind are entirely comprehensible. I feel no certainty that I should not act in the same way if I had been in their place long enough. But the impression remained that our social machinery is almost as blindly cruel as its steel machinery, and that it runs over the life of a poor man with scarcely a quiver.

There is certainly a great and increasing body of chronic wretchedness in our wonderful country. It is greatest where our industrial system has worked out its conclusions most completely. Our national optimism and conceit ought not to blind us longer to the fact. Single cases of unhappiness are inevitable in our frail human life; but when there are millions of them, all running along well-defined grooves, reducible to certain laws, then this misery is not an individual, but a social matter, due to causes in the structure of our society and curable only by social reconstruction. We point with pride to the multitude of our charitable organizations. Our great cities have annual directories of their charitable organizations, which state the barest abstract of facts and yet make portly volumes. These institutions are the pride and the shame of Christian civilization; the pride because we so respond to the cry of suffering; the shame because so much need exists. They are a heavy financial drag. The more humane our feeling is, the better we shall have to house our dependents and delinquents. But those who have had personal contact with the work feel that they are beating back a swelling tide with feeble hands. With their best intentions they may be harming men more than helping them. And the misery grows. The incapables increase faster than the population. Moreover, beyond the charity cases lies the mass of wretchedness that spawns them. For every half-witted pauper in the almshouse there may be ten misbegotten and muddle-headed individuals bungling their work and their life outside. For every person who is officially declared insane, there are a dozen whose nervous organization is impaired and who are centers of further trouble. For every thief in prison there are others outside, pilfering and defrauding, and rendering social life insecure and anxious. Mr. Hunter[19] estimates that about four million persons are dependent on public relief in the United States; that an equal number are destitute, but bear their misery in silence; and that ten million have an income insufficient to maintain them even in a state of physical efficiency to do their work. The methods by which he arrives at these results seem careful and fair. But suppose that he were a million or two out of the way, does that affect the moral challenge of the figures much?

Sir Wilfred Lawson told of a test applied by the head of an insane asylum to distinguish the sane from the insane. He took them to a basin of water under a running faucet and asked them to dip out the water. The insane merely dipped and dipped. The sane turned off the faucet and dipped out the rest. Is our social order sane?

THE WEDGE OF INEQUALITY

Approximate equality is the only enduring foundation of political democracy. The sense of equality is the only basis for Christian morality. Healthful human relations seem to run only on horizontal lines. Consequently true love always seeks to create a level. If a rich man loves a poor girl, he lifts her to financial and social equality with himself. If his love has not that equalizing power, it is flawed and becomes prostitution. Wherever husbands by social custom regard their wives as inferior, there is a deep-seated defect in married life. If a teacher talks down at his pupils, not as a maturer friend, but with an "I say so," he confines their minds in a spiritual straitjacket instead of liberating them. Equality is the only basis for true educational influences. Even our instinct of pity, which is love going out to the weak, works with spontaneous strength only toward those of our own class and circle who have dropped into misfortune. Businessmen feel very differently toward the widow of a businessman left in poverty than they do toward a widow of the poorer classes. People of a lower class who demand our help are "cases"; people of our own class are folks.

The demand for equality is often ridiculed as if it implied that all men were to be of identical wealth, wisdom, and authority. But social equality can coexist with the greatest natural differences. There is no more fundamental difference than that of sex, nor a greater intellectual chasm than that between an educated man and his little child, yet in the family all are equal. In a college community there are various gradations of rank and authority within the faculty, and there is a clearly marked distinction between the students and the faculty, but there is social equality. On the other hand, the janitor and the peanut vendor are outside of the circle, however important they may be to it.

The social equality existing in our country in the past has been one of the chief charms of life here and of far more practical importance to our democracy than the universal ballot. After a long period of study abroad in my youth I realized on my return to America that life here was far poorer in music, art, and many forms of enjoyment than life on the continent of Europe; but that life tasted better here, nevertheless, because men met one another more simply, frankly, and wholesomely. In Europe a man is always considering just how much deference he must show to those in ranks above him, and in turn noting jealously if those below him are strewing the right quantity of incense due to his own social position.

That fundamental democracy of social intercourse, which is one of the richest endowments of our American life, is slipping from us. Actual inequality endangers the sense of equality. The rich man and the poor man can meet on a level if they are old friends, or if they are men of exceptional moral qualities, or if they meet under unusual circumstances that reduce all things to their primitive human elements. But as a general thing they will live different lives, and the sense of unlikeness will affect all their dealings. With women the spirit of social caste seems to be even more fatally easy than with men. It may be denied that the poor in our country are getting poorer, but it cannot well be denied that the rich are getting richer. The extremes of wealth and poverty are much farther apart than formerly, and thus the poor are at least relatively poorer. There is a rich class and a poor class, whose manner of life is wedged farther and farther apart, and whose boundary lines are becoming ever more distinct. The difference in housing, eating, dressing, and speaking would be a sufficient barrier. The dominant position of the one class in industry and the dependence of the other are even more decisive. The owners or managers of industry are rich or highly paid; they have technical knowledge, the will to command, the habits of mind bred by the exercise of authority; they say "Go," and men go; they say "Do this," and an army of men obeys. On the other side is the mass who take orders, who are employed or dismissed at a word, who use their muscles almost automatically, and who have no voice in the conduct of their own shop. These are two distinct classes, and no rhetoric can make them equal. Moreover, such a condition is inseparable from the capitalistic organization of industry. As capitalism grows, it must create a proletariat to correspond. Just as militarism is based on military obedience, so capitalism is based on economic dependence.

We hear passionate protests against the use of the hateful word "class" in America. There are no classes in our country, we are told. But the hateful part is not the word, but the thing. If class distinctions are growing up here, he serves his country ill who would hush up the fact or blind the people to it by fine phrases. A class is a body of men who are so similar in their work, their duties and privileges, their manner of life and enjoyment, that a common interest, common conception of life, and common moral ideals are developed and cement the individuals. The businessmen constitute such a class. The industrial workers also constitute such a class. In old countries the upper class gradually adorned itself with titles, won special privileges in court and army and law, and created an atmosphere of awe and apartness. But the solid basis on which this was done was the feudal control of the land, which was then the great source of wealth. The rest was merely the decorative moss that grows up on the rocks of permanent wealth. With the industrial revolution a new source of wealth opened up; a new set of men gained control of it and ousted the old feudal nobility more or less thoroughly. The new aristocracy, which is based on mobile capital, has not yet had time to festoon itself with decorations, but likes to hasten the process by intermarriage with the remnants of the old feudal nobility. Whether it will ever duplicate the old forms in this country is immaterial, as long as it has the fact of power. In some way the social inequality will find increasing outward expression and will tend to make itself permanent. Where there are actual class differences, there will be a dawning class consciousness, a clear class interest, and there may be a class struggle.

In the past the sympathy between the richer and the poorer members of American society has still run strong. Many rich men and women were once poor and have not forgotten their early struggles and the simple homes of their childhood. As wealth becomes hereditary, there will be more who have never known any life except that of luxury, and have never had any associates except the children of the rich or their servants. Formerly the wealthiest man in a village or town still lived in the sight of all as a member of the community. As the chasm widens, the rich withdraw to their own section of the city; they naturally use means to screen themselves from the intrusive stare of the public which concentrates its gaze on them; they live in a world apart, and the mass of the people have distorted ideas about them and little human sympathy for them. There are indications enough how far apart we already are. We have a new literature of exploration. Darkest Africa and the polar regions are becoming familiar; but we now have intrepid men and women who plunge for a time into the life of the lower classes and return to write books about this unknown race that lives in the next block. It is amazing to note how intelligent men and women of the upper classes bungle in their judgment on the virtues and the vices of the workingpeople, and vice versa. Socialism is coming to be the very life-breath of the intelligent working class, but if all the members of all the social and literary clubs of a city were examined on socialism, probably two-thirds would fail to pass. Many are still content to treat one of the great elemental movements of human history as the artificial and transitory misbehavior of a few agitators and their dupes. The inability of both capital and labor to understand the point of view of the other side has been one chief cause of trouble, and almost every honest effort to get both sides together on a basis of equality has acted like a revelation. But that proves how far they have been apart.

Individual sympathy and understanding has been our chief reliance in the past for overcoming the differences between the social classes. The feelings and principles implanted by Christianity have been a powerful aid in that direction. But if this sympathy diminishes by the widening of the social chasm, what hope have we? It is true that we have an increasing number who, by study and by personal contact in settlement work and otherwise, are trying to increase that sympathetic intelligence. But it is a question if this conscious effort of individuals is enough to offset the unconscious alienation created by the dominant facts of life which are wedging entire classes apart.

Facts and institutions are inevitably followed by theories to explain and justify the existing institutions. In a political democracy we have democratic theories of politics. In a monarchy they have monarchical theories. Wherever inequality has been a permanent situation, theoretical thought has defended it. Aristotle living in a slaveholding society said: "There are in the human species individuals as inferior to others as the body is to the soul, or as animals are to men. Adapted to corporeal labor only, they are incapable of a higher occupation. Destined by nature to slavery, there is nothing better for them to do than to obey." Similarly in feudal society the lord regarded the serf as by nature little different from a beast of burden, and even the serf regarded oppression as a fixed fact in life, like cold and rain. If we allow deep and permanent inequality to grow up in our country, it is as sure as gravitation not only that the old democracy and frankness of manners will go, but that even the theory of human equality, which has been part of our spiritual atmosphere through Christianity, will be denied. It is already widely challenged.

THE CRUMBLING OF POLITICAL DEMOCRACY

Any shifting of the economic equilibrium from one class to another is sure to be followed by a shifting of the political equilibrium. If a class arrives at economic wealth, it will gain political influence and some form of representation. For instance, when the cities grew powerful at the close of the Middle Ages, and the lesser nobles declined in power, that fact was registered in the political constitution of the nations. The French Revolution was the demand of the business class to have a share in political power proportionate to its growing economic importance. A class which is economically strong will have the necessary influence to secure and enforce laws which protect its economic interests. In turn, a class which controls legislation will shape it for its own enrichment. Politics is embroidered with patriotic sentiment and phrases, but at bottom, consciously or unconsciously, the economic interests dominate it always. If therefore we have a class which owns a large part of the national wealth and controls nearly all the mobile part of it, it is idle to suppose that this class will not see to it that the vast power exerted by the machinery of government serves its interests. And if we have another class which is economically dependent and helpless, it is idle to suppose that it will be allowed an equal voice in swaying political power. In short, we cannot join economic inequality and political equality. As Oliver Cromwell wrote to Parliament, "If there be any one that makes many poor to make a few rich, that suits not a Commonwealth." The words of Lincoln find a new application here, that the republic cannot be half slave and half free.

The power of capitalism over the machinery of our government, and its corroding influence on the morality of our public servants, has been revealed within recent years to such an extent that it is almost superfluous to speak of it. If anyone had foretold ten years ago the facts which are now understood by all, he would have been denounced as an incurable pessimist. Our cities have surrendered nearly all the functions that bring an income, keeping only those that demand expenditure, and they are now so dominated by the public service corporations that it takes a furious spasm of public anger, as in Philadelphia, or a long-drawn battle, as in Chicago, to drive the robbers from their entrenchments in the very citadel of government; and after the victory is won there is absolutely no guarantee that it will be permanent. There is probably not one of our states which is not more or less controlled by its chief railways. How far our national government is constantly warped in its action, the man at a distance can hardly tell, but the public confidence in Congress is deeply undermined. Even the successful action against the meat-packers and against railway rebates only demonstrated what overwhelming popular pressure is necessary to compel the government to act against these great interests.

The interference of President Roosevelt in the great coal strike was hailed as a demonstration that the people are still supreme. In fact, it rather demonstrated that the supremacy of the people is almost gone. The country was on the verge of a vast public calamity. A sudden cold snap would have sent Death through our Eastern cities, not with his old-fashioned scythe, but with a modern reaper. The President merely undertook to advise and persuade, and was met with an almost insolent rejoinder. Mr. Jacob A. Riis, in his book *Theodore Roosevelt, the Citizen*, says that the President, when he concluded to interfere, set his face grimly and said: "Yes, I will do it. I suppose that ends me; but it is right, and I will do it." The Governor of Massachusetts afterward sent him "the thanks of every man, woman, and child in the country." The President replied: "Yes, we have put it through. But heavens and earth! It has been a struggle." Mr. Riis says, "It was the nearest I ever knew him to come to showing the strain he had been under." Now what sinister and ghostly power was this with which the President of our nation had wrestled on behalf of the people, and which was able to loosen even his joints with fear? Whose interests were so inviolable that they took precedence of the safety of the people, so that a commonsense action by the most august officer of the nation was likely to bring political destruction upon him? To what extent is a power so threatening able to turn the government aside from its functions by silent pressure, so that its fundamental purpose of public service is constantly frustrated? Have we a dual sovereignty, so that our public officers are in doubt whom to obey?

Here is another instance showing how political power is simply a tool for the interests of the dominant class. In 1891 the Working Women's Society of New York began to agitate for proper sanitary accommodations and seats for the female clerks in the department stores. This sensible bill was annually met and defeated at Albany by a lobby of the retail merchants. In 1896 it was at last enacted and the right of inspection and enforcement was given to the local boards of health. For eighteen months it was enforced in New York in the most tyrannical manner to make the law odious. The Tammany mayor then appointed one of the owners of a great department store as president of the Board of Health. This man said that he desired the position partly to quash an indictment against a certain philanthropic enterprise of his and partly to paralyze the Mercantile Inspection Law. The mayor suggested that the necessary appropriation be withheld, and so the law became a dead letter.

To secure special concessions and privileges and to evade public burdens have always been the objects for which dominant classes used their political power. For instance, the feudal nobility of France originally held their lands as franchises from the crown, in return for a tax of service, chiefly military, to be rendered to the nation. When the old feudal levies proved inefficient in the Hundred Years' War with England, a standing army was organized and supported by a money tax. The nobility were thereby relieved from their old obligation of levying and supporting soldiers, yet they successfully evaded their share of the tax. This is merely a sample case. It can safely be asserted that throughout history the strongest have been taxed least, and the weakest most. The same condition prevails in our country. The average homes in the cities are usually taxed to the limit; the most opulent homes, and especially their contents, are taxed lightly. Vacant lots, held for speculation, are often flagrantly favored, though they are a public nuisance. In 1856 taxes were paid in New York State on $148,473,154 worth of personal property over and above the capital of banks and trust companies. During the following forty years the increase in personal property in the State was immense, yet in 1896 the amount found for taxation had increased by only $66,000,000. In that year a study was made of 107 estates, taken at random in the State of New York and ranging from $54,559 to $3,319,500. After the death of the owners these estates disclosed personalty aggregating $215 to $132,366; but the year before their deaths the owners had been assessed only $3,819,412 on their personal property. Thirty-four of them had escaped taxation alto-gether.[20] An investigation by Professor E. W. Bemis in Ohio in 1901 showed that while farms and homes were assessed at about 60 percent of their value, railways were assessed at from 35 percent down to 13 percent of the market value of their stocks and bonds.[21] The interests which thus evade taxation have usually been enriched by public gifts, by franchises, mining rights, water rights, the unearned increment of the land, etc., and yet they allow the public burdens to settle on the backs of those classes who are already fearfully handicapped.

The courts are the instrument by which the organized community exercises its supremacy over the affairs of the individual, and the con-trol of the courts is therefore of vital concern to the privileged classes of any nation. Exemption from the jurisdiction of certain courts which would be troublesome, was a desirable privilege, and both the feudal aristocracy and the clergy had that privilege. To a wide extent the feudal nobles down to our own time had the right of jurisdiction within their own domains, and when they sat as judges, they were not likely to hurt their own interests. The English landowners long made the law in Parliament and interpreted it in their courts. The terrible punishments visited, for instance, on poaching are a demonstration how they dealt with offenses against their cherished class rights. In our own country all are equal before the law—in theory. In practice there is the most serious inequality. The right of appeal as handled in our country gives tremendous odds to those who have financial staying power. The police court, which is the poor man's court, deals with him very summarily. If a rich man and a poor man were alike fined $10 for being drunk and disorderly, the equal punishment would be exceedingly unequal. If the poor man is unable to pay the fine, he gets ten days; nothing likely to be inflicted on the rich man for a similar of-fense would hit him equally hard.

To what extent the judges are actually corrupt it is probably impos-sible to say. We have been trying to keep up our courage amid the general official corruption by asserting that the integrity of the judi-ciary at least is above reproach. But the only thing that would make them immune to the general disease is the spirit and the tradition of their profession. Class spirit and professional honor are a rather fragile barrier against the terrible temptations which can be offered by the great interests, and when that barrier is once undermined by evil example, it will wash away with increasing speed. Recent revelations have not been calculated to cheer us. The judge is frequently a successful politician before he sits on the bench. Is the sanctifying power of official responsibility so great that it will purge out the habits of mind acquired by a successful political career, as politics now goes? At any rate, it is safe to say that the study and practice of the law create an ingrained respect for things as they have been, and that the social sympathies of judges are altogether likely to be with the educated and possessing classes. This inward trend of sympathy is a powerful element in determining a man's judgment in single cases. That a man should be tried by a jury of his peers was so important a historical conquest because it recognized the bias of class differences and turned it in favor of the accused. Unless a judge is affected by the new social spirit, he is likely to be at least unconsciously on the side of those who have, and this is equivalent to a special privilege granted them by the courts. Connecticut alone, among English-speaking countries, has hitherto permitted the defendant in damage suits to transfer such suits from a jury to a bench of judges. When the constitution of Connecticut was revised in 1902, it was proposed to make jury trials mandatory in damage suits. The active "corporation group" in the convention bent its chief interest toward the defeat of this proposition. In the experience of corporations, judges must then be more favorably disposed to them than juries.

The ultimate power on which we stake our hope in our present political decay is the power of public opinion. Whenever some temporary victory has been scored by the people, the newspapers triumphantly announce that the people are really still sovereign, and that nothing can resist public opinion when once aroused. In reality this sheet anchor of our hope is as dependable as the wind that blows. It takes strenuous efforts to arouse the public. Only spectacular evils are likely to impress it. When it is aroused, it is easily turned against some side issue or some harmless scapegoat. And, like all passions, it is very short-lived and sinks back to slumber quickly. Despotic governments have always trusted in dilatory tactics, knowing well the somnolence of public opinion. The same policy is adroitly used by those who exploit the people in our country. To this must be added the fact that the predatory interests are tampering with the organs which create public opinion. If public opinion is indeed so great a power, it is not likely that it will be overlooked by those who are so alert against all other sources of danger. It will not be denied that some newspapers are directly in the pay of certain interests and are their active champions. It will not be denied that the counting-room standpoint is profoundly influential in the editorial policy of all newspapers, and that large advertisers can muzzle most papers if they are determined on a policy. Not only the editorials are affected, but the news matter. After the first great election in Chicago in 1902, in which the people by referendum decided for municipal ownership of street railways and of the gas and electric lighting plants by an astonishing majority, the Associated Press dispatches and the great New York dailies were almost or wholly silent on this significant demonstration of public ownership sentiment. After the presidential election of 1892, in which the Populist Party played so important a part, I was unable to find any figures on their vote in the New York dailies. The day after the presidential election of 1904, in which the Socialist vote took its first large leap forward, I traveled through several States, but no paper which I saw contained the statistics of the Socialist vote. The only fact mentioned was that their vote had declined in one or two cities. When the Mercantile Inspection Bill, to which reference was made above, was before the New York legislature, one of the most respectable metropolitan newspapers contained frequent articles and interviews opposing the bill from the point of view of the department stores. One of my friends, who championed the bill, spoke to one of his friends on the staff of this paper and asked him in fairness to print an interview on the other side. The man replied, "Certainly, that is only fair, I will go and arrange for it." He returned and said that absolute orders had come from the counting-room that nothing in favor of the bill was to be printed. Now the justice and efficiency of democratic government depend on the intelligence and information of the citizens. If they are purposely misled by distorted information or by the suppression of important information, the larger jury before which all public causes have to be pleaded is tampered with, and the innermost life of our republic is in danger.

In an address before the Nineteenth Century Club in 1904, Professor Franklin H. Giddings, one of the most eminent sociologists of our country, said: "We are witnessing today, beyond question, the decay—perhaps not permanent, but at any rate the decay—of republican institutions. No man in his right mind can deny it." We have, in fact, one kind of constitution on paper, and another system of government in fact. That is usually the way when a slow revolution is taking place in the distribution of political and economic power. The old structure apparently remains intact, but actually the seat of power has changed. The Merovingian kings remained kings long after all real power had passed to the Major Domo and they had become attenuated relics. The Senate of Rome and the consuls continued to transact business in the time-hallowed way, though they merely registered the will of the real sovereign. The president of a great university has predicted that we shall have an emperor within twenty years. We shall probably never have an emperor, but we may have a chairman of some committee or other, some person not even mentioned in any constitution or law, who will be the *de facto* emperor of our republic. Names are trifles. An emperor by any other name will smell as sweet. The chief of the Roman Empire was called Caesar or Augustus, which happened to be the names of the men who first concentrated power in that form. When the tottering Empire rested on military force alone, the prefect of the praetorian guard came to be the virtual prime minister, uniting the chief judicial and executive functions in his hands. The boss in American political life is the extra-constitutional ruler simply because he stands for the really dominant powers.

The political life of a nation represents the manner in which that nation manages its common affairs. It is not a thing apart from the rest of the national life. It is the direct outgrowth of present forces and realities, somewhat modified by past traditions, and in turn it intensifies the conditions which shape it. The ideal of our government was to distribute political rights and powers equally among the citizens. But a state of such actual inequality has grown up among the citizens that this ideal becomes unworkable. According to the careful calculations of Mr. Charles B. Spahr, 1 percent of the families in our country held more than half of the aggregate wealth of the country, more than all the rest of the nation put together.[22] And that was in 1890. Is it likely that this small minority, which is so powerful in possessions, will be content with 1 percent of the political power wherewith to protect these possessions? Seven-eighths of the families held only one-eighth of the national wealth. Has it ever happened in history that such a seven-eighths would permanently be permitted to wield seven-eighths of all political power? If we want approximate political equality, we must have approximate economic equality. If we attempt it otherwise, we shall be bucking against the law of gravitation. But when we consider what a long and sore struggle it cost to achieve political liberty; what a splendid destiny a true republic planted on this glorious territorial base of ours might have; what a mission of liberty our country might have for all the nations—it may well fill the heart of every patriot with the most poignant grief to think that this liberty may perish once more; that our birthright among the nations may be lost to us by our greed; and that already our country, instead of being the great incentive to political democracy in other nations, is a heavy handicap on the democratic movement, an example to which the opponents of democracy abroad point with pleasure and which the lovers of popular liberty pass with averted face.

THE TAINTING OF THE MORAL ATMOSPHERE

Our moral character is wrought out by choosing the right when we are offered the wrong. It is neither possible nor desirable to create a condition in which the human soul will not have to struggle with temptation. But there are conditions in which evil is so dominant and its attraction so deadly and irresistible, that no wise man will want to expose himself or his children to such odds. Living in a tainted atmosphere does not increase the future capacity of the body to resist disease. Swimming is hard work and therefore good exercise, but not swimming where the undertow locks the swimmer's limbs in leaden embrace and drags him down.

We cannot conceal from ourselves that in some directions the temptations of modern life are so virulent that characters and reputations are collapsing all about us with sickening frequency. The prevalence of fraud and the subtler kinds of dishonesty for which we have invented the new term "graft" is a sinister fact of the gravest import. It is not merely the weak who fall, but the strong. Clean, kindly, religious men stoop to methods so tricky, hard, and rapacious that we stand aghast whenever the curtain is drawn aside and we are shown the inside facts. Every businessman who has any finer moral discernment will realize that he himself is constantly driven by the pressure of business necessity into actions of which he is ashamed. Men do not want to do these things; but in a given situation they have to, if they want to survive or prosper, and the sum of these crooked actions gives an evil turn to their life.

If it were proposed to invent some social system in which covetousness would be deliberately fostered and intensified in human nature, what system could be devised which would excel our own for this purpose? Competitive commerce exalts selfishness to the dignity of a moral principle. It pits men against one another in a gladiatorial game in which there is no mercy and in which 90 percent of the combatants finally strew the arena. It makes Ishmaels of our best men and teaches them that their hand must be against every man, since every man's hand is against them. It makes men who are the gentlest and kindliest friends and neighbors, relentless taskmasters in their shops and stores, who will drain the strength of their men and pay their female employees wages on which no girl can live without supplementing them in some way. It spreads things before us and beseeches and persuades us to buy what we do not want. The show-windows and bargain-counters are institutions for the promotion of covetousness among women. Men offer us goods on credit and dangle the smallness of the first installment before our eyes as an incentive to go into debt heedlessly. They try to break down the foresight and self-restraint which are the slow product of moral education, and reduce us to the moral habits of savages who gorge today and fast tomorrow. Kleptomania multiplies. It is the inevitable product of a social life in which covetousness is stimulated by all the ingenuity of highly paid specialists. The large stores have to take the most elaborate precautions against fraud by their employees and pilfering by their respectable customers. The finest hotels are plundered by their wealthy patrons of anything from silver spoons down to marked towels. After the annual Ladies' Day at a prominent club in Chicago over 200 spoons and 237 sprigs of artificial decoration, besides miniature vases and bric-a-brac, were missing, and that is always the case after Ladies' Day, and never at other times. At a reform school for boys two lads were pointed out to me as the sons of two men of great wealth. They had been placed there by their parents to cure them of their inveterate habit of stealing. Their fathers were in the United States Senate. Our business life borders so closely on dishonesty that men are hardly aware when they cross the line. It is a penal offense for a government officer to profit by a contract which he awards or mediates; in business life that is an everyday occurrence. No wonder that our officials are corrupt when their corruption is the respectability of business life.

Gambling is the vice of the savage. True civilization ought to outgrow it, as it has outgrown tattooing and cannibalism. Instead of that our commercial life stimulates the gambling instinct. Our commerce is speculative in its very nature. Of course risk is inseparable from human life. It is the virtue of the pioneer to take risks boldly. Every field sown by the farmer represents a certain risk. But the element of labor is the main thing in the farmer's work and that makes the process wholesome. In the measure in which productive labor is eliminated and the risk taken becomes the sole title to the profit gained, the transaction approximates gambling. Above the entrance of an Eastern penal institution the motto has been inscribed, "The worst day in the life of a young man is when he gets the idea that he can make a dollar without doing a dollar's worth of work for it." That is good sense, but how would that motto look on the walls of the New York Stock Exchange or the Chicago Produce Exchange? If a man buys stock or wheat on a margin and clears a hundred dollars, what labor or service has he given for which this is the reward? In what respect does it differ from crap-shooting in which a boy risks his pennies and uses his skill just like the speculator? In Europe lotteries are state institutions and prized privileges of churches and benevolent undertakings. We have fortunately outlawed them in our country, but gambling is one of our national vices because our entire commerce is saturated with the spirit of it.

The social nature of man makes him an imitative creature. The instinct of imitation and emulation may be a powerful lever for good if individuals and classes set the example of real culture and refinement of manners and taste. But the processes of competitive industry have poured vast wealth into the lap of a limited number and have created an unparalleled lavishness of expenditure which has nothing ennobling about it. Those who have to work hard for their money will, as a rule, be careful how they spend it. Those who get it without effort will spend it without thought. Thus parasitic wealth is sure to create a vicious luxury, which then acts as a center of infection for all other classes. Fashions operate downward. Each class tries to imitate the one higher up, and to escape from the imitation of those lower down. Thus the ostentation of the overfull purses of the predatory rich lures all society into the worship of false gods. It intensifies "the lust of the eye and the pride of life" unnaturally, and to that extent expels "the love of the Father," which includes the love of all true values. Anyone can test the matter in his own case by asking himself how much of his money, his time, and his worry is consumed in merely "keeping up with the procession," and is diverted from real culture to mere display by the compulsion of social requirements about him. The man who lives only on his labor is brought into social competition with people who have additional income through rents and profits, and must break his back merely to keep his wife and children on a level with others. The very spirit of democracy which has wiped out the old class lines in modern life makes the rivalry keener. In Europe a peasant girl or a servant formerly was quite content with the dress of her class and had no ambition to rival the very different dress of the gentry. With us the instinct of imitation works without a barrier from the top of the social pyramid to the bottom, and the whole process of consumption throughout society is feverishly affected by the aggregation of unearned money at the top. The embezzlements of businessmen, the nervous breakdown of women, the ruin of girls, the neglect of home and children, are largely caused by the unnatural pace of expenditures. If the rich had only what they earned, and the poor had all that they earned, all wheels would revolve more slowly and life would be more sane.

Industry and commerce are in their nature productive and therefore good. But in our industry a strong element of rapacity vitiates the moral qualities of business life. A railway president in New York said to me, half in joke, of course: "The men who go downtown on the Elevated at seven and eight o'clock really make things. We who go down at nine and ten only try to take things away from one another." Supplying goods to the people is, of course, the main thing; but crowding out the other man, who also wants to supply them, takes a large part of the time and energy of business. Our competitive life has so deeply warped our moral judgment that not one man in a thousand will realize anything immoral in attracting another man's customers. "Thou shalt not covet thy neighbor's trade" is not in our decalogue.

The same instinct of rapacity cheats the consumer. They sell us fruit-jam made without fruit; butter that never saw the milk-pail; potted chicken that grunted in the barnyard; all-wool goods that never said "baah," but leave it to the buyer to say it. If a son asks for bread, his father will not offer him a stone; but ground soapstone is freely advertised as an adulterant for flour. Several years ago the Secretary of Agriculture, on the basis of an extensive inquiry, estimated that 30 percent of the money paid for food products in the United States is paid for adulterated or misbranded goods.[23] We are fortunate if the title of the food is false, but the food is wholesome. But when fruit flavors are made with coal-tar and benzoic acid, and when the milk for our children is preserved with formaldehyde, the rapacity becomes murderous. The life of a mother or a child may depend on the purity of a medicine administered at the critical stage of a disease; but we have very little guarantee that our medicines are not adulterated. In 1904 the Board of Health in New York City had a list of about three hundred druggists and dealers who had attempted to sell spurious mixtures to the very officers of the Board. Most of the patent medicines which our people trust are cheap and worthless concoctions. Others are insidious conveyors of narcotic poisons which are intended to set up a morbid appetite in the consumers for the profit of the dealers. And if patent medicines were as health-giving as they claim to be, the very principle of patenting and withholding from general use a beneficent invention for the saving of human life would be a shameful confession of selfish greed. The liquor traffic presents a striking case of a huge industry inducing people to buy what harms them. It is militant capitalism rotting human lives and characters to distill dividends. In the atrocities on the Congo we have the same capitalism doing its pitiless work in a safe and distant corner of the world, on an inferior race, and under the full support of the government. The rapacity of commerce has been the secret spring of most recent wars. Speculative finance is the axis on which international politics revolve.

The counts in the indictment against our marvelous civilization could be multiplied at pleasure. It is a splendid sinner, "magnificent in sin." The words which Bret Harte addressed to San Francisco in its earlier days characterize the whole of modern society:

I know thy cunning and thy greed,
Thy hard, high lust and willful deed,
And all thy glory loves to tell
Of specious gifts material.

It defrauds the customer who buys its goods. It drains and brutalizes the workman who does its work. It hunts the businessman with fear of failure, or makes him hard with merciless success. It plays with the loaded dice of false prospectuses and watered stock, and the vaster its operations become, the more do they love the darkness rather than the light. It corrupts all that it touches—politics, education, the Church. For a profession to be "commercialized" means to be demoralized. The only realms of life in which we are still glad and happy are those in which the laws of commerce are not practiced. If they entered the home, even that would be hell.

Industry and commerce are good. They serve the needs of men. The men eminent in industry and commerce are good men, with the fine qualities of human nature. But the organization of industry and commerce is such that along with its useful service it carries death, physical and moral. Frederick Denison Maurice, one of the finest minds of England in the Victorian Age, said, "I do not see my way farther than this, Competition is put forth as the law of the universe; that is a lie." And his friend Charles Kingsley added, "Competition means death; cooperation means life." Every joint-stock company, trust, or labor union organized, every extension of government interference or government ownership, is a surrender of the competitive principle and a halting step toward cooperation. Practical men take these steps because competition has proved itself suicidal to economic welfare. Christian men have a stouter reason for turning against it, because it slays human character and denies human brotherhood. If money dominates, the ideal cannot dominate. If we serve mammon, we cannot serve the Christ.

220   *Christianity and the Social Crisis in the 21st Century*

THE UNDERMINING OF THE FAMILY

We have purposely left to the last what properly comes first in any consideration of social life. The family is the structural cell of the social organism. In it lives the power of propagation and renewal of life. It is the foundation of morality, the chief educational institution, and the source of nearly all the real contentment among men. To create a maximum number of happy families might well be considered the end of all statesmanship. As President Roosevelt recently said, all other questions sink into insignificance when the stability of the family is at stake. The most significant part of that utterance was that such a thing had to be uttered at all.

Hard times are always marked by a downward curve in the percentage of marriages. In our country the decline has become chronic for some years past. Men marry late, and when the mating season of youth is once past, many never marry at all. In my city of Rochester, New York, with a population of 162,608, the census of 1900 showed 25,219 men between the age of 25 and 44, the years during which a man ought to be enjoying a home and rearing children, and 7,355 of them were still unmarried. There were 28,218 women of the same years, relatively further along in marriageable age than the men, and 8,109 were still unmarried.

Now the attraction between men and women is just as fundamental a fact in social life as the attraction of the earth is in physics, and the only way in which that tremendous force of desire can be prevented from wrecking lives is to make it build lives by home contentment. The existence of a large class of involuntary celibates in society is a more threatening fact even than the increase of divorces. The slums are aggregations of single men and women. If the monastic celibates of the Middle Ages, who had the powerful incentive of religious enthusiasm and all the preventives of isolation and supervision, could not keep chaste, is it likely that the unmarried thousands in the freedom of modern life will maintain their own purity and respect the purity of others? They are thrust into the lonely life through no wise resolve of their own, but mainly through the fear that they will not be able to maintain a family in the standard of comfort which they deem necessary for their life.

If a man and woman do marry, they do not yet constitute a true family. The little hand of a child, more than the blessing of a priest, consecrates the family. France has long been held up as furnishing the terrible example of a declining birthrate, but the older portions of our country are saved from the same situation only by the fertility of the immigrants. The native population of New England would not reproduce itself.

The chief cause for this profoundly important fact is economic fear. Whenever the economic condition of any class is hopeful and improving, there is an increase in the birthrate. Whenever there is economic disaster or increasing pressure, there is a decline. In the West, where land is still abundant, families are large. The immigrants, who feel the relative easement of pressure, multiply. The natives, who suffer by the competition of the immigrants and who feel the tightening grip of our industrial development, refuse to bring children into a world which threatens them with poverty.

Our cheerful newspaper optimists assure us that the American child makes up by quality what it lacks in numbers. They quote the reply of the lioness in the fable, "One, but a lion." But that is merely an effort to make an ugly fact look sweet. People hunting for apartments in a large city soon discover one cause. "As arrows in the hand of a mighty man, so are the children of youth," said the Psalmist. "Happy is the man that hath his quiver full of them; they shall not be put to shame when they speak with their enemies in the gate." But they shall talk very humbly and beseechingly when they speak with their prospective landlords nowadays. The concentration of population in the cities through competitive necessities, the consequent increase in rents, the enforced proximity to undesirable neighbors, the rise in the standard of luxury together with the decreased purchasing power of the average income — these account in the main for the declining birthrate. When men are hardly able to keep their head above water, they fear to carry a child on their back. Fear stands where the spring of life should bubble and freezes it into subsidence. That situation raises the most serious questions in the most intimate morality of human life. Moreover, the absence of children decreases the cohesive power of the married relation, the blitheness and youthfulness of life, the unselfishness of character, the insight into human nature; in short, it blights much of what is really fine and high in the souls and relations of men. The luxury and culture made possible by the absence of children is a glittering varnish to cover decaying wood.

The menace to the future of our nation is still greater through the fact that sterility is most marked among the able and educated families. The shiftless, and all those with whom natural passion is least restrained, will breed most freely. The prudent consider and shrink. The poor have little to lose. Children are their form of old-age pensions. The well-to-do see the possible depth to which they or their children may descend, and are afraid. Thus the reproduction of the race is left to the poor and ignorant. Unusual ability is not transmitted. The benefits of intellectual environment fail to be prolonged by heredity. The vital statistics of Harvard and Columbia graduates show a rapidly declining birthrate and complete failure to reproduce their own number.[24] I sat at a table with seven of the best and ablest men I know. We talked of children and found that only two had a child; one of the two was a Swede, the other the son of German immigrants. In a previous chapter we referred to the loss suffered by mankind through the sterility of its most ideal individuals while monasticism and priestly celibacy prevailed.[25] Here we have a fact of equal historical significance, but unrelieved by the idealism of the monastic vow. Education can only train the gifts with which a child is endowed at birth. The intellectual standard of humanity can be raised only by the propagation of the capable. Our social system causes an unnatural selection of the weak for breeding, and the result is the survival of the unfittest.

When the family is small, the influence of brothers and sisters on the formation of character is lacking. When the father has to work long hours and then spend additional time in traveling between his home and his work, the element of fatherhood in the home is reduced to a minimum. If the mother, too, goes out to work, the children are left to "the street," which is an educator of rather doubtful value. If boarders and roomers are taken in to help in paying the rent, an alien and often a demoralizing element enters the family. Thus the economic situation everywhere saps family life.

One family to one house is the only normal condition. When twenty families live in one tenement, twenty souls inhabit one body.

That was the condition of the demoniac of Gadara,[26] in whom dwelt a legion. He was crazy.

To be a home in the fullest sense, it must be loved with the sense of proprietorship. As cities grow, home ownership declines. A semi-vagrancy from one flat to the next grows up. In the borough of Manhattan only 6 percent of the homes are owned by those who live in them; in Philadelphia, a city of small houses, only 22 percent own their homes. Rochester is an almost ideal city for the development of homes, and the popular assumption is that nearly everybody owns his home. Yet the census of 1900 showed that of the 33,964 homes in the city only 12,290 were owned by the tenants, and half of these were mortgaged.

The condition of the home determines the condition of a woman. If girls are eagerly sought in marriage, they can choose the best. If few men can afford a good home, girls must take what offers or go without. If a man can easily make a living for a family, he can afford to be indifferent to anything but the person of the woman he loves. As the economic pressure tightens and social classes grow more clearly defined, American men, too, will begin to inquire what property comes to them with their bride. We shall have love modified by the "*dot*."

Our optimists treat it as a sign of progress that "so many professions are now open to women." But it is not choice, but grim necessity, that drives woman into new ways of getting bread and clothing. The great majority of girls heartily prefer the independence and the satisfaction of the heart which are offered to a woman only in a comfortable and happy home. Some educated girls think they prefer the practice of a profession because the dream of unusual success lures them; but when they have had a taste of the wearing routine that prevails in most professions, they turn with longing to the thought of a home of their own. Our industrial machine has absorbed the functions which women formerly fulfilled in the home, and has drawn them into its hopper because female labor is unorganized and cheap labor. They are made to compete with the very men who ought to marry them, and thus they further diminish their own chance of marriage. If anyone has a sound reason for taking the competitive system by the throat in righteous wrath, it is the unmarried woman and the mother with girls.

Girls go to work at the very age when their developing body ought to be shielded from physical and mental strain. Many are kept standing for long hours at a time. During rush seasons they are pushed to exhaustion. In few cases can they permit themselves that periodical easement which is essential to the continued health of most women. Many of them enter marriage with organic troubles that develop their full import only in later years. Girls pass from school to shop or store and never learn housekeeping well. If they marry, they assume charge of a manufacturing establishment in which all the varied functions are performed by one woman. They have to learn the work at an age when the body no longer acquires new habits readily. If the burden of maternity is added at the same time, the strain is immense, and is likely to affect the temper and the happiness of the home. It is thus our civilization prepares its women for the all important function of motherhood, for on the women of the working class rests the function of bearing and rearing the future citizens of the republic. Individually Americans are more tender of women than any other nation. Collectively we treat them with cruelty and folly.

A large proportion of working women are not paid wages sufficient to support themselves in comfort and to dress as the requirements of their position and of modern taste demand. In that case they must either suffer want or supplement their earnings. They are fortunate if fathers and brothers support the home. In that case they are able to underbid those who are dependent on their own labor alone. If the home does not thus shield them, what are they to do? There are numbers of unmarried and married men about them looking for transient love. The girls themselves have the womanly desire for the company and love of men. Satisfaction by marriage may not be in sight. They crave for the clothing, the trinkets, the pleasures that glitter about them. It is so easy to get a share. When I reflect on the unstained virtue and nobility of the great majority of working girls whom I have known, I feel the deepest respect for them. But some are always on the edge of danger. As the crocodile takes toll of the Hindu women at the river ford, so every now and then one of the girls throws up her hands and goes under. Those who are strong by personal vigor, or by religious training, can escape, and blessed is he who strengthens their hands. But that does not satisfy the situation. If a ship were wrecked and the passengers clinging to the tilted deck, the strongest would hold on best. If someone cheered their failing strength and showed them how best to cling, it would be a great service. But if the deck kept on tilting at a steeper angle, more still would go. There are employers in European cities who expect as a matter of course that their female clerks will give them more than the working capacity of their bodies. There are stores in New York and elsewhere where some girls get the easy positions and some are made uncomfortable for reasons well understood. That sort of oppression will be successful in the measure in which the girls fear to lose their positions. Woe to the weak! They are like birds fluttering in the hot hand of the pursuer. The most serious danger is not the increase of professional prostitutes, but the frequency with which women supplement their wages and secure their pleasures by occasional immorality. Prostitutes are ostracized by their class. It is worse if girls are tainted, but retain their standing and spread the contagion. The freedom of movement in American life and the growing knowledge of preventives makes sin easy and safe. To anyone who realizes the value of womanly purity, it is appalling to think that the standard of purity for their whole sex may drop and approximate the standard prevailing among men.

The health of society rests on the welfare of the home. What, then, will be the outcome if the unmarried multiply; if homes remain childless; if families are homeless; if girls do not know housework; and if men come to distrust the purity of women?

THE FALL OR THE RISE OF CHRISTIAN CIVILIZATION

The continents are strewn with the ruins of dead nations and civilizations. History laughs at the optimistic illusion that "nothing can stand in the way of human progress." It would be safer to assert that progress is always for a time only, and then succumbs to the inevitable decay. One by one the ancient peoples rose to wealth and civilization, extended their sway as far as geographical conditions would permit, and then began to decay within and to crumble away without, until the mausoleums of their kings were the haunt of jackals, and the descendants of their conquering warriors were abject peasants slaving for some alien lord. What guarantee have we, then, that our modern civilization with its pomp will not be "one with Nineveh and Tyre"?

The most important question which humanity ought to address to its historical scholars is this: "Why did these others die, and what can we do to escape their fate?" For death is not an inevitable and welcome necessity for a nation, as it is for the individual. Its strength and bloom could be indefinitely prolonged if the people were wise and just enough to avert the causes of decay. There is no inherent cause why a great group of nations, such as that which is now united in Western civilization, should not live on in perpetual youth, overcoming by a series of rejuvenations every social evil as it arises, and using every attainment as a stepping-stone to a still higher culture of individual and social life. It has never yet been done. Can it be done in a civilization in which Christianity is the salt of the earth, the social preservative?

Of all the other dead civilizations we have only scattered relics and fragmentary information, as of some fossil creature of a past geological era. We can only guess at their fate. But the rise and fall of one happened in the full light of day, and we have historical material enough to watch every step of the process. That was the Greco-Roman civilization which clustered about the Mediterranean Sea.

Its golden age, which immediately preceded its rapid decline, had a striking resemblance to our own time. In both cases there was a swift increase in wealth. The Empire policed the seas and built roads. The safety of commerce and the ease of travel and transportation did for the Empire what steam transportation did for the nineteenth century. The mass of slaves secured by the wars of conquest, and organized for production in the factories and on the great estates, furnished that increase in cheap productive force which the invention of steam machinery and the division and organization of labor furnished to the modern world. No new civilization was created by these improved conditions; but the forces latent in existing civilization were stimulated and set free, and their application resulted in a rapid efflorescence of the economic and intellectual life. Just as the nations about the Seven Seas are drawing together today and are sharing their spiritual possessions in a common civilization, so the Empire broke down the barriers of the nations about the Mediterranean, gathered them in a certain unity of life, and poured their capacities and thoughts into a common fund. The result was a breakdown of the old faiths and a wonderful fertilization of intellectual life.

Wealth—to use a homely illustration—is to a nation what manure is to a farm. If the farmer spreads it evenly over the soil, it will enrich the whole. If he should leave it in heaps, the land would be impoverished and under the rich heaps the vegetation would be killed.

The new wealth created in the Roman Empire was not justly distributed, but fell a prey to a minority who were in a position to seize it. A new money aristocracy arose which financed the commercial undertakings and shouldered the old aristocratic families aside, just as the feudal aristocracies were superseded in consequence of the modern industrial revolution. A few gained immense wealth, while below them was a mass of slaves and free proletarians. The independent middle class disappeared. The cities grew abnormally at the expense of the country and its sturdy population. Great fortunes were made and yet there was constant distress and frequent hard times. The poor had no rights in the means of production, so they used the political power still remaining to them to secure state grants of land, money, grain, and pleasures. There was widespread reluctance to marry and to rear children. Education became common, and yet culture declined. There were plenty of universities, great libraries, well-paid professors, and yet a growing coarseness of taste and a decline in creative artistic and literary ability. If the yellow newspaper could have been printed, it would have "filled a long-felt want." The social conditions involved a readjustment of political power. A strong centralized government was necessary to keep the provinces quiet while Rome taxed them and the bureaucracy grew rich on them. Government was not based broadly on the just consent of the governed, but on the swords of the legions, and especially of the praetorian guard. The old republican forms were long maintained, but Rome verged more and more toward despotic autocracy.

In a hundred ways the second century of our era seemed to be the splendid culmination of all the past. The Empire seemed imperishable in the glory of almost a thousand years of power. To prophesy its fall would have seemed like predicting the failure of civilization and humanity. The reverses which began with the death of Marcus Aurelius in AD 180 seemed mere temporary misfortunes. Yet they were the beginning of the end.

The German and Celtic tribes had long swirled and eddied about the northern boundary of the Empire, like the ocean about the dikes

of Holland. The little Rome of Marius a hundred years before Christ
had successfully beaten back the Cimbrians and Teutons. For two centuries the strong arm of the legions had dammed the flood behind the
Rhine and Danube. Rome was so much superior in numbers, in
wealth, in the science of war and all the resources of civilization, that
it might have continued to hold them in check and to turn their forward movements in other directions. But the decay at the center now
weakened the capacity for resistance at the borders. The farmers who
had made the legions of the Republic invincible had been ruined by
the competition of slave labor, crowded out by land monopoly, and
sucked into the ragged proletariat of the cities. The armies had to be
recruited from the conquered provinces and finally from barbarian
mercenaries. The moral enthusiasm of a citizen soldiery fighting for
their homes was gone. The impoverished and overtaxed provinces
were unable to respond to additional financial needs. Slowly the barbarians filtered into the Northern provinces by mass immigration. The
civilized population did not have vitality enough to assimilate the foreign immigrants. Slowly, by gradual stages, hardly fast enough for men
to realize what was going on, the ancient civilization retreated, and the
flood of barbarism covered the provinces, with only some islands of
culture rising above the yellow flood.

And how will it be with us? Will that vaster civilization which began
in Europe and is now spreading along the shores of all the oceans, as
Rome grew from Italy outward around the great inland sea, run
through the same stages? If the time of our weakness comes, the barbarians will not be wanting to take possession. Where the carcass is,
the vultures will gather.

Nations do not die by wealth, but by injustice. The forward impetus
comes through some great historical opportunity which stimulates the
production of wealth, breaks up the caked and rigid order of the past,
sets free the energies of new classes, calls creative leaders to the front,
quickens the intellectual life, intensifies the sense of duty and the ideal
devotion to the common weal, and awakens in the strong individuals
the large ambition of patriotic service. Progress slackens when a single
class appropriates the social results of the common labor, fortifies its
evil rights by unfair laws, throttles the masses by political centralization and suppression, and consumes in luxury what it has taken in

covetousness. Then there is a gradual loss of productive energy, an increasing bitterness and distrust, a waning sense of duty and devotion to country, a paralysis of the moral springs of noble action. Men no longer love the Commonwealth, because it does not stand for the common wealth. Force has to supply the cohesive power which love fails to furnish. Exploitation creates poverty, and poverty is followed by physical degeneration. Education, art, wealth, and culture may continue to advance and may even ripen to their mellowest perfection when the worm of death is already at the heart of the nation. Internal convulsions or external catastrophes will finally reveal the state of decay.

It is always a process extending through generations or even centuries. It is possible that with the closely knit nations of the present era the resistive vitality is greater than in former ages, and it will take much longer for them to break up. The mobility of modern intellectual life will make it harder for the stagnation of mind and the crystallization of institutions to make headway. But unless the causes of social wrong are removed, it will be a slow process of strangulation and asphyxiation.

In the last resort the only hope is in the moral forces which can be summoned to the rescue. If there are statesmen, prophets, and apostles who set truth and justice above selfish advancement; if their call finds a response in the great body of the people; if a new tide of religious faith and moral enthusiasm creates new standards of duty and a new capacity for self-sacrifice; if the strong learn to direct their love of power to the uplifting of the people and see the highest self-assertion in self-sacrifice—then the entrenchments of vested wrong will melt away; the stifled energy of the people will leap forward; the atrophied members of the social body will be filled with a fresh flow of blood; and a regenerate nation will look with the eyes of youth across the fields of the future.

The cry of "Crisis! Crisis!" has become a weariness. Every age and every year are critical and fraught with destiny. Yet in the widest survey of history Western civilization is now at a decisive point in its development.

Will some Gibbon of Mongol race sit by the shore of the Pacific in the year AD 3000 and write on the "Decline and Fall of the Christian

Empire"? If so, he will probably describe the nineteenth and twentieth centuries as the golden age when outwardly life flourished as never before, but when that decay, which resulted in the gradual collapse of the twenty-first and twenty-second centuries, was already far advanced.

Or will the twentieth century mark for the future historian the real adolescence of humanity, the great emancipation from barbarism and from the paralysis of injustice, and the beginning of a progress in the intellectual, social, and moral life of mankind to which all past history has no parallel?

It will depend almost wholly on the moral forces which the Christian nations can bring to the fighting line against wrong, and the fighting energy of those moral forces will again depend on the degree to which they are inspired by religious faith and enthusiasm. It is either a revival of social religion or the deluge.

Can These Dry Bones Live?

Cornel West

Walter Rauschenbusch was the most influential and important religious public intellectual in early-twentieth-century America. His prophetic ministry as pastor for over a decade at Second German Baptist Church adjacent to the impoverished Hell's Kitchen section of Manhattan and his prophetic writings as professor of church history at Rochester Seminary in upstate New York best exemplify the Social Gospel movement—a historic movement that wedded the Christian faith to social justice during the Gilded Age (Mark Twain's phrase) of imperial extension, corporate greed, and massive immigration.

In this classic work now a century old, Rauschenbusch tries to lay bare the ways in which the spiritual power and moral forces of the Christian tradition could be mobilized to revive and renew the democratic possibilities of American society. In his powerful chapter 5, entitled "The Present Crisis," Rauschenbusch welcomes the coming of the twentieth century with a parabolic dialogue between the Spirits of the Dead Centuries sitting on granite thrones together. As the Spirit of the Nineteenth Century enters, the others are eager to hear the report—"Tell thy tale, Brother. Give us word of the humankind we left to thee." And we hear a self-congratulatory tale of economic growth, scientific breakthroughs, technological innovation, and the proliferation of democratic regimes. The Spirit of the First Century then speaks—"Your words sound as if the redemption of man had come at last. Has it come?"

Needless to say, if we now follow the descent of the Spirit of the Twentieth Century to the "vaulted chamber of the past" and listen to the words of the major figures of our day, do they sound any different?

We have reached the end of history. There is no alternative to corporate capitalism. The era of racism and sexism is over. Americans are never aggressive imperialists, only democratic missionaries. These self-celebratory forms of rhetoric hide and conceal the social misery that constitutes the present crisis. Rauschenbusch goes on in the chapter to examine the devouring of land by corporate elites, the stagnation and decline of wages as profits soar, the dip in the morale of workers as capital becomes more mobile, the health-care shortage for Americans, the escalating wealth inequality alongside the crumbling of political democracy, the tainting of the moral atmosphere, and the market-driven undermining of the family. Does not our present moment echo Rauschenbusch's "present crisis"? Do not our contemporary troubles rooted in a free-market fundamentalism that idolizes a market way of life, an aggressive militarism that exalts violence as a preeminent way of solving conflicts, and an escalating authoritarianism that slowly yet surely attenuates our rights and liberties in the name of national security resonate with Rauschenbusch's prescient words:

> Nations do not die by wealth, but by injustice.... Progress slackens when a single class appropriates the social results of the common labor, fortifies its evil rights by unfair laws, throttles the masses by political centralization and suppression, and consumes in luxury what it has taken in covetousness. Then there is a gradual loss of productive energy, an increasing bitterness and distrust, a waning sense of duty and devotion to country, a paralysis of the moral springs of noble action.

For him, the function of prophetic religion in the present time is to promote a social awakening by means of concrete praxis—from personal prayer to political organization. This social awakening is predicated on regenerated personalities, on courageous and compassionate people who possess "a will which sets justice above policy and profit, and of an intellect emancipated from falsehood" (see chapter 7, "No Thoroughfare"). He argues that the future of American democracy—if not Western civilization—rests largely on the fighting energy of moral forces undergirded by prophetic religious vision. He states boldly, "It is either a revival of social religion or the deluge."

For those of us who critically—yet appreciatively—build on the precious legacy of Walter Rauschenbusch, Martin Luther King Jr., Dorothy Day, Rabbi Abraham Joshua Herschel, Mahmoud Mohamed Taha, and other prophetic religious giants, the present crisis is a terrifying one. Will the Religious Right along with conservative corporate elites and imperial politicians push us into an American-style neo-fascism in the name of "restoring morality," "market productivity," and the "war on terrorism"? Can an organized citizenry prevail over the chronic lying, massive spying, and green-lighted torturing in our day? Can we be awakened from the ubiquitous sleepwalking—a callous indifference to others' suffering reinforced by well-paid conservative pundits, professors, politicians, and preachers?

Rauschenbusch felt our same urgency and wrestled with our own despair. And he responded with a deep sense of hope—a hope based on our commitment to justice for all, service to others, and a love that counters unlovely persons and circumstances.

> In the last resort the only hope is in the moral forces which can be summoned to the rescue. If there are statesmen, prophets, and apostles who set truth and justice above selfish advancement; if their call finds a response in the great body of the people; if a new tide of religious faith and moral enthusiasm creates new standards of duty and a new capacity for self-sacrifice; if the strong learn to direct their love of power to the uplifting of the people and see the highest self-assertion in self-sacrifice—then the entrenchments of vested wrong will melt away; the stifled energy of the people will leap forward; the atrophied members of the social body will be filled with a fresh flow of blood; and a regenerate nation will look with the eyes of youth across the fields of the future.

The major lesson for us of Walter Rauschenbusch—the grandfather of my dear teacher and the towering philosopher Richard Rorty—is his profound commitment to moral maturity. He found this moral maturity most manifest in the life of Jesus—a life so shot through with love that "love with Jesus was not a flickering and wayward emotion, but the highest and most steadfast energy of a will bent on creating fellowship" (see chapter 2, "The kingdom of God and the ethics of

Jesus"). The very "tone of sadness in [Jesus's] later ministry" (chapter 2, "The purpose of Jesus: the kingdom of God") was due to the lack of moral maturity in his own people, community, nation, empire, and disciples. When it seemed as if all was lost, most had turned from him, and even close friends betrayed him; "unutterable sadness filled his soul, but he never abandoned his faith in the final triumph of that kingdom of God for which he had lived" (chapter 2, "The revolutionary consciousness of Jesus").

Like Antonio Gramsci in the face of fascism, Rauschenbusch counsels a robust willfulness in the face of corporate capitalism. Neither loses faith in the moral capacity of ordinary people to wake up and shake up the status quo. His optimism of the will against the grain of "tragic human life" is nurtured by "a revolutionary Christianity which will call the world evil and change it" (chapter 2, "The revolutionary consciousness of Jesus"). To be a Christian is to live dangerously, primarily owing to the narrow conformity of Constantinian Christendom, the powers of entrenched interest, and the comforting seductions of the idols of greed and bigotry. He writes:

> Jesus foresaw that the Christian movement would work incidental harm and pain.... Our argument here is simply this, that Christianity must have had a strong social impetus to evoke such stirrings of social unrest and discontent. It was not purely religious, but also a democratic and social movement. Or, to state it far more truly: it was so strongly and truly religious that it was of necessity democratic and social also. (chapter 3, "The leaven of Christian democracy")

For too long Rauschenbusch has been cast as a naive liberal Christian thinker unacquainted with the dark side of life or a sentimental Christocentric Protestant unaware of the formidable obstacles to pursuing the kingdom of God on earth. We should not be deceived by these clichés often attributed to giants like Reinhold Niebuhr or Karl Barth. Instead, we must see that he—like them—believed that the riches of the Christian tradition can be brought to bear on the social misery, spiritual vacuity, and political hypocrisy of our day—and that our very future depends on this precious yet fallible effort.

SIX

The Stake of the Church in
the Social Movement

The demoralization of society which we have tried to bring before us in the preceding chapter ought to appeal most powerfully to the Church, for the Church is to be the incarnation of the Christ-spirit on earth, the organized conscience of Christendom. It should be swiftest to awaken to every undeserved suffering, bravest to speak against every wrong, and strongest to rally the moral forces of the community against everything that threatens the better life among men.

But in addition to the call of unselfish duty, the Church may well hear in the present crisis the voice of warning to it to guard its own interests. The organized Church is a great social institution, deeply rooted in the common life of humanity, and if all other human life about it suffers through some permanent evil, the Church is bound to suffer with it. It holds property; it needs income; it employs men. Therefore whatever affects property and employment will affect the Church. Its work is done on human material; anything which deteriorates that material impedes the work of the Church. The warning of justifiable self-interest runs in the same direction with the call to duty and each reinforces the other.[1]

In this chapter I propose to set forth this aspect of the situation. It is not the highest line of appeal, but it well deserves consideration, not only by those whose professional interests are bound up with the Church, but by all who believe that the Church propagates and perpetuates the religious life, and that its vitality is of importance to the higher life of humanity.

THE CHURCH AND ITS REAL ESTATE

The Church is a large landowner. As soon as it gets beyond its first itinerant stage, it needs a permanent foothold on the land. Every enlargement of church work, every mission or parish-house, requires land. If land is cheap, church expansion is easy. If land prices are artificially high, expansion is checked. Land speculation, which checks and strangles every other business, hampers the Church, too.

The retarding influence of land prices is felt most in the founding of missions and young churches. It is a frost that nips the young shoots. A young church enterprise is usually feeble in its finances. If it has to pay a prohibitive price for a mere location, that may cripple it or frustrate it altogether.

Now, land prices are highest where population is densest. Consequently it is harder to plant new churches in large cities than in small. A hundred working people in a small town might easily unite in buying a lot for $1,000. The same hundred persons, if living in New York, might have to pay $10,000 for a lot of half the size. But the denser the population, the more unwholesome are the moral influences and the greater is the need of religious work. Thus land prices act as an automatic brake on church extension, and this brake presses the harder, the steeper the uphill grade is which the Church has to climb. This is one simple explanation of the fact so often lamented, that the Church does not keep pace with the population in large cities. A certain church in New York fifty years ago planted a number of missions in the growing suburbs of that day by holding cottage meetings in the homes of its members and renting vacant stores in which it organized Sunday-schools. Several of these missions developed into vigorous churches. Forty years later the same church desired to resume its early missionary career, but its members now lived in tenement houses, and the cheapest store in sight cost $600 a year. It was numerically and financially stronger than in its early days, but rent had increased faster than the ability of the church, and high rent quenched its missionary impulse. The pioneer work which formerly rested on the spontaneous zeal of plain people becomes dependent on the assistance of wealthy individuals or city mission organizations. That conduces to prudence, and also to officialism.

Of course single churches may profit by the land system which hampers the Church at large. A church occasionally sells its old site at an enormous increase and builds luxuriously in a new neighborhood on the proceeds. Several denominations in New York City are forging ahead of others, not simply by superior spiritual efficiency, but because they have long had an endowment in city land and are able to feed their religious work with the "unearned increment" created by the community. In general our land system works against the great majority of churches which have to live from hand to mouth. It has long seemed to me that the land-tax system advocated by Henry George would create almost ideal conditions for the ordinary church. A church would then pay an annual rental or tax on the site occupied, just as if it occupied land under a perpetual lease. It would not have to raise a large sum for the initial purchase of the land, but could devote its available capital to the church edifice, and hope to pay its annual land-tax from its current income, just as it now pays interest on the church debt.

The needs of modern industry shift and change the population. They denude the country and gather the people about the shops and mines. They invade a residence neighborhood with factories, scatter the old population, and fill the chinks between the shops and warehouses with a population of lower grade, and perhaps of alien faith and tongue. This affects the churches profoundly. Fine old country churches are left high and dry. When a trust transfers a shop to another city, some church may be left behind, like Rachel, mourning for her children. Protestant churches wake up and find themselves in an Italian or Jewish neighborhood. All the endless labor and love which pastor and people put into the erection of a new church home may serve only for a few years, and then the location will have to be abandoned and the edifice sold for second-hand building material. The interest of the Church is in stability of population. A permanent location builds up an invaluable "goodwill." People come to love the local church for the memories and traditions which cling about it and make it more beautiful than the ivy on its walls. Churches are long-lived organisms, like trees, and strike their roots deeper with the passing years. When a speculative and frantic commerce hustles the churches around, they owe it no thanks.

Competitive industry sweeps the people together in the great cities. Therewith it creates the problem of the downtown church. In a community of moderate diameter the people on the outskirts can easily reach a church built in the center. When a city grows very large, the outer fringe of homes drifts ever farther away from the ancient churches that stand in heroic loneliness like the Roman soldier dying on guard at Pompeii. Their problem is aggravated by land speculation, which usually lays a belt of sparsely settled land about the city and compels home-seekers to cross that belt to nuclei of social life still farther out.

These brief suggestions will suffice to show that at the bottom of some of the gravest problems that harass churches and pastors lies the land question in its relation to the complex total of modern life. The condition of the crowded and landless people ought long ago to have aroused the Church to examine the moral basis of our land system. Let it realize in addition that its own growth and stability is impaired by the same causes.

THE CHURCH AND ITS INCOME

The income of the Church in former times and in other countries was mainly derived from landed wealth or from state subsidies. In our country the churches with few exceptions are maintained by the current contributions of their living members. It is therefore of the utmost importance to the financial welfare of the churches that their members shall have a regular and secure income, from which they can readily support their church. Thus the Church has the greatest possible interest in a just and even distribution of wealth. The best community for church support at present is a comfortable middle-class neighborhood. A social system which would make moderate wealth approximately universal would be the best soil for robust churches. If, on the contrary, society tends to divide into a few rich families and a mass of poor wage-earners, the troubles of the Church are before it.

We all understand that a man receiving $500 a year cannot pay as much to religious institutions as a man receiving $5,000, but the universal impression seems to be that he can fairly be expected to contribute the same proportion of his income. The Old Testament law of tithing is very generally recommended as the ideal to be followed by all, on the supposition that 10 percent of an income of $500 is the same proportion as 10 percent of an income of $5,000. This commercial method of calculation leaves some fundamental facts of human nature out of account and has inflicted a grave wrong on the poorer portion of our churches. Dr. Ernst Engel, long the eminent chief of the Prussian Bureau of Statistics, compiled from a large number of family budgets the proportion expended for various purposes. The following table[2] contains the main results:

Item of Expenditures	Percentage of the Expenditure of a Family with an Income of		
	$225–$300 a year	$450–$600 a year	$750–$1100 a year
1. Subsistence	62.0% ⎫	55.0% ⎫	50.0% ⎫
2. Clothing	16.0% ⎪	18.0% ⎪	18.0% ⎪
3. Lodging	12.0% ⎬ 95%	12.0% ⎬ 90%	12.0% ⎬ 85%
4. Firing and lighting	5.0% ⎭	5.0% ⎭	5.0% ⎭
5. Education, worship, etc.	2.0% ⎫	3.5% ⎫	5.5% ⎫
6. Legal protection	1.0% ⎪ 5%	2.0% ⎪ 10%	3.0% ⎪ 15%
7. Care of health	1.0% ⎬	2.0% ⎬	3.0% ⎬
8. Comfort, mental and bodily recreation	1.0% ⎭	2.5% ⎭	3.5% ⎭

The minor items of this table will vary somewhat in different countries, according to local prices and customs; but the main deduction, which is known in political economy as "Engel's Law of Consumption," is as universal as human nature. It will be noticed that the first four items include those expenditures which satisfy the animal necessities of the body: food, shelter, and warmth. The other four satisfy the higher needs. As the income rises, the proportion spent on the first group sinks, and the proportion spent on the second group rises. Within the first group the proportion spent for lodging, heat, and light is the same in all classes, and the proportion for clothing nearly so. But the proportion spent for food is far larger with the poorest families.

The human body has certain imperious demands for its maintenance, and these demands cannot be compressed below a certain minimum. If the income is small, the largest part must go simply for stoking the human machine, and the higher needs of the social, intellectual, and religious nature must be starved. If food prices rise, that proportion will be still greater. The nearer the people descend toward the poverty line, the less will be available for the higher wants.

If, then, any average wage-earner in the churches has actually given a tenth of his income, he deserves profound respect. It is heroic giving for him. And if we have allowed the impression to prevail that the giving of one-tenth by all was equal giving for all, we have unwittingly inflicted a grievous injustice on the poorer church members.

In every church working among the poorer classes there are a number who contribute nothing or are dependents of the church instead of supporters. Every season of economic distress depresses additional families below this line. But some self-respecting people may choose a different line of action. If their church membership involves too heavy a tax, they drop away. Other causes and motives may work in the same direction, but the pressure exerted by the systematized giving of the modern church, and the insistence on this virtue in pulpit teaching, must alienate some. They simply cannot afford church life. The fraternal societies, which offer insurance and mutual help in sickness and death, have increased immensely among the wage-earners, while the Church confessedly has lost ground among them. Is this due merely to religious indifference and unbelief, or to poverty coupled with self-respect?

I am not in a position to prove this, but I offer it as a working hypothesis to explain in part the alienation of the working classes from the churches. Certainly the churches are deeply affected by the economic pressure resting on the wage-workers. Engel's Law deserves serious consideration from the point of view of church finances. I have never come across any discussion of it nor any indication that it is understood in its bearings on church life.

If the people become poor, they cannot afford to share in a self-supporting church. The unequal distribution of wealth thus tends to strip the churches of their poorer clientage. The same inequality of wealth threatens the churches in other ways on the side of the strong who profit by it.

If a church is composed of many wage-workers with a few well-to-do families, the contributions of these few will be of inordinate importance in the financial affairs of the church. The departure of a single family may mean that the church can no longer pay the minister's salary nor support itself. Such a condition will almost inevitably breed an unwholesome deference at some points and an unwholesome jealousy at others. It would be strange, too, if those who are the financial stays of the church did not have the feeling that their wishes ought to be decisive about the coming and going of the minister and other matters deeply affecting the spiritual life. But the preference of wealthy men and their wives may select a pastor who is more of a courtier than a saint. The fundamental evil in the union of Church and State is that worldly men with their interests and points of view dominate the life of the Church which ought to be guided by moral and Christian interests. The point of contact between the Church and the State was frequently the local nobleman, who had the right of "patronage" and could "present the living" to some candidate of his own selection. It was this which caused the Disruption of the Church of Scotland in 1843. Church and State are separate with us, but the essence of the evil may creep in once more as soon as the mass of church members are financially weak and a few persons hold the financial existence of the Church in their hands. Church democracy and voluntarism presuppose approximate financial equality.

The danger just described has been averted usually by the fact that in the larger cities, where there is more than one church of a denomination, the wealthier families do not remain in the poorer churches, but gravitate toward churches composed in the main of their own class. Water seeks its level and so do men. If a young man rises to wealth, and if he and his wife have social ambitions, or if they have intellectual and aesthetic tastes, the wealthy church attracts them. If a man from Christian motives remains in a church of poorer people and bears its burdens, he may find that undesirable associations threaten his growing children there. There are a hundred perfectly natural and legitimate reasons to recommend a transfer of membership to the more congenial surroundings. As fast as the social extremes draw apart and society stratifies in classes, the churches will pass through the same process. The very democracy of our intercourse in America makes it the more inevitable.

But this situation creates the same problem of dependence on a larger scale. The poorer churches become financially dependent on those which contain the wealth of the denomination. If a small church becomes a "mission" of a wealthy church, it thereby secures volunteer workers and a safe budget, but it loses its independence and something of its virility. If a city mission organization undertakes the support of the poorer churches, it is certain to draw its income chiefly from the wealthy churches, and the situation will again be essentially the same.

The inequality of wealth affects the churches on a still larger scale. Most denominations have a few very wealthy supporters. The yearly balance of the great denominational boards and institutions may depend on the singlehanded contributions of these large givers. The initiative in the larger religious enterprises will fall to them. If they hitch their steam-tug to the denominational canal-boat, it will float away to a prosperous voyage; if they hold off, it will stick on the mud-bank of poverty and all the poling of the crew may not get it afloat. They may, and often do, use their vast powers very wisely to develop the latent resources of their denomination. But it is at least conceivable that men whose character has been molded by commercialism may be guided by points of view very alien from the Christian spirit, and that personal dislikes or class prejudices may decide questions of the greatest spiritual importance. Thus the mere fact of great inequality of wealth injects a monarchical element into denominations with democratic government, and in bodies with episcopal government it creates a financial episcopacy back of the bishops.

Then there is always the danger of change. The rich man may grow weary of the constant demands on his help and the disheartening experiences of untruthfulness and parasitism which he is bound to make, and may slacken in his giving. It is not as delightful to be a god on a small scale as outsiders think. Or the children of the rich man may be debilitated by the atmosphere of wealth and be more interested in orchids or art curios than in the church their father and mother loved so well. Or they may follow the drift of their social set toward the ritualistic churches, which offer more aesthetic satisfaction and bring to this country some of the social prestige and antique grandeur which they have in older countries. In any of these contingencies the revenues of an entire denomination, which have been adjusted to these important contributions, may be upset and its missionary policies at home and abroad may suffer calamitous retrenchment. If wealth is in few hands, there is the pleasant possibility of very large and swift benefactions, but there is also a constant danger of instability. The safest income is from the moderately wealthy.

There is more to say, but this will suffice to show that the financial welfare of the churches is bound up with the economic health of society, and that its perils increase as wealth accumulates in few hands and the social extremes draw farther apart. Moreover, the finances of the Church have always affected its constitution and inner life in the subtlest ways.[3] The bishops probably rose to power in the early Church first of all by controlling the pursestrings of the churches. One cause for the rise of the papacy was the large wealth early controlled by the bishop of Rome. The history of the Church in the Middle Ages and its struggles with the secular powers were largely due to the fact that the Church was a great landowner and fought for its income. The corruptions of the papacy and its financial extortions, which alienated the Northern nations and prepared them for the schism of the Reformation, were due in part to the economic changes of the fourteenth and fifteenth centuries. The financial necessities of the Church even created new sacramental observances, and indirectly the doctrines based on them. In the Reformation financial interests played a decisive part throughout. The democratic polity of the various congregational bodies, which is most in harmony with the genius of American life, grew up in homogeneous bodies of plain people. It works best where social equality is greatest. Its essence is imperiled as soon as equality departs. Financial changes are apt to involve far more than anyone foresees at the time. When financial control shifts, other elements and functions of church life are sure to shift with it. The Church surely has an interest at stake in the distribution of social wealth.[4]

One of the finest results of our free church life is that it has developed the resources of the laity and has offered to the ordinary members the opportunity to express their Christian life in Christian work. The American conception of a church is not to have an active priest or

minister with a passive people. All recent movements in church organization, for instance the Endeavor Societies and Men's Clubs, have
tended to draw new groups of the membership into active participation in church work. Church work has been laicized. The instinct of
the leaders of these movements has been entirely right. In our schools
we have learned that a child profits not by what is said to it by the
teacher, but by what it says and does itself. In the volunteer work of
our churches lies their chief educational value, and the lay workers are
the main reservoir of religious strength.

It is, then, of the utmost importance to the churches to have a large
supply of intelligent and competent men and women, who have a
margin of leisure time and a reserve fund of physical and mental
strength which they can devote to church work. If these volunteer
workers labor in factories or stores all week for long hours, at a rapid
pace, and under unwholesome conditions, they cannot bring the same
physical and mental elasticity to their church work. While youth and
health last, they may manage; but when age approaches or ill health
drains their strength, they have to husband their forces for the task of
getting a living. They will henceforth come to church to be cheered
and helped, and can no longer put forth much service. If a young
woman is on her feet all day Saturday till late, her work in Sunday-
school must be impaired by it. Thus the churches are concerned in
the hours and conditions of labor. The exhaustion of the people drains
the churches of their working force.

Christian workers, to be effective, must also have some measure of
trained intelligence, managing ability, and resourcefulness. Those professions which develop these qualities furnish the ablest church workers. The business manager, the doctor, the school principal, make the
ideal Sunday-school superintendent or elder. Insofar as our industrial
life deprives the ordinary workers of all opportunity for executive plan-
ning and reduces them to automatic parts of the machinery, it fails to
develop their latent mental resources and thereby stunts their possibilities as Christian workers. Among the higher classes the churches can
lay hold of minds trained by their daily work and press them into Christian service. Among the lower classes it has to take minds blunted by
their daily work and itself train them. When the Church descends still
lower in the social scale, it works on material that has almost no capac-

ity for service. There the work falls back on a paid staff and officialism once more reigns in religion.

Thus the churches have an interest at stake in the prosperity, physical elasticity, mental efficiency, and leisure time of the people. As the modern factory and tenement stamp one generation after the other with the proletarian character, one of the most hopeful tendencies in the history of the Church will perforce be frustrated. Volunteer work will lessen, and the professional worker will carry the burden of work once more.

THE SUPPLY AND SPIRIT OF THE MINISTRY

"Like priest, like people." The condition of the Church depends on the character of the ministry, and the condition of the ministry depends on the social health of the people.

The ministry is recruited from the sons of the middle class, from the families of farmers, small businessmen, and the better grade of artisans. Students for the ministry rarely come from the homes of the very rich or the very poor. The boys of the poor may have fine native ability and piety, but if they are early forced to work, their educational chances are slighter and their minds are likely to be blunted. The country and the smaller cities furnish a larger proportion of the supply than the large cities, because there the wholesome conditions of middle-class life persist longer. The general shrinkage in the supply, which seems to be undeniable, is doubtless due to a combination of causes: theological unrest; the glamour of wealth in business life; the multiplied openings for intellectual work and social service; and the deterrent conditions existing in the ministry. But one chief cause for the shrinkage in the ministry must be the shrinkage of the class from which it is drawn. A spring will dry up if the rock formation is disturbed or removed within which the water collects. When the best elements of the country and village churches are drained off to the city; when the home life in the cities is narrowed and withered; when many of the most intelligent men of the middle classes have no children or very few of them—is not so far-reaching a social condition sure to affect the supply of young men drawn from these social classes?

The inequality of wealth has already lowered the spirit of the ministry. The most selfish church of wealthy people can offer a better salary and greater social advantages than the most generous church of working people. To get a warm berth, a man must get into the right stratum of society. Smoothness and courtly grace may count for more than spirituality and earnestness. Prophetic vigor may even be a disqualifying virtue. It is hard to make a comparative judgment of so elusive a thing as the spirit of a profession, but it does seem that a spirit of anxiety, ambition, and self-advancement is gaining ground and sapping one of the noblest of all professions of its power and its happiness. When lawyers, doctors, teachers, journalists, and artists have been "commercialized" to their inner loss, is it likely that the ministry can escape?

The chief reward of the ministry has always come to it in the affection and respect of the people. But our age is so drunk with the love of money that anything which does not pan out in cold cash has to take a backseat. Our newspapers constantly speak of college professors and ministers in a tone of patronizing condescension. The salaries of teachers are pitifully inadequate when compared with their value to the community. They turn boys and girls into nobler men and women; a successful writer of advertisements may turn a lie into dollars; clearly he deserves the higher pay. There have been times when the community had a truer judgment of comparative values and gave its spiritual leaders veneration and love. Our commercial system has begotten a fierce competitive thirst for wealth. It has concentrated all minds on money, and accordingly all callings which serve the intellectual and spiritual life have dropped in the relative importance and honor assigned to them. The ministry is one of them. It has lost its best perquisites.

Most ministers are proletarians. They live from hand to mouth on their wages like other wage-earners and have no share in the wealth-producing capital of the nation. They may not share in the class-consciousness of the wage-workers, but they do share in their sufferings. They, too, know the bitterness of hunting for a job and finding a long line of applicants ahead of them. Their tenure, too, has become insecure; what used to be a life-position has become a rapid shifting. Committees naturally tend to use the same methods in hiring or dismissing a minister which are used in hiring or "sacking" any other employee. Ministers, too, find that old men are not wanted, and that when the buoyancy of their youth has been used up, they are put aside with no provision for their age. They, too, find that the trusts can advance prices much more easily than the wage-worker can advance his wage. Thus the minister is dragged down with his class, even though he does not recognize that he belongs to that class.

Ill health, changes of belief, painful experiences in the pastorate, or inability to secure a position often make it seem desirable to a minister to earn his living in some other way. He casts his eye wistfully toward other professions. If there were an economical organization of the working ability of the community and a brisk demand for men, he might find an opportunity. If the labor market is overstocked, especially with elderly men, he finds himself shut up to the ministry and resumes his work there; but now no longer with the old sense of free dedication, but with the consciousness of economic compulsion. If a man knows that he can leave, he may not want to leave. If he knows that he never can leave, he may yearn to leave and pull his oar like a galley-slave. For the spirit of the ministry it is desirable that the door of exit shall be wide open. The old idea of "once a priest, always a priest" is a relic of sacerdotal religion which ascribed an indelible character to the ordained man. Thus the independence and joy of the ministry is subtly affected by the condition of the labor market. There are probably few preachers who can say that they have never been influenced by the fear of endangering their income when they shaped or delivered their message to the people. They, too, are "in bondage through fear."

THE CHURCH AND POVERTY

Other organizations may conceivably be indifferent when confronted with the chronic or acute poverty of our cities. The Christian Church cannot. The very name of "Christian" would turn into an indictment if it did not concern itself in the situation in some way.

One answer to the challenge of the Christian spirit has been the organization of institutional church work. A church perhaps organizes a day-nursery or kindergarten, a playground for the children, a meeting-place for young people, or educational facilities for those who are ambitious. It tries to do for people who are living under abnormal conditions what these people under normal conditions ought to do for themselves. This saving helpfulness toward the poor must be distinguished sharply from the money-making efforts of some churches called institutional, which simply run a continuous sacred variety performance.

Confront the Church of Christ with a homeless, playless, joyless, proletarian population, and that is the kind of work to which some Christian spirits will inevitably feel impelled. All honor to them! But it puts a terrible burden on the Church. Institutional work is hard work and costly work. It requires a large plant and an expensive staff. It puts such a strain on the organizing ability and the sympathies of the workers that few can stand it long. The Church by the voluntary gifts and labors of a few here tries to furnish what the entire cooperative community ought to furnish.

Few churches have the resources and leadership to undertake institutional work on a large scale, but most churches in large cities have some institutional features, and all pastors who are at all willing to do it have institutional work thrust on them. They have to care for the poor. Those of us who passed through the last great industrial depression will never forget the procession of men out of work, out of clothes, out of shoes, and out of hope. They wore down our threshold, and they wore away our hearts. This is the stake of the churches in modern poverty. They are buried at times under a stream of human wreckage. They are turned aside constantly from their more spiritual functions to "serve tables." They have a right, therefore, to inquire who is unloading this burden of poverty and suffering upon them by underpaying, exhausting, and maiming the people. The Good Samaritan did not go after the robbers with a shotgun, but looked after the wounded and helpless man by the wayside. But if hundreds of Good Samaritans traveling the same road should find thousands of bruised men groaning to them, they would not be such very Good Samaritans if they did not organize a vigilance committee to stop the manufacturing of wounded men. If they did not, presumably the asses who had to lug the wounded to the tavern would have the wisdom to inquire into the causes of their extra work.

THE CHURCH AND ITS HUMAN MATERIAL

An architect might have a Parthenon before his mind's eye, but unless he had quarries for the marble, he could not build it. A general might be a military genius, but if the recruits furnished to him were puny, spiritless, and sick with vices, he could make no forced marches nor fight long-drawn battles. Every human institution needs fit human material, as well as a great idea.

Clubs and fraternal societies can pick their material; the Church cannot. It must take in all sorts and conditions of men, and has a special call to seek out and draw in the most abandoned and lost. It has to take the material furnished to it by secular society. If that material is degenerate, the work of the Church is harder and there will be disastrous breaks. The lower the previous moral condition, the more frequent the backslidings. Native workers on foreign mission fields sometimes relapse into the most revolting vices, because their bodies and imaginations were saturated with contamination. Rescue missions are familiar enough with the pitiful attempts of broken human beings to rally faith and hope, and with the swift collapse of the enfeebled will. If large sections of the population should approximate the condition of the hobo, what chance would there be for church work among them?

Poverty does approximate that condition. It creates a character of its own. Constant underfeeding and frequent exhaustion make the physical tissues flabby and the brain prone to depression and vacillation, incapable of holding tenaciously to a distant aim. Mr. Jacob A. Riis says that street life develops in the child "dislike of regular work, physical incapability of sustained effort, misdirected love of adventure, gambling propensities, absence of energy, an untrained will, carelessness of the happiness of others." This characterization will apply to the human material produced by modern city poverty everywhere. Religious faith is the capacity for taking long outlooks and holding all minor aims under control to reach the highest. Poverty teaches men to live from hand to mouth, and for the moment. The experience of the Salvation Army shows that the poor need the strongest thrills of excitement and the most rigid discipline to arouse and hold them. The process of degeneration can be watched in acute form in times of industrial misery. If the decline of a social class is gradual, it escapes observation and only the final results appall us.

There is an old maxim current among religious workers that times of national disaster are followed by a revival of religion, for trouble drives men to God. It is true that in the lower stages of religion, famine, pestilence, and earthquake drove men to their temples and churches to plead with their angry gods. The priests of the temples would be likely to regard that as a hopeful revival of religion; we should call it a superstitious panic. It is true also that every deep emotion of joy or sorrow acts like the earthquake at Philippi: it opens the gates of the soul in the darkness, and then great things may happen. Both the birth and the death of a child may turn the parents to nobler thoughtfulness. But long-continued economic helplessness of entire classes acts differently. That bears the soul down with a numbing sense of injustice and despair. Israel in Egypt "hearkened not unto Moses for anguish of spirit and for cruel bondage." The industrial depression of the 90s was followed by moral disintegration and religious lethargy. It took the churches longer than commerce to recover from that paralysis of hopelessness. The maxim quoted is a relic of the ascetic view of life, which assumed that a man was closest to holiness when he was most emaciated and stripped of the joys of life.

The churches may well pray like the wise man, "Give me neither poverty nor riches" (Proverbs 30:8–9).[5] Poverty and luxury alike enervate the will and degenerate the human material for religion. Both create the love of idleness, vagrant habits, the dislike of self-restraint, and the inclination to indulge in the passing emotions. Ethical religion calls for precisely the opposite qualities. It is written large in the present conditions of the churches that they flourish best among people who have income enough for health and comfort, security enough for cheer and hope, and leisure enough to cultivate the higher sides of life. In London the type of religion represented by the Free Churches thrives best in the middle-class parishes.[6] When a certain line of poverty has been passed, the churches lose their hold almost completely, in spite of the most heroic efforts of Christian men and women. A social system which lifts a small minority into great wealth, and submerges a great number in poverty, is thus directly hostile to the interests of the Church. A system which would distribute wealth with approximate fairness and equality would offer honest religion the best working chance.

THE HOSTILE ETHICS OF COMMERCIALISM

Human nature is the raw material for the Christian character. The spirit of Christ working in the human spirit is to elevate the aims, ennoble the motives, and intensify the affections. This process is never complete. The Christian is always but in the making.

In the same way human society is the raw material for Christian society. The spirit of Christ is to hallow all the natural relations of men and give them a divine significance and value. This process, too, is never complete. The kingdom of God is always but coming.

The situation is changed when the individual presents not only the obstacles of raw human nature, a will sluggish to good, a preference for pleasure rather than duty, and the clogging influence of evil habits, but a spirit and principles consciously hostile to the influence of Christianity, and sets defiant pride and selfishness against the gentleness and unselfishness urged by the spirit of Jesus.

In the same way the situation is changed when the social relations are dominated by a principle essentially hostile to the social conceptions of Christ. Then the condition is not that of a stubborn raw material yielding slowly to the higher fashioning force, but of two antagonistic spirits grappling for the mastery. The more such a hostile principle dominates secular society, the more difficult will be the task of the Church when it tries to bring the Christ-spirit to victorious ascendancy.

Christianity bases all human relations on love, which is the equalizing and society-making impulse. The Golden Rule makes the swift instincts of self-preservation a rule by which we are to divine what we owe to our neighbor. Anything incompatible with love would stand indicted. Christ's way to greatness is through preeminent social service. Self-development is desirable because it helps us to serve the better. So far as the influence of the Christian spirit goes, it bows the egoism of the individual to the service of the community. It bids a man live his life for the kingdom of God.

In urging the social duty of love, Christianity encounters the natural selfishness of human nature. But this is not a hostile force. It is the instinct of self-preservation without which no child would survive. In a well-trained child the frank egoism of the baby is steadily modified by a growing sense of duty and of solidarity with the family and the little social group in which it moves. With the change of adolescence comes a powerful instinct of self-devotion to society. If the influence of Christianity accompanies the child during this development, and comes to conscious adoption in the adolescent period, it gives an immense reinforcement to the moralizing influence of the family and the school, and creates a character ready for real social life and service. If the larger human society into which the young man or woman then enters were adapted to continue the social training given in the family and the school; if the industrial life which molds the adult set tasks for conscious social service and inspired all workers with the sense of moral solidarity; social life would be so closely akin to the Christian conception that the task of Christianity would be easy, and comparative success would be within reach.

Instead of that the young adult in the most plastic time of his development is immersed in an industrial life which largely tends to counteract and neutralize Christian teaching and training. Competitive industry and commerce are based on selfishness as the dominant instinct and duty, just as Christianity is based on love. It will outbuy and outsell its neighbor if it can. It tries to take his trade and grasp all visible sources of income in its own hand. The rule of trade, to buy in the cheapest market and sell in the dearest, simply means that a man must give as little to the other man and get as much from him as possible. This rule makes even honest competitive trade—to say nothing of the immense volume of more or less dishonest and rapacious trade—antagonistic to Christian principles. The law of Christ, wherever it finds expression, reverses the law of trade. It bids us demand little for ourselves and give much service. A mother does not try to make as rich a living as possible, and to give a minimum of service to her children. It would be a sorry teacher who would lie awake thinking how he could corner the market in education and give his students as small a chunk of information as possible from the pedagogic ice-wagon. The relation between a minister and a church is Christian only when the church pays him as well as it can afford to do, and he gives as wholehearted and complete service as he can get out of himself. There are some professions and some social relations which are in the main dominated by the Christian conceptions of solidarity and service, and they are the only ones that arouse our enthusiasm or win our love. Industry and commerce are not in that class.

Commerce has moved away from the golden age of competition, when businessmen were like Ishmaels, with every man's hand against every other man. Large social groups are now working on the principle of cooperation in great corporations. That develops loyalty and human goodwill within the cooperative group. But only within it. Every trust still has a lot of outsiders whom it has to fight and tame into submission. The wonderful mechanism of a great department store is not directed merely to mutual service, but also to the undoing of its competitors. A board of directors may feel a sense of coherence — modified by a fear of treachery — but when they turn toward their employees and toward the public, the sense of solidarity ends. It is probably fair to say that the great business world is not appreciably influenced in its daily struggles by the consciousness that it exists to serve mankind. A minister, a doctor, a teacher, an artist, a soldier, or a public official may forget it often and may turn traitor to the principle altogether; but if he is good for anything, he will always feel the constraint of the higher principle upon him. In these callings it is comparatively easy for a man to realize the joy and strength of that principle, if he is only willing. In business life the constraint is all the other way. The social value of business is reserved for ornamental purposes in after-dinner speeches. There all professions claim to exist for the good of society. At a recent dinner of the Pawnbrokers' Association of New York, Mr. Abraham Levy spoke of the company as "the benefactors and bearers of the burdens of the poor," and doubtless he believed it when he said it.

Every human institution creates a philosophy which hallows it to those who profit by it and allays the objections of those who are victimized by it. Thus M. Pobiedonestzeff, the great procurator of the Holy Synod in Russia, taught the sacredness of the autocracy and thereby strengthened the hands of those who kept the people down. Where alcoholism dominates the customs of a people, it weaves a halo around itself in the songs and social observances of the people, till joy and friendship seem to be inseparable from mild narcotic paralysis of the nerve centers. Similarly, the competitive industry has its own philosophy to justify the ways of business unto men. "Competition is the life of trade." "If every man will do the best for himself, he will thereby do the best for society." In short, the surest way to be unselfish is to look out for Number One.

This individualistic philosophy was worked out at the end of the eighteenth century in order to cut away the artificial restraints inherited from a bygone period of industry. The noblest thinkers enthusiastically believed that the unfettered operation of self-love would result in happy conditions for all. Experience has proved this a ghastly mistake. Scientific thought and practical statesmanship have abandoned the policy of unrestrained competition. The more enlightened businessmen, too, view it with moral uneasiness and a certain shame. The selfish hardness of business life is to them a sad fact, but they feel they must play the game according to the rules of the game. Yet as long as competitive commerce continues and is the source of profit in the business world, competitive selfishness will be defended as the true law of life.

As soon as the competitive philosophy of life encounters an opposing philosophy in socialism, it is angrily insistent on its own righteousness. The same is the case when any attempt is made to urge the Christian law of life as obligatory for business as well as private life. "Don't mix business and religion." "Business is business." These common maxims express the consciousness that there is a radical divergence between the two domains of life, and that the Christian rules of conduct would forbid many common transactions of business and make success in it impossible. Thus life is cut into two halves, each governed by a law opposed to that of the other, and the law of Christ is denied even the opportunity to gain control of business. When a man lives a respectable and religious life in one part of the city and a life of vice in another part, he is said to live a double life. That is the heartbreaking condition forced upon Christian businessmen by the antagonism of Christianity and competitive commerce. They have to try to do what Christ declares impossible: to serve God and mammon. It is no wonder that many try to maintain their faith in their own integrity of character by denying that business life is antagonistic to Christianity at all. But the rest of the community judges differently. The moral sincerity of the most prominent members of the churches is impugned by the public, which has little sympathy with the tragic situation in which Christian businessmen find themselves. This deeply affects the moral prestige of the churches in the community. They are forced into the defensive instead of challenging the community to a higher standard of morals.

When two moral principles are thus forced into practical antagonism in daily life, the question is which will be the stronger. If the Church cannot Christianize commerce, commerce will commercialize the Church. When the churches buy and sell, they follow the usual methods and often drive hard bargains. When they hire and dismiss their employees, they are coming more and more to use the methods of the labor market. In the teaching of the Church those elements of the ethics of Jesus which are in antagonism to commercial life are toned down or unconsciously dropped out of sight. The Sermon on the Mount, in which Jesus clearly defines the points of difference between his ethics and the current morality, is always praised reverently, but rarely taken seriously. Its edge is either blunted by an alleviating exegesis, or it is asserted that it is intended for the millennium and not for the present social life. When the religious teachings of Tolstoi first became known in the 80s, they gave many of us a shock of surprise by asserting with the voice of faith that these were the obligatory and feasible laws of Christian conduct. Thus the principles of commerce affect the moral practice of the Church and silence its moral teachings insofar as they are antagonistic to business morality.

We pointed out that there are some departments of life which are to some degree under the actual dominion of the Christian principle, especially personal morality, the family life, and neighborly social intercourse. But the principle incorporated in business life is so deeply affecting the methods of action, the points of view, and the philosophy of life as preached in the press and in conversation, that it is encroaching even on those realms of life which have hitherto been blessed by Christ's law. If Christianity cannot advance, it will have to retreat even from the territory already claimed by it.

If the Church cannot bring business under Christ's law of solidarity and service, it will find his law not merely neglected in practice, but flouted in theory. With many the Darwinian theory has proved a welcome justification of things as they are. It is right and fitting that thousands should perish to evolve the higher type of the modern businessman. Those who are manifestly surviving in the present struggle for existence can console themselves with the thought that they are the fittest, and there is no contradicting the laws of the universe. Thus an atomistic philosophy crowds out the Christian faith in solidarity. The law of the cross is superseded by the law of tooth and nail. It is not even ideal and desirable "to seek and to save the lost," because it keeps the weak and unfit alive. The philosophy of Nietzsche, which is deeply affecting the ethical thought of the modern world, scouts the Christian virtues as the qualities of slaves. It glorifies the strong man's self-assertion which treads underfoot whatever hinders him from living out his life to the full. The philosophy regnant in any age is always the direct outgrowth of the sum total of life in that age. We view Neo-Platonism, for instance, as the necessary product of the third century. It is safe to say that students of some future century will establish an intimate causal connection between the industrial system which evolves the modern captain of industry and the philosophy of Nietzsche which justifies and glorifies him.

On the other hand, among the masses who are being ground up in this evolutionary mill there will be a growing sense of the inexorable cruelty of natural law and a failing faith in the fundamental goodness of the universe. And if the universe is not at bottom good, then the God who made it and who runs it is not good. Or perhaps there is no God at all. Goodness is folly. Force rules the world. Let us use what force we have, grasp what we can, and die. The Church in the past has been able to appeal to the general faith in a good and just God and to intensify that. If that half-unconscious religion of the average man once gives way to a sullen materialism, there will be a permanent eclipse of the light of life among us.

This is the stake of the Church in the social crisis. If one vast domain of life is dominated by principles antagonistic to the ethics of Christianity, it will inculcate habits and generate ideas which will undermine the law of Christ in all other domains of life and even deny the theoretical validity of it. If the Church has not faith enough in the Christian law to assert its sovereignty over all relations of society, men will deny that it is a good and practicable law at all. If the Church cannot conquer business, business will conquer the Church.

CHRISTIAN CIVILIZATION AND FOREIGN MISSIONS

The world is getting small. The shuttle of travel is weaving back and forth. The East and the West have met. We are camping in the front yard of the Hindu and Chinaman, and they are peering over the fence into our backyard. Never before since Islam contended with Christendom for the mastery of the Mediterranean world has the Church been compelled to confront the non-Christian religions as now.

The modern movement of foreign missions was the response of the spirit of Christ in the Church to the opportunity presented by the new worldwide commerce. From the outset the missionaries were put to it to explain what relation the white traders who sold the natives rum and brought them contagious diseases bore to the Jesus-religion taught by the missionaries. Trade made the way for missions, but traders also frustrated Christianity. Today commerce is bearing down on the non-Christian nations with relentless eagerness, breaking down their national independence at the cannon's mouth, breaking up their customs and tribal coherence, industrializing them, atomizing them, and always making profit on them. At the same time the non-Christian peoples are getting intimate information about Christianity as it works in its own home. They travel through our slums and inspect Packingtown.[7] They see our poverty and our vice, our wealth and our heartlessness, and they like their own forms of misery rather better. "By their fruits ye shall know them," when applied to religions, reads, "By their civilizations ye shall know them." The moral prestige of Christian civilization ought to be the most valuable stock in trade for the foreign representatives of Christianity; instead of that it is forcing missionaries into an apologetic attitude. With all the faults that anyone can point out in it, the foreign mission work of the modern Church is one of the most splendid expressions of the Christ-spirit in history, full of blessing for the Church at home, and fuller of historic importance for the future of mankind than any man can now foresee. Here the Church is really on the fighting-line. But here its sword-arm is paralyzed by the existence of a mass of un-Christianized life in its own camp. Our industrial life antagonizes our Christian gospel to non-Christian nations.

It even reacts on the faith of the people at home. The Japanese war has furnished a demonstration of the moral qualities of a heathen nation in an object lesson so brilliant that it has gone home with all the world. It has shaken our confidence in the easy moral supremacy of Christianity. We are gaining in respect for the spiritual forces resident in other nations at the same time that we are getting an ever more vivid sense of our evils at home and of our impotence in dealing with them.

Thus our unsettled social problems dog the footsteps of the Church wherever it goes. The social wrongs which we permit at home contradict our gospel abroad and debilitate our missionary enthusiasm at home. With what different confidence we should present the claims of our religion abroad if our missionaries went out from a nation of free men, living in social equality and organized fraternity!

To most thoughtful men today the social question is the absorbing intellectual problem of our time. To the working class it is more. Socialism is their class movement. The great forward movement inaugurated by the French Revolution was the movement of the businessmen who wrested political control from the feudal nobility and clergy. The wage-workers were then neither strong nor intelligent enough to force a readjustment of rights in their favor. That class is now in its birth-throes. The rest of us may be sympathetic onlookers and helpers, but to them it is a question of life and death.

Every great movement which so profoundly stirs men unlocks the depths of their religious nature, just as great experiences in our personal life make the individual susceptible to religious emotion. When the chaotic mass of humanity stirs to the throb of a new creative day, it always feels the Spirit of God hovering over it. The large hope which then beckons men, the ideal of justice and humanity which inspires them, the devotion and self-sacrifice to the cause which they exhibit— these are in truth religious.

As long as the people are still patriotic and religious, their first impulse is to march under the banner of their inherited religion, sure that it must be on their side. When the German peasants in 1525 set forth their simple and just demands in the celebrated "Twelve Articles," they based them all on the Bible and offered to surrender any demand which should be proved out of harmony with God's word.[8] Thus again the people of St. Petersburg on January 22, 1905, moved to the Winter Palace to present their petition to "the Little Father," led by a priest in the vestments of religion, and bearing before them the portrait of the czar and the cross of Christ. In both cases the response to their petition was a massacre.

It is humiliating to say that the confidence with which the people at the beginning of such risings have turned to their religion for moral backing has not been justified in the past. Luther had scant sympathy with the peasants at the outset, and as soon as they used force against the castles of the barons and the monasteries, he called for forcible repression in the most violent language. The pope, too, wrote a congratulatory letter to those who had been most active in repressing the movement. The state Church in Russia is certainly not on the side of the revolution, though many of her priests may be. The churches in Europe were almost universally hostile to the French Revolution.

When the people find their aspirations opposed and repudiated by their churches, they turn away chilled or angry. It is then a question whether the discipline of the Church is sufficiently strong to turn the people back from the popular movement and retain them in obedience to the Church. That is the problem which the Roman Catholic Church is now confronting in its opposition to socialism. It is trying to quarantine the Catholic workingmen in organizations of their own and to keep them immune from the bacillus of socialism. It is far fitter for such paternal repression than the Protestant churches, but its ultimate success is dubious. The mass of the people are more likely to sweep on and away from churchly religion. When the dearest ethical convictions of the people in such a crisis are brought into collision with organized religion, the result is sad for the people and disastrous for the Church.

In Germany the process has worked out its conclusions quite fully. For a long time the German state Church took no sympathetic interest in the socialist movement. It preached loyalty to the king, the divine necessity of social classes, submission, and godly patience. A socialist was a heathen and a publican. It was generally denied that a man could be both a socialist and a Christian. The socialists in their propaganda constantly encountered the Church as a spiritual and social force defending the existing social order, a bulwark of privilege and conservatism. They could gain a man for socialism only by undermining the authority of the Church over his mind. At the same time the leaders of the working class were drinking in eagerly the new results of natural science and philosophy, which at that time was baldly atheistic in Germany. "Science," as popularized in socialist literature and propaganda, was atheistic materialism. The German Social Democracy professes to be indifferent to religion and declares it a private affair, but actually it is a force hostile to religion. The tide of socialism has risen until now the Social Democratic Party is almost coextensive with the working class in the cities. Gradually the Church woke up. It tried to remedy the social misery of the people by charitable work and by alleviative legislation on the basis of the existing social order. In both directions splendid work has been done, but the allegiance of the people has not been regained. The clergy are now thoroughly awake to social questions. Many of them are more or less socialistic in their thought, but the State and the governing bodies of the Church have favored the social activity of the clergy only when it seemed likely to quiet the people and establish the existing order, and have been harshly repressive as soon as individual ministers went farther.

The Church in past centuries repeatedly lost the respect and affections of the people by its corruptions and the oppression which it sanctioned and intensified, but it was able to regain its hold when it repented and improved. It may be that in coming days the Church in Germany will regain its old influence in the life of the people. But the outlook is not sure. The old medieval reverence for the Church as the only mediator of salvation is gone, and the people are permanently critical in spirit. Formerly the Church was able to envelop itself in awe by the shimmering mist of idealized history which it spread about its past services. The people are now educated beyond that. So the future is somber. When a mountainside is once denuded of vegetation and the roots of the trees no longer lace the soil together and hold the rain, the soil is washed down into the valleys. The rocks are again corroded and might form new soil, but as it is formed, it is again washed away. Because the rocks are bare, they stay bare. From him that hath not is taken even that which he hath.

In our own country we are still at the parting of the ways. Our social movement is still in its earliest stages. The bitterness and anger of their fight has not eaten into the heart of the working classes as it has abroad. Many of them are still ready to make their fight in the name of

God and Christ, though not of the Church. Populistic conventions used to recite the Lord's Prayer with deep feeling. The Single Tax movement utilized religious ideas freely. A Cooper Union meeting cheered Father McGlynn when he recited the words: "Thy kingdom come! Thy will be done on earth!" Some of the favorite speakers and organizers of the socialists in our country are former Christian ministers, who use their power of ethical and religious appeal. In Labor Lyceums and similar gatherings, ministers are often invited as speakers, though perhaps quite as much in the hope of converting them as with a desire to hear what they have to say. The divorce between the new class movement and the old religion can still be averted.

It is a hopeful fact that in our country the Church is so close to the common people. In many of the largest denominations the churches are organized as pure democracies, and the people own and run them. Our ministry is not a hereditary pundit class, but most ministers have sprung from plain families and have worked for their living before they became ministers. The Church is not connected with the State and is not tainted, as in Europe, with the reputation of being a plainclothes policeman to club the people into spiritual submission to the ruling powers. The churches of monarchical countries have preached loyalty to the monarchy as an essential part of Christian character. The Church in America believes heartily in political democracy. But a Church which believes in political democracy can easily learn to believe in industrial democracy as soon as it comprehends the connection. It has one foot in the people's camp. The type of Christianity prevailing in America was developed in the Puritan Revolution and has retained the spirit of its origin. It is radical, evangelical, and has the strong bent toward politics which Calvinism has everywhere had. American ministers naturally take a keen interest in public life, and, as well as they know, have tried to bring the religious forces to bear at least on some aspects of public affairs.

As a result of these characteristics, the Christian Church in America is actually deeply affected by sympathy with the social movement. It stands now, at the very beginning of the social movement in America, where the repentant Church of Germany stands after a generation of punishment by atheistic socialism. No other learned profession seems to be so open to socialist ideals as the ministry. Several years ago the

New York Evening Post began to lament that the Church had gone over to socialism.

Nevertheless the working class has not as yet gained the impression that the Church is a positive reinforcement to them in their struggle. The impression is rather the other way. The eminent ministers whose utterances are most widely disseminated are usually the pastors of wealthy churches, and it is natural that they should echo the views taken by the friends with whom they are in sympathetic intercourse. Even those ministers who are intellectually interested in social problems are not always in sympathy with the immediate conflicts of the working class. They may take a lively interest in municipal reform or public ownership, and yet view dubiously the efforts to create a fighting organization for labor or to end the wages system. We are of a different class and find it hard to sympathize with the class struggle of the wage-workers.

In recent years many ministers have spoken frankly and boldly against the physical violence and brutality in connection with the great strikes, and against the denial of "the right to work." The former protest was made in the name of law and order, the latter in the name of liberty. No one who has ever seen the destruction of property in a riot, or the hounding of scabs by a mob, or the unleashing of the brute passions under the continued strain of a great industrial conflict, can help sympathizing with both contentions. And yet it is probable that when posterity looks back on the struggles of our day, it will judge that the righteous indignation of these protests was directed against a cause that was more righteous still.

Law is unspeakably precious. Order is the daughter of heaven. Yet in practice law and order are on the side of those in possession. The men who are out can get in only through the disturbance of the order now prevailing. Those who in the past cried for law and order at any cost have throttled many a newborn child of justice. The aristocracy and bureaucracy of Russia are all for law and order, for law and order mean the old law and their own order. When the German peasants in 1525, betrayed and murdered by their aristocratic enemies who scorned to keep faith with the canaille, used violence in turn, Luther lost all his former faint sympathy with their fair demands, and called for order at any price. He said they had forfeited all rights, and summoned the forces of order to kill them as one would kill a mad dog.

They did it. The princes and barons, assured that they were not only protecting their class interest, but serving God in the bargain, slaughtered probably a hundred thousand, devastated entire districts, broke the backbone of the German peasantry, and retarded the emancipation of a great and worthy class by centuries. It was a very righteous impulse with Luther, and yet we count it one of the darkest stains on his life. That class which he opposed in the blind agony of its emancipation is now rising to intelligence and power, and is forgetting all his great merits for this sin committed against the common people. When violence was used during the Brooklyn street-car strike in 1895, an eminent minister of that city used words that sounded strangely like Luther's fearful invective: "If clubs will not do, then bayonets; if bayonets will not do, then lead; if bullets will not do, then Gatling guns." He said he was willing to have the churches turned into hospitals to see order maintained.

Freedom, too, is a holy word. The right to labor is one of the fundamental rights of man. But the cry of "the right to work" in our country has been raised mainly by the employers on behalf of those who were willing to help them in breaking down the resistance of organized labor. Their interest seems to be more in the right to be worked for than in the right to work. Strike-breaking is now a highly organized business, and those who do it rank morally with the mercenaries kept by princes to subdue their people. For those workmen who under the pressure of need break away from the coherence of their class and take the job which is calling for them, the situation is indeed terrible. The "scab" may be actuated by fine motives. He may feel loyalty to the employer whose bread he has long eaten; he may be driven by the hunger and sickness of his family to provide bread for them at any cost; or he may disapprove of this strike or of labor-unions in general. But he breaks down the solidarity of his class, and his class will judge him by that standard alone.

There has never been a social class or group which has not punished to the best of its ability anyone who betrayed the interests of the class, and which did not visit bitterer condemnation on those actions which endangered its safety than on any others. A boy may steal apples and retain his moral standing with the other boys, but he must not "tell on a fellow." A cowboy could sin all around the compass with impunity, but if he stole a horse, he was hung; the safety of his class depended on the security of their horses. Militarism winks at gambling and lewdness, but strikes relentlessly at insubordination. The governing powers in Russia have been lenient on many things, but they tolerated no opinions which undermined the moral foundations of the autocracy. While the clerical hierarchy was dominant, it punished the schismatic and heretic, for he was the "scab" and "blackleg" of the Church. Each class regards the punishment visited on its traitors as just and natural, but regards with horror the class of offenses punished by the opposing class and its methods of getting even with its traitors. These observations have held true throughout human history, and have been deeply influential in the gradual formation of customary and statutory law.

The working class is now engaged in a great historic class struggle which is becoming ever more conscious and bitter. Their labor is all they have. Individually they are helpless. Their only hope for wresting better wages and conditions from the other side is in union of action. With infinite effort, with sacrifice of time, money, and chances of self-advancement, they create organizations which obey discipline and act together. Under certain circumstances anyone breaking away from their discipline may secure exceptional terms for himself, but he does so at the expense of all the efforts which the union has put forth. Others are laboriously erecting a dam to raise the water level so that all may irrigate their fields and raise better crops. This man breaks through the dam to get an immediate supply for his own field. If we expect the working class to be patient with those who sell out the interest of their class for personal advantage, and lend themselves as tools to those who seek to undermine the fighting force of the organization, we demand of one of the lowest groups of society a moral magnanimity and breadth of view which no other group has ever shown. The great sociologist Schaeffle, who was by no means a radical, said, "There is nothing more brutal than a moneyed aristocracy in persecuting those who dispute its dominion." The philosophy of all class movements is summed up in Kipling's Jungle Law:[9]

Now this is the Law of the Jungle—as old and as true as the sky;
   And the Wolf that shall keep it may prosper, but the Wolf that shall break it must die.

As the creeper that girdles the tree-trunk the Law runneth forward
  and back;
For the strength of the Pack is the Wolf, and the strength of the
  Wolf is the Pack.
Now these are the Laws of the Jungle, and many and mighty are
  they;
But the head and the hoof of the Law, and the haunch and the
  hump is—"Obey!"

In its struggle the working class becomes keenly conscious of the
obstacles put in its way by the great institutions of society, the courts,
the press, or the Church. It demands not only impartiality, but the
kind of sympathy which will condone its mistakes and discern the justice of its cause in spite of the excesses of its followers. When our sympathies are enlisted, we develop a vast faculty for making excuses. If
two dogs fight, our own dog is rarely the aggressor. Stealing peaches is
a boyish prank when our boy does it, but petty larceny when that drat-
ted boy of our neighbor does it. If the other political party grafts, it is a
flagrant shame; if our own party does it, we regret it politely or deny
the fact. If Germany annexes a part of Africa, it is brutal aggression; if
England does it, she "fulfills her mission of civilization." If the business interests exclude the competition of foreign merchants by a protective tariff, it is a grand national policy; if the trades-unions try to
exclude the competition of non-union labor, it is a denial of the right
to work and an outrage.

The working class likes to get that kind of sympathy which will take
a favorable view of its efforts and its mistakes, and a comprehension of
the wrongs under which it suffers. Instead of that the pulpit of late has
given its most vigorous interest to the wrongs of those whom militant
labor regards as traitors to its cause. It has been more concerned with
the fact that some individuals were barred from a job by the unions,
than with the fact that the entire wage-working class is debarred from
the land, from the tools of production, and from their fair share in the
proceeds of production.

It cannot well be denied that there is an increasing alienation between the working class and the churches.[10] That alienation is most
complete wherever our industrial development has advanced farthest

and has created a distinct class of wage-workers. Several causes have contributed. Many have dropped away because they cannot afford to take their share in the expensive maintenance of a church in a large city. Others because the tone, the spirit, the point of view in the churches, is that of another social class. The commercial and professional classes dominate the spiritual atmosphere in the large city churches. As the workingmen grow more class-conscious, they come to regard the businessmen as their antagonists and the possessing classes as exploiters who live on their labor, and they resent it when persons belonging to these classes address them with the tone of moral superiority. When ministers handle the labor question, they often seem to the working class partial against them even when the ministers think they are most impartial. Foreign workingmen bring with them the long-standing distrust for the clergy and the Church as tools of oppression which they have learned abroad, and they perpetuate that attitude here. The churches of America suffer for the sins of the churches abroad. The "scientific socialism" imported from older countries through its literature and its advocates is saturated with materialistic philosophy and is apt to create dislike and antagonism for the ideas and institutions of religion.

Thus in spite of the favorable equipment of the Church in America there is imminent danger that the working people will pass from indifference to hostility, from religious enthusiasm to anti-religious bitterness. That would be one of the most unspeakable calamities that could come upon the Church. If we would only take warning by the fate of the churches in Europe, we might avert the desolation that threatens us. We may well be glad that in nearly every city there are a few ministers who are known as the outspoken friends of labor. Their fellow ministers may regard them as radicals, lacking in balance, and very likely they are; but in the present situation they are among the most valuable servants of the Church. The workingmen see that there is at least a minority in the Church that champions their cause, and that fact helps to keep their judgment in hopeful suspense about the Church at large. Men who are just as one-sided in favor of capitalism pass as sane and conservative men. If the capitalist class have their court-chaplains, it is only fair that the army of labor should have its army-chaplains who administer the consolations of religion to militant labor.

Thus the Church has a tremendous stake in the social crisis. It may try to maintain an attitude of neutrality, but neither side will permit it. If it is quiescent, it thereby throws its influence on the side of things as they are, and the class which aspires to a fitter place in the organization of society will feel the great spiritual force of the Church as a deadweight against it. If it loses the loyalty and trust of the working class, it loses the very class in which it originated, to which its founders belonged, and which has lifted it to power. If it becomes a religion of the upper classes, it condemns itself to a slow and comfortable death. Protestantism from the outset entered into an intimate alliance with the intelligence and wealth of the city population. As the cities grew in importance since the Reformation, as commerce overshadowed agriculture, and as the business class crowded the feudal aristocracy out of its leading position since the French Revolution, Protestantism throve with the class which had espoused it. It lifted its class, and its class lifted it. On the other hand, the Anabaptist movement in Germany, which propagated within the lower classes, was crushed with the class that bore its banner. If the present class struggle of the wage-workers is successful, and they become the dominant class of the future, any religious ideas and institutions which they now embrace in the heat of their struggle will rise to power with them, and any institution on which they turn their back is likely to find itself in the cold. The parable of the Wise and Foolish Virgins holds of entire nations and institutions as well as of individuals.

THE FORWARD CALL TO THE CHURCH

We have seen that the crisis of society is also the crisis of the Church. The Church, too, feels the incipient paralysis that is creeping upon our splendid Christian civilization through the unjust absorption of wealth on one side and the poverty of the people on the other. It cannot thrive when society decays. Its wealth, its independence, its ministry, its social hold, its spiritual authority, are threatened in a hundred ways.

But on the other hand the present crisis presents one of the greatest opportunities for its own growth and development that have ever been offered to Christianity. The present historical situation is a high

summons of the Eternal to enter on a larger duty, and thereby to inherit a larger life.

In all the greatest forward movements of humanity, religion has
been one of the driving forces. The deadweight of hoary institutions
and the resistance of the caked and encrusted customs and ideas of the
past are so great that unless the dormant energies of the people are
awakened by moral enthusiasm and religious faith, the old triumphs
over the new. "Mighty Truth's yet mightier man-child" comes to the
hour of birth, but there is no strength to bring forth.

But in turn the greatest forward movements in religion have always
taken place under the call of a great historical situation. Religious
movements of the first magnitude are seldom purely religious in their
origin and character. It is when nations throb with patriotic fervor,
with social indignation, with the keen joy of new intellectual light,
with the vastness and fear of untried conditions, when "the energy sublime of a century bursts full-blossomed on the thorny stem of Time,"
that religion, too, will rise to a new epoch in its existence.

The Reformation of the sixteenth century is a classical illustration
of this fact. The popular view which regards it first of all as a restoration of evangelical doctrine on the basis of the open Bible is almost
wholly misleading.[11] The Reformation had been gathering headway
for four years before Luther put his hand to the translation of the
Bible, and then he had no clear foresight of the importance of that
work. He nailed up his Theses on indulgences in 1517 but he did not
begin to attack the doctrines of the Church till 1520. The prime cause
of the Reformation was the smoldering anger of the Northern nations
at their financial exploitation by the Italian papacy. Luther's great
manifesto "To the Christian Nobility of Germany" was a tremendous
social, educational, and ecclesiastical reform program. He secured the
support of the princes and nobles because he said with a thundering
voice what all felt about the extortion and oppression of the ecclesiastical machine. At the Diet of Worms in 1521 nearly all the German estates were friendly to him, but they cared nothing for his doctrinal
differences, and would have been best pleased if he had abjured them.
The glorious years of the Lutheran Reformation were from 1517 to
1525, when the whole nation was in commotion and a great revolutionary tidal wave seemed to be sweeping every class and every higher

interest one step nearer to its ideal of life. The mightiest years in the life of Luther were those same years when he was the spokesman of an awakened nation and grappled fearlessly with all the problems of human life.[12] Then came the reactionary turn in his life. He feared the spirit which he had helped to evoke. He disavowed the cause of the lower classes, distrusted the common people in Church and State, alienated their love and trust, and strengthened the wealth and power of the princes. By his theological dogmatism he repelled the men who had fought with him in the interests of education and science, and the Swiss reformers who differed with him on points of doctrine. He had been the leader of a nation; now he became the head of a sect. The Lutheran Reformation had been most truly religious and creative when it embraced the whole of human life and enlisted the enthusiasm of all ideal men and movements. When it became "religious" in the narrower sense, it grew scholastic and spiny, quarrelsome, and impotent to awaken high enthusiasm and noble life. The scepter of leadership passed from Lutheranism to Calvinism and to regenerated Catholicism. Calvinism had a far wider sphere of influence and a far deeper effect on the life of the nations than Lutheranism, because it continued to fuse religious faith with the demand for political liberty and social justice.

Similarly the religious reform movements of the Middle Ages were very closely connected with wider social causes: the changes created by the Crusades, the consequent rise of commerce, the growth of luxury, the transition to a money basis in industry, the rise of the cities and the development of a new city proletariat. The movement of Francis of Assisi, of the Waldenses, of the Humiliati and Bons Hommes, were all inspired by democratic and communistic ideals. Wiclif was by far the greatest doctrinal reformer before the Reformation; but his eyes, too, were first opened to the doctrinal errors of the Roman Church by joining in a great national and patriotic movement against the alien domination and extortion of the Church. The Bohemian revolt, made famous by the name of John Hus, was quite as much political and social as religious. Savonarola was a great democrat as well as a religious prophet. In his famous interview with the dying Lorenzo de' Medici he made three demands as a condition for granting absolution.[13] Of the man he demanded a living faith in God's mercy. Of the millionaire he demanded restitution of his ill-gotten wealth. Of the political usurper he demanded the restoration of the liberties of the people of Florence. It is significant that the dying sinner found it easy to assent to the first, hard to consent to the second, and impossible to concede the last.

Nations rise to the climax of their life, and humanity unfolds its enormous dormant capacities, only when religion enters into a living and inspiring relation to all the rest of human life. Under an impulse which was both religious and national the little Netherlands, hardly three million people on marshy soil, resisted the greatest and richest and most relentless power of Europe for eighty years, leaped to the van of European sea power, and became the leader in the great political coalitions of Europe. Under the same unity of religious and political enthusiasm Sweden, with only a million men on rocky and snow-bound soil, came to the rescue of Protestantism under Gustavus Adolphus and dictated terms to Europe. England would have been glad to help, but was held down by the selfish dynastic policy of James I. When the religious enthusiasm of the English did get a grip on the political machinery, it made England great. It developed an incomparable army, inspired a rough country gentleman to be the greatest ruler England has ever had, raised up such statesmen, and evoked such political ideas that England ever since has been carrying out the conceptions then born. The Puritan Revolution was the starting-point of modern democracy.

Thus in past history religion has demonstrated its capacity to evoke the latent powers of humanity, and has in turn gained a fresh hold on men and rejuvenated its own life by supporting the high patriotic and social ambitions of an age. We, too, are in the midst of a vast historical movement. The historians of the future will rank it second to none. It is one of the tides in the affairs of men. If rightly directed, a little effort in this time of malleable heat will shape humanity for good more than huge labor when the iron is cold. If Christianity would now add its moral force to the social and economic forces making for a nobler organization of society, it could render such help to the cause of justice and the people as would make this a proud page in the history of the Church for our sons to read. And in turn the sweep and thrill of such a great cause would lift the Church beyond its own narrowness. If it

would stake its life in this cause of God, it would gain its life. If it follows the ways of profit and prudence, it will find its wisdom foolishness. At the beginning of the modern foreign missionary movement
the Church was full of timid scruples about its call and its ability for
such a work. Today there are few things in the life of the Church
which so inspire its finest sons and daughters and so intensify the
Christ-spirit in its whole body as this movement in which it seems to
scatter its strength abroad. If the social movement were undertaken in
a similar spirit of religious faith and daring, it would have a similar
power to re-Christianize the Church.

Individuals have long felt the enlarging and uplifting touch of the
wider mission of the Church to society, and furnish a demonstration in
their lives of the effect which such a Christ-like task would have on the
Church at large. That quickening effect is sometimes met in the most
unexpected places. For instance, one of the influences which put fire
and passion into the heart of Dwight L. Moody was the reading of the
life of the Italian revolutionist Garibaldi. What movement would seem
more purely religious than the Welsh Revival of 1904? Yet it was kin-
dled by a revelation of human democracy. At Hafod, on December 16,
1904, Evan Roberts told how the revival first reached him. One evening while at Loughor he walked from his home down to the post-
office and on his way passed a gypsy woman, who saluted him with
"Good evening, sir." Her use of "sir" in addressing a mere miner went
straight to his heart, and he asked himself why he had not said "Good
evening, madam," to the gypsy. "From that moment I felt that my
heart was full of the divine love and that I could love the whole world,
irrespective of color, creed, or nationality."[14]

In our study of the Old Testament prophets we saw that it was their
participation and leadership in a national and patriotic movement
which first lifted the prophets of Israel above the level of the professional soothsayers and mantic clairvoyants of which the surrounding
nations had plenty. It is still true that the wider social outlook is almost
invariably the condition for the prophetic gift. The men of our own
age who have had something of the prophet's vision and power of
language and inspiration have nearly all had the social enthusiasm
and faith in the reconstructive power of Christianity. Maurice and
Kingsley, Ruskin and Carlyle, Lamennais and Mazzini and Tolstoi,

were true seers of God, and they made others see. On the other hand, individualistic evangelicalism, while rich in men of piety and evangelistic fervor, has been singularly poor in the prophetic gift. It has not even welcomed prophets when they did appear. It has had so little real understanding of the ways of God in contemporary history that it has misinterpreted many of his greatest acts completely. The French Revolution has long been viewed with horror by it as an anti-Christian fury which could be explained only on the supposition of Satanic agencies. The mechanical schemes borrowed from Jewish apocalypticism are its nearest approach to an interpretation of current history from the point of view of God. Religious individualism lacks the triumphant faith in the possible sovereignty of Jesus Christ in all human affairs, and therefore it lacks the vision and the herald voice to see and proclaim his present conquest and enthronement. It lacks that vital interest in the total of human life which can create a united and harmonious and daring religious conception of the world. To those Christian men who have that today it has usually come either along the avenue of world-wide missions or of the social movement.

"No religion gains by the lapse of time; it only loses. Unless new storms pass over it and cleanse it, it will be stifled in its own dry foliage." Men are so afraid of religious vagaries, and so little afraid of religious stagnation. Yet the religion of Jesus has less to fear from sitting down to meat with publicans and sinners than from the immaculate isolation of the Pharisees. It will take care of itself if mixed into the three measures of meal; but if the leaven is kept standing by itself, it will sour hopelessly. If the Church tries to confine itself to theology and the Bible, and refuses its larger mission to humanity, its theology will gradually become mythology and its Bible a closed book. "There is no creature more fatal than your pedant; safe as he esteems himself, the terriblest issues spring from him. Human crimes are many, but the crime of being deaf to God's voice, of being blind to all but parchments and antiquarian rubrics when the divine handwriting is abroad on the sky—certainly there is no crime which the Supreme Powers do more terribly avenge!"[15]

The gospel, to have full power over an age, must be the highest expression of the moral and religious truths held by that age. If it lags behind and deals in outgrown conceptions of life and duty, it will lose power over the ablest minds and the young men first, and gradually over all. In our thought today the social problems irresistibly take the lead. If the Church has no live and bold thought on this dominant question of modern life, its teaching authority on all other questions will dwindle and be despised. It cannot afford to have young men sniff the air as in a stuffy room when they enter the sphere of religious thought. When the world is in travail with a higher ideal of justice, the Church dare not ignore it if it would retain its moral leadership. On the other hand, if the Church does incorporate the new social terms in its synthesis of truth, they are certain to throw new light on all the older elements of its teaching. The conception of race sin and race salvation becomes comprehensible once more to those who have made the idea of social solidarity in good and evil a part of their thought. The law of sacrifice loses its arbitrary and mechanical aspect when we understand the vital union of all humanity. Individualistic Christianity has almost lost sight of the great idea of the kingdom of God, which was the inspiration and center of the thought of Jesus. Social Christianity would once more enable us to understand the purpose and thought of Jesus and take the veil from our eyes when we read the Synoptic gospels.

The social crisis offers a great opportunity for the infusion of new life and power into the religious thought of the Church. It also offers the chance for progress in its life. When the broader social outlook widens the purpose of a Christian man beyond the increase of his church, he lifts up his eyes and sees that there are others who are at work for humanity besides his denomination. Common work for social welfare is the best common ground for the various religious bodies and the best training school for practical Christian unity. The strong movement for Christian union in our country has been largely prompted by the realization of social needs, and is led by men who have felt the attraction of the kingdom of God as something greater than any denomination and as the common object of all. Thus the divisions which were caused in the past by differences in dogma and church polity may perhaps be healed by unity of interest in social salvation.

As we have seen, the industrial and commercial life today is dominated by principles antagonistic to the fundamental principles of Christianity, and it is so difficult to live a Christian life in the midst of it that few men even try. If production could be organized on a basis of cooperative fraternity; if distribution could at least approximately be determined by justice; if all men could be conscious that their labor contributed to the welfare of all and that their personal well-being was dependent on the prosperity of the Commonwealth; if predatory business and parasitic wealth ceased and all men lived only by their labor; if the luxury of unearned wealth no longer made us all feverish with covetousness and a simpler life became the fashion; if our time and strength were not used up either in getting a bare living or in amassing unusable wealth and we had more leisure for the higher pursuits of the mind and the soul—then there might be a chance to live such a life of gentleness and brotherly kindness and tranquillity of heart as Jesus desired for men. It may be that the cooperative commonwealth would give us the first chance in history to live a really Christian life without retiring from the world, and would make the Sermon on the Mount a philosophy of life feasible for all who care to try.

This is the stake of the Church in the social crisis. If society continues to disintegrate and decay, the Church will be carried down with it. If the Church can rally such moral forces that injustice will be overcome and fresh red blood will course in a sounder social organism, it will itself rise to higher liberty and life. Doing the will of God it will have new visions of God. With a new message will come a new authority. If the salt loses its saltness, it will be trodden under foot. If the Church fulfills its prophetic functions, it may bear the prophet's reproach for a time, but it will have the prophet's vindication thereafter.

The conviction has always been embedded in the heart of the Church that "the world"—society as it is—is evil and sometime is to make way for a true human society in which the spirit of Jesus Christ shall rule. For fifteen hundred years those who desired to live a truly Christian life withdrew from the evil world to live a life apart. But the principle of such an ascetic departure from the world is dead in modern life. There are only two other possibilities. The Church must either condemn the world and seek to change it, or tolerate the world and conform to it. In the latter case it surrenders its holiness and its mission. The other possibility has never yet been tried with full faith on a large scale. All the leadings of God in contemporary history and all the promptings of Christ's spirit in our hearts urge us to make the trial. On this choice is staked the future of the Church.

Sounding the Trumpet Today: Changing Lives and Redeeming the Soul of Society in the 21st Century

James A. Forbes Jr.

The validity of religion itself is called into question if the social dimension of faith is diminished. Claims to have a relationship with God are discredited if such encounters do not lead believers to work for the upgrading of the quality of life in human community. How we treat one another is the most telling witness to either genuine or hypocritical faith. Individuals may find inspiration and encouragement from spiritual experiences, but the true test of spiritual maturity is whether one is led to neighborliness, compassion, justice, and respect for others.

Walter Rauschenbusch took upon himself the challenge of calling the Church to its mission of upholding the prophetic tradition as an essential aspect of conscientious Christianity. The Hebrew prophetic tradition had passionately promoted a view of religion that could not neglect the ethical and social responsibilities of those who boasted of having a covenant relationship to the liberating God of Israel. The founder of our faith was a part of this stream of Judaism. No view of Jesus could be complete that did not acknowledge his call to prayer and fruitful actions to "transform human society into the kingdom of God by regenerating all human relations and reconstituting them in accordance with the will of God" (see Introduction).

Professor Rauschenbusch, out of his broad grasp of historical precedents, knew that a tradition rarely sustains the highest level of achievement mandated by its founding principles and that the social forces of the temporal realm always function to dilute loyalty to the noblest spiritual ideals. Yet he viewed the Church as a necessary influence on society's ability to cope with the emerging problematics of social, economic, and political developments. As the Church works to call the culture to reflect values inspired by the vision of the kingdom of God, it has to remember that it is also a social institution affected by the same necessities and dynamics faced by other areas of human community. The gospel mandate for the Church to be "in but not of" the world requires that it cultivate the art of challenging the very systems that regulate property, financial investments, neighborhood design, taxes, wages, political policies, and the distribution of wealth, educational opportunity, and work. The sensibilities and sensitivities awakened by *Christianity and the Social Crisis* stimulated the growth of the Social Gospel Movement and produced some of the finest efforts of the twentieth century to embody the ideals of a more just society.

One hundred years later, a refresher course in the prophetic justice impulses of the Social Gospel is urgently needed. The twenty-first century finds our nation with a widening of the gap between the haves and the have-nots. Poverty is largely ignored. Individualism has trumped the concern for the common good. Property rights are privileged, and human rights are pushed to the back burner. Labor as a movement has become a merely tolerated stepchild. The controlling alliance between government and business operates with almost unchallengeable power. The press seems to be losing its freedom through various forms of embeddedness. The military-industrial complex and oil interests are able to preempt other social and infrastructure necessities. The language of affirmative action, safety nets, and social responsibility seems anachronistic. Minorities are disproportionately populating our prisons. The lives of the elderly and children are imperiled by the lack of food, housing, and quality health care. Electoral politics is held hostage to influence-pedaling and money deals. The delicate checks and balances of the executive, legislative, and judicial branches of government are choreographed into an awkward waltz of calculated compromises. The special interests of the powerful few rule the day, while efforts to address the environmental challenges facing our generation and future ones are postponed for a more convenient time. This is a bleak picture indeed, especially when measured by the signs of the kingdom of God.

In the face of this long list of contemporary crises, where is the Church? As was the case in the last century, the Church is largely divided over which approach will lead us beyond the perils of the present to the hope for years to come. Supporters of the revivalist impulse believe that personal conversion will lift the fallen and renew in them the values and the vitality that lead to wholesome morals and spiritual integrity. Personal human sinfulness is viewed as the central factor in the depraved quality of life unfolding in the urban enclaves of the underclass. Charity and evangelistic outreach are expected to bring the necessary repair. "Save the sinner and the society will be healed."

On the other hand, Social Gospelers are convinced that the social forces in the postmodern world are creating an environment in which the evils of the day are generated faster than individual salvation can effectively address. The most serious need is to come to a clear understanding of the destructive by-products of social, economic, and political trends. Then the people must be educated and mobilized to address the social causes undermining the fabric of the society. "Save as many sinners as you can, but sanctify the systems that regulate their lives."

Members of these two camps of the Church need to heed the wisdom of Elton Trueblood, the Quaker philosopher, who taught that the most important word in the Bible is *and*. It is not *either* personal piety *or* social witness. It is both. In his first sermon, Jesus outlined the contours of his ministry by speaking of his anointing by the Spirit *and* by setting forth a liberating agenda that announced good news to the poor and set the captives free. He urged his disciples to pray for the coming of the kingdom of God on earth as in heaven, *and* he led them to work for a world in which there would be care for the "least of these." He was more concerned about pointing out the contamination of the ritual systems of his day than admonishing his disciples to be supersensitive to the ritual of hand-washing.

What is at stake in the Church today is finding the humility to acknowledge that the best prospect of leading our society to increased justice and compassion is to hold together in vibrant tension the need for both personal spiritual renewal and radical social critique, for both personal conversion and societal transformation for peace, compassion, and justice.

The social movement on which the ministry and scholarship of Walter Rauschenbusch had so powerful an impact helped to spark a great awakening in our country. Once again the future of our nation cries out for a great spiritual awakening in which religious energy, vision, and prophetic zeal will set in motion the reform of inequities, the alleviation of social ills, and the revitalization of moral and spiritual policies and practices.

Given the pluralistic nature of our society, it is likely that such an awakening will be an interfaith renewal movement. Each of the faith traditions will be urged to offer the best wisdom of their traditions and their discernment of the causes of the malaise we are experiencing. We will listen to our interfaith colleagues give their understanding of the sources of power for deliverance from the destructive patterns of moral and spiritual decadence.

An early venture toward interfaith revitalization took place at the Riverside Church in New York City in 2005. The Dalai Lama convened representatives of many different faith traditions from around the world. Part of the liturgy for the service was the reading from sacred writings of twelve major religions. Although the verses varied in form and emphasis, each reading held up the same central tenet for all the faithful: *treating others as one would like to be treated.* One-to-one contact with God that excludes consideration for other children of faith does not meet heaven's litmus test of righteousness. Nor does it measure up to the wisdom of the world's religions. The Golden Rule connects us all. During the service we were encouraged to covenant to turn the Golden Rule into a guiding principle by which we would seek to promote peace and compassion in this age of terror and war.

Walter Rauschenbusch sounded an alarm to awaken the Church to its social responsibility. That his efforts bore fruit can be seen in the rise of the New Deal, the strengthening of the labor movement, the expansion of women's rights, the sowing of the seed for the civil rights movement, and the various expressions of liberation theology.

The Church of today is being called to sound the trumpet, as well. We may vary in the analysis and the prescription we offer, but the issues that need to be addressed are threatening our well-being with ever-increasing urgency.

During the spring and fall of 2004, I was called to be part of the "Let Justice Roll" campaign of the National Council of Churches. Supported by my congregation, I traveled across our nation promoting what I call the prophetic justice principles. I experienced a general sense of acceptance of the list of specific points, but I felt that there was a need for undergirding the principles with a sound biblical and theological foundation. I invite progressive and conservative churches to give a critical reading of this list and offer wisdom regarding how best to prepare the churches of the nation to challenge their communities with bedrock moral and spiritual reasons to change prophetic justice principles into practical policy initiatives.

Seek the common good.
Be truthful in facts and motives.
Promote unity and inclusion.
Care for the poor.
Protect the vulnerable.
Guard freedom of thought and discussion.
Respect other nations and peoples.
Ensure the stewardship of creation.
Cherish the human family.
Provide moral leadership.

On a grander scale, there are the United Nations Millennium Development Goals:

Eradicate extreme poverty and hunger.
Achieve universal primary education.
Promote gender equality and empower women.
Reduce child mortality.
Improve maternal health.
Combat HIV/AIDS, malaria, and other diseases.
Ensure environmental sustainability.
Develop a global partnership for development.

How does our faith tradition call us to champion the causes set forth in this document?

In general, the churches are called to be salt and light—not just for religious communities but for the world. What can we contribute to our society in this time of mutation of values, class struggle, and clashes of religions and cultures? Is there any word from the Lord on race, class, taxes, wages, distribution of wealth, family values, democracy, imperialism, conflict resolution, consumption of natural resources, trade, environmental responsibility, population growth, health care, political rights, HIV/AIDS, nuclear warfare, peace, prosperity, compassion, education, or responsibility for our children and the children of the world?

No one branch of the church or denomination or congregation can respond to all these issues with equal depth. Yet whatever concerns the quality of life we share together on this planet is to some degree a part of our near or distant responsibility. We cannot abdicate that responsibility because the issues are complex or because addressing them requires sacrifice. Nor can we justify retreating into private religious experience divorced from confronting the principalities and powers of social systemic evil.

We can pray and listen to the voice of the Spirit to discern what our assignment is and with whom we may be able to partner to work on improving the health of our nation. As we awaken to the power of the Spirit, we will discern that we are not left at the limits of our own mere human powers. There is the promise that a Comforter is to be with us as we pray and work for the coming of the kingdom.

Let us in our time receive the baton of courageous social witness from Walter Rauschenbusch. Let us run the race with the assurance that our faith is strong enough to change the lives of individuals and also to redeem the soul of our society. Nothing less than demonstrating the truth of this hope is our stake in the social movement.

SEVEN

What to Do

We rest our case. We have seen that in the prophetic religion of the Old Testament and in the aims of Jesus Christ the reconstruction of the whole of human life in accordance with the will of God and under the motive power of religion was the ruling purpose. Primitive Christianity, while under the fresh impulse of Jesus, was filled with social forces. In its later history the reconstructive capacities of Christianity were paralyzed by alien influences, but through the evolution of the Christian spirit in the Church it has now arrived at a stage in its development where it is fit and free for its largest social mission. At the same time Christian civilization has arrived at the great crisis of its history and is in the most urgent need of all moral power to overcome the wrongs which have throttled other nations and civilizations. The Church, too, has its own power and future at stake in the issues of social development. Thus the will of God revealed in Christ and in the highest manifestations of the religious spirit, the call of human duty, and the motives of self-protection alike summon Christian men singly and collectively to put their hands to the plow and not to look back till public morality shall be at least as much Christianized as private morality now is.

The questions then immediately confront us: What social changes would be involved in such a religious reorganization of life? What institutions and practices of our present life would have to cease? What new elements would have to be embodied? What social ideal should be the ultimate aim of Christian men, and what practical means and policies should they use for its attainment?

These questions exceed the scope of this book. This closing chapter will merely undertake to suggest in what ways the moral forces latent in Christian society can be aroused and mobilized for the progressive regeneration of social life, and in what chief directions these forces should be exerted.

"NO THOROUGHFARE"

There are certain lines of endeavor which lead nowhere. Christian men have again and again attempted to find the way out of the maze in these directions, but experience has set up the sign, No THOROUGH-FARE.

One of these futile efforts is the attempt to make economic development revert to earlier stages. Christian men of conservative spirit recoil from the swift pace and impersonal hugeness of modern industry and look back to the simpler processes and more personal contact between master and men as a better and more Christian social life. The personal interest of the intelligent Christian middle class is likely to run in the same direction. Thus in our country we have the outcry of that class against the trusts and the department stores, and the insistence on returning to the simple competition of small concerns. But it is safe to say that no such return would be permanent. These great industrial undertakings extend the area within which cooperation and the correlation of forces rule, and competition is no match for cooperation. Our effort must rather be to preserve all the benefits which the elaboration of the productive machinery has worked out, but to make these benefits enrich the many instead of the few. Reform movements arising among the business class are often reactionary; they seek to revert to outgrown conditions and turn the shadow on the dial backward. Socialism is almost unique in accepting as inevitable and desirable the essential achievements of industrial organization, but only as halfway stages toward a vaster and a far juster social system.

For the same reasons it is futile to attempt to reform modern society on biblical models. The principle underlying the Mosaic land system is wholly right. The spirit pervading the Hebrew laws protecting the laborer and the poor is so tender and noble that it puts us to shame. But these legal prescriptions were adjusted to an agricultural and stationary population, organized under patriarchal and tribal coherence, and they would be wholly unworkable under modern conditions. It is rather our business to catch the bold and humane spirit of the pro-

phetic tribunes of the people and do as well in our day as they did in
theirs. Nothing could be more valuable than to understand the social
contents of the Bible in their historical setting, and press home on the
Christian Church the essential purpose and direction of its own inspired book. But here, too, it is true that "the letter killeth; it is the
spirit that quickeneth."

One of the most persistent mistakes of Christian men has been to
postpone social regeneration to a future era to be inaugurated by the
return of Christ. In former chapters the origin of this hope and its
original beauty and power have been discussed. It was at the outset a
triumphant assertion of faith against apparent impossibilities. It still
enshrines the social hope of Christianity and concedes that sometime
the social life of men is to pass through a radical change and be ruled
by Christ. But the element of postponement in it today means a lack
of faith in the present power of Christ and paralyzes the religious initiative. It ignores the revelation of God contained in nineteen centuries of continuous history. It is careful not to see the long succession of
men and churches and movements that staked all their hopes and all
their chances of social improvement on this expectation and were dis-
appointed. It is true that any regeneration of society can come only
through the act of God and the presence of Christ; but God is now
acting, and Christ is now here. To assert that means not less faith, but
more. It is true that any effort at social regeneration is dogged by perpetual relapses and doomed forever to fall short of its aim. But the
same is true of our personal efforts to live a Christ-like life; it is true,
also, of every local church, and of the history of the Church at large.
Whatever argument would demand the postponement of social regeneration to a future era will equally demand the postponement of personal holiness to a future life. We must have the faith of the apostolic
Church in the triumph of Christ over the kingdoms of the world, *plus*
the knowledge which nineteen centuries of history have given to us.
Unless we add that knowledge, the faith of the apostles becomes our
unbelief.

Another cul-de-sac of Christian endeavor is the organization of
communistic colonies. There is no reason why a number of Christian
people should not live in commons or organize for cooperative production if they can hope to make their life more comfortable, more

free from care, and more moral in its relations. But past experience does not show that such colonies served to Christianize social life at large. The example is not widely contagious, even if the colony is successful. If the experiment fails through any of a hundred practical causes, its failure is heralded as a convincing demonstration that competition is the only orthodox and successful basis of society. Settlements with some communistic features are likely to increase in the future as the eyes of cultured people are opened to the wastefulness and unhappiness of ordinary life, and they may be exceedingly useful if they gather like-minded men and women in groups, and thus intensify and clarify their convictions by intercourse. But they will be influential on a large scale only if the ideas and experiences wrought out in these settlements find channels to run out freely into the general unregenerate life through books, newspapers, or lectures issuing from the settlement. In the main, the salt of the earth will do its work best if it is not stored in casks by itself, but rubbed in evenly and generously where it is most needed. The mass of society will ponderously move an inch where a select colony might spurt a mile toward the future; but the total gain in foot-pounds will be greater in the mass-movement. The cooperative stores in England and on the continent are a far more hopeful and influential education in the cooperative principle than the communistic colonies have been, because they are built into the mass of the general life.

If the Church should in the future really seek to Christianize social life, it will almost certainly be tempted to make itself the chief agent and beneficiary of the process. Attempts will be made to organize ecclesiastical duplicates of fraternal insurance societies, cooperative undertakings, labor bureaus, etc. There will be Christian socialist parties in politics. The Church will claim to be the only agency through which social salvation can come. It will seek to keep the social movement under clerical control. This effort will be prompted partly by the desire to put its organized power at the service of the poor; partly by the fear of non-Christian or anti-Christian influences which may dominate social radicalism; and partly by the instinct of self-assertion, self-protection, and self-aggrandizement which resides in every social organization. Just as the desire to save individuals is now frequently vitiated by the anxiety to increase church membership, so the desire to save social life may be vitiated by the anxiety to keep the Church to the front. Those ecclesiastical bodies which have the strongest church-consciousness are most likely to insist that this work shall be done through them or not at all. The history of the social movement in Europe has furnished most interesting and significant demonstrations of this tendency. But it is full of peril not only to the Church, but to the social movement itself. It beclouds the social issues by ecclesiastical interests and jealousies. It subtly and unconsciously changes the aim from the salvation of the people to the salvation of the Church. The social movement could have no more powerful ally than religious enthusiasm; it could have no more dangerous ally than ecclesiasticism. If the Church truly desires to save the social life of the people, it must be content with inspiring the social movement with religious faith and daring, and it must not attempt to control and monopolize it for its own organization. If a man wants to give honest help, he must fill himself with the spirit of Jesus and divest himself of the ecclesiastical point of view.

SOCIAL REPENTANCE AND FAITH

In personal religion the first requirement is to repent and believe in the gospel. As long as a man is self-righteous and complacently satisfied with his moral attainments, there is no hope that he will enter into the higher development, and unless he has faith that a higher level of spiritual life is attainable, he will be lethargic and stationary.

Social religion, too, demands repentance and faith: repentance for our social sins; faith in the possibility of a new social order. As long as a man sees in our present society only a few inevitable abuses and recognizes no sin and evil deep-seated in the very constitution of the present order, he is still in a state of moral blindness and without conviction of sin. Those who believe in a better social order are often told that they do not know the sinfulness of the human heart. They could justly retort the charge on the men of the evangelical school. When the latter deal with public wrongs, they often exhibit a curious unfamiliarity with the forms which sin assumes there, and sometimes reverently bow before one of the devil's spiderwebs, praising it as one of the mighty works of God. Regeneration includes that a man must pass under the domination of the spirit of Christ, so that he will judge of life as Christ would judge of it. That means a revaluation of social values. Things that are now "exalted among men" must become "an abomination" to him because they are built on wrong and misery. Unless a man finds his judgment at least on some fundamental questions in opposition to the current ideas of the age, he is still a child of this world and has not "tasted the powers of the coming age." He will have to repent and believe if he wants to be a Christian in the full sense of the world.

No man can help the people until he is himself free from the spell which the present order has cast over our moral judgment. We have repeatedly pointed out that every social institution weaves a protecting integument of glossy idealization about itself like a colony of tent-caterpillars in an apple tree. For instance, wherever militarism rules, war is idealized by monuments and paintings, poetry and song. The stench of the hospitals and the maggots of the battlefield are passed in silence, and the imagination of the people is filled with waving plumes and the shout of charging columns. A Russian general thought Verestchagin's[1] pictures ought to be destroyed because they disenchanted the people. If war is ever to be relegated to the limbo of outgrown barbarism, we must shake off its magic. When we comprehend how few wars have ever been fought for the sake of justice or the people; how personal spite, the ambition of military professionals, and the protection of capitalistic ventures are the real moving powers; how the governing classes pour out the blood and wealth of nations for private ends and exude patriotic enthusiasm like a squid secreting ink to hide its retreat—then the mythology of war will no longer bring us to our knees, and we shall fail to get drunk with the rest when martial intoxication sweeps the people off their feet.

In the same way we shall have to see through the fictions of capitalism. We are assured that the poor are poor through their own fault; that rent and profits are the just dues of foresight and ability; that the immigrants are the cause of corruption in our city politics; that we cannot compete with foreign countries unless our working class will descend to the wages paid abroad. These are all very plausible assertions, but they are lies dressed up in truth. There is a great deal of conscious lying. Industrialism as a whole sends out deceptive prospectuses just like single corporations within it. But in the main these misleading theories are the complacent self-deception of those who profit by present conditions and are loath to believe that their life is working harm. It is very rare for a man to condemn the means by which he makes a living, and we must simply make allowance for the warping influence of self-interest when he justifies himself and not believe him entirely.[2] In the early part of the nineteenth century, when tiny children in England were driven to the looms with whips, and women lost even the physical appearance of womanhood in the coal mines, the owners insisted that English industry would be ruined by the proposed reform laws, and doubtless they thought so. If men holding stock in traction companies assert that municipal ownership is un-American; if the express companies say that parcels cannot be carried below their own amazing rates; if Mr. Baer[3] in the midst of the coal strike assured a minister that "God in his infinite wisdom had given control of the property interests of the country" to him and his associates and they would do all things well—we must simply allow for the warping effect of self-interest and pass on to the order of the day. Macaulay said that the doctrine of gravitation would not yet be accepted if it had interfered with vested interests.

The greatest contribution which any man can make to the social movement is the contribution of a regenerated personality, of a will which sets justice above policy and profit, and of an intellect emancipated from falsehood. Such a man will in some measure incarnate the principles of a higher social order in his attitude to all questions and in all his relations to men, and will be a well-spring of regenerating influences. If he speaks, his judgment will be a corrective force. If he listens, he will encourage the truth-teller and discourage the peddler of adulterated facts and maxims. If others lose heart, he will stay them with his inspired patience. If any new principle is to gain power in human history, it must take shape and life in individuals who have faith in it. The men of faith are the living spirits, the channels by which new truth and power from God enter humanity. To repent of our collective social sins, to have faith in the possibility and reality of a divine life in humanity, to submit the will to the purposes of the kingdom of God, to permit the divine inspiration to emancipate and clarify the moral insight—this is the most intimate duty of the religious man who would help to build the coming Messianic era of mankind.

SOCIAL EVANGELIZATION

The men who have worked out the new social Christianity in their own thinking and living constitute a new type of Christian. At a religious convention it is easy to single out the speakers who have had a vision of the social redemption of humanity. No matter what subject they handle, they handle it with a different grasp. Their horizon is wider; their sympathy more catholic; their faith more daring. It is significant that they predominate when speakers are selected for important occasions. The men of natural ability and idealism are most receptive to the prophetic ideas now dawning, and in turn these ideas enlarge and lift the mind that harbors them, so that even those who do not think that way pay the tribute of attention when they speak.

But that type propagates itself. Mankind is so closely bound together that no man lives to himself, and no man is saved to himself alone. The new salvation is contagious. Those who have wrought out a faith that embraces the salvation of all human relations make it easier for others to reach the same unification of all relations in the great aim of the kingdom of God. There will be a social evangelization, consciously and unconsciously. The believers will win other believers.

The young men will respond, and there is no telling to what a young man will rise if the divine aim and impulse are in him. "*L'homme, l'homme lui-même est une quantité indéterminable.*"[4] Such young minds are "the hidden germs of fresh humanities, the hidden founts of gathering river-floods." After twenty or thirty years the young men who now embrace the new social faith will be in the controlling positions in society and will carry into practice some fractional part of the ideals of their youth. Few may preserve them uncontaminated to the end; they will compromise; they may surrender; but they can never be quite the same again. The men and women of Brook Farm[5] did not all remain faithful to their early idealism, but they have left their impress on the country for good. The revolutionists of 1848 did not all remain revolutionists, but it is strange to see how many of the poets and statesmen and educators who had something of the divine afflatus in the latter half of the nineteenth century had nourished the revolutionary enthusiasm in their hearts in the earlier half of the century.[6] A surprising number of the men who are foremost in the present struggle in our own country to reconquer for the people some of the political powers and economic privileges bartered away by a former generation, have been under the influence of the movement led by Henry George and of the diluted socialism following that.

It has always been recognized that the creation of regenerate personalities, pledged to righteousness, is one of the most important services which the Church can render to social progress. But regeneration merely creates the will to do the right; it does not define for a man what is right. That is defined for him in the main by the religious community whose ideas he accepts. If his church community demands total abstinence from liquor, he will consider that as part of the Christian life; if it sanctions slavery or polygamy, he will consider them good. While the Church was swayed by ascetic ideas, the dedication of the will to God meant surrender to the monastic life. In the past the Church has largely connected the idea of religious duty with the service of the Church. It has made itself the *summum bonum*, the embodiment of all religious aims. To that extent it has monopolized for itself the power of devotion begotten in regenerated hearts and has not directed that incalculable force toward social and political affairs. Now that the idea of social salvation is taking hold of us, the realm of duty spread before a mind dedicating itself to God's service is becoming more inclusive. The social work of the YMCA and YWCA, of the Salvation Army and the Volunteers of America, of the social settlements and institutional churches, shows what is coming. It is significant that several new religious sects have embodied the social ideal in their religious aims. If the Church in any measure will lay consecrating hands on those who undertake social redemption, it will hallow their work and give it religious dignity and joy. And when politicians and social exploiters have to deal with the stubborn courage of men who pray about their politics, they will have a new factor to reckon with.

The older conception of religion viewed as religious only what ministered to the souls of men or what served the Church. When a man attended the services of the Church, contributed money to its work, taught in Sunday-school, spoke to the unconverted, or visited the sick, he was doing religious work. The conscientiousness with which he did his daily work also had a religious quality. On the other hand, the daily work itself, the plowing, building, cobbling, or selling, were secular, and the main output of his life was not directly a contribution to the kingdom of God, but merely the necessary method of getting a living for himself and his family. The ministry alone and a few allied callings had the uplifting consciousness of serving God in the total of daily work. A few professions were marked off as holy, just as in past stages of religion certain groves and temples were marked out as holy ground where God could be sought and served.

If now we could have faith enough to believe that all human life can be filled with divine purpose; that God saves not only the soul, but the whole of human life; that anything which serves to make men healthy, intelligent, happy, and good is a service to the Father of men; that the kingdom of God is not bounded by the Church, but includes all human relations—then all professions would be hallowed and receive religious dignity. A man making a shoe or arguing a law case or planting potatoes or teaching school could feel that this was itself a contribution to the welfare of mankind, and indeed his main contribution to it.

But such a view of our professional life would bring it under religious scrutiny. If a man's calling consisted in manufacturing or selling useless or harmful stuff, he would find himself unable to connect it with his religion. Insofar as the energy of business life is expended in crowding out competitors, it would also be outside of the sanction of religion, and religious men would be compelled to consider how industry and commerce could be reorganized so that there would be a maximum of service to humanity and a minimum of antagonism between those who desire to serve it. As soon as religion will set the kingdom of God before it as the all-inclusive aim, and will define it so as to include all rightful relations among men, the awakened conscience will begin to turn its searchlight on the industrial and commercial life in detail, and will insist on eliminating all professions which harm instead of helping, and on coordinating all productive activities to secure a maximum of service. That in itself would produce a quiet industrial revolution.

Scatter through all classes and professions a large number of men and women whose eyes have had a vision of a true human society and who have faith in it and courage to stand against anything that contradicts it, and public opinion will have a new swiftness and tenacity in judging on right and wrong. The murder of the Armenians, the horrors of the Congo Free State, the ravages of the liquor traffic in Africa, the peace movement, the protest against child labor in America, the movement for early closing of retail stores—all these things arouse only a limited number of persons to active sympathy; the rest are lethargic. It takes so long to "work up public sentiment," and even then it stops boiling as fast as a kettle of water taken off the fire. There are so many Christian people and such feeble sentiment on public wrongs. It is not because people are not good enough, but because their goodness has not been directed and educated in this direction. The multiplication of socially enlightened Christians will serve the body of society much as a physical organism would be served if a complete and effective system of ganglia should be distributed where few of them existed. The social body needs moral innervation; and the spread of men who combine religious faith, moral enthusiasm, and economic information, and apply the combined result to public morality, promises to create a moral sensitiveness never yet known.

THE PULPIT AND THE SOCIAL QUESTION

The new evangel of the kingdom of God will have to be carried into the common consciousness of Christendom by the personal faith and testimony of the ordinary Christian man. It is less connected with the ministrations of the Church and therefore will be less the business of the professional ministry than the old evangel of the saved soul. It is a call to Christianize the everyday life, and the everyday man will have to pass on the call and make plain its meaning. But if the pulpit is willing to lend its immense power of proclamation and teaching, it will immeasurably speed the spread of the new conceptions. "With the assistance of the clergy everything in matters of social reforms is easy; without such help, or in spite of it, all is difficult and at times impossible."[7]

None can deny that the pulpit has the teaching function, and that its obligation runs wherever a moral question can be raised. Those who think the institutional Church a departure from the spiritual mission of the Church, must concede all the more that the Church should teach plainly on the moral causes and remedies of social misery. If the Church is not to deal with mass poverty by its organized work, its obligation is all the greater to deal with it by the sword of the word. Preaching on social questions is not an innovation in the history of the pulpit. The Church Fathers, the great medieval preachers, the leaders of the Reformation—all dealt more boldly with public questions than the classical sermonizers of the generations just preceding ours.[8] In all the history of preaching the pulpit has perhaps never been so silent in this direction as in the nineteenth century before the social movement began to affect Christian thought.

Of all moral questions none are so pressing today as the questions of public morality. On none is there greater confusion of thought, less fixity of conviction, and greater need of clear thought and wise teaching. What right have Christian ministers to back away from these questions and refuse to contribute whatever moral discernment God has given them?

It is true enough that social preaching has often been badly done. It has often been ignorant, bitter, partisan, and nonreligious. But if it has been done badly by the few who stood alone in attempting it, that is all the more reason why all should develop greater wisdom by common experience.

There are preachers who undertake to discuss the largest social questions with the air of a specialist and the knowledge of a tyro. I knew a man who preached a course of sermons on social questions after reading his first book on the subject. He may have been equally rash in discussing the ways of the Almighty, but God is patient and does not talk back. Men are more sensitive when they hear a half-true dissection of the methods by which they get their living. If a lawyer misstates the facts in court, the attorney for the other side will be eager to point out his error. If a minister talks foolishness in the pulpit, his hearers have to suffer in silence without the satisfaction of setting him right. He has a perilous immunity from contradiction and for that very reason is in honor bound to be careful. In general, it is safe to advise a man who feels "the burden of the Lord" on social wrongs to go slowly and get adequate information, especially in political economy and the history of social institutions. It is more sensible in every sermon to show the larger application of the truth to social morality than to spill out the entire tub of his mind in a course of sermons on social subjects. The former is also a severer test of his comprehension of the subject. On the other hand, he should not let the fire of the Lord cool down. If he delays utterance, it should be to speak the more forcibly and wisely when he does speak. He should not take counsel of his timidity nor wait till he is infallible. Those who hold a brief for vested wrongs are not overconscientious.

Men who first begin to discuss social wrongs are likely to launch into personal invectives against prominent individuals. This tendency is in part a product of our religious individualism. We have always been told that if only all individuals were regenerated and lived right, all social questions would be solved. Consequently when we see wrong done, we feel that it must be due to the personal wickedness of individuals. But the farther a man goes in his comprehension of the questions before us, the more will he realize that the great leaders of industry are not committing mischief for the fun of it, but that they are themselves the victims of social forces. They are free only within very contracted limits. In underpaying and overworking his men, or in employing women and children, the man with kind intentions is pushed by the entire group to which he belongs. In competition the most ruthless man sets the pace. Corporate management eliminates personal sympathy and the individual sense of honor to a degree which many of us hardly understand. The moral code of the businessman is largely shaped for him by the moral code of his class. If he bribes public officials, it is often hard to say if he is a corrupter of innocence or the victim of blackmail. If he breaks the law, it may be because the law is a formulation of outgrown conditions which has to be broken if commercial development is to make headway.

A businessman may be the victim of evil hitherto done by all, or the cause of evil henceforth done by all. He may yield to the pressure of evil with alacrity because it offers him profit, or he may yield with a heavy heart because it seems the lesser evil of two between which he must choose. By these questions God will judge him. But if man undertakes to judge him, he must do it in love and mercy and with self-accusation, because we have all jointly spun the fatal web of temptation in which the sinner is entangled. The community is *particeps criminis* with the individual in almost every sin that is committed. The girl who drifts into shame because no happy marriage is open to her; the boy who runs into youthful criminality because he has no outlet for his energies except the street; the great financial operator who organizes deceptive moments in the stock market and fleeces the mass who are crazy for unearned gain—they can justly turn against us all and say, "You have led us into temptation."

It is not only unjust but unwise to make a prominent individual the scapegoat for the sin of all. If people are led to think that an evil is the personal product of one man or a small group of men, their attention will be diverted from the deeper causes which produced these men and would have produced others of the same kind if these had never existed.

Any preacher dealing with social questions is certain to be charged with partiality. The wider our social cleavage, the more difficult will it be to satisfy both sides. Nor is it his business to try trimming and straddling. He must seek to hew as straight as the moral law. Let others voice special interests; the minister of Jesus Christ must voice the mind of Jesus Christ. His strength will lie in the high impartiality of moral insight and love to all.

But if he really follows the mind of Christ, he will be likely to take the side of the poor in most issues. The poor are likely to be the wronged. Almost any man will concede that in past history the poor have been oppressed, and that in foreign countries they are now being oppressed. Wherever the situation is far enough away to allow us to be impartial, we see correctly. But that constitutes a presumption that the same situation exists in our own country. The saying of Mirabeau is as true as any other historical maxim, "When the people have complained, the people have always been right." The strong have ample means of defending all their just interests and usually enough power left to guard their unjust interests, too. Those who have been deprived of intelligence, education, and property need such championship as the ministers of Jesus Christ can give them, and any desire to pardon and excuse should be exercised on their belief.

As things are, a minister will have to make a conscious effort if he is to be fair to the poor. The daily press, public opinion, custom, literature, orthodox economic science, and nearly all the forces which shape thought, are on the side of things as they are. Unless a minister consciously puts himself into contact with the working classes by attending their meetings and reading their literature, he will assume that he is judging fairly, whereas he has never heard more than one side. If he attends the dinners of the Chamber of Commerce, he must take socialist street meetings as an antidote. Socialism has fully as much claim on his intellect as Robert Browning.[9]

If a man follows the mind of Jesus Christ in his judgments, he will have to appear partial in a social world which is by no means built on a line with the mind of Christ. It is a different matter entirely for a minister to follow the mind of a political party and make himself liable to the charge of partisanship. It may happen at long intervals in the history of a nation that a political party so thoroughly embodies the righteous instincts of the nation that its cause is almost identified with the triumph of justice. In such a juncture a minister may wisely decide that he must throw his influence publicly with that party and risk a loss of influence in other directions. But it is questionable if that situation has confronted ministers in our country these many years. A man may well doubt if the machinery of our great parties has ground out social progress or ground it up, and whether party loyalty has propagated patriotism or poisoned it.

A minister has no business to be the megaphone of a political party and its catchwords. He should rather be the master of politics by creating the issues which parties will have to espouse. Questions are usually discussed a long time before they become political issues. Old political parties are controlled by conservative forces and will take up progressive measures only when it is necessary to retain their followers or outbid another party. The time for the pulpit to do its best work is before a question is torn to tatters on the platform. A Christian preacher should have the prophetic insight which discerns and champions the right before others see it. If he has honestly done that, he can afford to be silent when the "practical men" grumblingly enter to finish up the job which he has helped to lay out for them. Hail to the pioneers! The early work is the formative work. Embodying a moral conviction in law is the last stage of a moral propaganda. Laws do not create moral convictions; they merely recognize and enforce them.

Moreover, there are important political questions which never become party issues. The eradication of tuberculosis, for instance, is a public task for the next decade. But the creation of public sanitariums for the infected, and the enforcement of sanitary regulations for the prevention of the disease, will never become a party question. Strong pressure will be brought to bear on legislatures and public officials to protect the financial interests of tenement-house owners who propagate tuberculosis by their death-traps, but no party will dare openly to champion their cause. If the pulpit creates the public sentiment which will insist on the enactment and enforcement of such laws and ordinances, it will not be meddling with party politics.

One of the most serious charges that can be raised against preaching on social questions is that it is unreligious. It is the business of a preacher to connect all that he thinks and says with the mind and will of God, to give the religious interpretation to all human relations and questions, and to infuse the divine sympathy and passion into all moral discussions. If he fails in that, he is to that extent not a minister of religion. It is the highest test of his influence if his pastoral visits, his chance conversations, and his pulpit teachings somehow help men and women to take the high and divine view of their past and their future, of their joys and their sorrows, of their labors and their pleasures. That test is justly applied to his teachings on social questions, too. Others can talk from the point of view of economic and political expediency; does the minister talk from the point of view of the eternally true and right?

In passing judgment on a preacher's work by that canon we shall have to remember, however, that religion and public questions have so long been divorced that it requires a strong and independent religious nature to carry the religious spirit freely into the discussion of public questions. If a man can make his hearers feel that they are in the presence of God when he discusses the condition of the working girls or the drift of the city administration, he gives proof of unusual qualities. It was evidence of religious genius when Jeremiah carried religion out of national life into the experiences of the suffering individual soul. Today it is evidence of spontaneous religious power if a man can carry religion from private experience into national life.

His hearers, too, are likely to mistake their own customs for the whole range of religion. Because they have not been accustomed to hear such questions discussed in the pulpit, they feel that the preacher is dragging in alien and nonreligious matters. When the "Evangelical movement" swept over the Church of England, and ministers once more preached personal repentance and conversion, Lord Melbourne is said to have risen from his pew and stalked down the aisle, angrily exclaiming, "Things have come to a pretty pass when religion is made to invade the sphere of private life."

At any rate, social questions cannot be more nonreligious than many of the things about which ministers have to talk in the pulpit. If it is religious to advocate rebuilding a church, why is it nonreligious to advocate tearing down and rebuilding slum districts? If it is religious to encourage the church to recarpet the aisles and cushion the seats for the feet and backs of the worshipers, why is it nonreligious to speak of playgrounds for young feet and old-age pensions for aged backs?

Social preaching has come under suspicion because experience has shown that when a preacher begins to speak on social questions, he is apt to veer away from the established course and fly off on a tangent. The new ideas take such hold on him that all other Christian truth seems stale and outworn in comparison. His preaching becomes one-sided. He twangs on a harp of a single string, and it becomes a weariness. If he encounters coldness, he may shake the dust of the Church from his feet in witness that it has once more cast out its prophets.

Such cases are held up as proof that social questions are forbidden ground. They are indeed profoundly pathetic. These men are the explorers who travel along the unblazed trails where in coming days the highways of the Church will run, and explorers are apt to leave their graves as way-marks for those who come after. It is easy enough to march steadily on a beaten road and in the rank and file of a regiment. If these social preachers were not so alone, they would not go astray as they do. If they found many other ministers thinking the same thoughts, they could exchange and correct their ideas, and the future would not seem so dark. Thus the guilt for their aberrations rests in part on all of us who have shirked our duty and lagged behind. It may be that some of these men are naturally unstable and self-confident. But that is the stuff of which pioneers are usually made. Our Western pioneers were the venturesome pick; the solid people stayed at home. Abraham, who was the father of all men of faith, was also the father of pioneers, striking off into the unknown at the call of an inner voice, and perhaps some of his friends in Haran hinted that he was a rolling stone and "lacked common sense." It may be that God will find more virtue in the impetuous faults of these pioneers of social Christianity than in the faultless prudence of their critics. Balance was hardly the distinguishing quality of the Old Testament prophets, and yet they are commonly supposed to have been good for something.

It is doubtless true that the interest in the social question is apt to overshadow the other aspects of religion. Absorbed in public questions, such men may forget to appeal to the individual soul for repentance and to comfort those in sorrow. That is a sore defect. The human soul with its guilt and its longing for holiness and deathless life is a permanent fact in religion, and no social perfection will quench its hunger for the living God. There was no chance for Christianizing public life on the island where Robinson Crusoe lived alone with his parrot and his cats, but when Crusoe began to read his Bible and won through to repentance for his past and faith in God, it was a triumph of religion.

There are two great entities in human life—the human soul and the human race—and religion is to save both. The soul is to seek righteousness and eternal life; the race is to seek righteousness and the kingdom of God. The social preacher is apt to overlook the one. But the evangelical preacher has long overlooked the other. It is due to that protracted neglect that we are now deluged by the social problem in its present acute form. It is partly due to the same neglect that our churches are overwhelmingly feminine. Woman nurtures the individual in the home, and God has equipped her with an intuitive insight into the problems of the individual life. Man's life faces the outward world, and his instincts and interests lie that way. Hence men crowd where public questions get downright discussion. Our individualistic religion has helped to feminize our churches. A very protracted one-sidedness in preaching has to be balanced up, and if some now go to the other extreme, those who have created the situation hardly have the right to cast the first stone.

It seems likely that even after this present inequality of emphasis is balanced, some preachers will put more stress on the social aspects of religion. In that case we must apply Paul's large and tolerant principle, "There are diversities of gifts, but the same Spirit." Some by nature and training have the gift of dealing with individuals and the loving insight into personal needs; others have the passionate interest in the larger life and its laws. The Church needs evangelists and pastors, but it needs prophets, too.

If a minister uses the great teaching powers of the pulpit sanely and wisely to open the minds of the people to the moral importance of the social questions, he may be of the utmost usefulness in the present crisis. Intelligent men who live in the midst of social problems do not yet know that there is a social problem, just as one may pass among the noises and sights of a city street without noticing them.[10] If the minister can simply induce his more intelligent hearers to focus what is in their very field of vision, thereafter they cannot help seeing it, and information will begin to collect automatically in their minds. The Church itself has riveted the attention of the people on other aspects of life hitherto and thereby has diverted their attention from the social problems. It ought to make up for this.

A minister mingling with both classes can act as an interpreter to both. He can soften the increasing class hatred of the working class. He can infuse the spirit of moral enthusiasm into the economic struggle of the dispossessed and lift it to something more than a "stomach question." On the other hand, among the well-to-do, he can strengthen the consciousness that the working people have a real grievance and so increase the disposition to make concessions in practical cases and check the inclination to resort to force for the suppression of discontent. If the ministry would awaken among the wealthy a sense of social compunction and moral uneasiness, that alone might save our nation from a revolutionary explosion. It would be of the utmost importance to us all if the inevitable readjustment could be secured by a continuous succession of sensible demands on the one side and willing concessions on the other. We can see now that a little more wisdom and justice on both sides might have found a peaceable solution for the great social problem of slavery. Instead of that the country was plunged into the Civil War with its fearful cost in blood and wealth. We have been cursed for a generation with the legacy of sectional hatred, and the question of the status of the black race has not been solved even at such cost. If Pharaoh again hardens his heart, he will again have to weep for his firstborn and be whelmed in the Red Sea. It is a question if we can rally enough moral insight and goodwill to create a peaceable solution, or if the Bourbon spirit is to plunge our nation into a long-continued state of dissolution and anarchy which the mind shrinks from contemplating. The influence of the Christian ministry, if exercised in the spirit of Christian democracy, might be one of the most powerful solvents and the decisive influence for peace.

THE CHRISTIAN CONCEPTION OF
LIFE AND PROPERTY

The spiritual force of Christianity should be turned against the materialism and mammonism of our industrial and social order.

If a man sacrifices his human dignity and self-respect to increase his income, or stunts his intellectual growth and his human affections to swell his bank account, he is to that extent serving mammon and denying God. Likewise if he uses up and injures the life of his fellow men to make money for himself, he serves mammon and denies God. But our industrial order does both. It makes property the end, and man the means to produce it.

Man is treated as a *thing* to produce more things. Men are hired as hands and not as men. They are paid only enough to maintain their working capacity and not enough to develop their manhood. When their working force is exhausted, they are flung aside without consideration of their human needs. Jesus asked, "Is not a man more than a sheep?" Our industry says, "No." It is careful of its livestock and machinery, and careless of its human working force. It keeps its electrical engines immaculate in burnished cleanliness and lets its human dynamos sicken in dirt. In the Fifteenth Assembly District in New York City, between Tenth and Eleventh Avenues, 1,321 families in 1896 had three bathtubs between them. Our industrial establishments are institutions for the creation of dividends, and not for the fostering of human life. In all our public life the question of profit is put first. Pastor Stöcker,[11] in a speech on child and female labor in the German Reichstag, said: "We have put the question the wrong way. We have asked: How much child and female labor does industry need in order to flourish, to pay dividends, and to sell goods abroad? Whereas we ought to have asked: How ought industry to be organized in order to protect and foster the family, the human individual, and the Christian life?" That simple reversal of the question marks the difference between the Christian conception of life and property and the mammonistic.

"Life is more than food and raiment." More, too, than the apparatus which makes food and raiment. What is all the machinery of our industrial organization worth if it does not make human life healthful and happy? But is it doing that? Men are first of all men, folks, members of our human family. To view them first of all as labor-force is civilized barbarism. It is the attitude of the exploiter. Yet unconsciously we have all been taught to take that attitude and talk of men as if they were horsepowers or volts. Our commercialism has tainted our sense of fundamental human verities and values. We measure our national prosperity by pig-iron and steel instead of by the welfare of the people. In city affairs the property owners have more influence than the family owners. For instance, the pall of coal smoke hanging over our industrial cities is injurious to the eyes; it predisposes to diseases of the respiratory organs; it depresses the joy of living; it multiplies the labor of housewives in cleaning and washing. But it continues because it would impose expense on business to install smoke consumers or pay skilled stokers. If an agitation is begun to abolish the smoke nuisance, the telling argument is not that it inflicts injury on the mass of human life, but that the smoke "hurts business," and that it really "pays" to consume the wasted carbon. In political life one can constantly see the cause of human life pleading long and vainly for redress, like the widow before the unjust judge. Then suddenly comes the bass voice of Property, and all men stand with hat in hand.

Our scientific political economy has long been an oracle of the false god. It has taught us to approach economic questions from the point of view of goods and not of man. It tells us how wealth is produced and divided and consumed by man, and not how man's life and development can best be fostered by material wealth. It is significant that the discussion of "Consumption" of wealth has been most neglected in political economy; yet that is humanly the most important of all. Theology must become Christocentric; political economy must become anthropocentric. Man is Christianized when he puts God before self; political economy will be Christianized when it puts man before wealth. Socialistic political economy does that. It is materialistic in its theory of human life and history, but it is humane in its aims, and to that extent is closer to Christianity than the orthodox science has been.

It is the function of religion to teach the individual to value his soul more than his body, and his moral integrity more than his income. In the same way it is the function of religion to teach society to value human life more than property, and to value property only insofar as it forms the material basis for the higher development of human life. When life and property are in apparent collision, life must take precedence. This is not only Christian but prudent. When commercialism in its headlong greed deteriorates the mass of human life, it defeats its own covetousness by killing the goose that lays the golden egg. Humanity is that goose—in more senses than one. It takes faith in the moral law to believe that this penny-wise craft is really suicidal folly, and to assert that wealth which uses up the people paves the way to beggary. Religious men have been cowed by the prevailing materialism and arrogant selfishness of our business world. They should have the courage of religious faith and assert that "man liveth not by bread alone," but by doing the will of God, and that the life of a nation "consisteth not in the abundance of things" which it produces, but in the way men live justly with one another and humbly with their God.

THE CREATION OF CUSTOMS AND INSTITUTIONS

When the social activity of the Church is discussed, it is usually assumed that the churches are to influence legislation and to watch over the execution of the laws. The churches are within their rights in doing both. There are probably few denominations which would hesitate a moment to fling their full force on a legislature if the tenure of their property or the freedom of their church administration were threatened. If it is right to lobby in their own behalf, it cannot well be wrong to lobby on behalf of the people.

But we have an exaggerated idea of the importance of laws. Our legislative bodies are the greatest law factories the world has ever seen. Our zest for legislation blinds us to the subtle forces behind and beyond the law. Those influences which really make and mar human happiness and greatness are beyond the reach of the law. The law can compel a man to support his wife, but it cannot compel him to love her, and what are ten dollars a week to a woman whose love lies in broken shards at her feet? The law can compel a father to provide for his children and can interfere if he maltreats them, but it cannot compel him to give them that loving fatherly intercourse which puts backbone into a child forever. The law can keep neighbors from trespassing, but it cannot put neighborly courtesy and goodwill into their relations. The State can establish public schools and hire teachers, but it cannot put enthusiasm and moral power into their work; yet those are the qualities which distinguish the few true teachers to whom we look back in after years as the real makers of our lives. The highest qualities and influences are beyond the law and must be created elsewhere.

The law is a moral agency, as effective and as rough as a policeman's club, sweeping in its operation and unable to adjust itself to individual needs and the finer shadings of moral life. It furnishes the stiff skeleton of public morality which supports the finer tissues, but these tissues must be deposited by other forces. The State is the outer court of the moral law; within stands the sanctuary of the Spirit. Religion creates morality, and morality then deposits a small part of its contents in written laws. The State can protect the existing morality and promote the coming morality, but the vital creative force of morality lies deeper.

The law becomes impotent if it is not supported by a diffused, spontaneous moral impulse in the community. If religion implants love, mutual helpfulness, and respect for the life and rights of others, there will be little left to do for the law and its physical force. The stronger the silent moral compulsion of the community, the less need for the physical compulsion of the State. If parents have to resort to physical punishment constantly, it furnishes presumptive evidence that their training has been defective in its moral factors. If we have to order out the militia frequently to quell riots and protect property, it constitutes a charge of inefficiency against the religious and educational institutions of the community.

Thus it is clear that the Church has a large field for social activity before touching legislation. It cannot make laws, but it can make customs, and *quid leges sine moribus?* Of what avail are laws without customs? Our two words *morals* and *ethics*, the one from the Latin and the other from the Greek, both mean "that which is customary." There

is a singular lack of appreciation in American thought for the importance of custom; possibly because in our new and plastic life customs
are less rigid and formative than anywhere on earth. Yet our life, too, is
ruled largely by unenacted laws. Our helpfulness toward children and
old people, our respect for womanhood and the consequent unparalleled freedom of woman's social intercourse, the comparative disappearance of profanity and obscenity from conversation—all this rests
on custom and not on law, and these customs are in large part the
product of purified modern religion. The disappearance of alcoholic
liquors from the homes of great strata of our people is in most locali-
ties due to custom rather than law. Religion first demanded it, and educational, scientific, and economic motives have since reinforced the
custom. Religion first created the custom of Sunday rest and the law
then protected it. The weekly rest day is a gift of religion to the people.
If it was not already so firmly established in our life, it would be almost
impossible to wrest one full day from the whirl of modern commercialism. The law did not create Sunday rest; neither is it able to maintain its finer qualities. It can prohibit work, but it cannot prescribe
how the day shall be spent.

It is entirely feasible for the Church to mitigate the social hardships
of the working classes by lending force to humane customs. Its help
would make the Saturday half holiday in summer practicable. It could
ease the strain of the Christmas shopping season. It could secure seats
and restrooms for the girls in the department stores. It could counteract the tendency of tenement owners to crowd the people. It could
encourage employers in making a place for their aged employees and
discourage the early exploitation of children. A single frank and prayer-
ful discussion of one of these questions in a social meeting of the
church or its societies would create more social morality and good
custom than many columns in the newspapers. Such an activity would
not solve the fundamental questions of capitalism, but it would ease
the pressure a little and would save the people from deterioration,
while the social movement is moving toward the larger solution.

Good customs are perpetually in danger, and the Church can act as
a conservative influence in guarding them against hostile inroads. For
instance, the custom which barred alcoholic drinks from respectable
and educated homes is now being undermined by the influence of the

idle upper class which needs stimulants and copies their use from foreign society, and the Church should undertake a new temperance crusade with all the resources of advanced physiological and sociological science. The head of an important Eastern institution a few years ago proposed to introduce beer in the social gatherings of students in order to make them more sociable. Such an innovation would not merely create the habit of moderate drinking in many young men, but would introduce a foreign custom into American life. Many of our public dinners are now wholly free from the flush of wine or beer. The excellence of American after-dinner speaking, and the prevalence of real humor and fun at our public dinners, are mainly due to the fact that both speaker and audience are in full control of their critical faculties and therefore demand fine intellectual work and are in condition to appreciate it. The alcoholic paralysis begins with the brain and lessens the capacity for self-scrutiny and self-restraint. An alcoholized audience will howl at anything unseemly and be too dull for anything really witty. Even if the students of that institution should all stop drinking when they graduated, a lasting damage would be done to American college life if it became customary for the college community to pass into partial narcosis as a preparation for social enjoyment. Against all such corruptions of good custom the Church should do sentinel duty.

Any permanent and useful advance in legislation is dependent on the previous creation of moral conviction and custom. It is a commonplace that a law cannot be enforced without the support of public opinion, and that an unenforced law breaks down the usefulness of all related laws and the reverence for law in general. If the law advances faster than the average moral sense, it becomes inoperative and harmful. The real advance, therefore, will have to come through those social forces which create and train the sense of right. The religious and educational forces in their totality are the real power that runs the cart uphill; the State can merely push a billet of wood under the wheels to keep it from rolling down again. Some of the gravest evils of our day are either not covered by enacted law or the law against them does not work. In such cases the forces which create active moral conviction are under accusation for neglect of duty.

The process of guarding, creating, or strengthening useful institutions is similar to the process of creating good customs. It is a function in which religious sentiment and the organized Church can work freely. For instance, our public parks are an institution of the highest value to the physical and moral life of the cities. About fifty years ago no city in the United States had purchased an acre of land for park purposes. Mainly through the influence of public-spirited men, supported by enlightened moral sentiment, parks have been created and are now not only increasing their acreage and their beauty, but their usefulness. They are beginning to offer sand-hills for the little children, swimming baths in summer, skating in winter, music on holidays, gymnastic apparatus, and open-air games. Instead of warning the people to "keep off the grass," they are bidding for the inflow of the people. Yet it is safe to say that every one of these advances cost some struggle and effort, and at every such moment of struggle a lift from the powerful shoulders of the organized religious community would be practically decisive.

The Hague Tribunal is an institution of far-reaching historical importance which has grown up under our eyes. Its real origin was in the hearts of idealists who supported their protest against war and armed peace by scientific reasoning. These ideas found lodgement in the mind of Czar Nicholas, and by the power of initiative vested in a great monarch he was able by a single manifesto to compel worldwide attention to the question and force a theory into the field of practical politics. But the suspicion and non-ideal conservatism of governments is so great that they would have let the movement die stillborn, if it had not awakened the moral enthusiasm of the common people in those countries in which democracy had trained the people to act, and in which purified religion had stored the strongest ethical dynamic. English and American public sentiment were probably the decisive factor which made the first conference at the Hague more than a dress parade. The aim for which the Conference was really called was not accomplished; the increase in armaments was not checked. Instead of that a permanent tribunal of international arbitration was created. For a time no use was made of it. Many made mock of this puny outcome of a movement which had been mistakenly heralded as a proposition for universal peace. Many religious journals sat on the seats of the scornful. Then another strong man with convictions put his hand on the idle machinery and set it in motion. President Roosevelt secured the reference of the "Pious Fund"[12] dispute with Mexico and later the reference of the Venezuelan disputes, and therewith the Hague Tribunal became an operative force in history. Andrew Carnegie, that one of our great millionaires who has the strongest leaven of democratic idealism, has undertaken to house the Tribunal in adequate splendor. It is safe to say that the institution will now perpetuate itself and gradually enlarge its functions.

Here we have under our eye the various forces which cooperate to advance humanity; the dissemination of ideas by idealistic thinkers, the action of individuals strong by hereditary position, personal character or wealth, and the support of enlightened public opinion. History will do the rest. It will be immeasurably easier to assign additional powers to the Tribunal than to create it in the first place. These forces triumphed over the sullen reluctance and cynical doubt of some governments and the amused ridicule of many "practical men." Many religious people looked askance, because peace on earth can be established only by the coming of Christ. Others hailed it with a shout of triumph as another step in the coming of Christ. The future will probably look back to it as the faint beginning of a new era in international relations and will marvel that any doubted the clear call of Christ at such a turning-point.

> "In the years that have been I have bound man closer to man
> And closer woman to woman;
> And the stranger hath seen in a stranger his brother at last
> And a sister in eyes that were strange.
> In the years that shall be I will bind me nation to nation
> And shore unto shore," saith our God.
> "Lo! I am the burster of bonds and the breaker of barriers,
> I am he that shall free," saith the Lord.
> "For the lingering battle, the contest of ages is ending,
> And victory followeth me."
>   —*Stephen Philips*

Such a cooperation of the religious and political forces of the community furnishes the positive solution of the problem of Church and State. Historical experience has compelled us to separate Church and State because each can accomplish its special task best without the interference of the other. But they are not unrelated. Our life is not a mechanical duality, built in two airtight compartments. Church and State both minister to something greater and larger than either, and they find their true relation in this unity of aim and service. When the State supports morality by legal constraint, it cooperates with the voluntary moral power of the Church; but if it should seek to control the organization and influence of the Church by appointing its officers or interfering with its teaching, it would tamper with the seedplot of moral progress. When the Church implants religious impulses toward righteousness and trains the moral convictions of the people, it cooperates with the State by creating the most delicate and valuable elements of social welfare and progress; but if it should enter into politics to get funds from the public treasury or police support for its doctrine and ritual, it would inject a divisive and corrosive force into political life. The machinery of Church and State must be kept separate, but the output of each must mingle with the other to make social life increasingly wholesome and normal. Church and State are alike but partial organizations of humanity for special ends. Together they serve what is greater than either: humanity. Their common aim is to transform humanity into the kingdom of God.

Jesus in his teachings alluded with surprising frequency to the use and abuse of entrusted wealth and power. In the parables of the talents and pounds (Matthew 25:14-30; Luke 19:11-27), he evidently meant to define all human ability and opportunity as a trust. His description of the head servant who is made confident by the continued absence of his master, tyrannizes over his subordinates, and fattens his paunch on his master's property, is meant to show the temptation which besets all in authority to forget the responsibility that goes with power (Matthew 25:14-30). His portrayal of the tricky steward who is to be dismissed for dishonesty, but manages to make one more grand coup before his authority ends, not only shows the keen insight of Jesus into the ways of the grafter, but also shows that he regarded all men of wealth as stewards of the property they hold (Luke 16:1-15). The parable of the peasants who jointly rent a vineyard and then try to do their absent owner not only out of his rent, but out of the property itself, was meant by Jesus to condense and dramatize the whole history of the ruling class in Israel (Matthew 21:33–46). The illustration of the fig tree which has had all possible advantages of soil and care without returning fruit, and which merely gets a year's reprieve through the hopeful pleading of the gardener, expresses the indignation of Jesus against the waste of entrusted opportunity (Luke 13:6–9). The terrible invective against the scribes and Pharisees is directed against teachers who had misused their influence to darken truth and leaders who had treated their leadership as a chance to get profit and honor for themselves (Luke 13:6–9).

The fact that Jesus in his diagnosis of wrong moral relations so often puts his finger on trust abused and betrayed, is proof of his penetrating social insight. Nearly all powers in society are essentially delegated powers. The more complex society becomes, the less will it be possible for the individual to attend to all his needs himself, and the more will he have to entrust others with specialized functions and powers. When a savage killed an animal for food and dressed its hide for clothing, he knew what he was getting. When a man buys canned meat and a ready-made suit, he has to trust to the honesty of others for what he gets. When a man deposits money in a savings bank or pays an insurance premium, he exercises trust. When he engages a lawyer to conduct a suit or search a title, the lawyer is a steward of entrusted power. When he submits the body of his child to a surgeon's knife, or its intellect to a schoolteacher, or its soul to a preacher, he trusts, and these professional men are his trustees. Our life is woven through with such relations. Trust is the foundation of all higher social life. Life is good and restful in the measure in which it is safe to trust. Life turns back to the haunting suspicion and fear of the savage when man can no longer safely trust man.

On the other hand, the more complex society becomes, the more difficult is it to watch over the fidelity of all the trustees, and the greater is the temptation of a trustee or steward to divert the trust to his own use. A farming community in New England can watch how the selectmen of the township use their delegated powers. The ordinary citizen in our great cities does not understand the machinery of the government and has only a shadowy idea of what is really being done by public officers with his property and under his authority. He is, in effect, the absentee landlord whose servants are made bold to pilfer and cheat because the eye of the owner is not on them.

Moreover, it is only when society arrives at wealth and power that
"grafting" comes to pay. In a poor and savage community the individual has so little that the only way to get wealth without work is by
downright robbery of the weak. As the average of wealth rises, and the
aggregate of wealth becomes more enormous, a mere "rake-off" is
enough to enrich the grafter. Hence in a savage community we have
robbers and bandit chiefs; in a civilized community we have a parasitic
class who live in idleness and splendor by converting to their own use
some kind of entrusted wealth or delegated power. "Grafting" is a
highly perfected modern sin. Its essence is not stealing, but the corruption of a steward by one party and the betrayal of trust by a second
party, who together profit at the expense of a third party, most frequently the public.

The scale on which the parable of the wicked husbandmen has
been reenacted in human history is stupendous. For instance, the king
or duke in primitive Teutonic life was simply a capable man chosen
for temporary leadership in war. This temporary power tended to
become permanent. This permanent power tended to become hereditary. Tenure by capable service tended to become tenure "by divine
right." The limited monarchy tended to shake off its limitations, to
suppress coordinate forces of government, and to become absolutism.
When Louis XIV asserted, *"L'État, c'est moi,"* the steward was calmly
facing the owner and asserting that the owner existed by leave of the
steward. The steward had embezzled the property so long that the relationship between owner and steward had been turned upside down in
his mind. When Frederick the Great of Prussia said, on the other
hand, that "the king is the foremost servant of the State," the royal philosopher felt the breath of the coming French Revolution fanning his
brow. But the fact that so obvious a truth had to be stated at all is the
most convincing proof that the stewardship of kings had long been a
buried idea. The great movement of modern democracy, which is still
so far from its goal, is simply an effort to bring one set of faithless stewards to terms and restore their power to the people from whom it was
alienated.

The great feudal system, under which medieval society lived and
did business just as we live under capitalism, was fundamentally a systematized network of stewardship. A great noble was given a province

by the crown on condition that he render certain services, usually the military protection of public peace and safety. He in turn conferred smaller domains on smaller lords under similar conditions. But just as in the case of the kings, the feudal lords tended to shake off the obligation incurred and to strengthen their hold on the power conferred. Feudal stewardship turned into ownership and then shifted its fundamental military duties and taxes on other classes of the population, until the people, who were the owners of the land, sat shivering on the doorsteps of the stewards and made obeisance when they were kicked.

These are simply two illustrations on a large scale to show how vast have been the embezzlements of power from the people, and what a long historical struggle is necessary to oust the fraudulent steward and regain possession for the people. It would be easy to multiply the illustrations from history. It is more to the point to mark the same process today.

When a public officer secures government positions for his relatives or for those who worked for his election, or succulent contracts for the patriotic businessmen who put up campaign funds, he uses the property of the people to pay for services rendered to himself. That is essentially embezzlement by an agent. When President Cleveland solemnly announced that "public office is a public trust," it was greeted as a noble assertion of a great principle. What would be the condition of mathematical science in a nation if the solemn announcement that "two times two is four" should be hailed as an enlightening utterance? The standard of honor in public life has fallen so low in our country that it is very difficult to secure the conviction of even flagrant offenders because the official world, by community of sin, has lost its capacity for moral indignation. When the law touches one man on the shoulder, a shiver of apprehension runs down the whole line. Our political parties, at least in their local administration, are largely held together by the cohesive necessities of common plunder. Democracy is paralyzed by the party managers. The owner is once more being ousted by the steward.

Our public service corporations exist because the community grants them the use of public property and exercises the sovereign right of eminent domain on their behalf. They are stewards of public property and powers. But we have all seen in recent years that they have been very close to forgetting that they are stewards and have acted as if they were the owners. The present movement for rate-regulation, for instance, is simply an effort to assert the rights of the owner over the steward, and the aggrieved astonishment with which this movement has been met by the class that owns the railways is interesting proof that the usual historical process was very far advanced.

It has gone much farther in the case of mining rights. Our laws have been exceedingly open-handed to those who discovered and developed the mineral resources of our country. But this generosity has always been based on the tacit assumption that it was a good thing for the entire community to have the minerals brought out and cheapened, and that the grantees of mining rights would hasten to bring them out and compete in selling them. Mining rights are a form of public franchise and are conditioned on public service. It is preposterous to think that an individual or a corporation can ever have absolute ownership in a vein of coal or copper. A mining company owns the holes in the ground, for it made the holes; it does not own the coal, for it did not make the coal. The coal is the gift of God and belongs to the people. If the people entrust the mining of the coal to anyone, it is a delegated right and can be recalled if the stewardship is abused. If mining rights are now used to keep coal in and make it dear, instead of bringing coal out and making it cheap, that would be ample moral ground for canceling all rights.

The present movement for federal and state interference and control over corporations, of which President Roosevelt is the most eminent exponent and leader, is an effort to reassert the ownership and mastership of the people and to force these stewards of public powers back into the position of public servants. The next decade will probably show whether they are willing to take the position of well-paid servants and cease from ousting the owner. If not, the people will have to say, "Render the account of thy stewardship, for thou canst no longer be steward."

This movement is of far-reaching historical significance. It could be immensely quickened if the moral forces of the community would strengthen it by stiffening public sentiment on stewardship. The Church should turn whatever advanced moral insight it possesses, like a searchlight, on everything that claims to be ownership and scrutinize it to see if it is not in fact merely stewardship which has thrown off its responsibility and is running away with the property. It is said that all the cordage used by the English navy has a red thread running through the hemp, which proves that it is public property wherever it may be found. It would be interesting if the rigging of our private commercial craft could be overhauled to find the red thread of public ownership. We all draw our life, our safety, our intellect, our information, our organizing ability, from the common fund of the community, and we have not paid our obligations when we have settled our tax bill. The community could well turn on each of us and ask: "What hast thou that thou didst not receive? But if thou didst receive it, why doest thou boast as if thou hadst not received it?"

The doctrine of "Christian stewardship" has been strongly emphasized in church life in recent years, but mainly from the churchly point of view. It is a new formula designed to give our modern men of wealth a stronger sense of responsibility and to induce them to give more largely to the Church and its work. But if a rich man withdraws a million from commerce and gives it to a missionary society or a college, that simply shifts the money from one steward to another, and from one line of usefulness to another. The ecclesiastical idea of stewardship needs to be intensified and broadened by the democratic idea. Every man who holds wealth or power is not only a steward of God, but a steward of the people. He derives it from the people and he holds it in trust for the people. If he converts it to his own use, the people can justly call him to account in the court of public opinion and in the courts of law. If the law has hitherto given an absolute title to certain forms of property and has neglected to insist on the ingredient of public property and rights involved in it, that does not settle the moral title in the least. The people may at any time challenge the title and resume its forgotten rights by more searching laws. The Christian Church could make a splendid contribution to the new social justice if it assisted in pointing out the latent public rights and in quickening the conscience of stewards who have forgotten their stewardship. In turn, the religious sense of stewardship would be reinforced by the increased sense of social obligation. Our laws and social institutions have so long taught men that their property is their own, and that they can do what they will with their own, that the Church has uphill work in teaching that they are not owners, but administrators. Our industrial individualism neutralizes the social consciousness created by Christianity.

SOLIDARITY AND COMMUNISM

It is assumed as almost self-evident in popular thought that communism is impracticable and inefficient, an antiquated method of the past or a dream of Utopian schemers, a system of society sure to impede economic development and to fetter individual liberty and initiative. Thus we flout what was the earliest basis of civilization for the immense majority of mankind and the moral ideal of Christendom during the greater part of its history. Communistic ownership and management of the fundamental means of production was the rule in primitive society, and large remnants of it have survived to our day. For fifteen centuries and more it was the common consent of Christendom that private property was due to sin, and that the ideal life involved fraternal sharing. The idea underlying the monastic life was that men left the sinful world and established an ideal community, and communism was an essential feature of every monastic establishment. The progressive heretical movements in the Middle Ages also usually involved an attempt to get closer to the communistic ideal. It is a striking proof how deeply the ideas of the Church have always been affected by the current secular thought, that our modern individualism has been able to wipe this immemorial Christian social ideal out of the mind of the modern Church almost completely.

The assumption that communistic ownership was a hindrance to progress deserves very critical scrutiny. It is part of that method of writing history which exalted the doings of kings and slighted the life of the people. For the grasping arm of the strong, communistic institutions were indeed a most objectionable hindrance, but to the common man they were the strongest bulwark of his independence and vigor. Within the shelter of the old-fashioned village community, which constituted a social unit for military protection, economic production, morality, and religion, the individual could enjoy his life with some fearlessness. The peasant who stood alone was at the mercy of his lord. Primitive village communism was not freely abandoned as an inefficient system, but was broken up by the covetousness of the strong and selfish members of the community, and by the encroachments of the upper classes who wrested the common pasture and forest and game from the peasant communities. Its disappearance nearly everywhere marked a decline in the prosperity and moral vigor of the peasantry and was felt by them to be a calamity and a step in their enslavement.

But we need not go back into history to get a juster verdict on the practicability and usefulness of communism. We have the material right among us. Ask any moral teacher who is scouting communism and glorifying individualism, what social institutions today are most important for the moral education of mankind and most beneficent in their influence on human happiness, and he will probably reply promptly, "The home, the school, and the church." But these three are communistic institutions. The home is the source of most of our happiness and goodness, and in the home we live communistically. Each member of the family has some private property, clothes, letters, pictures, toys; but the rooms and the furniture in the main are common to all, and if one member needs the private property of another, there is ready sharing. The income of the members is more or less turned into a common fund; food is prepared and eaten in common; the larger family undertakings are planned in common. The housewife is the manager of a successful communistic colony, and it is perhaps not accidental that our women, who move thus within a fraternal organization, are the chief stays of our Christianity. Similarly our public schools are supported on a purely communistic basis; those who have no children or whose children are grown up are nevertheless taxed for the education of the children of the community. The desks, the books to some extent, the flowers and decorations, are common property, and it is the aim of the teachers to develop the communistic spirit in the children, though they may not call it by that name. Our churches, too, are voluntary communisms. A number of people get together, have a common building, common seats, common hymn-books and Bibles, support a pastor in common, and worship, learn, work, and play in common. They are so little individualistic that they fairly urge others to come in and use their property. Private pews and similar encroachments of private property within this communistic institution are now generally condemned as contrary to the spirit of the Church, while every new step to widen the communistic serviceableness of the churches is greeted with a glow of enthusiasm.

Thus the three great institutions on which we mainly depend to train the young to a moral life and to make us all good, wise, and happy, are essentially communistic, and their success and efficiency depend on the continued mastery of the spirit of solidarity and brotherhood within them. It is nothing short of funny to hear the very men who ceaselessly glorify the home, the school, and the church, turn around and abuse communism.

It can fairly be maintained, too, that the State, another great moral agent, is communistic in its very nature. It is the organization by which the people administer their common property and attend to their common interests. It is safe to say that at least a fourth of the land in a modern city is owned by the city and communistically used for free streets and free parks. Our modern State is the outcome of a long development toward communism. Warfare and military defense were formerly the private affair of the nobles; they are now the business of the entire nation. Roads and bridges used to be owned largely by private persons or corporations, and toll charged for their use; they are now communistic with rare exceptions. Putting out fires used to be left to private enterprise; today our fire departments are communistic. Schools used to be private; they are now public. Great men formerly had private parks and admitted the public as a matter of favor; the people now have public parks and admit the great men as a matter of right. The right of jurisdiction was formerly often an appurtenance of the great landowners; it is now controlled by the people. The public spirit and foresight of one of the greatest of all Americans, Benjamin Franklin, early made the postal service of our country a communistic institution of ever increasing magnitude and usefulness. In no case in which communistic ownership has firmly established itself is there any desire to recede from it. The unrest and dissatisfaction is all at those points where the State is not yet communistic. The water-works in most of our cities are owned and operated by the community, and there is never more than local and temporary dissatisfaction about this great necessity of life, because any genuine complaint by the people as users of water can be promptly remedied by the people as suppliers of water. On the other hand, the clamor of public complaint about the gas, the electric power and light, and the street railway service, which are commonly supplied by private companies, is incessant and increasing. While the railway lines were competing, they wasted on needless parallel roads enough capital to build a comfortable home for every family in the country. Now that they have nearly ceased to compete, the grievances of their monopoly are among the gravest problems of our national life. The competitive duplication of plant and labor by our express companies is folly, and their exorbitant charges are a drag on the economic welfare and the common comfort of our whole nation. This condition continues not because of their efficiency, but because of their sinister influence on Congress. They are an economic anachronism.

Thus the State, too, is essentially a communistic institution. It has voluntarily limited its functions and left many things to private initiative. The political philosophy of the nineteenth century constantly preached to the State that the best State was that which governed least, just as the best child was that which moved least. Yet it has almost imperceptibly gathered to itself many of the functions which were formerly exercised by private undertakings, and there is no desire anywhere to turn public education, fire protection, sanitation, or the supply of water over to private concerns. But the distinctively modern utilities, which have been invented or perfected during the reign of capitalism and during the prevalence of individualistic political theories, have been seized and appropriated by private concerns. The railways, the street railways, the telegraph and telephone, electric power and light, gas—these are all modern. The swift hand of capitalism seized them and has exploited them to its immense profit. Other countries have long ago begun to draw these modern public necessities within the communistic functions of the State. In our country a variety of causes, good and bad, have combined to check that process; but the trend is manifestly in the direction of giving state communism a wider sweep hereafter.

Private ownership is not a higher stage of social organization which has finally and forever superseded communism, but an intermediate and necessary stage of social evolution between two forms of communism. At a certain point in the development of property primitive communism becomes unworkable, and a higher form of communism has not yet been wrought out; consequently men manage as best they can with private ownership. To take a simple illustration: on the farm or in a country village the creek is common property for bathing purposes; the "swimmin'-hole" is the communistic bathtub for all who want to refresh their cuticle. As the village grows, the march of the houses drives the bathers farther out; the pervasiveness of the "eternally feminine" robs the boys of their bath; the primitive communism of the water ceases. Some families now are wealthy enough to install private bathtubs and have the increased privilege of bathing all the year around. The bulk of the people in the cities have no bathing facilities at all. At last an agitation arises for a public bath. A beginning is made with enclosed river-baths, perhaps, or with shower-baths. At last a plunge-bath is built and opened summer and winter. The bathing instinct of the community revives and increasingly centers about the public bath. The communism of the water has returned. From the communistic swimming-hole to the marble splendor of the communistic bath the way lay through the individualistic tub of the wealthy and the unwashed deprivations of the mass. In the same way there is no need of parks in primitive society, because all nature is open. As cities grow up, the country recedes; a few are wealthy enough to surround their homes with lawns and trees; the mass are shut off from nature and suffocate amid brick and asphalt. Then comes the new communal ownership and enjoyment of nature: first the small square in the city; then the large park on the outskirts; then the distant park on the seashore or by the river and lake; and finally the state or national reservation where wildlife is kept intact for those who want to revert to it. Thus we pass from communism to communism in our means of enjoyment, and that community will evidently be wisest which most quickly sees that the old and simple means of pleasure are passing, and will provide the corresponding means for the more complex and artificial community which is evolving. The longer it lingers in the era of private self-help, the longer will the plain people be deprived of their heritage, and the more completely will the wealthy minority preempt the means of enjoyment for themselves.

Everywhere communism in new forms and on a vaster scale is coming back to us. The individualistic pump in the backyard is gone;

the city water-works are the modern counterpart of the communistic village well to which Rebekah and Rachel came to fill their water-jar. The huge irrigation scheme of our national government in the West is an enlarged duplicate of the tanks built by many a primitive community. The railway train carrying people or supplies is a modernized form of the tribe breaking camp and carrying its women and children and cattle and tents to better grazing or hunting grounds. Compared with the old private vehicle, the railway carriage is a triumphant demonstration of communism. Almost the only private thing about our railways is the dividends. The competitive individualism of commerce is being restricted within ever narrower limits. State supervision and control is a partial assertion of the supremacy of communistic interests. It is probably only a question of time when the private management of public necessities will be felt to be impossible and antiquated, and the community will begin to experiment seriously with the transportation of people and goods, and with the public supply of light and heat and cold.

How far this trend toward communistic ownership is to go, the common sense of the future will have to determine. It is entirely misleading to frighten us with the idea that communism involves a complete abolition of private property. Even in the most individualistic society there is, as we have seen, a large ingredient of communism, and in the most socialistic society there will always be a large ingredient of private property. No one supposes that a man's toothbrush, his love-letters, or the shirt on his back would ever be common property. Socialists are probably quite right in maintaining that the amount of private property per capita in a prosperous socialist community would be much larger than it is now. It seems unlikely even that all capital used in production will ever be communistic in ownership and operation; a socialistic State could easily afford to allow individuals to continue some private production, just as handicraft lingers now amid machine production. It will never be a question of having either private property absolute or communism absolute; it will always be a question of having more communism or less.

The question then confronts Christian men singly and the Christian Church collectively, whether they will favor and aid this trend toward communism, or oppose it. Down to modern times, as we have seen, the universal judgment of Christian thought was in favor of communism as more in harmony with the genius of Christianity and with the classical precedents of its early social life. Simultaneously with the rise of capitalism that conviction began to fade out. Protestantism especially, by its intimate alliance with the growing cities and the rising business class, has been individualistic in its theories of Christian society. The question is now, how quickly Christian thought will realize that individualism is coming to be an inadequate and antiquated form of social organization which must give place to a higher form of communistic organization, and how thoroughly it will comprehend that this new communism will afford a far nobler social basis for the spiritual temple of Christianity.

For there cannot really be any doubt that the spirit of Christianity has more affinity for a social system based on solidarity and human fraternity than for one based on selfishness and mutual antagonism. In competitive industry one man may profit through the ruin of others; in cooperative production the wealth of one man would depend on the growing wealth of all. In competitive society each man strives for himself and his family only, and the sense of larger duties is attenuated and feeble; in communistic society no man could help realizing that he is part of a great organization, and that he owes it duty and loyalty. Competition tends to make good men selfish; cooperation would compel selfish men to develop public spirit. The moral and wholesome influences in society today proceed from the communistic organizations within it; the divisive, anarchic, and destructive influences which are racking our social body today proceed from those realms of social life which are individualistic and competitive. Business life today is organized in growing circles within which a certain amount of cooperation and mutual helpfulness exists, and to that extent it exerts a sound moral influence. Insofar as it is really competitive, it engenders covetousness, cunning, hardness, selfish satisfaction in success, or resentment and despair in failure. It is a marvelous demonstration of the vitality of human goodness that a system so calculated to bring out the evil traits in us still leaves so much human kindness and nobility alive. But the Christian temper of mind, the honest regard for the feelings and the welfare of others, the desire to make our life serve the common good, would get its first chance to control our social life in a society organized on the basis of solidarity and cooperation.

It would seem, therefore, that one of the greatest services which Christianity could render to humanity in the throes of the present transition would be to aid those social forces which are making for the increase of communism. The Church should help public opinion to understand clearly the difference between the moral qualities of the competitive and the communistic principle, and enlist religious enthusiasm on behalf of that which is essentially Christian. Christian individuals should strengthen and protect the communistic institutions already in existence in society and help them to extend their functions. For instance, the public schools can increasingly be made nuclei of common life for the district within which they are located, gathering the children for play out of school hours, and the adults for instruction, discussion, and social pleasure in the evenings. The usefulness of the public parks as centers of communal life can be immensely extended by encouraging and organizing the play of the children and by holding regular public festivals. Simply to induce the crowd listening to a band concert in the park to join in singing a patriotic song, would convert a mass of listening individuals into a social organism thrilled with a common joy and sensible of its cohesion. Public ownership of the great public utilities would be desirable for the education it would give in solidarity, if for no other reason. Even if a street railway should be run at a loss for a time under city management, it would at least draw the people closer together by the sense of common proprietorship and would teach them to work better together to overcome the trouble. Every step taken in industrial life to give the employees some proprietary rights in the business, and anything placing owners and employees on a footing of human equality, would deserve commendation and help.

The Christian spirit of fraternity should create fraternal social institutions, and the fraternal institutions may in turn be trusted to breed and spread the fraternal spirit. It is a most hopeful fact that the communistic features of our government are awakening in some public officials a whole-hearted and far-seeing devotion to the public welfare. A number of our public health officers have thrown themselves into the crusade against tuberculosis and infant mortality with a zeal more far-sighted and chivalrous than is usually called out in the ordinary doctor who cures patients on the individualistic plan. When men at the head of some department of city government realize the immense latent capacity of their department to serve the people, they are fired with ambition to do what they see can be done. Their natural ambition to make themselves felt, to exert power and get honor, runs in the same direction with the public needs. Such men are still scarce, but they are a prophecy of the kind of character which may be created in a communistic society and of the power of enthusiastic work which may hereafter be summoned to the service of the people. The vast educational work done by some departments of our national government, for instance the Department of Agriculture, furnishes similar proof of what may be done when we abandon the policeman theory of government and adopt the family theory. Certainly it would be no betrayal of the Christian spirit to enter into a working alliance with this great tendency toward the creation of cooperative and communistic social institutions based on the broad principle of the brotherhood of men and the solidarity of their interests.

THE UPWARD MOVEMENT OF THE WORKING CLASS

The ideal of a fraternal organization of society is so splendid that it is today enlisting the choicest young minds of the intellectual classes under its banner. Idealists everywhere are surrendering to it, especially those who are under the power of the ethical spirit of Christianity. The influence which these idealists exert in reinforcing the movement toward solidarity is beyond computation. They impregnate the popular mind with faith and enthusiasm. They furnish the watchwords and the intellectual backing of historical and scientific information. They supply devoted leaders and give a lofty sanction to the movement by their presence in it. They diminish the resistance of the upper classes among whom they spread their ideas.

But we must not blink at the fact that the idealists alone have never carried through any great social change. In vain they dash their fair ideas against the solid granite of human selfishness. The possessing classes are strong by mere possession long continued. They control nearly all property. The law is on their side, for they have made it.

They control the machinery of government and can use force under the form of law. Their self-interest makes them almost impervious to moral truth if it calls in question the sources from which they draw their income. In the past they have laughed at the idealists if they seemed harmless, or have suppressed them if they became troublesome.

We Americans have a splendid moral optimism. We believe that "truth is mighty and must prevail." "Truth crushed to earth shall rise again." "The blood of the martyrs is the seed of the Church." In the words of the great Anabaptist Bailthasar Hübmaier, who attested his faith by martyrdom, "Truth is immortal; and though for a long time she be imprisoned, scourged, crowned with thorns, crucified and buried, she will yet rise victorious on the third day and will reign and triumph." That is a glorious faith. But the three days may be three centuries, and the murdered truth may never rise again in the nation that crucified it, but may come to victory in some other race and on another continent. The Peasants' Rising in 1525 in Germany embodied the social ideals of the common people; the Anabaptist movement, which began simultaneously, expressed their religious aspirations; both were essentially noble and just; both have been most amply justified by the later course of history; yet both were quenched in streams of blood and have had to wait till our own day for their resurrection in new form.

Truth is mighty. But for a definite historical victory a given truth must depend on the class which makes that truth its own and fights for it. If that class is sufficiently numerous, compact, intelligent, organized, and conscious of what it wants, it may drive a breach through the entrenchments of those opposed to it and carry the cause to victory. If there is no such army to fight its cause, the truth will drive individuals to a comparatively fruitless martyrdom and will continue to hover over humanity as a disembodied ideal. There were a number of reformatory movements before 1,500 which looked fully as promising and powerful as did the movement led by Luther in its early years; but the fortified authority of the papacy and clergy succeeded in frustrating them, and they ebbed away again. The Lutheran and Calvinistic Reformation succeeded because they enlisted classes which were sufficiently strong politically and economically to defend the cause of

Reformed Religion. It was only when concrete material interests entered into a working alliance with Truth that enough force was rallied to break down the frowning walls of error. On the other hand, the classes within which Anabaptism gained lodgement lacked that concrete power, and so the Anabaptist movement, which promised for a short time to be the real Reformation of Germany, just as it came to be the real Reformation of England in the Commonwealth, died a useless and despised death. In the French Revolution the ideal of democracy won a great victory, not simply because the ideal was so fair, but because it represented the concrete interests of the strong, wealthy, and intelligent business class, and that class was able to wrest political control from the king, the aristocracy, and the clergy.

The question is whether the ideal of cooperation and economic fraternity can today depend on any great and conquering class whose self-interest is bound up with the victory of that principle. It is hopeless to expect the business class to espouse that principle as a class. Individuals in the business class will do so, but the class will not. There is no historical precedent for an altruistic self-effacement of a whole class. Of the professional class it is safe to expect that an important minority—perhaps a larger minority in our country than in any country heretofore—will range themselves under the new social ideal. With them especially the factor of religion will prove of immense power. But their motives will in the main be idealistic, and in the present stage of man's moral development the unselfish emotions are fragile and easily chafe through, unless the coarse fiber of self-interest is woven into them. But there is another class to which that conception of organized fraternity is not only a moral ideal, but the hope for bread and butter; with which it enlists not only religious devotion and self-sacrifice, but involves salvation from poverty and insecurity and participation in the wealth and culture of modern life for themselves and their children.

It is a mistake to regard the French Revolution as a movement of the poor. The poor fought in the uprising, but the movement got its strength, its purpose, and its direction from the "third estate," the bourgeoisie, the business class of the cities, and they alone drew lasting profit from it. That class had been slowly rising to wealth, education, and power for several centuries, and the democratic movement of the nineteenth century has in the main been their march to complete ascendancy.

During the same period we can watch the slow development of a new class, which has been called the fourth estate: the city working class, the wage-workers. They form a distinct class, all living without capital merely by the sale of their labor, working and living under similar physical and social conditions everywhere, with the same economic interests and the same points of view. They present a fairly homogeneous body and if any section of the people forms a "class," they do. The massing of labor in the factories since the introduction of power machinery has brought them into close contact with one another. Hard experience has taught them how helpless they are when they stand alone. They have begun to realize their solidarity and the divergence of their interests from those of the employers. They have begun to organize and are slowly learning to act together. The spread of education and cheap literature, the ease of communication, and the freedom of public meeting have rapidly created a common body of ideas and points of view among them.

The modern "labor movement" is the upward movement of this class. It began with local and concrete issues that pressed upon a given body of workingmen some demand for shorter hours or better wages, some grievance about fines or docking. The trades-unions were formed as defensive organizations for collective action. It is quite true that they have often been foolish and tyrannical in their demands, and headstrong and even lawless in their actions; but if we consider the insecurity and narrowness of the economic existence of the working people, and the glaring contrast between the meager reward for their labor and the dazzling returns given to invested capital, it is impossible to deny that they have good cause for making a strenuous and continuous fight for better conditions of life. If Christian men are really interested in the salvation of human lives and in the health, the decency, the education, and the morality of the people, they must wish well to the working people in their effort to secure such conditions for themselves and their dear ones that they will not have to die of tuberculosis in their prime, nor feel their strength ground down by long hours of work, nor see their women and children drawn into the merciless hopper of factory labor, nor be shut out from the enjoyment of the culture about them which they have watered with their sweat.

But the labor movement means more than better wages and shorter hours for individual workingmen. It involves the struggle for a different status for their entire class. Other classes have long ago won a recognized standing in law and custom and public opinion—so long ago that they have forgotten that they ever had to win it. For instance, the medical profession is recognized by law; certain qualifications are fixed for admission to it; certain privileges are granted to those inside; irregular practitioners are hampered or suppressed. The clerical profession enjoys certain exemptions from taxation, military service, and jury duty; ministers have the right to solemnize marriages and collect fees therefore; railways give them half fares, and these privileges are granted to those whom the clergy themselves ordain and admit to their "closed shop." A lawyer who is admitted to the bar thereby becomes a court officer; the bar association, which is his trades-union, takes the initiative in disbarring men who violate the class code, and the courts take cognizance of its action; in the state of New York the bar associations have assumed some right to nominate the judges. As for the business class, it is so completely enthroned in our social organization that it often assumes that it is itself the whole of society.

On the other hand, the working class has no adequate standing as yet. It did have in the guilds of former times, but modern industry and modern law under the *laissez-faire* principle dissolved the old privileges and reduced the working class to a mass of unrelated human atoms. Common action on their part was treated in law as conspiracy. In our country they have not yet won from their employers, nor from public opinion, the acknowledged right to be organized, to bargain collectively, and to assist in controlling the discipline of the shops in which they have to work. The law seems to afford them very little backing as yet. It provides penalties for the kind of injuries which workingmen are likely to inflict on their employers, but not for the subtler injuries which employers are likely to inflict on their workingmen. Few will care to assert that in the bitter conflicts waged between labor and capital the wrong has always been on one side. Yet when the law bares its sword, it is somehow always against one side. The militia does not seem to be ordered out against capital. The labor movement must go on until public opinion and the law have conceded a recognized position to the labor-unions, and until the workingmen interested in a given question stand collectively on a footing of equality with the capitalists interested in it. This means a curtailment of power for the employers, and it would be contrary to human nature for them to like it. But for the working class it would be suicidal to forgo the attempt to get it. They have suffered fearfully by not having it. All the sacrifices they may bring in the chronic industrial warfare of the present will be cheap if they ultimately win through to an assured social and legal status for their class.

As long as the working class simply attempts to better its condition somewhat and to secure a recognized standing for its class organization, it stands on the basis of the present capitalistic organization of industry. Capitalism necessarily divides industrial society into two classes—those who own the instruments and materials of production, and those who furnish the labor for it. This sharp division is the peculiar characteristic of modern capitalism which distinguishes it from other forms of social organization in the past. These two classes have to cooperate in modern production. The labor movement seeks to win better terms for the working class in striking its bargains. Yet whatever terms organized labor succeeds in winning are always temporary and insecure, like the hold which a wrestler gets on the body of his antagonist. The persistent tendency with capital necessarily is to get labor as cheaply as possible and to force as much work from it as possible. Moreover, labor is always in an inferior position in the struggle. It is handicapped by its own hunger and lack of resources. It has to wrestle on its knees with a foeman who is on his feet. Is this unequal struggle between two conflicting interests to go on forever? Is this insecurity the best that the working class can ever hope to attain?

Here enters socialism. It proposes to abolish the division of industrial society into two classes and to close the fatal chasm which has separated the employing class from the working class since the introduction of power machinery. It proposes to restore the independence of the workingman by making him once more the owner of his tools and to give him the full proceeds of his production instead of a wage determined by his poverty. It has no idea of reverting to the simple methods of the old handicrafts, but heartily accepts the power machinery, the great factory, the division of labor, the organization of the men in great regiments of workers, as established facts in modern life, and as the most efficient method of producing wealth. But it proposes to give to the whole body of workers the ownership of these vast instruments of production and to distribute among them all the entire proceeds of their common labor. There would then be no capitalistic class opposed to the working class; there would be a single class which would unite the qualities of both. Every workman would be both owner and worker, just as a farmer is who tills his own farm, or a housewife who works in her own kitchen. This would be a permanent solution of the labor question. It would end the present insecurity, the constant antagonism, the social inferiority, the physical exploitation, the intellectual poverty to which the working class is now exposed even when its condition is most favorable.

If such a solution is even approximately feasible, it should be hailed with joy by every patriot and Christian, for it would put a stop to our industrial war, drain off the miasmatic swamp of undeserved poverty, save our political democracy, and lift the great working class to an altogether different footing of comfort, intelligence, security, and moral strength. And it would embody the principle of solidarity and fraternity in the fundamental institutions of our industrial life. All the elements of cooperation and interaction which are now at work in our great establishments would be conserved, and in addition the hearty interest of all workers in their common factory or store would be immensely intensified by the diffused sense of ownership. Such a social order would develop the altruistic and social instincts just as the competitive order brings out the selfish instincts.

Socialism is the ultimate and logical outcome of the labor movement. When the entire working class throughout the industrial nations is viewed in a large way, the progress of socialism gives an impression of resistless and elemental power. It is inconceivable from the point of view of that class that it should stop short of complete independence and equality as long as it has the power to move on, and independence and equality for the working class must mean the collective ownership of the means of production and the abolition of the present two-class arrangement of industrial society. If the labor movement in our country is only slightly tinged with socialism as yet, it is merely because it is still in its embryonic stages. Nothing will bring the working class to a thorough comprehension of the actual status of their class and its ultimate aim more quickly than continued failure to secure their smaller demands and reactionary efforts to suppress their unions.

We started out with the proposition that the ideal of a fraternal organization of society will remain powerless if it is supported by idealists only; that it needs the firm support of a solid class whose economic future is staked on the success of that ideal; and that the industrial working class is consciously or unconsciously committed to the struggle for the realization of that principle. It follows that those who desire the victory of that ideal from a religious point of view will have to enter into a working alliance with this class. Just as the Protestant principle of religious liberty and the democratic principle of political liberty rose to victory by an alliance with the middle class which was then rising to power, so the new Christian principle of brotherly association must ally itself with the working class if both are to conquer. Each depends on the other. The idealistic movement alone would be a soul without a body; the economic class movement alone would be a body without a soul. It needs the high elation and faith that come through religion. Nothing else will call forth that self-sacrificing devotion and lifelong fidelity which will be needed in so gigantic a struggle as lies before the working class.

The cooperation of professional men outside the working class would contribute scientific information and trained intelligence. They would mediate between the two classes, interpreting each to the other, and thereby lessening the strain of hostility. Their presence and sympathy would cheer the working people and diminish the sense of class isolation. By their contact with the possessing classes they could help to persuade them of the inherent justice of the labor movement and so create a leaning toward concessions. No other influence could do so much to prevent a revolutionary explosion of pent-up forces. It is to the interest of all sides that the readjustment of the social classes should come as a steady evolutionary process rather than as a social catastrophe. If the laboring class should attempt to seize political power suddenly, the attempt might be beaten back with terrible loss in efficiency to the movement. If the attempt should be successful, a raw governing class would be compelled to handle a situation so vast and complicated that no past revolution presents a parallel. There would be widespread disorder and acute distress, and a reactionary relapse to old conditions would, by all historical precedents, be almost certain to occur. It is devoutly to be desired that the shifting of power should come through a continuous series of practicable demands on one side and concessions on the other. Such a historical process will be immensely facilitated if there are a large number of men in the professional and business class with whom religious and ethical motives overcome their selfish interests so that they will throw their influence on the side of the class which is now claiming its full rights in the family circle of humanity.

On the other hand, the Christian idealists must not make the mistake of trying to hold the working class down to the use of moral suasion only, or be repelled when they hear the brute note of selfishness and anger. The class struggle is bound to be transferred to the field of politics in our country in some form. It would be folly if the working class failed to use the leverage which their political power gives them. The business class has certainly never failed to use political means to further its interests. This is a war of conflicting interests which is not likely to be fought out in love and tenderness. The possessing class will make concessions not in brotherly love but in fear, because it has to. The working class will force its demands, not merely because they are just, but because it feels it cannot do without them, and because it is strong enough to coerce. Even Bismarck acknowledged that the former indifference of the business class in Germany to the sufferings of the lower classes had not been overcome by philanthropy, but by fear of the growing discontent of the people and the spread of social democracy. Max Nordau meant the same when he said, "In spite of its theoretical absurdity, socialism has already in thirty years wrought greater amelioration than all the wisdom of statesmen and philosophers of thousands of years." All that we as Christian men can do is to ease the struggle and hasten the victory of the right by giving faith and hope to those who are down, and quickening the sense of justice with those who are in power, so that they will not harden their hearts and hold Israel in bondage, but will "let the people go." But that spiritual contribution, intangible and imponderable though it be, has a chemical power of immeasurable efficiency.

SUMMARY OF THE ARGUMENT

We undertook in this chapter to suggest in what ways the moral forces latent in Christian society could be mobilized for the progressive regeneration of social life, and in what directions chiefly these forces should be exerted.

We saw that some lines of effort frequently attempted in the past by Christian men and organizations are useless and misleading. It is fruitless to attempt to turn modern society back to conditions prevailing before power machinery and trusts had revolutionized it; or to copy biblical institutions adapted to wholly different social conditions; or to postpone the Christianizing of society to the millennium; or to found Christian communistic colonies within the competitive world; or to make the organized Church the center and manager of an improved social machinery. The force of religion can best be applied to social renewal by sending its spiritual power along the existing and natural relations of men to direct them to truer ends and govern them by higher motives.

The fundamental contribution of every man is the change of his own personality. We must repent of the sins of existing society, cast off the spell of the lies protecting our social wrongs, have faith in a higher social order, and realize in ourselves a new type of Christian manhood which seeks to overcome the evil in the present world, not by withdrawing from the world, but by revolutionizing it.

If this new type of religious character multiplies among the young men and women, they will change the world when they come to hold the controlling positions of society in their maturer years. They will give a new force to righteous and enlightened public opinion, and will apply the religious sense of duty and service to the common daily life with a new motive and directness.

The ministry, in particular, must apply the teaching functions of the pulpit to the pressing questions of public morality. It must collectively learn not to speak without adequate information; not to charge individuals with guilt in which all society shares; not to be partial, and yet to be on the side of the lost; not to yield to political partisanship, but to deal with moral questions before they become political issues and with those questions of public welfare which never do become political issues. They must lift the social questions to a religious level by faith and spiritual insight. The larger the number of ministers who attempt these untrodden ways, the safer and saner will those be who follow. By interpreting one social class to the other, they can create a disposition to make concessions and help in securing a peaceful settlement of social issues.

The force of the religious spirit should be bent toward asserting the supremacy of life over property. Property exists to maintain and develop life. It is un-Christian to regard human life as a mere instrument for the production of wealth.

The religious sentiment can protect good customs and institutions against the inroads of ruthless greed, and extend their scope. It can create humane customs which the law is impotent to create. It can create the convictions and customs which are later embodied in good legislation.

Our complex society rests largely on the stewardship of delegated powers. The opportunities to profit by the betrayal of trust increase with the wealth and complexity of civilization. The most fundamental evils in past history and present conditions were due to converting stewardship into ownership. The keener moral insight created by Christianity should lend its help in scrutinizing all claims to property and power in order to detect latent public rights and to recall the recreant stewards to their duty.

Primitive society was communistic. The most valuable institutions in modern life—the family, the school, and the church—are communistic. The State, too, is essentially communistic and is becoming increasingly so. During the larger part of its history the Christian Church regarded communism as the only ideal life. Christianity certainly has more affinity for cooperative and fraternal institutions than for competitive disunion. It should therefore strengthen the existing communistic institutions and aid the evolution of society from the present temporary stage of individualism to a higher form of communism.

The splendid ideal of a fraternal organization of society cannot be realized by idealists only. It must be supported by the self-interest of a powerful class. The working class, which is now engaged in its upward movement, is struggling to secure better conditions of life, an assured status for its class organizations, and ultimately the ownership of the means of production. Its success in the last great aim would mean the closing of the gap which now divides industrial society and the establishment of industry on the principle of solidarity and the method of cooperation. Christianity should enter into a working alliance with this rising class, and by its mediation secure the victory of these principles by a gradual equalization of social opportunity and power.

THE NEW APOSTOLATE

The first apostolate of Christianity was born from a deep fellow-feeling for social misery and from the consciousness of a great historical opportunity. Jesus saw the peasantry of Galilee following him about with their poverty and their diseases, like shepherdless sheep that have been scattered and harried by beasts of prey, and his heart had compassion on them. He felt that the harvest was ripe, but there were few to reap it. Past history had come to its culmination, but there were few who understood the situation and were prepared to cope with it. He bade his disciples to pray for laborers for the harvest, and then made them answer their own prayers by sending them out two by two to proclaim the kingdom of God. That was the beginning of the worldwide mission of Christianity (Matthew 9:32–10:42).

The situation is repeated on a vaster scale today. If Jesus stood today amid our modern life, with that outlook on the condition of all humanity which observation and travel and the press would spread before him, and with the same heart of divine humanity beating in him, he would create a new apostolate to meet the new needs in a new harvest-time of history.

To anyone who knows the sluggishness of humanity to good, the impregnable entrenchments of vested wrongs, and the long reaches of time needed from one milestone of progress to the next, the task of setting up a Christian social order in this modern world of ours seems like a fair and futile dream. Yet in fact it is not one tithe as hopeless as when Jesus set out to do it. When he told his disciples, "Ye are the salt of the earth; ye are the light of the world," he expressed the consciousness of a great historic mission to the whole of humanity. Yet it was a

Nazarene carpenter speaking to a group of Galilean peasants and fishermen. Under the circumstances at that time it was an utterance of the most daring faith—faith in himself, faith in them, faith in what he was putting into them, faith in faith. Jesus failed and was crucified, first his body by his enemies, and then his spirit by his friends; but that failure was so amazing a success that today it takes an effort on our part to realize that it required any faith on his part to inaugurate the kingdom of God and to send out his apostolate.

Today, as Jesus looks out upon humanity, his spirit must leap to see the souls responsive to his call. They are sown broadcast through humanity, legions of them. The harvest-field is no longer deserted. All about us we hear the clang of the whetstone and the rush of the blades through the grain and the shout of the reapers. With all our faults and our slothfulness we modern men in many ways are more on a level with the real mind of Jesus than any generation that has gone before. If that first apostolate was able to remove mountains by the power of faith, such an apostolate as Christ could now summon might change the face of the earth.

The apostolate of a new age must do the work of the sower. When the sower goes forth to sow his seed, he goes with the certainty of partial failure and the knowledge that a long time of patience and of hazard will intervene before he can hope to see the result of his work and his venture. In sowing the truth a man may never see or trace the results. The more ideal his conceptions are, and the farther they move ahead of his time, the larger will be the percentage of apparent failure. But he can afford to wait. The powers of life are on his side. He is like a man who has scattered his seed and then goes off to sleep by night and work by day, and all the while the seed, by the inscrutable chemistry of life, lays hold of the ingredients of its environment and builds them up to its own growth. The mustard-seed becomes a tree. The leaven assimilates the meal by biological processes. The new life penetrates the old humanity and transforms it. Robert Owen was a sower. His cooperative communities failed. He was able to help only a small fraction of the workingmen of his day. But his moral enthusiasm and his ideas fertilized the finest and most self-sacrificing minds among the working classes. They cherished his ultimate hopes in private and worked for realizable ends in public. The Chartist movement was filled with his spirit. The most influential leaders of English unionism in its great period after the middle of the nineteenth century were Owenites. The Rochdale Pioneers were under his influence, and the great cooperative movement in England, an economic force of the first importance, grew in some measure out of the seed which Owen had scattered. Other men may own the present. The future belongs to the sower—provided he scatters seed and does not mistake the chaff for it which once was so essential to the seed and now is dead and useless.

It is inevitable that those who stand against conditions in which most men believe and by which the strongest profit, shall suffer for their stand. The little group of early Christian socialists in England, led by Maurice, Kingsley, and Hughes, now stand by common consent in the history of that generation as one of its finest products, but at that time they were bitterly assailed and misunderstood. Pastor Rudolf Todt, the first man in Germany who undertook to prove that the New Testament and the ethics of socialism have a close affinity, was almost unanimously attacked by the Church of Germany. But Jesus told his apostles at the outset that opposition would be part of their day's work. Christ equipped his Church with no legal rights to protect her; the only political right he gave his disciples was the right of being persecuted.[13] It is part of the doctrine of vicarious atonement, which is fundamental in Christianity, that the prophetic souls must vindicate by their sufferings the truth of the truth they preach.

> Disappointment's dry and bitter root,
> Envy's harsh berries, and the choking pool
> Of the world's scorn, are the right mother-milk
> To the tough hearts that pioneer their kind
> And break a pathway to those unknown realms
> That in the earth's broad shadow lie enthralled;
> Endurance is the crowning quality,
> And patience all the passion of great hearts;
> These are their stay, and when the leaden world
> Sets its hard face against their fateful thought,
> And brute strength, like a scornful conqueror,
> Clangs his huge mace down in the other scale,

The inspired soul but flings his patience in,
And slowly that outweighs the ponderous globe—
One faith against a whole earth's unbelief,
One soul against the flesh of all mankind.

—*James Russell Lowell, "Columbus"*

The championship of social justice is almost the only way left open to a Christian nowadays to gain the crown of martyrdom. Theological heretics are rarely persecuted now. The only rival of God is mammon, and it is only when his sacred name is blasphemed that men throw the Christians to the lions.

Even for the social heretics there is a generous readiness to listen which was unknown in the past. In our country that openness of mind is a product of our free intellectual life, our ingrained democracy, the denominational manifoldness of our religious life, and the spread of the Christian spirit. It has become an accepted doctrine among us that all great movements have obscure beginnings, and that belief tends to make men respectful toward anything that comes from some despised Nazareth. Unless a man forfeits respect by bitterness or lack of tact, he is accorded a large degree of tolerance, though he will always be made to feel the difference between himself and those who say the things that please the great.

The certainty of opposition constitutes a special call to the strong. The ministry seems to have little attraction for the sons of rich men. It is not strange when one considers the enervating trials that beset a rich man in a pastorate. But here is a mission that ought to appeal to the rich young man if he has heroic stuff in him. His assured social standing would give him an influence with rich and poor alike which others attain but slowly if at all. The fear of being blacklisted for championing justice and mercy need have no terrors for him. To use his property as a coat of mail in fighting the battles of the weak would be the best way of obeying Christ's command to the rich young ruler to sell all and give it to the poor. When Mr. Roosevelt was still police commissioner in New York, he said to the young men of New York: "I would teach the young men that he who has not wealth owes his first duty to his family, but he who has means owes his to the State. It is ignoble to go on heaping up money. I would preach the doctrine of work to all, and to the men of wealth the doctrine of unremunerative work."[14] The most "unremunerative work" is the work that draws opposition and animosity.

Mr. Roosevelt implies here that a man's duty to his family is the first and dominant duty, and that this exempts him in some measure from service to the larger public. It follows that the childless have a call to the dangerous work of the kingdom of God. A man and woman who are feeding and training young citizens are performing so immense and absorbing a service to the future that they might well be exempt from taxes to the State and from sacrificial service to the kingdom of God. If nevertheless so many of them assume these duties in addition, the childless man and woman will have to do heroic work in the trenches before they can rank on the same level. It is not fair to ask a man with children to give his time and strength as freely to public causes as if he had none. It is still more unfair to expect him to risk the bread and the prospects of his family in championing dangerous causes as freely as if he risked only himself. The childless people should adopt the whole coming generation of children and fight to make the world more habitable for them as for their own brood. The unmarried and the childless should enlist in the new apostolate and march on the forlorn hopes with Jesus Christ.

In asking for faith in the possibility of a new social order, we ask for no Utopian delusion. We know well that there is no perfection for man in this life: there is only growth toward perfection. In personal religion we look with seasoned suspicion at anyone who claims to be holy and perfect, yet we always tell men to become holy and to seek perfection. We make it a duty to seek what is unattainable. We have the same paradox in the perfectibility of society. We shall never have a perfect social life, yet we must seek it with faith. We shall never abolish suffering. There will always be death and the empty chair and heart. There will always be the agony of love unreturned. Women will long for children and never press baby lips to their breast. Men will long for fame and miss it. Imperfect moral insight will work hurt in the best conceivable social order. The strong will always have the impulse to exert their strength, and no system can be devised which can keep them from crowding and jostling the weaker. Increased social refinement will bring increased sensitiveness to pain. An American may suffer as much distress through a social slight as a Russian peasant under the knout. At best there is always but an approximation to a perfect social order. The kingdom of God is always but coming.

But every approximation to it is worthwhile. Every step toward personal purity and peace, though it only makes the consciousness of imperfection more poignant, carries its own exceeding great reward, and everlasting pilgrimage toward the kingdom of God is better than contented stability in the tents of wickedness.

And sometimes the hot hope surges up that perhaps the long and slow climb may be ending. In the past the steps of our race toward progress have been short and feeble, and succeeded by long intervals of sloth and apathy. But is that necessarily to remain the rate of advance? In the intellectual life there has been an unprecedented leap forward during the last hundred years. Individually we are not more gifted than our grandfathers, but collectively we have wrought out more epoch-making discoveries and inventions in one century than the whole race in the untold centuries that have gone before. If the twentieth century could do for us in the control of social forces what the nineteenth did for us in the control of natural forces, our grandchildren would live in a society that would be justified in regarding our present social life as semi-barbarous. Since the Reformation began to free the mind and to direct the force of religion toward morality, there has been a perceptible increase of speed. Humanity is gaining in elasticity and capacity for change, and every gain in general intelligence, in organizing capacity, in physical and moral soundness, and especially in responsiveness to ideal motives, again increases the ability to advance without disastrous reactions. The swiftness of evolution in our own country proves the immense latent perfectibility in human nature.

Last May a miracle happened. At the beginning of the week the fruit trees bore brown and greenish buds. At the end of the week they were robed in bridal garments of blossom. But for weeks and months the sap had been rising and distending the cells and maturing the tissues which were half ready in the fall before. The swift unfolding was the culmination of a long process. Perhaps these nineteen centuries of Christian influence have been a long preliminary stage of growth, and now the flower and fruit are almost here. If at this juncture we can rally sufficient religious faith and moral strength to snap the bonds of evil and turn the present unparalleled economic and intellectual resources of humanity to the harmonious development of a true social life, the generations yet unborn will mark this as that great day of the Lord for which the ages waited, and count us blessed for sharing in the apostolate that proclaimed it.

What to Do

Jim Wallis

In the one hundred years which have passed since the publication of Walter Rauschenbusch's *Christianity and the Social Crisis*, much has changed and much has not. Upon reflection, a century later, this remarkable and milestone book helps us to understand both what to do and also what not to do in our twenty-first century.

When I first read the book, as an evangelical seminary student in the 1970s, I immediately appreciated his central theme: that Christian faith has a social ethic. In my own evangelical tradition, faith had been narrowly privatized and had an implicit conservative political ethic which resisted any impulse toward social justice. Then, just a few years later, that same tradition produced a very active but reactionary social ethic that focused on the moral issues of abortion and family values, while endorsing the wealth, power, and military policies of the American State. As a young evangelical, I was hungry for a Christian social ethic that focused on the poor, on social and racial equality, and on peace. Walter Rauschenbusch was a breath of fresh air.

Reading him again, on the occasion of the book's centennial edition, has been a very instructive experience. I again appreciated how directly and explicitly he saw the social ethics of Christianity. He asks what the "social ideal" of Christians ought to be and how we could be "mobilized for the progressive regeneration of social life." He calls for a society that might "enrich the many instead of the few" and speaks against the "mistakes" of many to "postpone social regeneration to a future era to be inaugurated by the return of Christ" as he reminds us that "God is now acting."

I still like his clarity in linking personal and social religion. "In personal religion," he says, "the first requirement is to repent and believe the gospel." But then, "social religion, too, demands repentance and faith: repentance for our social sins." Faith requires, he said, "a revaluation of social values." He says there are "two great entities in human life—the human soul and the human race—and religion is to save both."

The Church's role, in Rauschenbusch's view, is "inspiring the social movement with religious faith and daring." But in the practicing of its social ethic, he warns, "it must not attempt to control and monopolize [that movement] for its own organization"—a critical counter to the kind of religion today that seeks political power and domination for its own agenda. He also insists that the exercise of Christian social conscience not be bound by partisan motivations and goals—also a needed corrective to the so-called Christian politics of some today.

The wholeness of the biblical vision and the depth of classical Christian orthodoxy come through when he says that "all human life can be filled with divine purpose; ... God saves not only the soul, but the whole of human life." "The kingdom of God," he reminds us, "is not bounded by the Church, but includes all human relations." Yet his strategy is to exhort believers with a Christian social ethic ("salt and light") to infiltrate society, rather than make power grabs or seek political certainties. To move from Christian social ethics to easy political solutions was not his instruction, but rather, "it is safe to advise a man who feels 'the burden of the Lord' on social wrongs to go slowly and get adequate information"—again a needed corrective to the ideological Christian politics we have seen too much of in recent years.

He also cautions against the use of "personal invective" against individuals, so common in religious pronouncements in politics today. Rather he speaks of the "pressure of evil" that causes powerful leaders in society to act unjustly and notes that they, too, are the "victims of social forces."

I love how Christocentric Rauschenbusch is when he says, "Let others voice special interests; the minister of Jesus Christ must voice the mind of Jesus Christ." But if the Christian "really follows the mind of Christ, he will be likely to take the side of the poor in most issues. The poor are likely to be the wronged." He calls on pastors in particular not to worry about being charged with being "partial" to the poor, because "the daily press, public opinion, custom, literature, orthodox economic science, and nearly all the forces which shape thought, are on the side of things as they are." Be partial, and yet not "partisan" by following "the mind of a political party." These are all solid principles for social engagement today.

Rauschenbusch shows great insight into the limitations of the State to change social opinion and behavior and says the Church must change the "customs" that can prepare the way for real social change. It is his way of making the point that we often must change culture and public opinion before we can change politics, as shown by great practitioners of Christianity since then like Dr. Martin Luther King Jr. Rauschenbusch endorses the separation of Church and State, but cautions that their tasks are "not unrelated." Church and State do not live in "two airtight compartments" and together must both "serve what is greater than either: humanity."

In an era of rampant consumerism and almost continuous corporate scandal, Rauschenbusch's call sounds utterly contemporary: "The spiritual force of Christianity should be turned against the materialism and mammonism of our industrial and social order." In our own time, when even politics treats people as consumers more than citizens, his observation cuts right to the heart of the matter: "Man is treated as a *thing* to produce more things." As he uses the injunctions of the Sermon on the Mount ("life is more than food and raiment") to challenge his own society, ours today stands equally implicated: "Our industrial establishments are institutions for the creation of dividends, and not for the fostering of human life. In all our public life the question of profit is put first." In a populist critique, he asks how the economy of his day could be "organized in order to protect and foster the family, the human individual, and the Christian life"—a better family and spiritual values question than we often hear from some today. He even names the economy as "an oracle of the false god" and says that it is the "function of religion to teach society to value human life more than property, and to value property only insofar as it forms the material basis for the higher development of human life."

One hundred years later, theologians today, echoing Rauschenbusch's warnings, warn that with the onset of globalization the market is now god—complete with the characteristics of all-powerful, all-knowing, and omnipresent. Similarly, Rauschenbusch's call for the proper "stewardship" of resources and public power anticipates the Christian concern today for both the economy and the environment.

When Rauschenbusch speaks of the essential "communism" of the church's history and calls for an expansion of it in the public square, he is really calling for a theology and politics of the common good and an expansion of what we today sometimes call "the commons"—the places that bring us together and serve our collective needs and interests, like parks, public protection and social services, transportation networks, communication networks, and health-care plans. The home, the public schools, and the church are all examples of "communistic institutions" for him.

But his continual use of the word *communism* is jarring to modern readers, who know the terrible costs to human freedom and human rights later perpetrated by systems with that name. Rauschenbusch was writing in 1907, ten years before Lenin and the Bolshevik Revolution in Russia and the onset of totalitarian communism as a political ideology, system, and threat. It is fair to say that he not only failed to anticipate any of that history but also generally missed communism's potential for collective evil. His almost Utopian dreams for the future, at the height of the progressive era and at the beginning of the century, reveal a naïveté about human nature and sin that was characteristic of the time.

The century after *Christianity and the Social Crisis* was written witnessed the horrors of Nazism and fascism, the Holocaust, communism, the Cold War, Western imperialism, other genocides, and now global terrorism—all perpetrated by states or groups in the name of religion. None of these were anticipated by Rauschenbusch's projections of unmatched human progress.

On the contrary, he thought that, "with all our faults and our slothfulness we modern men in many ways are more on a level with the real mind of Jesus than any generation that has gone before." He went further to say that "perhaps these nineteen centuries of Christian influence have been a long preliminary stage of growth, and now the flower and fruit are almost here. If at this juncture we can rally sufficient religious faith and moral strength to snap the bonds of evil and turn the present unparalleled economic and intellectual resources of humanity to the harmonious development of a true social life, the generations yet unborn will mark this as that great day of the Lord for which the ages waited." Then came the atrocities of the twentieth century.

Near the end of the final chapter, he tries a little more modesty and self-correction.

> In asking for faith in the possibility of a new social order, we ask for no Utopian delusion. We know well that there is no perfection for man in this life: there is only growth toward perfection. In personal religion we look with seasoned suspicion at anyone who claims to be holy and perfect, yet we always tell men to become holy and to seek perfection. We make it a duty to seek what is unattainable. We have the same paradox in the perfectibility of society. We shall never have a perfect social life, yet we must seek it with faith.

Perhaps a better way to say it—and one that presents a clearer corrective to Rauschenbusch's social optimism at the beginning of the twentieth century—comes from the French theologian Jacques Ellul: in 1948, after witnessing the brutalities of the first half of the century, he asserted that the Christian must maintain a "perpetually revolutionary posture" that never puts faith in ideological systems and Utopian dreams.

Walter Rauschenbusch's articulation of a Christian social ethic is an eloquent and necessary corrective to privatized religion. But his view of history sometimes misses the biblical reality of evil and the Christian notion of the kingdom of God that is both "already" and "not yet." Motivated and energized by the Christian ethic of social justice, we can make concrete and dramatic social reforms—the abolition of slavery, the victories of the civil-rights movement, the fall of the Berlin Wall, the end of South African apartheid, the establishment of democracies, the advancements of human rights, the protection of the environment, the peaceful resolution of conflicts—but never can we bring in social Utopias. Human revolutions and ideologies ultimately disappoint and fall far short of their promises and can often lead to more injustice. But the reforms are worth all the effort and sacrifice, and they point to the ultimate reign of God. In the meantime, our hopes for social transformation must be tempered by Christian realism and by a social and religious pluralism—both of which preclude the "Christianizing" of society for which Rauschenbusch hoped.

Near the end of the book, Rauschenbusch says it himself: "At best there is always but an approximation to a perfect social order. The kingdom of God is always but coming. But every approximation to it is worthwhile." Amen.

Buds That Never Opened

Richard Rorty

Secular humanists like myself think of the doctrine of original sin as having, disastrously, diverted the attention of Christians from the needs of their neighbors to the state of their own souls. So what we like best about Rauschenbusch's *Christianity and the Social Crisis* is its dismissal of the Pauline claim that we are corrupt and in desperate need of purification. "The ascetic ideal," Rauschenbusch argues, was "originally due to non-Christian influences." He deplores the fact that that ideal has "so long been able to pose as almost the essence of Christian morality" (chapter 4, "The ascetic tendency").

Rauschenbusch was well aware that many readers would accuse him of ignoring, as he put it, "the sinfulness of the human heart" (chapter 7, "Social repentance and faith")—a charge that Niebuhr and other critics later reiterated. But he hoped to persuade them that it was society, rather than individual souls, that stood in need of redemption—that they should not think of Jesus as their *personal* savior. Jesus did not come to save you, but to teach that you and your neighbor, working together, can create a just society. "Religious individualism," Rauschenbusch claims, "was a triumph of faith under abnormal conditions, and not a triumph of religious life" (chapter 1, "Summary"). He asked Christians to "have faith enough to believe that ... God saves not only the soul, but the whole of human life; that anything which serves to make men healthy, intelligent, happy, and good is a service to the Father of men" (chapter 7, "Social evangelization").

Rauschenbusch urged us to think of Jesus as the successor of the Hebrew prophets, whose great theme—at least before the national catastrophe to which Jeremiah was reacting (chapter 1, "The later religious individualism")—was social justice. He wanted us to think of Christ not as our link with another, better world—the immaterial world dreamed up by Plato—but as having shown us how to live worthwhile lives in this world. We should turn away from the Platonized, logocentric Gospel of John, in which "the divine figure of the Son of God moves through the doubts and discussions of men like the silver moon sailing serene through the clouds." Instead, we should read Luke, who "alone reports the parables of the rich fool, the unjust steward, and Divus and Lazarus" (chapter 2, "His teaching on wealth").

Rauschenbusch disliked millenarianism and apocalypticism almost as much as asceticism and individualism. He would have been as appalled by the popularity of the Left Behind novels as by the televangelists' suggestion that making Christ one's business partner ensures success. He loathed the idea that the task of Christians is to keep themselves clean while awaiting the Second Coming. He rejected the idea that there is a Divine Plan working itself out in history and, more generally, that only divine intervention can make a significant difference to the human condition. He hoped that Christians would come to believe that they might, by their own efforts, create the kingdom of God here on earth.

Rauschenbusch urged Christians to set aside hopes for eternal life (hopes that he himself does not seem to have shared) and to focus instead on the suffering being inflicted daily by the strong upon the weak. Once they had done so, the Christian churches would try to "mitigate the social hardships of the working classes by lending force to humane customs." The churches might, for example, campaign to "secure seats and restrooms for the girls in the department stores." That sort of reform, he said, "would not solve the fundamental questions of capitalism, but it would ease the pressure a little and would save the people from deterioration, while the social movement is moving toward the larger solution" (chapter 7, "The creation of customs and institutions"). He believed that this larger solution would require "collective ownership of the means of production and the abolition of the present two-class arrangement of industrial society" (chapter 7, "The upward movement of the working class").

The hope that Christian churches might take the lead in radical social change links *Christianity and the Social Crisis* with another bestseller, published more than half a century later: Gustavo Gutierrez's *A Theology of Liberation*. Gutierrez had the same hopes for the Catholic priests ministering to the poor of Latin America that Rauschenbusch had had for the Protestant clergy of the United States. Both men hoped that what Rauschenbusch called "ecclesiasticism" could finally be overcome, leaving the clergy free to become agents of social change.

Had Karol Wojtyla and Joseph Ratzinger embraced rather than suppressed liberation theology, the Catholic Church might have not only redeemed itself but set an example for the rest of Christendom. But they reacted to Gutierrez's book with distrust and fear, and so his hopes were short-lived. Rauschenbusch's vision, however, was more viable. For some fifty years after his death, American politicians trying to cobble together a welfare state could rely on the support of tens of thousands of Christian ministers who had been inspired by *Christianity and the Social Crisis*. During that half-century, the Social Gospel was a force in political life. But by the 1970s religious individualism had begun to stage a comeback. Nowadays American Protestantism is once again dominated by the apocalyptic millenarianism against which Rauschenbusch struggled.

One hundred years ago, there was still a chance that the Christian churches would play a central role in the struggle for social justice — that Christian, rather than Marxist, ideas would inspire radical sociopolitical change. One can imagine a twentieth century in which the two World Wars and the Great Depression were avoided, the Bolshevik Revolution collapsed, and social democrats like Eugene Debs and Jean Jaures were elected to high office, thanks to the enthusiastic support of the Christian clergy. Decolonialization and the entrance of India and China on the international stage could then have taken place against the background of a consensus, in the West, that building a global egalitarian society was a moral obligation. With a bit more luck, Rauschenbusch's dream could have come true, despite "the sinfulness of the human heart."

But our luck was bad, and Christianity has probably missed its chance. The likelihood that religion will play a significant role in the struggle for justice seems smaller now than at any time since *Christianity and the Social Crisis* was published. In Western Europe, where the influence of social democratic ideas has been greatest, there has been no return to religion; the term *Christian Socialism* no longer has resonance. In the United States and various other places in the world, such a return is indeed taking place, but it is producing forms of religiosity that have little to do with hopes for a cooperative commonwealth.

In the last paragraph of his book, Rauschenbusch writes that "perhaps these nineteen centuries of Christian influence have been a long preliminary stage of growth, and now the flower and fruit are almost here" (chapter 7, "The new apostolate"). Even unbelievers like myself can agree that without that influence—without all those sermons on Rauschenbusch's favorite texts from Luke—we would have had neither the democratic revolutions of the eighteenth century nor the rise of socialist ideals in the nineteenth. It was no accident that the push for socioeconomic equality first gained momentum in a part of the world where such sermons had been preached, generation after generation. By 1907 centuries of such preaching had created a climate of opinion in which it was reasonable to anticipate flowers and fruit. Rauschenbusch and his contemporaries could not have foreseen the fierce, blighting storms that were to come.

Notes

CHAPTER 1: THE HISTORICAL ROOTS OF CHRISTIANITY: THE HEBREW PROPHETS

1. See also Psalm 40:6, 50:8–15, 51:16–17.
2. Kautzsch, *Geschichte des alttestamentlichen Schrifttums*.
3. See also Micah 2:2.
4. James F. McCurdy, *History, Prophecy, and the Monuments* (1894), II, 206–13.
5. Buhl, *Die socialen Verhaeltnisse der Israeliten*, pp. 4–9.
6. Philo, *Who Is an Heir of Divine Things?* (Bohn's edition), II, p. 33.
7. Edward McGlynn (1837–1900), a Catholic priest in New York City, gave such strenuous support to the political campaigns and economic ideas of Henry George that he was, for a brief period, excommunicated.
8. See also Exodus 23:11; Buhl, *Die socialen Verhaeltnisse der Israeliten*, p. 22.
9. See also Leviticus 19:9–10, 23:22.
10. See also Leviticus 19:13.
11. Kautzsch (*Geschichte des alttestamentlichen Schrifttums*) translates it beautifully: "einmal aufatme."
12. McCurdy, *History, Prophecy, and the Monuments*, II, 175–76.
13. George Adam Smith, *The Book of the Twelve Prophets* (1898–99), I, 23.
14. Smith, *The Book of the Twelve Prophets*, I, 25.
15. Kuenen, *Prophets and Prophecy in Israel*, 60.
16. For the ordinary reader who may wish to follow up the subject, I know no book more generally accessible and more delightful than the two volumes in the *Expositor's Bible* on *The Book of the Twelve Prophets* by George Adam Smith, especially the introductory chapters in each volume.

    I think it is only honest to state that the Old Testament has never been my professional specialty and the foregoing discussion lays no claim to authority. Doubtless the expert student will notice inaccuracies in detail. But if he differs in fundamentals, the difference is not likely to be due to such minor points of information, but to his general conceptions of history and religion.

CHAPTER 2: THE SOCIAL AIMS OF JESUS

1. Those who read only English are fortunate in having at their command two excellent books on the subject of this chapter: *Jesus Christ and the Social Question* (1900) by Professor Francis G. Peabody of Harvard, and *The Social Teaching of Jesus* (1897) by Professor Shailer Mathews of the University of Chicago. The former is very sympathetic in its treatment; the latter perhaps more incisive in its methods.
2. Mark 1; Matthew 3; Luke 3; John 1.
3. See also Matthew 11:2–19; Luke 7:18–35.

4. Josephus, *Antiquities*, XVIII, 5, 2.

5. Ernest Renan, *Life of Jesus* (1864), 152–53.

6. This superiority is beautifully expressed in Julius Wellhausen's *Israelitische und Jüdische Geschichte* (1914), Chap. XXIV.

7. See the list of definitions in Mathews, *The Social Teaching of Jesus*, 53, n. 1.

8. On the later Messianic hope of the Jewish people, see Shailer Mathews, *The Messianic Hope in the New Testament* (1905); Schürer, *The Jewish People in the Time of Jesus Christ*, p. 29; see also p. 32, V.

9. The parables of Matthew 13; see also Mark 4:26–29.

10. On the Sabbath: Matthew 12:1–14; Luke 13:10–17. On fasting: Mark 2:18–22. On tabooed food and ceremonial lustrations: Mark 7:1–23; Matthew 15:1–20.

11. The parable stops with verse 9. What follows seems to consist of kindred sayings of Jesus which the editor has grouped here.

12. Compare Matthew 5:1–12 with Luke 6:20–26.

13. The Ebionites were a Jewish Christian sect of the first century AD, some of whom held extremely uncompromising notions about the Mosaic Law.

14. A very ancient proverb which may be translated "By his claws one knows the lion."

15. A legend referred to in Dante, and elaborated in Longfellow's "A Sicilian's Tale."

16. See the whole of Matthew 23.

17. The English translation, "exercise authority over them," is far too weak to do justice to the preposition in κατεξουσιάζουσιν. Weizsaecker translates it *vergewalligen*; the Twentieth Century New Testament, "oppress." It carries the meaning both of injustice and coercion.

18. See James Bryce, *Holy Roman Empire* (1886), 112–13.

19. Peabody, *Jesus Christ and the Social Question* (1900), 89.

CHAPTER 3: THE SOCIAL IMPETUS OF PRIMITIVE CHRISTIANITY

1. Elias (c. 1180–1253), a companion of St. Francis's, governed the Franciscan order after Francis's death until he was deposed for despotism.

2. See Paul Sabatier, *Life of St. Francis* (1902).

3. Adolf Harnack, *The Expansion of Christianity in the First Three Centuries* (1904), Bk. III, Chap. V.

4. This line of investigation is followed with great skill and effectiveness in Weizsaecker, *History of the Apostolic Age*.

5. Hilgenfeld, *Novum Testamentum extra canonem*, 16; E. B. Nicholson, *The Gospel According to the Hebrews* (London, 1879).

6. See especially 1 Corinthians 15 and Romans 8:18–25. For a summary of Paul's eschatology, see Bernhard Weiss, *Biblical Theology of the New Testament* (1893), Chap. X.

7. See the gorgeous imaginings of Papias, a man of the second generation of Christians, quoted by Irenaeus, *Heresies*, Bk. V, Chap. 33, 3–4. See *Ante-Nicene Fathers*, I, 562–63. Papias was so sure that this was part and parcel of Christianity that he claimed this as a saying of Jesus.

8. Eusebius, *Life of Constantine*, Chap. 32.

9. See Mathews, *The Messianic Hope in the New Testament*; Schürer, *The Jewish People in the Time of Jesus Christ*, p. 29 and p. 32, V.

10. Under Nero AD 64; under Domitian AD 95 or 96.

11. There are historical scholars who are so impressed by the latent hostility of the Christians to Rome that they incline to think some of them may have been guilty of setting Rome on fire, as was charged at the time. Cf. Tacitus, *Annales*, XV, 44.

12. Chapter 1, "The prophetic hope of national perfection."

13. Chapter 2, "The purpose of Jesus: the kingdom of God."

14. In the following sections I am greatly indebted to Harnack, *Expansion of Christianity*, Bk. II, Chap. VI.

15. See, for instance, Wilhelm Windelband, *History of Philosophy* (1893), p. 21.

16. 1 Peter 2:9: γένοζ, ιεράτευμα, έθνοζ, λαόζ.

17. See Allan Menzies, *History of Religion* (1903), Chap. VI.

18. Luke 2:1; Melito, quoted in Eusebius, *Church History*, IV, 26, 7–11.

19. Justin, *Apology*, I, Chap. 12.

20. *Epistle to Diognetus*, Chap. VI.

21. Ernst von Dobschütz, *Christian Life in the Primitive Church* (1904), 186–87.

22. Rudolf Sohm, *Kirchenrecht*, I, 71.

23. See Edwin Hatch, *Organization of the Early Christian Churches* (1881), 36–39.

24. In Acts 11:27–30, we find "elders" at Jerusalem doing the very thing the Seven were elected to do.

25. See Gerhard Uhlhorn, *History of Christian Charity in the Ancient Church*; Harnack, *Expansion of Christianity*, Bk. II, Chap. III.

26. See the account of the pestilence in Alexandria, AD 259, in Eusebius, *Church History*, VII, 22. See also Cyprian's letter to the Numidian bishops, forwarding a gift of 100,000 sestertia from the church at Carthage to redeem the captives of brigands. *Ante-Nicene Fathers*, V, 355.

27. Harnack quotes from the *Pseudo-Clementine Homilies* (Ep. Clem. 8) the fine maxim: τεχνίτη έργον, αόργανεί έλεοζ, "to the workman a job, to the man unable to work pity," i.e., alms.

28. Clement of Rome (about AD 96) always couples faith and hospitality in characterizing the Old Testament saints. I Clement, X–XII, *Ante-Nicene Fathers*, 1, 7–8.

29. The word ὃñâόôâôêὃ used by Paul, in Romans 16:1–2, is the feminine of ὃñïόôÜôçὃ, the Greek equivalent of *patronus*.

30. Harnack, *Expansion of Christianity*, Bk. II, Chap. III.

31. Hermann Schiller, *Geschichte der römischen Kaiserzeit* (1883), I, 461–62.

32. Karl Kautsky, *Die Vorläufer des neueren Sozialismus* (1909), 23, 32.

33. See Ephesians 6:5–9; 1 Peter 2:18–25; 1 Timothy 6:1–2.

34. Cyprian, Epistle 51, 9, *Ante-Nicene Fathers*, V, 329.

CHAPTER 4: WHY HAS CHRISTIANITY NEVER UNDERTAKEN THE WORK OF SOCIAL RECONSTRUCTION?

1. For a fine, popular statement of these changes, see Charles Loring Brace, *Gesta Christi* (1883).

2. This holds true not only of Brace, *Gesta Christi*, but of such solid and admirable works as Doellinger, *Gentile and Jew*, and Gerhard Uhlhorn's *Conflict of Christianity with Heathenism* (1879) and his *History of Christian Charity*.

3. See chapter 3, "The hope of the coming of the Lord."

4. See chapter 3, "The revolutionary character of the millennial hope."

5. Harnack, *Expansion of Christianity*, Bk. II, Chap. II, has an Excursus about this belief and its influence on ancient Christianity. Many of the most interesting passages in the Fathers are quoted there.

6. Irenaeus unconsciously; Clement of Alexandria and Origen consciously.

7. See Brace, *Gesta Christi*, Chaps. III–IV.

8. Epistle 14, 2.

9. On the entire subject, see Henry Charles Lea, *History of Sacerdotal Celibacy in the Christian Church* (1907).

10. Chapter 1, "Religion ethical and therefore social."

11. Epistle of Barnabas I, 6.

12. In the papal penitentiary of the fourteenth century the gravest crimes were those involving insubordination to the Church. A priest who admitted an excommunicated man to worship

had to pay a penalty equal to that of a parricide and greater than that of a perjurer. A priest giving Christian burial while a country was under the interdict was still more severely punished.

13. Gregory of Tours, *Historia Francorum*, II, 40, and III, 1.
14. Hermann Schiller, *Geschichte der römischen Kaiserzeit*, I, 916.
15. See Hatch, *Organization of the Early Christian Churches*.
16. See Harnack, *Contemporary Review*, December 1904.
17. Schiller, *Geschichte der Römische Kaiserzeit*, I, 911ff.
18. See the little book of the eminent Belgian economist Émile de Laveleye, *Protestantism and Catholicism in Their Bearing upon the Liberty and Prosperity of Nations* (1875).
19. De Laveleye, *Protestantism and Catholicism*, 34.
20. See Charles Bigg, *The Church's Task Under the Roman Empire* (1905), Lecture I, "Education."
21. This method of interpretation is still sanctioned by what is probably the most widely used book on the parables in English, Archbishop Trench's *Notes on the Parables of Our Lord*.
22. Two versions of the Arian heresy, one of which contended Christ was "like" God the Father, the other that he was "like in substance."
23. James Russell Lowell, *The Present Crisis*.

CHAPTER 5: THE PRESENT CRISIS
1. R. T. Ely, *Outlines of Economics* (1893), 5.
2. See Arnold Toynbee, *The Industrial Revolution in England*. For a popular summary, see Ely, *Outlines of Economics*, Chaps. I–IX.
3. See Thorold Rogers, *Six Centuries of Work and Wages* (1891); L. Brentano, *On the History and Development of Guilds*.
4. F. Engels, *Condition of the Working Class in England in 1844* (1887).
5. Gustav Schmoller, *Grundriss der allgemeinen Volkswirtschaftslehre*, II, 453.
6. See the great works of Sir Henry Maine, *Village-Communities in the East and West* (1871) and *Lectures on the Early History of Institutions* (1875).
7. F. Seebohm, *The English Village Community* (1890).
8. Émile de Laveleye, *De la propriété et de ses formes primitives* (1874).
9. Schmoller, *Grundriss der allgemeinen Volkswirtschaftslehre*, II, 450.
10. The brilliant books of Henry George, *Progress and Poverty* (1882) and *Social Problems* (1884), are still worth reading. In his main contentions he has never been answered.
11. *The Outlook*, March 19, 1904, 692.
12. Rodbertus and Adolf Wagner in their edition of *Rau's Lehrbuch der Nationalökonomie*.
13. See the admirable book by John Graham Brooks, *The Social Unrest* (1907).
14. Charles W. Eliot (1834–1920) was President of Harvard from 1869 to 1909.
15. This proportion of wages paid and wages retained is simply assumed for the sake of concreteness in the argument. The actual proportion, of course, will vary with the "profits" of a concern. The Census of 1900 estimated the average per capita production at $12 to $14 a day, and the average wage at $1.38.
16. Professor Nicholas P. Gilman, *Methods of Industrial Peace* (1904), computes the number of strikes, 1881 to 1900, at 22,793, and the lockouts at 1,005. The total number thrown out of work was 6,610,000. The loss to the men was $306,683,233; to the employers, $142,659,104.
17. On this entire section, see Robert Hunter, *Poverty* (1904).
18. The reduction in some cases has been from fifty-five to fourteen per thousand.
19. Robert Hunter, *Poverty*, Chap. I.
20. From an article by Comptroller Roberts, *Forum*, May 1897.
21. *The Outlook*, September 21, 1901, 150.

22. Charles B. Spahr, *An Essay on the Present Distribution of Wealth in the United States* (1896). See also George K. Holmes, *Political Science Quarterly*, 1893, 591.

23. Senator McCumber, in a speech in the Senate, January 23, 1906. He added that if we reduced the estimate to 15 percent to be conservative, the amount would be about $1,750,000,000. Today it would be safely estimated at $3,000,000,000. Our people would then annually pay for fraudulent and adulterated goods enough to pay the national debt thrice over. We shall wait to see how much permanent change the new Pure Food Law will make.

24. President Eliot, in the annual report of Harvard, 1903, gives the vital statistics of six classes more than twenty-five years out of college. They fell about 28 percent short of reproducing themselves. Professor Thorndike of Columbia University finds that there has been a steady decline of the average number of children from 5.6 in the classes graduating 1803–1809 down to 1.8 in the classes graduating 1875–1879.

25. Chapter 4, "Monasticism."

26. A madman, in whom devils dwelt until they were cast out by Christ.

CHAPTER 6: THE STAKE OF THE CHURCH IN THE SOCIAL MOVEMENT

1. An article in which I set forth this line of thought in more rudimentary form was published in the *American Journal of Sociology*, July 1897.

2. Report of the Massachusetts Bureau of Statistics of Labor, 1885. Dr. R. T. Ely has a brief discussion of the table in his *Outlines of Economics*, 243–45.

3. See an article by Professor Harnack, "The Relation Between Ecclesiastical and General History," *Contemporary Review*, 1904, 846.

4. On this entire subject, see *The Captive City of God* (1904) by my friend Mr. Richard Heath, a book written with searching insight and prophetic power.

5. Proverbs 30:8–9.

6. Charles Booth, *Life and Labor in London*, third series.

7. A slang name for the meat-packing areas of Chicago, at this time much in the public mind as the result of Upton Sinclair's muckraking novel, *The Jungle* (1905).

8. E. Belfort Bax, *The Peasants' War in Germany* (1899); Zimmermann, *Geschichte des Bauernkrieges*.

9. Rudyard Kipling, *The Second Jungle Book* (1895).

10. On the extent and causes of this alienation, see Richard Heath's *Captive City of God*.

11. H. C. Lea, *Cambridge Modern History*, I, 653: "The religious changes incident to the Reformation … were not the object sought, but the means for attaining that object…. The overthrow of dogma was the only way to obtain permanent relief from the intolerable abuses of the existing ecclesiastical system." This statement is extreme, but it is nearer the truth than the popular view.

12. Harnack, *History of Dogma* (1896), VII, 168ff.

13. Villari, *Life and Times of Savonarola*, I, 148.

14. From a pamphlet published by the *Western Mail* of Cardiff, and giving current reports of the meetings in Wales.

15. Carlyle, *Oliver Cromwell's Letters and Speeches* (1885), Part VI, in the beginning.

CHAPTER 7: WHAT TO DO

1. Vasily V. Verestchagin (1842–1904) was a Russian painter best known for his harshly realistic pictures of the horrors of war.

2. John Graham Brooks, in the introductory chapter to *The Social Unrest*, gives very interesting testimony to this fact.

3. George F. Baer (1842–1914), president of the Reading Railroad, made this statement on the eve of the Anthracite Strike of 1902.

356 *Notes*

4. Galiani, quoted by Martin von Nathusius, *Die Mitarbeit der Kirche an der Lösung der sozialen Frage* (1897), 68.
5. The Utopian community, founded in West Roxbury, Massachusetts, in 1841 by leading transcendentalists, had to disband in 1847.
6. For instance, in Germany the poets Uhland, Freiligrath, and Kinkel; the philosophers Feuerbach and Ruge; the scientist Virchow; the musician Wagner.
7. De Laveleye, *Protestantism and Catholicism*, 56.
8. Nathusius, *Mitarbeit der Kirche*, 487.
9. The English poet enjoyed an enormous popularity in America in the late nineteenth century, and "Browning Clubs," formed to discuss his poetry, were highly fashionable.
10. John Morley, *The Life of Cobden:* "Great economic and social forces flow with a tidal sweep over communities that are only half conscious of that which is befalling them."
11. Adolf Stöcker (1835–1908) was a minister of the German Evangelical Church, founder of the Christian Socialist party, and a noted anti-Semite.
12. The claim of the American Catholic hierarchy, after the Mexican Cession in 1848, to a share of the "Pious Fund of the Californias" developed into a long dispute between the American and Mexican governments; eventually it was referred to the Hague Tribunal.
13. Nathusius, *Mitarbeit der Kirche*, 476.
14. Jacob A. Riis, *Theodore Roosevelt, the Citizen* (1904).

Contributors

THE REV. DR. TONY CAMPOLO

Tony Campolo is professor emeritus at Eastern University and founder of the Evangelical Association for the Promotion of Education, an organization that develops schools and social programs in various third world countries and in cities across North America. He is the author of many books, his most recent being *Speaking My Mind*.

SISTER JOAN CHITTISTER

Joan Chittister, OSB, is a member and past prioress of the Benedictine sisters of Erie. Sister Joan is past president of the Conference of American Benedictine Prioresses and of the Leadership Conference of Women Religious, and has been a leading voice on spirituality for over twenty-five years. She is presently executive director of Benetvision: A Resource and Research Center for Contemporary Spirituality, located in Erie, Pennsylvania.

THE REV. DR. JAMES A. FORBES JR.

James Forbes served as senior pastor for The Riverside Church in New York City for seventeen years before stepping down in 2007. Rev. Forbes is internationally known as the "preacher's preacher," and served as the Harry Emerson Fosdick Adjunct Professor of Preaching at Union Theological Seminary. He was twice hailed as one of America's greatest black preachers by *Ebony Magazine*.

DR. STANLEY HAUERWAS

Stanley Hauerwas is currently the Gilbert T. Rowe Professor of Theological Ethics at Duke Divinity School. Dr. Hauerwas delivered the prestigious Gifford Lectureship at the University of St. Andrews, Scotland, in 2001. He was named "America's Best Theologian" by *Time Magazine* that same year. His book *A Community of Character: Toward a Constructive Christian Social Ethic* was selected as one of the one hundred most important books on religion of the twentieth century.

REV. PAUL BRANDEIS RAUSHENBUSH

Paul Raushenbush is the associate dean of religious life at Princeton University. He is an ordained American Baptist minister and has served at The Riverside Church, Madison Avenue Baptist Church, and First Baptist Church in Seattle, Washington. He is a contributing editor for Beliefnet.com and authored *Teen Spirit: One World, Many Paths*. He is the great-grandson of Walter Rauschenbusch.

DR. RICHARD RORTY

Richard Rorty taught philosophy at Wellesley for three years, at Princeton for twenty-one years, at the University of Virginia for fifteen years, and at Stanford for seven years. His books include *Philosophy and the Mirror of Nature; Contingency, Irony and Solidarity;* and *Achieving Our Country.* He is the grandson of Walter Rauschenbusch.

DR. PHYLLIS TRIBLE

Phyllis Trible is a professor of biblical studies at Wake Forest University Divinity School. A past president of the Society of Biblical Literature, she is the author of the books *God and the Rhetoric of Sexuality, Texts of Terror: Literary-Feminist Readings of Biblical Narrative,* and *Rhetorical Criticism: Context, Method, and the Book of Jonah.* She is the Baldwin Professor of Sacred Literature Emerita at Union Theological Seminary.

REV. JIM WALLIS

Jim Wallis is president and executive director of Sojourners/Call to Renewal, where he is editor-in-chief of *Sojourners* magazine. He convenes a national network of churches, faith-based organizations, and individuals working to overcome poverty in America. He is the author of *God's Politics: Why the Right Gets It Wrong and the Left Doesn't Get It.*

DR. CORNEL WEST

Cornel West is the Class of 1943 University Professor of Religion at Princeton University. He is the author of numerous articles and books, including *The American Evasion of Philosophy: A Genealogy of Pragmatism, The Cornel West Reader, Race Matters,* and *Democracy Matters.*

Index

lotteries, prevalence of in Europe, 216
Louis XIV, 310
love
    effect on society of, 57
    instinct of, 56
    social duty of, 251–252
Lowell, James Russell, 335–336
Luke
    accuracy of Gospels of, 65–66
    as church historian, 101
Luke 1:52–53, 68
Luke 1:74–75, 47–48
Luke 3:10–14, 44
Luke 4:16–22, 66
Luke 10:25–37
Luke 11:1, 43
Luke 12:15, 60
Luke 13:6–9, 309
Luke 13:32, 69
Luke 14, 57
Luke 14:12–14, 67
Luke 14:15–24, 67
Luke 15:1–10, 66
Luke 16:1–9, 63
Luke 16:1–15, 308
Luke 16:14, 64
Luke 16:15, 68
Luke 16:16, 43
Luke 16:19–21, 67
Luke 17:20–21, 49
Luke 17:21, 53
Luke 18:1–8, 67
Luke 19:11–27, 308
Luke 19:41–44, 54
Luke 22:24–30, 57
Luke 22:25, 69
Luke 22:35
Luther. See also *specific religious movements*
    view of peasants by, 259, 262–263, 269
Lycurgus, 1

man
    enemies of, 178–179
    objectivation of, 300–301
    original state of, 143
Marius, Rome of, 228
Mark 1:15
Mark 2:18–19, 57
Mark 7:1–13, 59
Mark 9:33–37, 57
Mark 10:17–31, 61
Mark 10:23, 61
Mark 10:31, 68
Mark 11:15–19, 58
Mark 12:37, 67
Mark 12:40, 67
Mark 12:41–44, 67
Mark 14:3–9, 56
marriage
    assessment of by early Church, 139
    Paul's recommendation about, 131
    as a sacrament, 140
marriage rates, in Rochester, New York, 220
martyrdom, 323
martyrs, reanimation of, 90
Mary of Bethany, instinct of love and, 56
materialism, evils of, 300–302
materialism *vs.* religiosity, 256
material world, and the return of Christ, 89–90
Matthew 3:5–12, 43
Matthew 4:10–12, 48–49, 49
Matthew 5:3–12, 68
Matthew 5:23–24, 56
Matthew 5:38–42, 56
Matthew 5:43–48, 56
Matthew 6:19–34, 60
Matthew 8:10–12, 51
Matthew 9:14, 43
Matthew 9:32–10:42, 333
Matthew 11:2–5, 66

Index